CITROËN
THE COMPLETE STORY

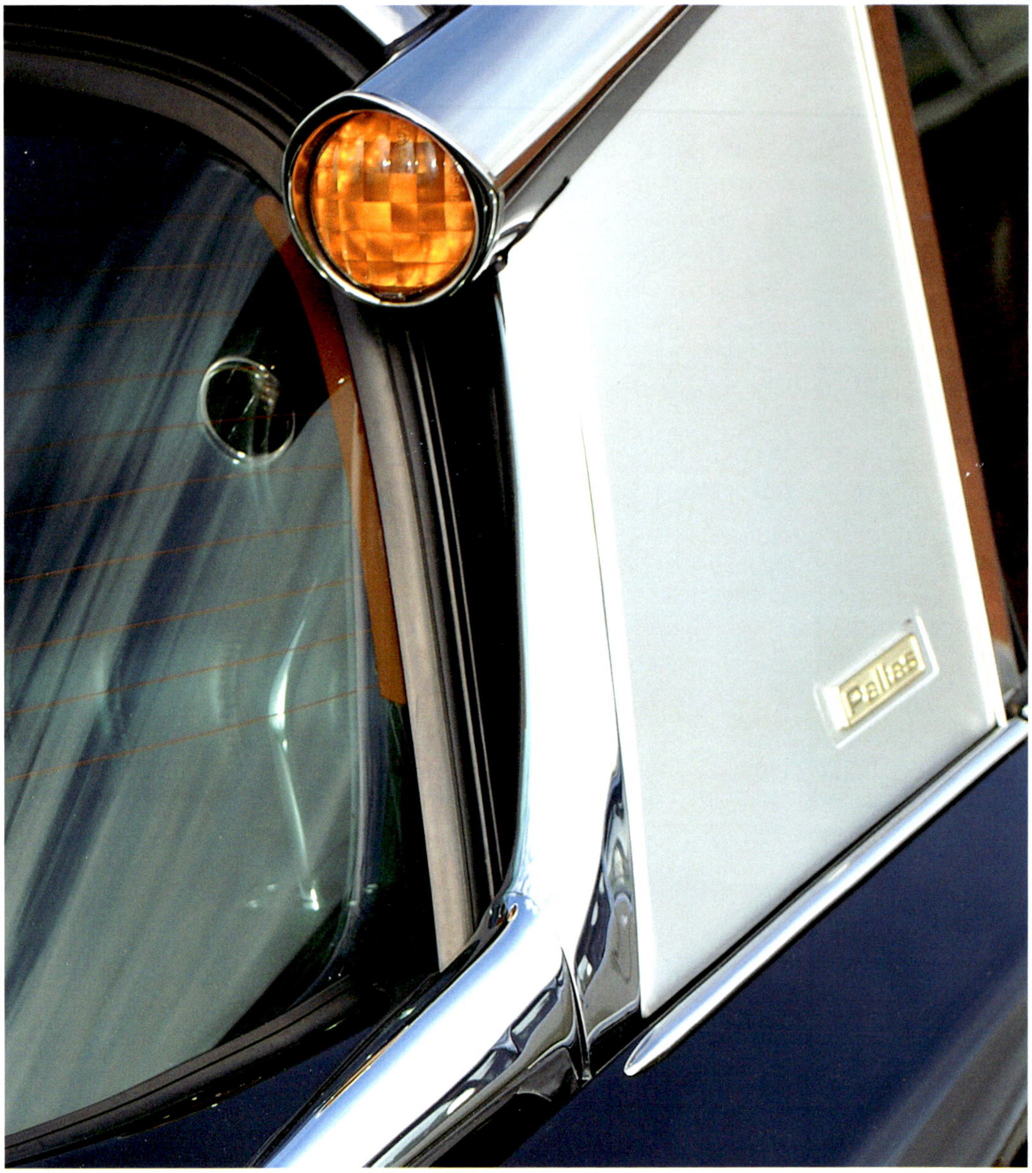
Pallas

CITROËN
THE COMPLETE STORY

LANCE COLE

THE CROWOOD PRESS

First published in 2014 by
The Crowood Press Ltd
Ramsbury, Marlborough
Wiltshire SN8 2HR

www.crowood.com

© Lance Cole 2014

All rights reserved. No part of this publication may be reproduced or transmitted in any form or by any means, electronic or mechanical, including photocopy, recording, or any information storage and retrieval system, without permission in writing from the publishers.

British Library Cataloguing-in-Publication Data
A catalogue record for this book is available from the British Library.

ISBN 978 1 84797 659 8

Photography by the author with additional photography by C. David Conway, Franklin Rugg, Pierre Jammes, Martijn van Well. Archive images from Citroën Communications photographers and Conservatoire Citroën.
Citroën cars artwork by Russell Wallis.
Frontispiece: DS Pallas – The grand legend.

Typeset by Shane O'Dwyer, Bristol, Avon
Printed and bound in India by Gopsons Papers Ltd

ALSO BY THE AUTHOR

Saab Cars, the Complete Story

Saab 99 and 900, the Complete Story

Vickers VC10

Secrets of the Spitfire

Long Haul

Heavies

Jetliners

The New Illustrated Encyclopaedia of the Automobile

DEDICATION

For my children, **EMILY** and **JACK**, as always.

Also for my Citroën DS-owning grandfather, **TOM GODDEN** (RAF). And in memory of the late **INNES IRELAND**, who was instrumental in launching my writing career, and who taught me to drink single malt with nothing added.

ACKNOWLEDGEMENTS

I HAVE BEEN ENCOURAGED and helped by many people in this new view of Citroën, and my biggest thanks and admiration go to the following: C. David Conway, John Sobey, Clive Hamilton Gould, Patrick Rugg, Reg Winstone, Citroën Communications/Conservatoire. Other key contributors, notably for access to cars and photographs, include Franklin Rugg, Brian Cass, Darrin Brownhill, Richard Biddulph, Vintage and Prestige Cars. Pierre Jammes of DsinAsia.com, Julian Marsh, Graham H. Wilson, the Reverend Mike Johnson. Mark Furneaux Pioneer Automobiles. Clarke and Rodway. Brian Drummond, and members of the Citroën Car Club in the UK. Wouter Jansen in The Netherlands, Roger Brioult, Dirk Walter, Steve Berry, Sander Aalderink: Brittany Ferries.

The wonderful artwork featured in the chapter openers is by auto designer Russell Wallis.

Much of the photography in this book, including the cover, is my own, but other significant contributions come from David Conway (2CV and others), Franklin Rugg (selected BX and CX), Pierre Jammes (DS in Asia), Martijn van Well (Ami, DS USA spec), Simeon Criddle (Eclectic Cars), Dan Stuart (GS Break), Eoin Sloan and the Citroën Archive photographers: Nicholas Zwickel, Patrick Legros, Jerome Lejeune, Laurent Nivalle via Citroën Communications agreement.

There have been numerous books published on Citroën, and many authors have cross-referenced others. The bibliography credits all the sources dating from 1911, and I have consulted many people and publications; however, I wish to specifically identify and thank the following as respected supplementary references: C. David Conway; Roger Brioult and his *L'Histoire et les Secrets de son Bureau d'Etudes*; *Bertoni – 30 Ans de Style Citroën* by Fabien Sabatés and Leonardo Bertoni; *André Lefebvre and the cars he created for Voisin and Citroën* by Gijsbert-Paul Berk; *My 1000 Cars* by Gabriel Voisin; English Reference Edition and Gerin both by Reg Winstone. Acknowledgement must also go to Julian Marsh and his Citroënet website, which makes so much information available to all Citroënistes.

CONTENTS

	Introduction	7

CHAPTER 1	THE ORIGINS OF CITROËNISM	17
CHAPTER 2	GENESIS OF AN ETHOS: LEFEBVRE UNDER VOISIN AND BEYOND	35
CHAPTER 3	TRACTION AVANT: THE FRONT-WHEEL-DRIVE PIONEER	51
CHAPTER 4	2CV: NOT BASIC AT ALL	63
CHAPTER 5	THE MAN WITH A VAN: COMMERCIALS	83
CHAPTER 6	DS: THE WORLD'S MOST ADVANCED CAR?	93
CHAPTER 7	BRAVE SIBLINGS: AMI AND DYANE	113
CHAPTER 8	SM: THE WORLD'S FIRST HYPER CAR	127
CHAPTER 9	GS: GENIUS	149
CHAPTER 10	CX: COEFFICIENT OF EXCELLENCE	167
CHAPTER 11	BASIC TO BRILLIANT: FROM LN TO VISA	183
CHAPTER 12	BX: THE CAR THAT SAVED CITROËN	201
CHAPTER 13	XM AND C6: UNDERESTIMATED GRANDES ROUTIÈRES	211
CHAPTER 14	AX TO ZX: VIA XANTIA AND XSARA	229
CHAPTER 15	C-SERIES CARS	241
CHAPTER 16	CITROËN CONCEPT CARS AND DS-LINE: A NEW HALLMARK	251

	References	269
	Bibliography	269
	Index	270

The 2013 Cactus Concept hints at a new model design from Citroën. Note the newly revised chevron motif and DS-inspired 'floating' roof and stylized C-pillar. All pointers to a new shape for a new model expected onto the market in 2014.

INTRODUCTION

CITROËN: A DESIGN PHILOSOPHY THAT CREATED CARS

Why are Citroëns designed as they are? Surely despite all the claims, Citroëns are just cars like any others? The answers to such questions are that Citroën design *is* unique, and no, the Citroën is *not* just a car like any other.

There are other questions about the why and how, and not just the when of Citroën. What does 'old Citroën' now mean, what mental picture does the phrase engender? Once it meant a Traction Avant, and to a wider audience it means a DS or 2CV, but to some, 'old Citroën' might now mean something else entirely. Beyond the world of the DS and 2CV there is a whole new generation of Citroën enthusiasts who have little experience of these icons: Citroënism to such people means a CX, GS, BX, XM or C6 or DS3. So would it not be better if Citroënism *also* meant the more recent cars, as well as the cars from Citroën's deeper past?

Some Citroën enthusiasts dismiss so-called 'lesser' Citroëns, and a few are contemptuous of anything produced after the Peugeot takeover of Citroën. Yet surely Citroëns are not just classic cars – they are new, current production cars, too. Therefore, amidst many books on the marque, this text is an attempt to reframe a sometimes tribal debate amid Citroënistes and to provide a new reference point for a wider readership who, like me, are fascinated as to the *why* of Citroën – old or new.

Citroën has been the subject of many words, but some commentators have followed the fashion to see certain examples of the Citroën marque in isolation, however splendid. Could it be that a differing analysis might reveal new or obscured strands of the Citroën helix? Creating a book that crosses boundaries and tries to blend various aspects of Citroënism is not easy, but herein is an attempt to weave history with the 'atmosphere' of Citroën. The reader seeking every single production, ownership, or restoration detail of a specific Citroën model will need to consult the individual books that cater solely for each model respectively. Herein, the narrative highlights key design aspects, their causes and effects, and the creators of such facets of the cars.

The Citroëniste must ask difficult questions. For example, will the gorgeously sculpted C6 of *circa* 2005–2012 become a 'classic' in years to come? Perhaps it could, and maybe it is just a matter of time and patination: imagine, if you will, a young enthusiast dreaming of restoring a faded, down-on-its-suspension stops, flaky old C6 found in a barn in 2030. What joy might that engender in the mind of a future not yet cast – and would that young enthusiast, discoverer of a curved behemoth of a barn find, ever wonder what made the car what it

The legend. As fitted to British-built 2CVs.

was? He or she would have to look backwards, not just to the DS, but far back into a magical age of metal bashing and sculpted carrosserie to understand the ethos of Citroën.

Citroën's early rear-wheel-drive exploits, and the aeronautical and engineering tutelage of the 1920s that so crucially informed it, and its resultant ethos, are less commonly subjected to discussion. Such vital ingredients of the story are also rarely considered in relevance to the more contemporary Citroën cars. The fact is that without these early events, the revolutionary Traction Avant, the DS and all that flowed therefrom, could not have occurred: yet the relevance of early aviation, and the role of French education, architecture and design in Citroën's history, are often obscured by more modern and apparently 'iconic' Citroëns amidst writers' stories of them.

Perhaps a wider perspective can lead us to realize that today's Citroën, *and* the Citroën of distant decades ago, are undeniably linked by a founding ethos that is still manifested in the now. Citroën's current designers have recently begun to remind us of the marque's aeronautical heritage through the new DS-line cars, especially the DS5. Architectural influences are also now deemed relevant to today's Citroën design, just as they were eight decades ago when the likes of Le Corbusier inspired design. Architecture seems to be a strong theme in the lives of Citroën stylists and their training, and even today the names of Gropius, Wright, van der Rohe and Hadid are cited by Citroën designers. And fine art – from Chagall, Kandinsky, to the impressionists and to Picasso and beyond – is also relevant to what happened at Citroën. Frédéric Soubirou, the new DS5's body designer, recently said:

> *We've been inspired by our past and aviation, but also by the rest of the automotive industry. A few years ago this was a UFO, we had no experience on this, we wanted a new story for the DS, we wanted heritage. The DS should be recognizable from a distance, but it has to be consistent with the entire line. It is an architectural object*[1].

INTRODUCTION

DS design on the move. A late model DS in black flies the French flag in an evocation of the atmosphere of Citroën and Bertoni, as its double-lobed ellipsoid styling makes its definitive statement.

Such words prove that a resurgence of the origins of the early ethos is upon us at the same time that this book is written, with its own examination of that very genesis.

Because the key to Citroën's identity is design led, this book has a design focus – how can it not, for it can be argued that industrial design as we know it stemmed in part from André Citroën's actions as a founding father of the motor car and in the design innovations of his cars.

Those brilliant Citroënistes the Dutch, with their love affair for Citroën, enthuse about all types of Citroëns old and new – but it seems that based on certain other interpretations you could be forgiven for thinking that the rear-wheel-drive world of Citroën before 1934 had little to do with the subsequent front-wheel-drive cars. Other opinions seem to suggest that life begins and ends with the DS, or that the last 'real' Citroën was built prior to 1976 upon the Peugeot involvement.

Yet the reality is that today's Citroën is one grown from the earlier foundations of its DNA as the soul of Citroën engineering and design. From 1919 to the current reincarnation of the 'DS' branding, the spirit of Citroën has never died – it may have

A rare, red SM gets going. The SM's six Cibie headlamps under a glass fairing still astounds today's observers.

INTRODUCTION

faded for a time, but the essence of Citroën is unbroken. And while the DS – 'La Déesse' (the Goddess) – may be famous, there was advanced Citroënism both *before* and *after* the DS, something a few Citroën commentators sometimes forget.

If the DS frames an image of Citroën, as it quite rightly does, then we should not be blinkered by its halo, because *other* wonderful Citroëns exist, both old and new, and good as the DS is, Citroën as a marque is about something wider. This is a statement that will infuriate those who inhabit the DS 'cocoon', but there is a balancing to be asserted. However, be under no illusion, for the DS was, and remains, a defining event in automotive history – maybe even in history itself. But the complexity of Citroënism and its construction *does* embrace a bigger picture.

Conversely, neither is Citroën solely about the 2CV – which really ought to be the 'Deudeuche' as it is known in colloquial French by those who love it.

Without the earlier experiences of 1919 to 1933, André Citroën, his company, and the men he drew to him to create all the subsequent cars, could never have become what they later became. The Citroën design 'dream team' amidst the Bureau d'Etudes did not just occur overnight: it took years of growth and learning amidst a rare tutelage. Was the Citroën philosophy, the unique ethos, solely of André's hand? The answer is no, for it stemmed both from him and others: André's dynamism created the story, but others fuelled the plot.

In terms of his own psyche and actions, there was indeed something unusual about André Citroën's shaping of his company and its cars. He seems to have part created, part landed upon a maverick marketing or branding profile that was an early example of the unique selling point, and a niche identity that most other mass car makers often failed to achieve. Amidst the great landscape around this very clever man, his incredible energy and open-minded attitude, there can be found a substrata of men and deeds who themselves were vital to the cars that resulted. And these men were cast into a time and place in history and society that was unique.

While *not* in any way undermining the genius of André Citroën as the true hero of the marque, the fact remains that his cars were designed and detailed by other men when he was alive, and after he was dead. Such men may well have been responding to André's innovative, maverick future vision and his determination, but nevertheless, it is they who actually thought out the cars and the specific engineering and design features. After André's demise, his ethos and that of his team carried on and seeded a future cast upon the wings of the wind – wind being a key Citroën element.

So it is clear that while some Citroënistes see André as the sole cause and effect of Citroën, this cannot be wholly accurate. And some say that André Lefebvre, as Citroën's first great design pioneer, was in some sense the protégé or pupil of

Citroën and architecture have long-established links. Here the SM sits under the entrance to Gloucester Cathedral.

André Citroën. But the two Andrés, Citroën and Lefebvre, only worked together for under three years before Citroën's early death, whereas Lefebvre had come to Citroën after more than a decade of creating experimentation and innovation for Gabriel Voisin amidst an explosion of knowledge. Lefebvre and his colleagues were *all* the product of an amazing era in French engineering, design, art, architecture and philosophy that they were born into, educated within, and emerged from.

Any reader who doubts the effect upon Citroën of Gabriel Voisin as claimed in this book, needs to investigate just how many of the men of Citroën and its Bureau d'Etudes had come through the French colleges (notably as 'Ingenieurs Arts le Metiers') and then worked for, or near Voisin in his aviation arena after graduation and before finding their way to André Citroën's employment. Even a later President of Citroën, Robert Puiseux, had worked for Voisin. Again, today many of Citroën's designers have an interest in aerospace technology and architecture.

INTRODUCTION

TUTELAGE OF THE BEST

The role of the grand engineering schools and design institutions of France – the École des Arts le Metiers, the École Centrale des Arts et Manufactures, the École des Beaux Arts, the École Grande Polytechnique, and the École Nationale Suprieure de l'Aeronautique et de Construction Mecanique (Sup'aéro) – play a significant yet rarely credited role in Citroën's development as a company. Nearly all the men of Citroën from 1920 to 1970 had graduated from the education of these great colleges.

Today, Citroën's engineers and designers come from such schools and their modern equivalents such as the École Nationale Supérieure des Arts Appliqués et des Métiers d'Art, the Insitut Supérieur de Design, the École Superieure d'Arts Graphiques et Architecture Interieur et Design, and of course, from the Royal College of Art's Vehicle Design Unit, the Los Angeles Art Centre Car Body Design Unit, and a small and select band of transportation design courses at various colleges in places such as Lyon, Coventry, Detroit, Turin, Milan, Zurich, and Stuttgart.

Amid all this education, France in the early years of the twentieth century saw the birth of world famous artistic and intellectual movements. André Citroën and his men were witness to the techniques and effects of everything from Impressionism, Cubism, Art Nouveaux, Art Deco, Modernism and the streamlining movement, to the philosophy and science of France's greatest period of intellectualism and open-minded innovation. France *circa* 1900 to 1930 was the centre of an explosion of artistic, architectural, engineering, medical and social revolution. Other nationalities and their efforts were for some time eclipsed by the incredible multi-disciplinary talents of the French. Many great advances that touched the world came from France at this time. And there was a reason why Wilbur and Orville Wright went to stay in France – at the heart of early aviation.

How many people know that Citroën (at Pierre Boulanger's lead) funded the pioneer aviator Sensaud de Lavaud in the 1930s, to develop not just his gearbox ideas, but also his now long-forgotten rotary-cycle engine, and encouraged diesel engine development by de Lavaud. This was decades before others leapt aboard the 'rotary' bandwagon, which Citroën re-joined in 1964 to explore Wankel-cycle technology. And Citroën's first diesel-powered vehicles were pre-World War II.

Given all the advanced thinking evident, it becomes clear that Citroënism does *not* begin with front-wheel-drive cars: it is the earlier developments of Citroën via its early history amidst the aeronautical innovations of the 1920s that led to the front drive, aerodynamic, ingenious ethos that so encapsulates Citroënism

A 1927 C-Type displays the earlier version of the Citroën corporate branding. This car spent much of its life in Australia before arriving in Great Britain.

today. Citroën and Citroënism is all about thinking and doing the previously-assumed-to-be-impossible – or achieving the not-even-thought-about: Citroën is daring, different and brave, just like André Citroën its founder, and his men.

THE ELEMENTS OF ALCHEMY – VOITURE AERODYNAMIQUE

What is the act of studying aerodynamics: is it an aeromancy? The dictionary says that 'aeromancy' is 'divination conducted by interpreting atmospheric conditions'; how apt, then, for Citroën's famed aerodynamicists that such study and use of the wind should be a lead strand in the DNA of Citroën. As Citroën stated in 1984:

> *Aerodynamics – recently this facet of the motor car has received much attention. Citroën has been building aerodynamic body shapes for production cars of increasing and tested aerodynamic efficiency since 1934. Citroën is now responsible for an entire marquee, which, in genuine realistic terms of total drag and aerodynamic efficiency, is superior to any rival, class by class.*

Was this extravagant engineering taken to the edge of complicated confusion – or entirely rational genius stemming from superior IQ?

The Details of Design Research

There are only so many ways you can say the same thing, whoever the author might be, but what of a new analysis? Does the known story of Citroën support a more extensive automotive archaeology?

The answer is a resounding yes, for having studied the well recognized and profound effect of Gabriel Voisin upon André Lefebvre (and then the influence on Citroën of Pierre Jules Boulanger), it was correct to go deeper still because it is unlikely that Lefebvre, Voisin, Cayla, Mages or Boulanger assumed anything from perceived evidence. It is clear that they avoided this dangerous practice, and instead thought new thoughts, and that this design research psychology or philosophy underpins Citroën. And the revelation that Voisin luminary Pierre Cayla had invented not just aeroplanes, but an oleo-pnuematic self-regulating braking system for cars, and that Jacques Gerin had created an 'Aerodyne' that was a precursor to the DS, should both be food for thought.

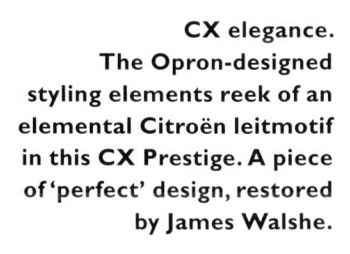

CX elegance. The Opron-designed styling elements reek of an elemental Citroën leitmotif in this **CX Prestige**. A piece of 'perfect' design, restored by James Walshe.

THE JOY OF CITROËNISM

We Citroënistes may well suffer from OCD, or 'Obsessive Citroën Disorder', or a Citroën psychosis. Perhaps it should be called *Citroënitis*, for it is a strange condition whose symptoms include staring at your Citroën from the kitchen or living room window, or worse, the bedroom (but not if you are French!). Those with Citroënitis are very protective about their cars. Maybe one can even be a *Citroholic*? No recovery programme is known.

I have owned many Citroëns: some have frustrated me with their foibles, but all have charmed me with their characters. Many Citroënistes have a passion for old Saabs and often refer to them as 'those Swedish Citroëns'. Few people know that in 1973 Citroën designed and built a 180bhp Wankel rotary cycle-engined helicopter, and subcontracted Saab to help build it. The helicopter, which had alloy blades, flew 200 hours test flying before the economic crisis of the 1970s and Citroën's debts effectively killed it.

Having been brought up from early childhood with my grandfather's Slough-built Citroën DS, I can be forgiven for my first car being a Citroën GS (accompanied by a Saab 99), and then a GSA, CX, Visa, ZX, and more recently a BX restoration project that resulted in a 'daily driver' for over a year. My GS derivative, the GSA, was a perfect car, totally reliable and strangely rust free. Today, motoring writers effuse about Subaru's flat-four horizontally opposed engines – yet Citroën has been designing them for decades.

Behind the Wheel

Driving a Citroën gives one a range of feelings. On starting up a hydro-pneumatic Citroën, one hears a gurgling and belching of the oleo-pneumatics as the mineral mix oozes through the many metres of pipework that course around the car carrying the fluid to its function. Then there is a clicking from behind the bulkhead as the suspension pump energizes as the engine revs rise, and suddenly the car levitates and there is a gushing sound of oil in pipework. This borborygmus rumbling of gas and oil in the car's intestines signals that the system is ready. Such is the Citroën, a wonderfully tactile, rewarding experience like no other.

What of the joy of driving and owning the twin-pot Visa? Whatever its 'humble' Peugeot origins, which might offend certain Citroën purists, this car was a superb device. My blue Visa was, with its pin-sharp steering, expertly tuned with conventional suspension, and brilliant body and cabin design, a real highlight, all without hydro-pneumatics. What a car, and a small, cheap one at that; for those in the know, and those who are not Citroën elitists, the Visa in 2- and 4-cylinder forms was one of the best small cars of its era, a real piece of design thinking. The fact that *CAR* magazine's George Bishop, at the time one of the top motoring writers in Britain, purchased a Visa for his personal use despite having access to any car he desired, spoke volumes of the Visa's design brilliance. And Visa's half-brother the Oltcit/Axel is an even more intriguing beast because it really was the last Citroën from the Bureau d'Etudes legacy.

Another significant figure of the greatest period in motoring writing, Ronald 'Steady' Barker, still cherishes his 2CV. The superb writer the late Phil Llewellin also preferred Citroëns, and in Andrew Brodie's exquisite and essential book, *An Omelette and Three Glasses of Wine – en Route with Citroëns*, Llewellin and photographer Martyn Goddard (with Brodie) recounted the affair of Citroënism. The writings of L. J. K. Setright and, more recently, Stephen Bayley, also populate Citroënism. Setright always said you could judge a car by its steering: he was correct, and the art of steering quality is a key Citroën parameter. At the revered *Octane* magazine, editor David Lillywhite, who can get his hands on any supercar he wants, runs an SM.

The Martians have landed. A British DS 'moment' made different.

INTRODUCTION

My next affair with Citroën was with the CX – an intergalactic star cruiser of a car. Rashly I bought a pale metallic lilac blue one, a 'Pallas', which was a Citroën trim level stemming from the DS Pallas within DS or 'Déesse', meaning Goddess, to the derivation to Athene and Pallas of Greek legend. Later CXs were of 'Athena' in trim nomenclature. With vivid blue interior trim, ellipsoid furnishings, and chromed, Art Deco-style wheel trims, the CX Pallas was a styling sensation; it rusted, of course, yet when it worked it was motoring like none other. You had to re-learn how to drive in order to extract the best from its vari-power steering and suspension set-up. Once mastered, this new driving technique (inherited from the DS and the SM) created in the conductor a perhaps delusional sense of grandeur. And yet such sweeping, smooth progress in a big Citroën *was* majestic: had not the CX's antecedent the SM, been coined 'Se Majeste'?

Driving the SM was incredible, but the CX was also a sensation. You had to slide yourself into the CX, as you slide into a sports car – yet there was plenty of room. No wonder French Presidents rode in them. The delusion was delightful – but although that 'CX' attitude was of course irrational, at least it was different, a sense of a very special occasion. Could *that* be achieved in its contemporaries?

The 2CV, DS and SM are revered in such places as Indonesia, Laos, Vietnam, Hong Kong, Malaysia, Zimbabwe, Uruguay, and other unexpected places where many examples of these cars lie awaiting their fate under tropical skies. There is even a website run by Pierre Jammes, dedicated to the DS in Asia (wwwDSinAsia.com).

There *are* other good French cars, but the Citroën, ancient or modern, has something special, that spirit of a car, that sense of occasion that marks a true automotive experience. Thus Citroëns could be exotic, grandes routières of aero-weapons with style, or they could be curious oddball little cars designed for the rural peasant: whichever, they were often very bizarre by the standards of perceived normality.

However, experiences of the previous Citroën capacity for rust and electrical temper tantrums will be very familiar to older Citroën enthusiasts. Yet underneath there was the design ingenuity that kept us hooked. More recently my ZX diesel was totally fault and rust free – yet as this is written my BX leaves a trail of green LHM 'life-blood' fluid (the blood that courses through its pipework) on the driveway, and it has also cooked its wiring with a lovely little fire. One day I shall write a book entitled *The Last Citroën on the Road to Rack and Rouen*, but in the meantime, I still adore my Citroëns and now covet, with some abandon, an M35 rotary Citroën to go with an XM V6.

To Citroënistes (never people to assume anything) there is nothing unusual, nor abnormal about having a relationship with an inanimate metal object. Ask a French farmer or his wife

Paris: Citroën Revolte concept car makes its stunning mark as another pointer to Citroën's design resurgence.

about their white Citroën van or the XM hidden in the barn, question an Alfa Romeo owner, or VW camper-van enthusiast, or ask a sailor or a pilot, for *they* will know what the elusive yet elemental allure of a hull is about. Indeed, we must surely consider *if* a sucking, wheezing, whirring (and *sometimes* hydraulic) Citroën is inanimate? For a Citroën is, above all, a sometimes recalcitrant, stylish, extraordinarily engineered, living, French mechanical device bearing the badge of the chevron.

We should not confabulate the failings of Citroën's past problems with build quality to any failing in design. The men of the Citroën studio – the Bureau d'Etudes designed cars – did not make them. The responsibility for poor quality and poor reliability was not theirs, so it is utterly incorrect to say that the act of advanced designs caused problems. It was the standards of the era, the manufacturing process and the weaknesses in execution that created the problems from which Citroën's cars sometimes used to suffer: one could apply the same reasoning to many of the American car marques, or FIAT, or worse British Leyland and what it did to Jaguar and Rover.

Despite the intelligence of the SM and the brilliance of the GS, followed by the architectural CX, Citroën's costs were huge. Teething problems were overcome, of course, and the cars' essential correctness shone through (just as with the earlier Traction Avant), but the issues of development costs and build quality failings did, in the end, take Citroën to the edge of the financial precipice in the 1970s. Despite all this, the band of followers across the social spectrum, across the class divides, remained: there was an emotional bond between Citroën owners and their cars.

INTRODUCTION

THIS PAGE:
With body design by Kevin Nougarede, *Wild Rubis* was Citroën's 2013 iteration of a 4×4 crossover-type concept. *Wild Rubis* is set to form the basis of the new DS7 model and may be seen in Citroën's 'DS-World' showroom in Shanghai before going on sale in Europe.

OPPOSITE PAGE:
The Henri Chapron SM 'Opera' four-door saloon was launched in late 1972. Eight were built. This one is at Gloucester Cathedral during the 2013 European SM Club tour. Carrossiere Chausson also built a one-off SM saloon prototype; although stillborn, it influenced the later Maserati Quattroporte.

Owning a Citroën still makes a statement. No wonder Jean-Jacques Burnell, the lead guitarist of *The Stranglers* drove a black CX Gti – and what of Russian President Leonid Brezhnev, who ordered a bright green-hued SM – champagne Citroënism at its height, it seems. The James Bond 007 music composer John Barry drove an SM, and so should have James Bond himself, but the closest he got was Roger Moore in a 1981 2CV.

DOUGLAS BADER AND A DYANE 6!

A surprising Citroëniste was Sir Douglas Bader, the aviator and World War II fighter pilot who so tragically lost both legs. One might have expected him to drive a Rover V8, or something with the status to match his powerful personality – yet Bader, at least in his later years, owned more than one Citroën Dyane. He could get from his West Berkshire home to London's West End in just over forty-five minutes going 'flat out' (as he described it to this author) up the M4 motorway in the Dyane, with his pipe bellowing smoke and the police eventually giving up the chase in Hammersmith. What a contrast the likes of Bader, the belligerent RAF fighter pilot of 1930s construction, is to the C6 owner, DS3 fan, thespian and satirist Alexei Sayle. Therein lies part of the paradox of Citroënism amidst those of polar opposites, yet who make the same Citroën choice.

There are also the celebrity Citroën owners and enthusiasts (or the infamous), a roll-call that includes Idi Amin, John Barry, Stephen Bayley, Raymond Blanc, Steve Berry, Leonid Brezhnev, Jean Jacques Burnell, Lee J. Cobb, Monty Don, the Shah of Iran, Peter Cook, Johan Cruyff, Sebastian Faulks, Graham Greene, Lorne Greene, Alec Guinness, Mike Hailwood, Erich Honecker, Saddam Hussein, the last King of Laos, Jay Leno, Robert Lutz, Lee Majors, Jonathan Meades, Manuel Norriega, Burt Reynolds, King Haile Selassie, Will Self, Charlie Watts, Orson Welles. McLaren Formula One team boss Martin Whitmarsh owns a Mehari.

In royal circles Prince Rainer and King Harald of Norway both owned personal CXs: as a young princess, the later HRH Queen Elizabeth II had a Citroën pedal car, as did her sister the Princess Margaret, both courtesy of a royal visit to Paris in the 1930s.

CITROËNS AT THE PALAIS

France's presidents mostly preferred Citroëns: Presidents Coty, De Gaulle, Pompidou and Chirac preferred Tractions, DSs and CXs, and an elongated SM and an XM also graced the presidential stables.

Back in the 1950s President Coty ordered a special long-wheelbase Traction Avant 15 Six H, a hydro-pneumatic Traction limousine built in 1955. President De Gaulle loved his DS, and his car saved his life with its abilities. Some presidents seemed to like the elegant Peugeot 604, but there were still Citroëns at the Palace. Jacques Chirac drove a CX Prestige Turbo for ten years before he got to the Palais de l'Elysée as president, while President Sarkozy left office in a C6, and President Hollande arrived in a C5 and took to the streets in a new DS5 – continuing the tradition irrespective of politics. Perhaps the next president of *la crise economique* will turn up in a 2CV!

A large number of British MPs also purchased CXs, and psychiatrists, too, often seem fond of them. Pilots loved the CX and the SM, and Lufthansa's former senior Boeing 747 captain, Jürgen Renner, is a well known SM owner and ex-head of the German SM Club.

INTRODUCTION

In truth, it cannot be denied that there was a time when Citroën slumped in the doldrums of product-minded, bean-counter control – but that was no more than a temporary moment. The smartly styled but tamely engineered Xsara felt more like a Ford, while the Saxo was Peugeot marketing and badge-engineering gone mad – but they sold and earned money for Citroën at a crucial period. It should not be forgotten that the so-called 'normal' BX was the car that saved Citroën in fiscal terms, a fact often ignored by the BX's critics.

AT THE SIGN OF THE CHEVRON – DARING BY DELIBERATE DESIGN

Citroën design past and present is a forensic research psychology like no other, and I have tried to follow such thinking in this text. I have given *some* of the more modern Peugeot-derived cars less space than other Citroëns. That is my prerogative and my choice, because the real design interest lies in the older Citroëns and the recent designs, and less in certain 1990s Peugeot seeded devices. But as you will see, Citroën is back from the doldrums and is once again a shining diamond in the automotive design landscape.

Re-inventing tradition amid innovation is the true secret of Citroën past and present. The point is that it illustrates that the French are still better at intellectualizing things than everyone else. What other race would have put so much effort into something so mundane as a car? This intellectual ability, born of the grand colleges of France, is how and why the art movements, architecture, even French garden design, all came about from an ability to see things differently and innovate without prejudice; such behaviours are also the core of Citroënism, proof then of a distinct design thinking, a philosophy that happened to build cars.

It may be said by some observers that this book is as complicated as the cars it describes and the men it follows. That would be good, for it *has* to be so to do them justice, because they were different, and sometimes very complicated. Even the French have on occasion raised their eyes and sighed at the bizarre nature of certain Citroën design details.

Crediting the figures in the Citroën story is important, and I have tried to name the main players and the less well known supporting cast; any errors or omissions in the names of Citroën employees are unintended, and simply reflect just how hard it is to research events that took place decades ago. Clearly the entire cast of the factory or the service or dealer departments cannot all be named, but alongside the men of the Bureau d'Etudes we should not forget the welders, trimmers, testers, mechanics, service agents, dealers, mechanics and garagistes who were also members of the great family of Citroën across France, Europe and the world.

This is a book for the Citroën fanatic: it has been written for those who seek discussion of cars and their design. As a book in the 'Complete Story' series I am a hostage to such a claim, but herein subject to the limitations of space and personal choice is one Citroëniste's version of a wonderful story. Not all will agree with the content or this author's views and for those that do not, well, they have the opportunity to research and write their own Citroën books.

Here, in a new text unlike any other about Citroën, it is time to embark, ease into the rich brown leather and raise up the suspension, slide a chromed gear selector into its machined-alloy gate and begin your traverse across the seas of normality to arrive in the land of Citroën and its thinking.

Lance Cole
Redon, Bretagne Sud, France

Tobacco brown leather, polished alloy and ellipsoid mouldings can only mean one thing: SM supercar interior and the atmosphere of Citroën.

CHAPTER ONE

THE ORIGINS OF CITROËNISM

THE ORIGINS OF CITROËNISM

THE CITROËN JOURNEY began with one man, André Gustave Citroën (1878–1935). He is our hero, but he did not do it all alone, and although loyally French, he was not actually French by DNA. Citroën as a brand and as a family may well be perceived as utterly French, the widely written truth upon which we must briefly alight is that this family were Dutch and Polish in their original DNA. André was born in Paris on 5 February 1878, but his diamond dealer father Levi Bernard was of Dutch-Jewish origins and his mother Masza Amalie Kleinmann was of Polish-Jewish extraction. Today the Dutch have a special affection for Citroën, and this should not be a surprise, for André was, in part, one of their own.

The name 'Citroën' is said to derive from a name change that stemmed from his grandfather's origins named as 'Limoenman' – literally 'lemon man' in Dutch. The link to citrus fruit or '*citron*' becomes obvious, but on moving up the social ladder the family created the name 'Citroën'. The name was initially spelt as 'Citroen', being devoid of the ¨ or diaeresis over the e, the addition of which creates a phonological change in sound by separating the spoken letters.

In Dutch, oe is pronounced as 'oo', so it is not unusual to hear a Dutch Citroën owner refer to a 'Citroon'. The correct French pronunciation of the name is Cit-ro-ën with emphasis on the last syllable 'ën', therefore it is *not* pronounced as the English say, 'Cit-chrun' nor 'Cit-rown'. Nor is it to be confused with *citron* in French as meaning lemon, nor is it 'Cityoen' meaning people or citizen.

So, 'Cit-ro-ën' (Si-tro-en) it is.

André Citroën was one of five children. His mother died when he was small, his father died in 1884, and his brother Bernard was killed in World War I; André was educated by relatives. After a sojourn in America as early as 1913, in 1914, young André married a Giorgina Bingen, who was of Italian extraction but a French citizen; Perhaps it was his DNA that made André who he was, a genius of future vision, seeded in French thinking and culture, yet unblinkered by not having a sole, single strand of thought or national stereotype. Tellingly, André was also fascinated by the futuristic ideas of Jules Verne.

Citroën's tutelage began at the Lycée Concordat upon the death of both his parents before he was ten years old, and then at the Lycée Louis le Grand. Next stop was the École Polytechnique, which was the principal technical school of Paris, from which he graduated as a young engineer in 1901. By 1905, Citroën's active brain had led to the idea to found his own engineering company. This company was 'André Citroën et Cie'. He was soon to make a clever business move by becoming involved in the small engineering concern, the Mors car company, owned by Emile and Louis Mors.

Prior to 1904, Mors (with input into its cars by Henri Brasier) was a success, and continued to make small runs of cars up until late 1906. Mors is said to have run into trouble due to design and production faults in its cars. Liquidation of the Mors concern was demanded by its Board, but one of the Mors directors had the better idea of bringing in a dynamic new force named André Citroën to do something new with their investment *circa* early 1907. Citroën was close to the director in question, and through Mors, André Citroën truly entered the motor industry. This was in fact André's second foray into automobile interests, because his first involvement with cars had been in 1905 via a commission to build a series of engines for the Sizaire-Naudin company.

There was a fight for Mors, and a Lyons-based company named Rochet-Schneider wanted to purchase the outfit, but Citroën and another investor got in first. Intriguingly it was the Mors factory and Mors machinery that latterly helped Citroën earn profile and profit from his wartime armaments business, both factors in his advancement towards becoming a mass-production car maker.

Another company, Le Zebre, had been small but had made basic early cars and turned in a profit from the approximate 1,000 cars it is reputed to have constructed between 1909 and 1912. Le Zebre's engineering brains came from Jules Saloman – who would soon work for André Citroën.

The man himself – hero, genius, maverick, engineer, paradox, and the person who helped create the dawning of a global industrial design movement: ANDRÉ CITROËN.

A less well known tangent to the story occurred in 1912, when André Citroën worked with his old college friends André Boas and Paul Hinstin to create a company Citroën-Hinstin. Here the three friends experimented with early ideas for gears and cogs in a small factory in the Parisian suburb of Faubourg Saint-Denis; this was a stepping stone to a larger facility near the Mors factory and the Quai de Javel. Citroën's new gear cogs were made in all sizes, and were first used in domestic appliances such as food mixers.

KNOWN PERSPECTIVES

In World War I, having been called up for military service, Citroën used his connections (via Louis Loucheur) to secure an audience high up in the French government, where he persuaded the Minister for Production to let him set up a munitions company and greatly improve national output; in doing so he laid the foundations for his car business (the Minister was Albert Thomas). The French government organized the use of 12,000sq m of land for Citroën to set up his armaments factory on the banks of the Seine, and soon the dynamic André Citroën was building and delivering vast numbers of military shells – as he had promised he would.

After World War I, in 1919 he operated as 'André Citroën: Ingenieur-Constructeur'. By 1924 Citroën's own business was registered as 'Société Anonyme des Engrenages Citroën'.

In the office *circa* 1921, André Citroën and his closest associates.

Therein lay the clue, as 'engrenage' is French for 'cog' – cogs as found in gear drives and transfer mechanisms. Citroën's cog company and its 'usine' (factory) was turning out machined cogs and drive bezels, the essential ingredients of Citroën's growth, and reflecting the brief Citroën-Hinstin company interlude. Some of these gear or cog drive mechanisms were twice the height of a man, as real heavyweight industrial toolings. André's story was that he saw some wooden helical gear cogs when visiting some of his Polish relatives in Lodz, and this set him thinking to build cogs in heavy metal and alloy. So helical gear drive bezels, aero engines and the cogs and drives within them also became a Citroën speciality.

To this day, the Citroën emblem is a stylistic rendition of the chevron pattern of gear cogs.

During the war years Citroën produced armaments under military commission; 23 million shells were made at his Quai de Javel premises (later renamed in Citroën's honour), and this armament output later created a car production-line process that was influenced by Henry Ford's early practices, of which Citroën was aware not least through his association with Gabriel Voisin the French aero-engineer; Citroën had met Ford as early as 1912–13, and soon, Citroën was the first European to make cars this 'Ford' way on a production line. And the war production had allowed André to create both personal profile and fiscal security to mimic Ford's idea.

As a parallel, another company name lies hidden in the genesis of the Citroën story, that name being Adolphe Clement. Grown from origins making bicycles and a tyre company that had moulded licence-built Dunlop tyres – or 'pneu' as they became known – Clement built a company that had further English connections when the firm produced 'Gladiator'-branded motorcycles. Clement also had a part share in René Panhard and Emile Levassor's fledgling company *circa* 1897. By 1903 Adolphe Clement had struck out on his own, and had formed a new company with a new name: Clement-Bayard. This company built cars, motorbikes and automobile parts for domestic and export markets.

By 1913 the company was part of the rapid expansion of French aeronautical knowledge and production through the building of aero engines. The Great War of 1914–18 saw Clement-Bayard move into munitions production, yet despite its previous experience, upon the coming of peace the company failed to return to its core business of aero-auto-mobilia. But there was a riddle in the story, for Clement-Bayard and its vital factory capacity was bought out by André Citroën. This was to become the site of the famous Levallois factory of 54 Quai Michelet, which complemented Citroën's existing Quai de Javel factory. Citroën's first cars from Levallois were produced in 1921, and the last on 29 February 1988, when the final 2CV from Paris was built.

In a parallel with other car makers, the expansion of military production created the factories and funding to think about post-war needs and opportunities. By 1919, Citroën – whose factory would soon employ nearly 12,000 men and women, provided his workers with food, child care and a medical centre – turned his engineering brain to the thought of cars. But these thoughts were not of some grand limousine of a 'land-yacht' car for the rich and powerful, at that time the only people who owned cars, but instead a car for the people.

THE PARADOX AND THE EFFECT OF ANDRÉ CITROËN

Although he wanted to do things for ordinary working people, André Citroën also lived well; he used the beautiful villa *Les Abeilles* at Deauville, Normandy, close to his favourite casinos, where on one occasion he won a very large amount of money. He also bought La Ferté-Vidame's chateau and grounds near Paris, which became Citroën's secret test track. Yet contrary to some misconceptions, André Citroën was not a property speculator nor a collector of expensive trinkets; a gambler perhaps, but he was *not* a playboy, in fact André was a trained engineer, a serious thinker, and a devoted husband and father. He may have been touched by the then mood of anti-semitism, but he proved his detractors wrong with his cars. As a supporter of music and art, he sponsored those less fortunate than himself. Like his cars he was, it seems, a touch paradoxical.

For André, innovation without prejudice was the key thinking. Could André Citroën, in branding terms, be framed as not just a maverick, but the first such entrepreneur? As we will see, André Citroën was a father of design, one of the creators of what we now call industrial design, and his effect even touched the development of American design and marketing. Today, few people realize how important André's wider effect was on our everyday lives and the products we use.

Citroën's links to, and enthusiasm for, aviation were also very significant. Not only did his engineering company supply the emerging aeronautical industry, he was embedded amongst its pioneers, and worked and socialized with them. Many of André's engineers and designers had aviation backgrounds, and the 'greats' of early aviation touched André Citroën and his thinking; he was also a friend of Charles Lindbergh, and hosted Lindbergh in Paris. Perhaps most importantly, André was close to Gabriel Voisin, a friendship that would lead to the defining event of another André – Lefebvre – joining Citroën.

From such aeronautical engineering practice emerges a question for the observer, namely why are some Citroën cars large extravagant behemoths, and others small economy cars, yet ones with special ingredients? And did Citroën start as a maker of small cheap cars, and then become an exotic big-car brand? The answer is no, for after its initial cars Citroën did not make standard, 'basic' small cars, nor did it create conventionally engineered big cars. All André Citroën's cars, whether large or small, were *designed to be different*.

The 1934 Traction Avant was a revolution, and the Deux Chevaux (or 2CV as it appears we must call it) may have been basic, but both were designs of brilliance that defied, and paradoxically even created, conventions. And therein was the quandary, the paradox, and one of the key ingredients of the uniqueness of Citroën as a total design entity and as a brand philosophy.

EARLY CITROËN CARS

The true beginning of Citroën cars began in 1918 when in a very short time, André Citroën produced his first 'Citroën'-branded car for release in the summer of 1919. It was based on a chassis design by Jules Salomon, the engineer he had recruited from Le Zebre. In truth, that first car was quite conventional in its appearance. Citroën is reputed to have initially commissioned an engine design of large capacity from Louis Dufresne, and then the building of the car known as the Artaud-Dufresne 'ADC' prototype which had originally been offered to the Mors company: Dufresne later worked for a certain Gabriel Voisin.

Citroën had nearly fallen for the high-powered limousine-thinking of the era, but he side-stepped it in a change of mind. Jules Salomon and the engine designer Edmond Moyet, both ex-Le Zebre, were the other engineering brains soon to become the boffins behind André Citroën's first car thoughts, which Georges Haardt would subsequently input as lead production manager.

At this time most cars were built as running chassis and then sent off to an independent coachbuilder who would create the design or bodywork, a process known as carrosserie – that is, a specially created or chosen body style would be designed and built by the carrosserie as coachbuilder. Many standard chassis had unique or low-volume produced special bodies. But Citroën produced the whole, clothed car ready for delivery to its new owner. In a rare sop to fashion, Citroën offered six different body styles, *his* factory styles.

So was born the Citroën Type A, as a fully kitted out, 4-cylinder powered, 1327cc rated car. This was the first low-cost car, which retailed at FF950 and would be offered with self-starting using an electric starter. It boasted powered lamps and a spare wheel, and it was, of course, rear-wheel drive. Of interest, the car was the first French production car to be left-hand

HOW ANDRÉ CITROËN'S FIRST CAR WAS NOT A CITROËN

André Citroën's first 'car' was not a Citroën – it was a Mors, yet a Mors that was never produced beyond prototype stage, but yet which did actually exist.

In 1917, when Ernest Artaud, a former motorcycle rider and mechanic, who had then worked for Panhard from 1914 onwards, met a certain Gabriel Voisin, Voisin had discussed his own plans to build a car rather than his usual aeroplanes, with Artaud. Artaud had teamed up with Louis Dufresne and created a modified Panhard-based car design. Artaud and Dufresne secured the rights to this lightweight, modified car and discussed it within the crucible of French engineering concerns at Issy-les-Moulineaux, Paris. There, Gabriel Voisin took a close interest, as he was in the process of creating his car. Artaud and Dufresne also had a Monsieur Cabaillot working with them, so the car became an 'ADC' in its nomenclature (Cabaillot went on to race Peugeots).

Artaud and Dufresne knew that André Citroën was also experimenting with thoughts of car design, and Dufresne had shown his early car plans to Citroën for consideration as a car for the Mors company, which at that time Citroën had had an expanding control over and a record of success in reviving – notably with new, quieter and more efficient 'Knight'-designed, sleeve-valve engines. Citroën wanted to produce a 'people's' car, yet the Dufresne design was not a car for the masses – few cars were.

In 1917, André Citroën commissioned Artaud and Dufresne to build three prototypes of the single, original version – three real rolling cars to be built in the Citroën workshops. So the first car to be built by André Citroën in his own Citroën factory was an Artaud-Dufresne creation and was intended as a post-war Mors company product. In total there were four of these working completed prototypes. But Citroën decided the design was too complex, and side-stepped the car. By March 1918, Artaud and Dufresne had taken the car, with Citroën's blessing, and offered it to Gabriel Voisin who used it as a development base.

Some degree of confusion exists over the chronology of the above car and its process as three rolling prototypes. Source references suggest that in mid-1917, André Citroën himself offered the Artaud-Dufresne design to Gabriel Voisin. At the same time, with munitions contracts soon to cease, both the Voisin company and the Citroën company were searching for a project to diversify into: there were factories and workforces to run, especially so for the more established Voisin company.

Whatever these circumstances and their exact dates, the fact is that André Citroën's first 'car' was an Artuad-Dufresne-Cabaillot design that became a Citroën-funded series of prototypes built in a Citroën-owned factory, and intended as a Mors car, yet which became a Voisin. Perhaps above all, in this vignette of early Citroënism, we see once again more proof of just how close were the aviation and automobile communities of engineering graduates, and how the process of Citroën was touched by the hand of Gabriel Voisin.

---

drive – something that was not then a set specification in France or anywhere. Announced in May 1919, Citroën manufactured 400 cars in just a few months after the first delivery in July 1919; less than a year later production figures had touched 12,000 units.

With its rather rakish front and rear wings or mudguards, there was something just a little revolutionary in this small car's appearance; but the mass-produced Citroën was a cheaper car, not a limousine nor a laundaulette. The car had a touch of Ford Model T to it, and the frontal treatment mainly had the feel of an early car, as did the windscreen and cabin design of this 'soft'-top, convertible-roofed car. Small, easily mass-produced like no other in Europe, the Citroën Type A was a basic yet clever little thing that had steel disc wheels as opposed to wooden or metal spokes. The car's Citroën double chevron badge was blue – not far off Ford blue, it should be noted.

The car was solid, roomy and well engineered; Citroën sold Type A cars as Parisian taxis, earning valuable income and PR for the fledgling car company: it is reputed that Citroën had financed his own taxi company to promote his cars with drivers and passengers alike. Before long London's taxis would be Citroëns.

The Type A was not as basic as has been often been suggested. It had expensive engineering within it that signalled techniques often only associated with the later, more obviously advanced Citroëns post-1934. The Type A had a pressurized crankshaft, expensive long-life bronze bearings, and improved oil flow pattern in the cylinder head. All these meant that the engine ran more smoothly and cooler, and lasted longer. Fittings

Type A and 5CV cabriolet owned by Clive Hamilton Gould: although styled in the idiom of their era, a great deal of high quality engineering went into these rear-driven cars and their resultant capabilities.

were of high quality and the car had excellent handling and steering. Citroën's engineers put significant effort into setting the car up, even if it was 'only' a 1.3-litre car. Given such factors, it should be realized that Citroën's advanced design behaviour stemmed from his first car, not just in the 'belle epoch' years of the mid-twentieth century: so the seeds of a specific design research culture were sown far earlier than is fashionably perceived.

In 1920, André Citroën also experimented with a half-tracked car based on the Type B that had agri-utilitarian or military possibilities. This design was known as the 'Autochenille' (caterpillar), and used the patented track-driven ideas of

Adolphe Kégresse. In rural France and Switzerland this 'soft-roader', as we might term it today, sold well and built up the brand name profile of Citroën. The French army and the farmers of rural France loved the half-tracked Citroëns and their capabilities.

By 1921 André Citroën had recruited his first technical director, a Louis Guillot who had also graduated from the École des Arts le Metier and, of significance, had worked on aeronautical designs for the Morane company. It was Guillot who would also recruit Maurice Broglie from La Regie (Renault) to manage the Citroën drawing office in 1924.

For 1922, Citroën had produced his Type B with a larger 1452cc engine, and 89,841 cars were sold across five years and in a multiplicity of body styles. Then came the cars that included a two-seat sports body with a cross between boat-tailed and torpedo styling. This was the famous 'jaune' or yellow car, as the only paint scheme offered was a strong hue of lemon yellow, a citron Citroën! One version of the B2 car was a two-door, with stylish, elliptically shaped side windows – perhaps the first hint at a Citroënesque style. For 1925 Henri Jouffret had designed a 1579cc L-head engine for the B12/B14 cars; Citroën's cars may also have been the first to be attractive to the emergent class of female drivers of the 1920s.

The nomenclature of early rear-wheel-drive Citroëns are framed by the French fiscal tax rating created in 1925 as a 'Systeme des Chevaux' originating from a *chevaux vapeur*, then defined as steam power; this confusingly led to a 'CV' as a taxable rating band that was streamed across various set 'CV' ratings such as 2, 3, 5, 7, and so on. However, it did *not* indicate the exact rated power of the engine in the English sense of brake horse power (bhp), as defined in the later Society of Automotive Engineers (SAE), or the Deutsche Industrie Normalen (DIN) definitions. So a '5CV' Citroën can even be called a '5HP' car in the context of its CV band rating, but that is not to define it as a '5hp' (bhp) car in the output-rated sense. So HP derived from CV is not hp as in bhp; a later Type A described as a '10HP' was actually a '10CV' and in reality had 18bhp. Such confusion perplexes observers to this day.

Similarly, the definitions of British-built Citroëns do not always agree with the French nomenclature, and this applies not just to rear-driven cars but also to the Traction Avant. Differing engine options created much confusion amongst badging.

The 5CV Type C2 of 1922 was given a longer chassis in 1923, and developed into the C3. By 1924, the Type C two-seater had grown a centrally positioned third seat just behind the front seats, giving rise to an early 'cloverleaf' or three-petal pattern-related Citroën name: the 'Trefle'. The period had also seen the B2 become a Citroën 'Caddy', as the company's first small sportster, of which only 226 were built; soon after, another sub-1.0-litre car emerged as the 5CV.

Classic French advertising for the 5HP with magneto for the 1923 model year.

Citroëns from the early period 1920–23 differed in specifications as the company developed. For example wire wheels were optionally fitted in place of steel wheels. Early Type C vehicles had coil ignitions, but later cars had magnetos; a resultant 'old' and 'new' model definition has been applied to these Type C cars. The B14 Taxi *circa* 1925 was a typical example of opportunistic marketing, with its upright stance, real wickerwork side panels, and large blue- and gold-painted ovaloid chevron badges mounted on each side.

By the mid-1920s, Citroën had opened up not just new factories such as the one at Levallois, but had also decided to address and re-frame the needs of the car market and its various sectors. Citroën also employed Lucien Rosengart as finance and planning director, to address his projects and marketing pitches (Rosengart put up Citroën car prices). In 1923, Citroën employed Maurice Norroy as a business executive, and recruited another engineer, a Paul Laubard. Also employed was Georges Sallot who had worked with Salomon on the B series cars.

Citroën dropped the 5CV car in August 1926 as the company moved upmarket to cars not just with larger engines, but also with steel bodies. Thus the B10 was the first fully steel-

LEFT: **The essential 5CV 'Trefle'.**

BELOW: **Roof up, the car looks decidedly 'vintage'.**

bodied car in Europe (using American-supplied Budd Company pressed steel), not in a monocoque sense, but as a steel-clad coachwork. This stemmed from André Citroën studying and having discussions with the American Budd company, who made steel shells for railway carriages and supplied all-steel car bodies in the USA (André's first visit to America was in 1912). In fact it was a Budd-licensed process that allowed Citroën to explore all-steel body construction. Citroën erected a steel-stamping or pressing plant at St Ouen-Gare, and then employed J. Paul Vavon as technical director for the newly titled 'Société Anonyme' that was the Citroën company.

Citroën also bought land and factory floor space to allow for expansion, and built a foundry at Clichy. Clearly this was a period of massive expansion under a determined personality, with some degree of a desire for self-publicity. For 1925, the B10 Type was a Citroën 'first' with all-round disc brakes. Then a new 9CV-rated L-type engine of 1539cc boosted the B14 model, which had shades of American styling in its looks; the engine had been designed by a Henri Joufret, another aeronautical engineer who had graduated to automobiles (via Peugeot). Citroën manufactured 50,526 B14s in 1926–27.

UPON BECOMING INDIVIDUAL

For the middle years of the decade, Citroën turned out the B12, the B14 of 1538cc and 22bhp. These, like the later B18 model, were upright and staid in their styling, aping British Edwardian 'Landaulette' coachbuilt shapes that the English upper classes favoured. Then came the C12/27, the C4, and leading to the first 6-cylinder powered Citroën, the 2442cc, C6 and then the C8/C12. A hint of a more modern, more defined style of Citroën design motif began to emerge in around 1929, when a slightly raked-back ovaloid grille design bearing the Citroën chevron became the first visage or graphic of Citroën.

The cars of 1929–30 also developed a sculpted, compound curve shape to the joining of the front body and windscreen pillars, but in other respects, even these larger, more contemporary Citroëns still lacked a defining essence. It was upon the front grille of the 1932 Rosalie two-door (but not on the smaller 1933 Rosalie 10L Faux Cabriolet) that the first major iteration of the chevron logo would appear as two large inverted V-angled chrome bars emblazoned across the radiator grille (this was before the Traction Avant made such a technique more obvious), and would also appear as a defining styling element on the Type 23 commercial vehicle in the early 1930s.

Good cars though the early Citroëns were, the brand Citroën had yet really to fully define itself or its image. The cars were not revolutionary, and some were basic, but Citroën was en route to the definition of its own motifs: yet could it be that the brand Citroën was André *himself*, and that his product was in part secondary? This would soon reverse itself with a product that defined the brand and led to further identity of product, not of name or badge.

Ever the astute marketeer, Citroën seized upon the popularity of his half-tracked cars and devised overland treks to prove the concept and raise profile during the 1920s. Citroën offered seats to scientists and journalists on a series of adventures using the half-tracks, and the ensuing PR coverage was worth millions.

From December 1922 to January 1923, a Citroën half-track expedition had crossed the Sahara Desert from Algiers to Tomboctou (Timbuktu). The Autochenille, driven by Georges Marie Haardt and Louis Audouin Dubreuil, led the first trans-Sahara crossing by car. Their 10bhp-powered B2 half tracks traversed 3,200km (1,990 miles), achieving an incredible 150km (93 miles) per day in the shifting, unmarked sand ways. From October 1924 to June 1925 another Citroën half-track expedition drove from Algeria to the southern Cape of Africa via Kenya. This was the journey so unfortunately titled the 'Black Journey' or 'Croisere Noire'. Asia beckoned as late as April 1931 for a 'Yellow' trip – the 'Croisere Jaune' – starting in Beirut using C4 and C6 half-tracks. This pair made it as far as what was then Peking, via the high mountain passes of the Himalaya. At one point both Citroëns had to be dismantled and hand-portered across the impassable mountain tracks. But they were re-built and drove on to China.

Pierre Louÿs

Citroën also created an in-house PR or 'propaganda department' in the 1920s, and its first director was Pierre Louÿs (another graduate of the École des Beaux Arts) who oversaw a mass advertising campaign using art and poster design as an innovative marketing tool; Louys drew many of the famous adverts used by Citroën.

Pierre Louÿs had joined Citroën as a draughtsman and emergent stylist, but would become a vital figure as the firm's first artistic director. He provided a further link to great design when he married Jeanne Morel, one of Chanel's top designers. Louÿs' assistant was Eugene Michel, and from 1924 Citroën had an atelier or studio for its artistic output and in-house car-body design, led by Louis Theux. André Martin was a senior figure in the project planning office.

By 1925 Citroën was a household name, not just through its cars but through André Citroën's clever marketing, which included hiring aircraft to write his name in contrails in the sky over Paris, and fitting 200,000 light bulbs and many kilometres of electric cabling to the Tour Eiffel.

Citroën and Lalique

André Citroën was a man who played for high stakes, and in business terms often won. His marketing skills may have been extravagant, but his sponsorship activities certainly encouraged creative works.

In 1925 Citroën sponsored the *Exposition Internationale des Arts Decoratifs et Industriels Modernes*. This major Paris exhibition

Art Deco extravagance: aping the Lalique influence, this 1930s mascot mounted on a Traction Avant Roadster encapsulates the style of the era.

led to the illumination of the Eiffel Tower in its sponsor's colours – thousands of light bulbs that read CITROËN. At the same time, André Citroën sponsored the glass artist René Lalique, maitre-verrier, and it was with Citroën's encouragement and sponsorship that Lalique began his creation of a series of exquisite car mascots that took the design of this device to a new relevance in automobilia. Naturally Lalique was commissioned by André Citroën to produce a stunning sculpture of five horses as 'Cinq Chevaux': this was applied to a 5CV Citroën. Lalique went on to create car mascots for the height of the Art Deco period to complement his previous works with Coty sponsorship.

The exhibition and its exhibits of advanced design stunned the world and had a major effect upon the emergence of American industrial design.

AUSTRALIA AND AN AFFAIR WITH 'LES ANGLAIS'

Somehow, a Citroën C-type 'Torpedo' found itself in Australia as early as 1925. There it was driven by a Mr Neville Westwood as a used, secondhand, high-mileage car all the way around the available roads of remote outback Australia. This proved the toughness of Citroën's components. Preston Motors of 114–122 Franklin Street, Melbourne, Victoria, were the main Citroën

RIGHT: **This 1927 C12/24** was originally exported to Australia from Great Britain and returned in recent years. It is rust free and original. With steel wheels, wide running boards and upright style it is conventional yet has a certain stance and economy of line.

LEFT: **Still in regular use, this car displays its astounding condition as an original pale blue Citroën.**

BELOW: **Well built in steel, is there something of the Ford Model T to the effect?**

A classic original Australian handbook from Preston Motors Pty.

A scene from the early days of Citroën production.

agents at the time; by 1927 there was even a Citroën dealer in Adelaide. Citroëns were made in Victoria State until 1966.

Of curious interest, Sneddons Motors of Brisbane, Queensland, advertised the Traction Avant for sale in Australia as 'the British Citroën' and as the 'only British car in Australia with Floating Power!' How strange that the delusion of a Slough-built, French car being touted as 'British' should be foisted upon the 'Empire' set of the then pro-British Australian psyche. A 12-volt Traction Avant sold for £430 in 1950s Australia – a huge sum, but sheep farmers were rich, and if a Mercedes, Jaguar or 'British' Citroën succumbed in the outback, the car was dumped and a new one purchased.

One of the earliest exponents of Citroën in Australia and New Zealand was the New Zealander Jack Weaver, who became well known campaigning his Traction Avant faux coupé in rallies and trials in the marque's early years 'down under'. In 1949–50 Jack Weaver even constructed his own Traction Avant fastback in the early 1950s as a real coupé with an air of Bertoni-esque style and a shortened wheelbase. Incredibly Jack Weaver nearly gave Citroën its one and only Grand Prix reference when he entered a self-designed car with a modified Traction Avant engine and gearbox in the 1960 New Zealand Grand Prix. Sadly he failed to qualify. Weaver had used a supercharged Citroën engine taken from a British-built 'Light Fifteen' 4-cylinder, yet converted to deliver rear-wheel-drive power through his adapted gearbox design. With stronger bearings, pinnions and casing, and an internal redesign, Weaver's gearbox stopped the Traction gearbox from self-destructing, and the concept was later added to restored Traction Avants.

An Australian who cut her racing teeth on a Citroën in Australia was the famous 1920s female driver Jean Richmond. She drove a 5CV-rated Citroën tourer fitted with an overhead-valve conversion of the type most numerously sold by F. Crespelle; Crespelle was an orignal French tuning manufacturer who 'improved' power output.

Maybe it was the early Australian exposure that brought Citroën to General Motors' (GM) attention in the late 1920s? At this time GM was seeking European investments, and would soon swallow Opel AG. Talks between André Citroën and GM were rumoured, but GM side-stepped the chance to gain a foothold in 1920s France.

Citroën began importing cars via Gaston and company at its first British base in Hammersmith/Acton in Britain in 1923 – to beat tough new import duties imposed by the British government at the time – and soon moved to a large Citroën-built factory in Slough for 1925. So Citroën and 'les Anglais' have had a long and enduring affair. Before 1936 a Danish Citroën factory produced cars from its own production line (latterly, Citroën produced cars in Chile, Argentina, Australia, Ireland, Romania, South Africa, Spain, Thailand, Yugoslavia, Zimbabwe, and elsewhere).

Japan

As an example of André Citroën's global ambitions, the first representatives of the Citroën company arrived in Tokyo as early as 1921. Felix Schugs and Alfred Scellier arrived as André's envoys to set up what became Citroën's furthest outpost, as the *Nichu-Jutsu Citroën Jidosha Kaishe* or the Franco-Japan Corporation for the selling of Citroën Ltd. By 1925, Citroën had sent fifty cars (nearly all 5CV models) by ship to Japan, and Alfred Dommiec had organized the first Citroën Japan car rally by the Nippon Citroën club from Tokyo to Osaka.

An intriguing legal dispute lasting several years took place when it was discovered that a Japanese citizen, a Mr Yamanouchi, had, without prior communications with André Citroën, registered the use of the Citroën trademark name in Japan in early 1920 in what can only be called a clever and audacious move.

Citroën has nevertheless enjoyed a long relationship with Japan; it has sold many DS, GS, CX and SM in Japan, and today is a revered marque with an active Japanese owners' club.

Across the Pacific Ocean, the Traction Avant soon found its way to pre-World War II America, and it would not be long before Citroën officially existed in America.

LUCIEN ROSENGART

Alongside these names there was a man who both influenced and worked for a period with André Citroën. This was Lucien Rosengart, a Frenchman from the east of the country. Like Citroën himself, Rosengart was a self-publicist and an engineer. It is accepted that Rosengart had some influence on André Citroën's fledgling business, and it is reputed that he assisted the emerging Citroën company because he was invited to be a Board member of S. A. André Citroën, and worked as a financial director in about 1923. In the 1920s he was also a consultant to the Peugeot family after severing his Citroën affiliation.

In 1928, Rosengart used ex-Citroën man Jules Saloman to design and engineer a new small car: this was intended to be the first Rosengart-branded car. Yet he then took a different route, and got Saloman to re-engineer a licensed version of the Austin Seven. It was a first foray into car making, albeit one with British ancestry. Rosengart then created a front-drive car that followed Citroën's lead. Strangely it was one part-based on a German license-built Adler car of Hans Rohr design. But in 1938 Rosengart returned to the Citroën idiom, for he took a Citroën Traction 11CV and restyled it with a special body that looked like a cross between a Citroën and a Mercedes with the addition of a new Rosengart design hallmark – a sharply angled 'V' frontal design that aped certain themes from the American Cord marque.

CITROËN AND ADOLPHE KÉGRESSE

Adolphe Kégresse was the pioneering figure behind the Citroën half-track type vehicles. Although French, his early engineering works included a stint in Russia building half-track expedition cars (including an early modification on a Packard, a British-originated Austin–Kégresse armoured car, and a Rolls-Royce Silver Ghost half-track conversion in 1916 that was later used by Lenin) for Tsar Nicholas II. After the Russian Revolution and World War I, Kégresse returned to France, and resumed his friendships with Jacques Hinstin and André Citroën. It was the 'Systeme Kégresse-Hinstin' and its combination of rubber, alloys, belts and pulleys that was the key to the success of the Citroen half-tracks – being lighter, easier to make and service, and much quieter (albeit of shorter life than metal-based mechanisms).

Kégresse had patented his tracked vehicle idea as early as 1913, but he was soon to be welcomed into the Citroën fold. In a wise move André Citroën realized that Kégresse and his half-tracked vehicles would have a wide variety of money-making applications ranging from military use, across agricultural, local

Autochenille – the Citroën half-track as used on the various 'Raids' of the 1920s.

business, ambulance, alpine and tropical or desert needs. Military variants were sold to the armies of Poland, Belgium, The Netherlands, Spain, and to Great Britain.

Kégresse's system used metal tracks mounted in a composite device of pulleys, rubber blocks and steel pins that were driven as a tractive force from a power take-off device from the engine. The early Kégresse system vehicles featured a rear half-track mechanism that was driven from a rear-mounted differential that took its supply from a prop-shaft equipped engine. However, Kégresse and Hinstin soon modified the system, and by the mid-1920s the tractive force drive mechanism operated on the front section of the half-track, yet still configured from a front-mounted, in-line, rear-drive, prop-shaft type layout. With the front of the tack unit powered and the rear axle riding free, significant weight was saved, along with a shorter drive mechanism with fewer power losses and better traction. By 1927 Kégresse had redesigned his tracks so that a new steel belt and pulley and rubber cone system reduced the risks of the tracks coming off, and created more efficient pulleys.

Apart from the well publicized Citroën 'Raids', the Kégresse-equipped Citroën half-tracks were used not just by the French military and other desert-roaming adventurers (including the Alaskan Raid Croisere Blanche), but also by the famed explorer Admiral Richard E. Byrd in his 1934 Antarctic Expedition. This created further profile for brand Citroën on an international scale.

To further promote the idea, Citroën created the 'Citracit' (Citroën trans-African transport) concern as a sub-division to promote the range of half-tracked vehicles. The engineering that went into the range was intriguing: for example, the Citracit P6 used a 15CV 4-cylinder in-line engine of a massive 2.8ltr cubic capacity, originally a Mors-designed engine from over a decade earlier. Panhard were also involved in the later P16, which was a small armoured car to a Panhard design constructed by the Schneider et Cie company. The Citroën B and C series ranges provided the basis for the Kégresse range, and the C6 took over as the 6-cylinder based P-series range.

Kégresse Models

Uses: Tourism/commercial/agricultural/industrial/military/expeditions

Type	Production period	Type	Production period
K1	1921–24	P17	1929–34
P4T	1924–25	P15N	1928–36
P7/T	1925–27	P19	1929–35
P7B	1927–28	P20	1936
P10	1928–29	P107	1935–40
P14	1926–40		

Notes:
- P16 as Panhard/Schneider armoured vehicle
- P21 and P112 special-build vehicle series in low numbers
- B2, P14, P17, P19 variants all saw service in the Polish Army

Early Citroënism: the view from the large steering wheel and open cabin.

COACHBUILT HEYDAYS: CREATIVE CARROSSERIE

Although André Citroën created whole cars as packages that were ready to drive, the fashion for adding special one-off or limited-series bodies to chassis did not leave Citroën untouched — indeed, many coachbuilders and body designers took the early cars for the basis of their creations, and André was hardly likely to complain.

Henri Labourdette and Son

Henri Labourdette was the son of a carriage maker. Henri founded his own role as a carrossier, and the first Labourdette cars were bodies built upon Panhard-Levassor chassis. Henri's son Jean-Henri had a flair for design and an interest in early aviation. As early as 1910 he developed an interest in aerodynamics – or aerodonetics, as the science was then termed. Jean-Henri fitted rounded, smooth fronts to his cars and pointed 'torpedo' tails, and he created a series of swept and sculpted open bodies known as 'skiff' cars based on Panhard-Levassor chassis. His first Citroën body was a boat-tailed B2, in 1922.

Labourdette also worked for Farman and Voisin, so he too was a Voisiniste. In 1933 he created a streamlined body for a Renault chassis – but perhaps his company's wildest moment was the spectacular body for the Delage DS-120 chassis. Jean-Henri Labourdette also invented and patented a unique windscreen mechanism that dispensed with the A-pillar, and wrapped and sealed the windscreen glass smoothly into the side window glass at the point where the door glass met the windscreen. He called this the 'Vutotal' and it was a redesign of the 'montant de para-brise' – a pillarless windscreen that allowed the driver to see a 'total view' without obstruction by the A-pillar.

A Driguet-bodied Car

Also associated with Citroën were the brothers René and Alexandre Driguet, who build bodies for Citroën and Voisin in their own carrosserie works. The Driguet-bodied Citroën B2 of 1924 had touring or 'torpedo'-style bodywork, and a V-shaped split windscreen. This rakish car had a 'duck's back', or semi boat-tailed rear and four seats, yet only two doors, access to the rear being between the front seats. Of note were the flowed or angled front wings. The car was rare at the time, and is even rarer today.

In 1931 Marcel Le Tourneur, son of Jean-Marie Le Tourneur, joined the Le Tourneur and Marchand carrosserie and brought in Carlo Delaisse as chief designer. Cars for every major French chassis builder resulted. Le Tourneur created a 'Unic' coupé in 1938 – and to say that it had shades of the Traction Avant 15/Six would be an understatement. The famed carrosserie of Franay built a limousine-type body on a Citroën Traction Avant 15/Six.

There was also a notable carrosserie named Mannessius. Derived from the name of the founder, Manès Lévy, who was of Latin lineage, this body design company was founded in 1919 at Levallois-Perret, Seine. It created its own all-metal body construction technique, and as early as 1925 invested in state-of-the-art metal presses using the patented Baehr techniques. Contracts from Fiat came in, as did one from André Citroën, who tasked Mannessius with building the bodies for his 'Rosalie' cars – which a certain Flaminio Bertoni styled long before he became famous for the DS.

The small carrosserie company of Bourgeois-Luchard had worked for Voisin and created an obliquely sliding partition that was patented; but Bourgeois-Luchard were soon to create a body of 'coupé des dames' style on a 5CV Citroën.

Other later Citroën 'specials' from external carrosserie would include the Robert de Clabot Citroën 11 CV coupé of 1937 that used a Traction Avant as a base. De Clabot added an American-style front bonnet and grille, and new side panels leading to a pointed tail and spatted rear wheels. Only the Traction's windscreen and scuttle remained.

Figoni and a Prize-winning Citroën Design

In later years, even Guiseppe (or Joseph) Figoni, the stylist of Figoni and Falaschi and of Talbot fame, would build a special body for a Citroën. This would be a 'shark-nosed' variant of the Traction in its 1950s 15/Six guise. This 1952 design would win a design prize – the Prix de l'Art et de l'Industrie. But before that came Jean Andréau, Pierre-Jules Boulanger, Georges Paulin, Flaminio Bertoni, Sixten Sason, Battista 'Pinin' Farina (whose company latterly became known as 'Pininfarina', but only after fraternal merger with the family Farina firm of 'Stablimenti Farina'), and a host of design 'greats' across an Art Deco Europe.

There were two famous carrosserie names that did not work either for or with Citroën at this time, yet their influence on the aerodynamics and design movements cannot be irrelevant to design or to Citroën. First was Iakov Saoutchick – or Jacob Saoutchik as he later styled himself. Saoutchik's styling specials were 'leading edge' design, often assisted by input from other themes, leading to his trademark wildly curvaceous and perhaps over-chromed detailing on Delahaye and Tabot-Lago chassis. Saoutchick also created a body for a V12 Voisin-engined Bucciali.

The other important name of influence was that of Georges Paulin, the dentist turned brilliant car stylist and aerodynamicist, whose work with the Parisian carrosserier Marcel Portout would include the Embiricos Bentley streamliner, prior to his untimely death in World War II.

From de Lavaud and Eiffel, to Panhard, Penaud and Tatin

From 1870 onwards the likes of Louis Blèriot, Pierre Cayla, Henri Coanda, Gustave Eiffel, Leon Levavsseur, Emile Levassor, Otto Lilienthal, Frederick Lanchester, René Panhard, Ettiene Bunau Varilla, Alphonse Penaud, Victor Tatin, Nikolai Zhukovskii, to name some key players, had paved the way. The Hungarian-Swiss-French Paul Jaray would soon soar above many of these names with his aerodynamic car designs (these were redesigns of car bodies upon existing car chassis, as opposed to entirely newly engineered cars in total). Yet it was the French pioneers who were the first generation of aerodynamic car designers (with Tatra being owed an honourable mention), before the advances of German car design and aerodynamics of the 1930s.

Two further projects framed the technical advances: Rumpler's Tropfen-Auto, and Auriel Persu's sleek, aerodynamically sculpted 'Correct Car' concept.

Circa 1914–25 there were other names with Voisin links that would end up with Citroën links – notably the Paulin-Ratier aviation company and its engineer Paul Dreptin. The Paulin-Ratier company would soon manufacture the *Citroënette*, a half-scale pedal car with which André Citroën would market his brand to the minds of French children, who would, of course, grow up to buy his full-scale cars. Citroën would in the 1920s also produce so-called 'toy' cars in the form of the accurate tin-plate *Jouets Citroën*, with which he would pre-condition his future clients. Production ceased during World War II.

Pierre Delcourt was an aero-engineer who privately made the first aerodynamic Citroën saloon – a papier-mâché and wooden built boat-tailed affair on a C4 chassis in 1928.

Other significant early explorers of aerodynamics were Ettiene Bunau Varilla, Marcel Riffard and Gaston Grummer. Grummer would build a series of early aerodynamic car bodies, notably for Voisin. The Spaniard Jean Antem would influence Panhard design, and in the 1930s build his own design on Citroën Traction Avant underpinnings: the carrosserier Henri Esclassan would do likewise with his modified Traction Avant 'Splendilux'.

France was at the heart of advances in structures and aerodynamics amidst an engineering explosion of ideas. But then came the 1929 economic crisis that began in America and shook the world. Just as it took hold in the early 1930s, André Citroën tore down his factory and rebuilt it to cope with ever-increasing demand, spending millions of francs in the process. He also sat down with his team and decided to create a whole new range of cars, and dreamed up a way of taking a massive leap forwards in design terms. It was a big risk, yet one that may not have been as obvious as hindsight might suggest.

As Europe's economies faltered, so too did orders for new cars. Yet at exactly this time Citroën had launched two cars that were arguably its first real attempt at defining a true Citroën style in design terms. These cars were the Citroën 8, a small, low-slung, two-door sports-type coupé; and the large, upper-class limousine Citroën 15, as the 'haut de gamme' range-topper.

Moteur Flottant and a Swan

In 1932, André Citroën marked a future thought by mounting the engines of his cars independently from the chassis. Iron-to-steel mountings were eliminated for the engine block to chassis joining. Instead, a 'floating' rubber absorber or cushion was made to carry the engine to body linkage. This 'moteur flottant' reduced vibration and resonance in the chassis and body to a remarkable degree. Suddenly Citroën had developed a notable characteristic in its cars. It was in fact an American-owned, but French-created idea that Citroën used under patent license from Chrysler. The system was the brainchild of Pierre Lemaire and Paul d'Aubarède, who had sold the patent to Chrysler – but perhaps the French public did not know that!

André Citroën coined a graphic icon of a swan, serenely sailing along unruffled by its unseen paddling. It was an inspired piece of alliteration, and the swan 'flottant' badge was featured on the front of Citroën cars, and so equipped the revised C4G

This Jouet Citroën model depicts an early C6 camion.

THE ORIGINS OF CITROËNISM

De Lavaud's Citroën-supported Advanced Designs

Another great early pioneer of all things aeronautical and automotive was Dimitri Sensaud de Lavaud, a Brazilian who moved to Paris in the 1920s. De Lavaud is well known for his subsequent designs for the speed-sensitive self-changing gearbox mechanism, and a patent for independent front suspension. He had made Brazil's first powered flight in 1909, and built several prototype cars in the late 1920s, including a steam-powered device and a cast alloy mono-piece chassis in 1927. These were constructed in Paris, and André Citroën took a close interest – indeed we can speculate as to whether de Lavaud's advanced thinking may have been part of the catalyst for André's own thoughts. Early de Lavaud gearboxes were fitted to the prototype Traction Avant (but not for production), thus proving how close Citroën was to de Lavaud, and the importance of the obscured influence of the latter.

What is less well known is that with the Citroën company's financial support (approved by Pierre Boulanger), de Lavaud designed and built a rotary-cycle engine in the years 1937 to 1941. The use of a diesel-fuelled rotary engine was also considered at this time by de Lavaud. This unique project was, after the Traction Avant's front-driven ohv powertrain, a significant example of Citroën's interest in advanced and alternative engine technology.

Jaeger instruments and chevron motifs amidst an elliptical instrument panel mark a proper Citroën dashboard.

and the 2.6-litre C6G of 1932. And if the engine could be isolated from the chassis, could not the suspension? Now there was a thought for the future...

Le Mans – Just

As the 1930s dawned, there came about the strange tale of how in 1932 a Citroën C4 Roadster entered by a young man named Henri de la Sayette competed at Le Mans at the Grand Prix d'Endurance. The C4's co-driver was to be a Charles Wolf. Sadly the C4 consumed its electrics after just three laps, with Wolf at the wheel. Henri de la Sayette never got to drive a Citroën at Le Mans, and it would be decades before another Citroën attempted the race. Recently this happened in the hands of Antonia Loysen and Celia Stevens in July 2010. On that date, Loysen's privately created 1932 Citroën C4 racer came home in forty-seventh place in the Le Mans Classic race, giving Citroën only its third Le Mans appearance in eighty-seven years[2].

The second appearance was in 1972 by a privately entered SM driven by Guy Verrier. Citroën had refused Verrier permission to drive a new SM at Le Mans (not least after an SM had expired at the Spa endurance race in late 1971), but in the end Verrier's Ligier-tuned SM did enter Le Mans. A second private entry has also been claimed for the same year.[3]

Citroën's 1920s competition cars (often racing at Montlhéry) carried the brand logo of the *Yacco* oil company whose sponsorship of Citroën competition cars continued for decades, including the 1972 SM at Le Mans.

ROSALIE – THE LAST OF A FOUNDING LINE

In 1932 the last of the pre-fwd revolution Citroëns, the Types 8–15, and the delightful 'Rosalie' range, heralded the initial run of early Citroën design motifs. The 'Rosalie' range was inspired by a number of tuned roadsters that set endurance records using streamlined bodies of varying forms, notably the 'Petite Rosalie 8', a wonderful blue-painted, boat-tailed racing machine which created illustrious speed record-breaking scenes at Montlhéry as late as 1933, when the car covered 300,000km (186,420 miles) in 134 days of near-continuous running at an average speed of 93km/h (58mph).

There were definite hints of late-1920s American styling to the Rosalie saloons and the decidedly Packard-esque Rosalie 15CV Coach Grand Luxe coupé of 1933, and the designation NH, or *Nouvel Habbilage*, was used to signal these new, larger, revised Citroëns. A key figure in the development of the Rosalie cars (and the engineering of the subsequent Traction Avant) was Jean Daninos, who joined Citroën in 1928 as a body structures specialist (Daninos went on to found FACEL).

For the rather upright Rosalie range it was the 'CV' rating rather than styling that set the marketing trends – people wanted more power. Citroën fettled and modified these cars, even restyling them and adding his new independent front suspension to the last 226 of the 54bhp, 2650cc, 15CV-rated variant.

A series of special streamlined bodies adorned a few of these later revised Rosalie chassis, and lightweight or 'légère' versions of smaller, shorter Rosalie bodies were also produced as 15CV cars with large engines but smaller bodies from the 10CV Rosalie. Confusingly there was also a 10CV Légère. A brief closing highlight for the Rosalie range was to see the car fitted with the larger overhead-valve engine from the Traction Avant in 7CV and 11CV rating. These engines had to be turned around – 'moteur inverse' – in order to work in the rwd configuration. The 1628cc from the Traction 7 had its capacity increased to provide a higher cruising speed.

André Citroën also allowed the use of externally designed coachbuilt special body designs on a series of late model cars. Contributing carrosserie included companies such as Sical, Manessius and Millon Guillet. It is reputed that over fifty specialist body designs were applied to Citroën Rosalie chassis up to 1937. Incredibly, in 1935 even an early diesel engine was fitted, after development by Ricardo in England. Later Rosalies were also fitted with the new torsion bar suspension designed for the Traction Avant. However, a plethora of body styles, and large modifications in parts that became model specific and not interchangeable, had since the late 1920s created a huge operating cost base: it was a symptom, and one perhaps of no surprise.

The larger Rosalie cars were the first 'big' Citroëns in the fashionable sense of the term, and were manufactured until late 1938 alongside the new Traction Avant until it gained wider acceptance – a wise move on the part of the Michelin directors who by this time controlled Citroën.

Soon André Citroën would go the whole way and create a car with everything that was so new, so unheard of, that it marked a new chapter in his company's life and in car design, and finally reflected both himself and the times he loved, and those people that surrounded him. It also reflected his admiration for American practices, and his effect upon America and the consequences that created car design.

There was the matter of world economic difficulties, cash-flow interruptions, and the need to seek further investors to stay afloat. This was because the new car that Citroën would soon launch, would also fail to take off immediately – not through any fault of its design (although there were teething problems with the car), but because of the economic crisis. Buyers all but dried up for several months, and not least overseas due to exchange controls and poor fiscal rates. Citroën's expenses in building factories, creating cars, and maintaining

Circa 1930, a 'Rosalie' leaves the Agence Citroën at Grand Garage Vienne in Brest, Finisterre, Brittany.

KEY MEMBERS OF THE DESIGN/ENGINEERING TEAM PRE-WORLD WAR II

Flaminio Bertoni	Pierre Louÿs
Gustave Behr	André Martin
Maurice Broglie	Paul Mages
Charles Brull	Pierre Mercier
Jean Cadiou	Eugene Michel
Marcel Chinon	M. Monteil
Pierre Louis Cordier	Edmond Moyet
Raoul Cuinet	Jean Muratet
Paul d'Aubaurd	Theo Nordinger
Jean Daninos	Maurice Norroy
Alfred Dommiec	Roger Prud'homme
Henri Dufresne	Pierre Provost 'le Colonel'
Alphonse Forceau	
Pierre Franchiset	Leon Renault
Raphael Fortin	Louis Robin
Louis Guillot	Jules Salomon
Georges Haardt	Georges Sallot
Charles Houdin	Maurice Sainturat
Henri Jouffret	André Sellier
Maurice Julien	Pierre Terrason
M. Kazimierczak	Louis Theux
André Lefebvre	J. Paul Vavon
André Louis	

an international profile had been huge, running into hundreds of millions of francs: the company owed its suppliers and its bank, and a rare strike at the factory also upset the financiers.

As the major French national corporate entity, Citroën may have been at risk of investor speculation, and the thought of a foreign investor getting their hands on a French institution must have caused concerns at the highest level. The possibility of investment in Citroën from Opel, Chrysler, Volvo and Skoda were all rumoured[4]. France was also in the midst of industrial and political crisis at this time, and the expensive employment laws that were imposed on major companies via the Front Populaire were not insignificant to the Citroën story.

By 1933, through various contacts and discussions, Citroën found himself selling a major share of his creation to the Michelin family concern. The Michelin family knew what Citroën was capable of, and also what waited in the wings. Nevertheless, that did not stop them pruning the number of employees at Citroën, and invoking cost-cutting measures which some have described as a 'purge'. But had Citroën been top heavy and over-staffed?

Inside Michelin was the future Citroën luminary of Pierre-Jules Boulanger, a man with a massive brain and huge engineering/architectural/design-minded talent. What was about to happen at Citroën under Michelin had the roots of its revolution in the often ignored beginnings of Citroën, and the influences of an important age in social, artistic, cultural and engineering advancement.

Before embarking upon the Citroën journey post-1934, the genetics of its latter progeny need to be understood. We need to know what made Citroën, what *created* the mindset of its just-about-rational engineering extravagance – it was not *just* André Citroën and his interesting personality with its expansive lateral thinking. As the Citroën story evolves to 1934 and the Traction Avant, we have to go back to the roots of the Citroën tree, and dig up the deep, often hidden layers of what made Citroënism, for therein lies the often ignored DNA of the Traction Avant, the marque itself and its later ideology, even of today's Citroën cars.

MICHELIN: DYNAMIC DYNASTY

The Michelin family and their business based in Clemont-Ferrand were another tangent of early French industrial excellence. They were also major supporters of early aviation, and suppliers of the prestigious Michelin Trophy awards to early aeronautical pioneers; this also touched the development of British aviation through Samuel Cody, who won two Michelin awards.

In the latter part of the nineteenth century the brothers Edouard and André Michelin started a business importing rubber, and creating and manufacturing a new range of products. It was not long before the idea to produce car and aircraft tyres became obvious. During World War I Michelin built over 1,850 aircraft in its factories; by 1930 it was a household name in France, and Citroën's supplier of tyres. When Citroën went bankrupt in 1934,

Michelin's Monsieur Bibendeum mascot was a marketing icon across the decades.

Michelin was its largest creditor. Almost overnight, Michelin took the reins of Citroën, and Pierre Michelin became the guiding hand that oversaw the Traction Avant and placed Pierre-Jules Boulanger into Citroën. Sadly Pierre was killed in an accident in 1938, leaving Boulanger to master Citroën.

In 1946 the Michelin 'X' tyre was developed for Citroën; it was applied to the Traction Avant and 2CV, and was used on the DS. This tyre broke new ground in terms of its construction, webbing, fibres and compounds.

Without Michelin, Citroën as a marque would have died in December 1934. In 1974 Michelin sold 50 per cent of its interest in Citroën, and when Peugeot took full control of Citroën in 1976, Michelin gained 10 per cent of Peugeot Société Anonyme shares, thus continuing an involvement with the beloved marque of Citroën.

CHAPTER TWO

GENESIS OF AN ETHOS

*LEFEBVRE UNDER
VOISIN AND BEYOND*

GENESIS OF AN ETHOS

LEFEBVRE UNDER VOISIN AND BEYOND

FROM 1919 TO his death in 1935 André Citroën created the beginnings of the fantastic legend of Citroën, but it took a series of circumstances to bring together the alchemy of themes, talents and knowledge that resulted in the brew that became the magic of Citroën's design revolution for small as well as big cars.

The essential, elemental Citroënism stemmed from just a few men. André Lefebvre was in 1933 the man of the moment for Citroën, but he had been trained and influenced before that point. Lefebvre was, after all, an aeronautical engineer, car designer, road racer and innovative genius prior to his arrival at Citroën, and he is rightly credited as the man behind the advancement of Citroën's ethos of front-wheel drive, and the early consideration of aerodynamics, clever packaging and exquisitely intelligent engineering. From Traction Avant to the DS, Lefebvre surely became the embodiment of an identity for Citroën.

But did Lefebvre just wake up one morning and announce his Citroën design direction? Of course not, for behind Lefebvre's thinking lay years of training, and the influence of one incredibly driven character, a man who was more than a genius, a personality of the polymath, that of Eugène Gabriel Voisin. Voisin was a man whose defining influence upon Citroën design is cited by a few but not known by many. And Lefebvre was not the only man to be trained by Voisin and to have influenced Citroën: there were others, long forgotten and rarely named.

André Citroën had been impressed by front-wheel drive in America where he had seen a front-driven, alloy V8 prototype of W. J. Muller chassis design at the Budd factory in 1931, and also the Gregoire 'Tracta' car, with its front-driven emphasis. Clearly, front-wheel drive was a meeting of minds for the two Andrés.

FROM BOATS TO WHEELED SKIFFS

How did Lefebvre get to Citroën? The answer is that he started out as a young engineer with Gabriel Voisin's aeroplane company in Paris just after World War I. It was here, working for an aviation manufacturer, that Lefebvre was trained and conditioned into the thinking of aeronautical engineering standards and into aerodynamics and handling. Lefebvre worked on the design of the Voisin bomber in 1919, so his thinking, his own design research psychology, began when the evolving art of aerodynamics was born from hydrodynamics: the beginnings of aerodynamic flow studies lay in boats and their flow dynamics, and many of the early proponents of car design reached back into boat hull or yacht research for their stepping stones into creating early aviation.

Streamed Lines

The new term for smooth design was soon to be 'streamlining', and it would reach its peak of public perception in the 1930s when Art Deco and its ability to transform the mundane into the elegant via reshaping or reskinning became not just a fashion but a design language. But what was 'streamlining'? It was a term that was conceived to describe the path that molecules or particles of air followed as they flowed over or from an object, so it was a line or track that they streamed along from a trigger or reference point so the air particles followed a streaming line – a streamline. The terminology stemmed from the early studies of water and fluid flows or hydrodynamics in the period 1875 to 1920.

The nautical influence was evident in terms such as 'skiff' and 'torpedo', which were applied to early attempts at automotive streamlining from about 1905 to 1925. So sailing, yachting and then sail planing (gliding) and motor-powered boating led to powered flight and onwards to car design. If an engineer knew about an aeroplane's centre of gravity, its centre of aerodynamic pressure and its lift pattern, not to mention longitudinal stability and undercarriage suspension issues, then these things were an essential precursor to knowing the same things about a car – principally a Voisin/Lefebvre racing car, and ultimately a Citroën saloon car. Lefebvre is reputed even to have made an attempt at starting his own aeronautical company.

The fact that there was an aeronautical engineer behind Citroën's design lineage and research psychology is of great note in the Citroën story. Both André Citroën and André Lefebvre were close to Gabriel Voisin and his aero-auto-mechanical output and influence.

A Beginning and the 'Sup'aéro'

Voisin's later pupil and Citroën's future star Lefebvre was born in August 1894, of a well-to-do family. By the age of twenty-two he was an early graduate of the École Nationale Supérieure de l'Aeronautique et de Construction Mecanique (the 'Sup'aéro') at the highlight of French design growth, and mirrored in output by the Grand École Polytechnique.

In April 1931, after many years working with Gabriel Voisin, André Lefebvre had accepted the security of an offer to join Louis Renault to develop the 'Reinastella' model. Lefebvre spent two years at Renault, and reputedly there were rows with Louis Renault who had no interest in new technology: the 'mindset' was different, and Lefebvre was keen to move on.

Lefebvre was still a close friend of Voisin, and expressed his feelings to him. Coincidentally, Voisin was talking to André Citroën about the future of the Voisin company – but Lefebvre,

ANDRÉ LEFEBVRE (1894–1964)

Born near Paris in 1894, few men have influenced not just French automotive design, but also international engineering as much as André Lefebvre. His initial studies were into early dirigibles or hot air ballons, and this led to a fascination for all things aeronautical; from this stemmed his growth under Voisin, and his vital role in the creation of the ethos of Citroën. He was the passionate visionary of the Traction Avant, the 2CV, DS, and more.

Under Voisin as his chief engineer, Lefebvre created grand prix cars and racers, and established the principles that touched not just Citroën, but later car design on the road and on the circuit. So advanced was the Lefebvre-Voisin C6 Laboratoire wood and aluminium monocoque, composite-constructed aerofoil-shaped racer, that the authorities reacted against it. Others such as Jaray and Rumpler may have created early aerodynamic cars, but they built tall and large re-creations on exisiting chassis. Only Lefebvre at Voisin investigated the low-built, low c.g, small cross-sectional area thinking that was the true advance of such work in the 1920s.

At Voisin, Lefebvre was working on large, high-powered, front-wheel-drive cars, but the idea failed – only to reappear as part of Citroën's Traction Avant of 1934. Citroën was defined as such until the 2CV and DS, both of Lefebvre, challenged that definition. Yet the Traction Avant was a car years ahead of its time, as the DS also later became. Few other designers can claim such a record of this kind of astounding future vision and engineering capability. The Traction Avant was a seminal moment in automotive history, and Lefebvre was its father – and the DS, however advanced, was in its wake.

Lefebvre is said to have been constantly driven, a man who poured out thousands of ideas, some of which were too much even for Citroën. Perhaps other engineers were ordered by Pierre-Jules Boulanger to rein in Lefebvre's creations a touch, but the facts are that Lefebvre never stopped. In the mid-1930s after the success of the Traction he was working long hours to create a new derivation of his ideas. These included a CVT transmission, on which he worked for over two decades before it was perfected by Van Doorne/DAF; there was a Lefebvre-conceived electrically powered car; and before that, and of great note in 1936, a small transversely mounted 1000cc engine with its gearbox mounted *in situ*, again an idea that pre-dated others – significantly the Issigonis use of such a layout two decades later in the Mini. Lefebvre also considered the use of a radial engine, and a de Lavaud rotary cycle in a car in the 1930s.

From aircraft to cars, and even to furniture and the advanced use of early plastics technology, Lefebvre can only be described as a total genius, a polymath engineer with a calculating brain, yet one with artistic flair and the capability to see beyond the dangerous, rigid, entrenched thinking of perceived wisdom and all its blinkered orthodoxy.

André Lefebvre, whose story is enmeshed in the narrative of this book, lived life at Citroën to the full. His home in the Department Var was where the DS was secretly tested. Lefebvre's *Coccinelle* design project, although unrealized, was a true future vision before and beyond the DS, one that may yet define the future of rational, eco-relevant car design. His life was wonderfully celebrated in a book by Gisbert-Paul Berk[5].

André Lefebvre's time at Citroën's Bureaux d' Etudes remains a defining moment in automotive history. And if ever there was a spirit of Citroënism, then Lefebvre was the genie who blended the essential elements into an alchemy of automotive passion.

Timeline of Lefebvre's Innovative Design Research Thinking

1916: Early interest in architecture and hot air balloons is manifested as design work on brakes and suspension components for Avions Voisin bomber.

André Lefebvre, genius, visionary engineer and designer, and one of the greatest, yet most obscured names in European car design.

Continued overleaf

ANDRÉ LEFEBVRE (1894–1964)

1919: Assists Voisin to improve the efficiency of Voisin's Knight-derived sleeve-valve engine; begins early research into aerodynamics and structures.

1923–24: Designs Voisin's C6, C8, C9, C10 grand prix racing cars. Drives and competes in numerous races and trials events. Hones aerodynamics and drivetrain dynamics research; creates forward bias braking ideas. Develops low c.g. design concepts with Voisin. Researches centre of aerodynamic pressure effects and in-board roll centres and c.g. tuning; begins to develop low frontal area design thinking.

1925–29: Designs Voisin 4-cylinder and 8-cylinder world speed/endurance record-braking cars. Leads 'Laboratoire' car thinking, and conducts experiments into all aspects of car design. Wins the Monte Carlo rally in 1927. Designs and constructs nearly all components in the Voisin 12-cylinder V12 record-breaking car of 30,000km (18,640 miles) over ten days at an average speed of 133.53km/h (82.98mph). Works on Voisin-funded front-wheel-drive car. Innovates use of the aviation material duralumin in car design.

1932–33: Brief spell as designer/engineer with Louis Renault, and develops the 4CV Reinstella range. Renault rejects Lefebvre's idea for a small front-wheel-drive car.

1933–34: Joins André Citroën; goes on to create the advanced Traction Avant in a matter of months – innovates the monocoque construction body; creates subsequent Traction Avant variants.

1936: Investigates radial engine design concepts, and suggests its use in a small car of approximately 1.0ltr capacity. Devises forward underslung clutch gearbox theory for transverse in-line engines.

1938: Draws up CVT transmission theories.

1939: TUB design van proposal, and early TPV–2CV concepts.

1940–45: Experiments with alternative fuels and electric car designs. Creates 2CV-derived agricultural vehicles and implements.

1946: Design work on H van, and rekindles 2CV with Bertoni.

1948–55: Explores VGD large car design concepts, culminating in the DS. Researches plastic, nylon, synthetic composite technologies.

1958: Creates advanced aerodynamic *Coccinelle* eco-car of great efficiency using plastics technology; designs furniture using plastics.

---

the brilliant mind that Citroën required, was working at Renault. Within days Voisin had told Citroën that the man he needed to advance his engineering was Lefebvre, now at Renault. Strings were quickly pulled, and Lefebvre left Renault's employment at Billancourt near Paris and by March 1933, within weeks, he had joined Citroën.

Given that Lefebvre had been one of the brains behind some of the Voisin company's list of aeronautical and automotive patents, the advanced thinking that soon became manifest at Citroën should not be seen as an 'overnight' revelation: it had been decades in the brewing under development at the Voisin company's Issy-les-Moulineaux laboratory in Paris.

Lefebvre was a keen car racer, driving Voisin's ever-larger cars in races, and was best known for his stints at the wheel of the Voisin C6, a car known as the 'Laboratoire' for the simple reason that it sported aerodynamic fairings, a pre-Kamm, pointed torpedo tail and some clever 'lightweight' – 'légère' or 'leggerra' – construction techniques. Lefebvre also worked on Voisin's record-breaking speed trials cars, and through to the Voisin C12. The pair also studied handling, as well as the effects of low-speed aerodynamics and lightweight chassis-less design. Henri Rougier was a lead driver for Voisin, and a man with aeronautical experience, and he was key to the development of Voisin and Lefebvre's ideas on the race track. It was Rougier who won the first Monte Carlo rally. And Lefebvre had, of course, worked on a Voisin front-wheel-drive engine.

ART DECO DESIGN – BEFORE AND AFTER

From the developments of the early aero-auto era before World War I came the cultural steps that led to an 'industrial' practice of art and engineering: this became industrial design as an entity. Art Deco was more than just a passing moment, because it taught designers and consumers about design and the language of design by turning normal everyday items into exquisite forms and shapes, yet which retained their function. From Art Deco came a new age of design and industrial and product design, as well as building design. Car design as product design was a vital activating component in the wider history of design, yet is often ignored by some Art Deco specialists. French design and Citroën design were an essential cog in this greater mechanism.

The 'Aerodyne' Era

In these early years of the nineteenth century, other names would populate the Parisian design enclave which was so vital to the creation of the knowledge that became the DNA of Citroën. For instance, the English-born, but French-speaking and Paris-based Henri Farman would emerge as an aeroplane maker. By 1908 Farman was the first man in the world to fly a closed 1km circuit – and he did it in a Voisin-engineered aircraft. He also flew in America and created an aerodynamic car body design. Also in 1910, the esoteric French engineer Robert Esnault-Peltrie created a part-metal, streamlined monoplane. Like André Citroën, Esnault-Peltrie was a fan of Jules Verne, and he would also be a pioneer of rocket research, also the study of space travel, and the use of nuclear power – all before 1925.

In 1911, streamlining was taken a step further by the shape of the Tatin-Paulhan-designed 'Aero Torpille', or Torpedo. By 1913, the world's first monocoque, aerodynamically streamlined wooden monoplane would emerge, not in Britain, nor in Germany, but in France as Deperdussin's 'Monocoque', a truly revolutionary, high speed device that would later influence Lefebvre's automotive thinking. In 1910 Armand Jean Auguste Deperdussin had employed Louis Becherau to create an advanced monocoque monoplane. The Deperdussin had a Swiss-French engineer as its father in Monsieur Ruchonnet. Little did Deperdussin know that his early craft with its single self-supporting 'mono-coque' (one-shell) body would soon influence a car – the Citroën.

FROM MONCOQUE TO POD, AND COANDA'S TAILPIECE

Levasseur's 'Monobloc', Bechereau's monocoque Deperdussin, and other French designs such as the single pod 'one-box' car of Emile Claveau, were decades ahead –and although this lead would be smothered by the industrial might of conventional practice, the French nevertheless had a lead that found itself expressed in cars.

Henri Coanda is remembered for his jet-type engine designs of 1910, but he, too, was a car enthusiast, and he brought aerodynamics knowledge from aviation to car design as early as 1911. Having learned about the importance of streamlining at the front of a fuselage or body, Coanda had also studied very early smoke and tuft testing techniques and early wind-tunnel findings, and realized that the manner in which airflow leaves the rear end of a car is a vital and important technique in overall drag reduction. In the early days of car design the phenomenon of this rear end wake drag was confusingly cited as a form of 'cavitation'.

Coanda realized that upright, perpendicular rear body designs to cars were leaving a large, low pressure drag envelope, or wake, trailing behind the car. This was often exacerbated by having panels that had no defined airflow separation point. This lack of a separation point meant that the air would 'break' inconsistently, and its trailing vortices would be uncontrolled and both dirt-, drag- and lift-inducing. By adding a defined point of airflow separation, Coanda created a tuned and set separation characteristic and known drag and lift values.

In his remarkably prescient *Torpille*, as a faired-in torpedo-tailed car design of 1911, Coanda took the torpedo tail design concept one step further by placing the spare wheel horizontally in a specially shaped fairing near the base of the curved tail section of the car, as a horizontal airflow separation point or de facto 'slicer' ridge. The French called it an 'aileron', and it worked as air cleaved off the *Torpille*'s domed roof and stern.

Elliptical Excellence

Although the Swiss-German Wunibald Kamm is credited through his 1930s and 1950s work with defining the rear airflow separation design technology used by car makers since the 1960s, we can look to Coanda as another of the aeronauts of Paris who *circa* 1910 made the first explorations into a design technique that ultimately led to the teardrop school of design that made the car a singular, blended one-piece sculpture – or at least, *certain* cars.

In Britain, Frederick Lanchester was pioneering British elliptical studies, and as early as 1894 he had built elliptically winged craft with lower induced drag and better glide ratios: Lanchester went on to publish his results and create a car company. Ludwig Prandtl and Hugo Junkers also explored the ellipse, and in London, 'one off' aerodynamic car body study had also been built by Oliver North as the North-Lucas Radial (NLR). North had visited the epicentre of aeronautical and automotive convergence at Issy-les-Moulineaux, Paris (home of Avions Voisin) and been inspired into the aero-auto thinking.

Key to these early streamliners, and the later works of Lefebvre and Gerin, was the shape, form and beneficial aerodynamic (and structural) qualities of the ellipse. By 1927–28, advanced cars, and advanced aircraft such as R. J. Mitchell's Supermarine S.5, the Short Bristow Crusader, and Giovanni

Pegna's PC.7 racing float planes for the Schneider Trophy races, were setting a trend for ellipsoid aerodynamic styling. The 1936 Supermarine Spitfire's unique, asymmetric, conjoined double-ellipse-formed wing with incredibly low drag was shaped by the Canadian Beverley Shenstone and bore no link to previous symmetrical single ellipse wings such as those seen in the Heinkel output. The French soon turned out a Dewotine with their own version of the Spitfire wing.

Of intriguing Anglo-French relevance, Nigel Gresley's A4 class 203.4km/h (126.4mph) ellipsoid streamliner steam

DATELINE 1925: FROM CITROËN TO BEL GEDDES

In 1925 the city of Paris staged a massive and lavish design exhibition entitled *Exposition Internationale des Arts Decoratifs et Industriels Modernes*; this exhibition spurred American design into life. André Citroën was a major force and the principal sponsor behind this important event, where the French displayed their innovative intellectual designs, created with free thinking. The exhibits stunned the world, and leading designers and engineers travelled to Paris, including American practitioners and manufacturers.

The Paris exhibition of 1925 was a turning point in global design. Those who attended it rushed home with tales of seeing a new 'product design' look and a new functionality, as well as the Art Deco fixtures and fittings that had been exhibited. Paris 1925 was a wake-up call to the world's designers. By the early 1930s, some American designers had also embraced this new thinking and developed their origination of 'industrial' design. Through aviation, architecture and Art Deco, the car was becoming an art form.

One designer stood tall amongst the others: Norman Bel Geddes, an ex-advertising creative who had become a theatrical set designer; he was also trained as an architect. In the late 1920s Bel Geddes started turning out elliptical, podded monocoque vehicle designs with highly aerodynamic or hydrodynamic anthropomorphic shapes, some of which were taken up by the Graham Paige concern. His car designs were cab-forward, and tear-dropped with curved turrets and sloping tails that were very similar to Bertoni's ideas. Almost overnight, Bel Geddes became one of the new industrial designers who stemmed from the need to advertise the new era of products.

From his own beginnings, the pioneering Norman Bel Geddes had adapted his early avant-garde designs from the innovations he had seen in France where the revolution in design had inspired him. Of significance, he had made a special study of French design in all its forms, ranging from interiors, to J. Corot's paintings, to the dirigibles of H. Fressyinet, and the architecture of Rheims Cathederal.

Raymond Loewy, the Frenchman in America, became well profiled, as did Walter Dorwin Teague, Henry Dreyfuss (an apprentice of Bel Geddes), Harley Earl and others – but Norman Bel Geddes was the first futurist and of massive social influence. These other designers were the first true industrial designers of America, and it is of significance that the drive to create industrial design in America is linked directly to the great French design exhibition of 1925, which had made the Americans wake up to design.

The blend of men and their ideas resulted in a new, American design quality, as did the design of the 1935 Lincoln-Zephyr aerodynamically shaped car, as derived from the Briggs streamliner penned by the Dutchman, Johan Tjaarda van Starenborgh. The Tjaarda-shaped Lincoln Zephyr, with input from Citroën-owning designer Eugene Gregoire, was an early US attempt at an aerodyne-type car amid the early dawning of the Harley Earl GM influence of applied curves and chrome – the Chrysler Airflow notwithstanding.

The effect of the French design revolution on America's emergent first designers is a little known tangent of the story of design itself. The birth of industrial design and of aerodynamic car styling in America has proven links from French innovations and advances in design, and principally the effects of the 1925 Paris exhibition, an event which would not have happened without André Citroën. André had already adopted American production practices, and was fully aware of the new pace of design development in America that had resulted from the 1925 Paris exhibition. This knowledge spurred him on to create something so advanced that it would wipe out even the ever-rising threat of the new American competition: the design he had in mind was the Traction Avant.

The significance of Citroën's often ignored early history is once again evidenced as being vital not just to a later Citroën ethos, but to global design itself.

locomotive that shattered the world speed record took direct inspiration from the cars of Bugatti and Voisin which Gresley studied closely, notably the wedge-fronted 'Laboratoire' cars.

The late 1930s riot of streamlining would surely never have been born without Citroën, Voisin, Lefebvre and the 1925 Paris design exhibition (*opposite*). From boats to aircraft to car design, the ellipse, with all its drag-reducing, wake-tuning advantages, soon translated itself into the *goutte d'eau* (drop of water) school of 'teardrop' car design – and never more so than in the 1930s streamliner cars and the Citroëns that followed, notably the DS and Lefebvre's *Coccinelle*.

Any observer in any doubt of such effects at the time of these developments only had to stand in Paris and look up at the elliptically shaped and structured Eiffel Tower, looming over them all with its grand parabolic arrogance. And the first wind tunnel in France was built by André Citroën's friend, Gustave Eiffel, underneath the Eiffel Tower in 1912, where it provided early access to technology never before known, and well in advance of others.

The Crucial Difference

The point about André Citroën and his 'dream team' was that few of the mainstream industrial designers did what Voisin, Lefebvre and Citroën did. Whilst others tweaked or modified *existing* themes, or made exotic cars for the rich, Voisin, Lefebvre and then Citroën created entire engineering themes – new innovations as whole new cars, not just restyles on old chassis. In such types of innovation lies the subtle yet *vital* overarching importance of the Voisinistes and their subsequent Citroënism.

Jaray, or any other thinker, could clothe an existing car or concept in a wind-cheating body, but the likes of Lefebvre at Voisin and Citroën did more than reclothe existing chassis: they created the *whole* car as a new, single entity that encompassed not just aerodynamic innovation, but structural, suspension, and engine innovation too. This was the crucial difference, with the new car concept as a whole process, not just as an applied engineering tweak to cheat the wind. And it may be conjectured that Jacques Jean-Marie Jules Gerin was the 'missing link' between the first and second generation of aerodynamic car design movements: Gerin proponent and author D. R. A. Winstone provides us with compelling evidence that Gerin and his elliptical monocoque Aerodyne car of the mid-1920s was just that[6].

Like Voisin, Cayla, Gerin, and so many others, André Lefebvre and André Citroën were, by fate of birth and era, cast deep into the thinking of these years and these events. Therein lie the strands of design ethos, the attention to advanced and complex engineering detail and to aerodynamics, that later became the essence of Citroën. Gabriel Voisin and his aeronautical influence upon Lefebvre and Citroën *was* significant, but there were other aeronautically influenced engineers at Citroën. Louis Guillot as Citroën's technical guru had started his career with the Morane brothers – aeroplane builders; Henri Jouffret, the Citroën engine designer, had created a 16-cylinder aero-engine for Peugeot; and Citroën's Henri Dufresne was chief engineer at Martini before working at Citroën.

Thus many of Citroën's men were steeped in aeronautical engineering through their high education and early junior career roles with the French aeronautical movement *circa* 1910–20.

The Influence of the École

The École des Arts le Mëtiers, the École Centrale des Arts et Manufactures, the École des Beaux Arts, the École Grande Polytechnique, and the École Nationale Suprieure de l'Aeronautique et de Construction Mecanique (Sup'aéro) were the key institutions that trained many of Citroën's men. It was the high engineering standards of French education, and the thinking and forensic tolerances of the *aeronautical* engineering mindset that drove the advanced thinking of the time and place – leading to advanced *automotive* ideas. In the halls of these 'Beaux Arts' educational centres, and in the aeronautical firms they fed with talent, is where the ethos of Citroën was seeded.

The Voisin brothers; Gabriel (*left*) carved a huge niche in the annals of early aviation and automotive engineering.

EUGÈNE GABRIEL VOISIN – VISIONARY GENIUS AND CITROËN INFLUENCE

No study of the origins of Citroën should avoid a detailed review of the work of Gabriel Voisin (1880–1973), who it is said was a man who never worried about how previous thinking had solved problems because he was unconstrained by the blinkers of received wisdom. This led to his free thought, his fresh innovative thinking of great originality.

In 2011, Peter Mullin's Voisin C25 Aerodyne was the 'Best in Show' at the Pebble Beach Concours in California. In 2012, the Mullin museum celebrated Voisin design in a grand 'one-off' exhibition. Having invested millions in his vital foundation, Mullin, like others, has become fascinated with the style and genius of Voisin, and the cascade of effects that stemmed therefrom. Even to those like Mullin and his devotees who today are 'in the know' about Voisin's cars, the C25 stuns them with its amazing blend of style and engineering.

And perhaps the even rarer, less well known Voisin 'Aiglée' coupé C28 Aerosport, and its one-piece, sculpted ellipsoid body, was more influential than the C25. And the effect of the C30 – a last grand-coupé saloon product of the Voisin brand (by this time the Garabeddian-Voisin) – might have been far reaching, as this car had elements of later Citroëns within it, notably the DS's clad or flocked structural frame technique.

The Voisin C25 was a very large car, yet few realize that the Citroën 2CV would appear to resemble it slightly, in a shrunken form. The Voisin C25 has a kinked 'A' pillar; it also has a secondary front bonnet line that dives down from the windscreen between the front wings, and extends the nose line in a manner reflected by the 2CV. At the rear, podded rear wings and a 'C' pillar and roof shape of incredible similarity to the original, 'four-light' 2CV are very obvious. But the C25 came first – over five years before Boulanger, Lefebvre and Bertoni created the 2CV.

Seen beside each other, it is clear that the 2CV looks like a C25 that shrank in the wash – the key styling elements of both cars are graphically close in all except dimensions. In fact the *prototype* 2CV is more organic, more curved, and features a stunning 'hip' joint between the bonnet and windscreen junction, one that was lost in Bertoni's 1947 restyle. The 2CV has a roll-back roof, just like the Voisin C25. Did the C25 take any styling hints from the Voisin–Le Corbusier small car project *circa* 1931, which itself *may* have influenced the later 2CV's own shape?

Few Citroënistes have been prepared to voice such apparent heresy, but dispassionate observation can only lead to noting the extraordinary close relationship between the shape of the Voisin C25 and the smaller, later Citroën 2CV. Gabriel Voisin it seems is an often forgotten and sometimes maligned figure of Citroën influence, *unless* Bertoni or Lefebvre secretly influenced the shapes of the C25 or the Le Corbusier small car proposal. Therein lies an unsolved riddle.

AERO-AUTO-MARINE

After the early aerodynamics experiments of the likes of the French-American Octave Chanute (1832–1910), in the years 1905 to 1910 the French raced ahead. With the exception of a few notables, not least the aforementioned Frederick Lanchester, the British remained in a torpor of conceit, failing to achieve powered flight, to the point where the British press attacked the sloth of British aviation, despite its vast library and its heroes of research. Indeed, it was in a Voisin aeroplane that an Englishman, J. T. Moore-Brabazon, made the first piloted powered flight by an English subject, on 1 December 1908.

Meanwhile the French – and notably Ferdinand Ferber, the early French exponent of the hang glider, the car fanatic Levassor, and the separate, streamlining Levavasseur, with Louis Blèriot and Gabriel Voisin – were all racing ahead, ultimately to create the monoplane. So the cauldron of design began to bubble.

Any reader in doubt of, or sceptical about, the importance of Voisin, is asked to consider the fact that so advanced was French aviation and Voisin in particular, that on 15 March 1911, the British Bristol Company, purveyors of aircraft (and decades later, cars), signed a contract with Gabriel Voisin to employ him as a 'consultant expert' on the development of their first monoplane. The British had to resort to asking a 'foreigner' for help. Even Rolls-Royce sent a delegation to see Voisin's V12 engine work after Mr Minchin, Rolls-Royce's Parisian agent, noticed Voisin's work.

Voisin evolved in the Paris-based centre of learning, as did latterly his pupil Lefebvre, not to mention Gerin and the older, ex-naval officer Cayla. This was the hub of the revolution in aeronautical design that soon embraced Citroën in car design. Paris and the years 1905 to 1920 were the key to what Citroën cars became in design: advanced, and utterly daring.

From Architecture to Automotive

As a student Gabriel Voisin had studied architecture (as did Lefebvre, Bertoni, Boulanger), and had trained with the architectural office of Godefroy et Freynet before he switched passions to engineering. He then founded an aircraft company that defined design evolution, and had produced fifty-nine aircraft by 1911. Then in 1917 Voisin turned to cars, and persued his obsession with automobilia up until the 1960s.

From tracked vehicles, a 1929 front-drive transmission, a fully sliding roof section, an electromagnetic gearbox and clutch, and self-limiting brakes: these and dozens of other ideas were Gabriel Voisin's patents between 1908 to 1966. And it was Voisin, with Lefebvre at his side, who investigated front-wheel drive and an idea for an aluminium panelled body without a frame (which itself mirrored the 'De Vizcaye' registered system of self-supporting alloy panelwork), and Voisin who also came up with a version of the Franco-American 'Weyman' body construction techniques of Charles Terres Weyman.

Voisin called his aeroplane company *Avions G. Voisin*, but the subtitle said it all: 'Aéronautique–Automobile–Mécanique' – and *Automobiles G. Voisin* would not be long in coming. Prior to yet another, ultimate reincarnation in Paris, the various Voisin companies led turbulent commercial lives yet were packed with advanced thinking.

ENGINEER EXTRAORDINAIRE

Voisin's three areas of design thinking – drivetrain, structure and aerodynamics – were his passion. He occupied similar engineering ground to his friend, Ettore Bugatti, but went his own way, writing his own script of modernist industrial design (Jean Bugatti included). From incredible aircraft to cars that included the 'Aerodyne', the 'Aerosport' as Art Deco land yacht cars, and through to the 1960s with post-2CV-esque ideas such as his 'Biscooter' economy car for the masses, Voisin left a legacy that was not reflected by the small number of cars he made.

Voisin's early 1920s cars were upright and elegant with a hint of both American and English styling known as 'razor-edged'. However, this style would soon be superseded by Voisin's growing passion for sleek torpedo shapes. Engine design excellence at Voisin came from Marius Bernard who had trained at Panhard and joined the Voisin company in 1918; he had also latterly worked at Lancia before returning to the French fold. Fernand Viallet and André Lefebvre were the next names to make their mark upon what would become Voisin's crucible of advanced design excellence, though it was to have 'money' troubles (and even transfer briefly in the early 1930s to a short period of Dutch-Belgian ownership). Inside Voisin's company were René Panhard's 'Systeme Panhard' engineers, men who would later work for Citroën.

Some have questioned Voisin's claims, but surely they cannot deny his advanced, forensic, exquisite engineering thinking – be it his, or that of his colleagues.

The Voisin-Cayla Hydraulic Braking System

Voisin and Lefebvre promoted an early form of differential or 'almost' anti-skid braking that was regulated by the pre-setting of the brake bias. But it was the ex-French Navy engineering officer Voisin director Pierre A. F. Cayla who created a self-adjusting, hydraulically driven braking regulator for each wheel of a car; this idea, in its ultimate modern-day incarnation via the Dunlop 'Maxarat' anti-skid system for aircraft, evolved into today's ABS systems.

This hydraulically actuated and self-setting braking system was patented by Cayla, the man from southern Brittany, and it was Cayla who really conceived the idea of having individually 'driven' brake pumps at each wheel. In Cayla's braking system every wheel had a closed circuit hydraulic pump driven and ratified by its own speed, and a self-limiting valve. Key to the system was an oil reservoir with a pump actuation using a delivery pipe with a by-pass return route via a suction orifice that could be set to open or closed ratings by the driver. This system received US Patent No. 1,548,349 on 4 August 1925[7].

As mentioned above, this system incorporated the beginnings of the famed ABS or 'Anti-Blocker-System', and perhaps led Citroën to the totality of its hydro-pneumatic system. Thus

Pierre Cayla (*left*) was the now forgotten pilot, engineer and inventor who worked with Gabriel Voisin (*right*) to patent many ideas in the 1920s.

Pierre Cayla and his Voisin-funded system incorporated the genesis not just of ABS, but also of Citroën's integrated braking, steering, suspension design of oleo-pneumaticism latterly developed from 1944 by Citroën and brought to fruition by three men: Mages, Maignan and Dascotte.

Pierre Cayla and Jacques Gerin devised such systems where oil and air were mixed to produce an effect. In that blend they were in advance of the simple air-regulated pneumatic suspension that the French company Delpeuch had devised in 1910. British pressurized air springing experiments emanated from the Cowey company in 1915. It would surely be wrong to link simple, fluidless air pressure regulating systems to the creation of a blended oleo-pneumatic system such as those devised by Cayla, Gerin and ultimately Citroën, who made the idea work on a mass industrial scale. The only other relevant, known, fluid-air experiments in shock absorbing were in France *circa* 1925 from the Messier company (now famous for aircraft undercarriages), which devised its own pressurized shock-absorbing suspension oil-bathed strut just after the early Cayla ideas.

In summary, Cayla designed and patented his braking system. Perhaps by simply entitling it 'hydraulic braking system' he concealed its real significance and its later relevance to Citroën. For there were many attempts at hydraulic braking systems by many men, but the details of Cayla's design may constitute a precursor to anti-lock brakes and to Citroën's own hydro-pneumatic, pump-driven, self-regulating, 'closed'-circuit hydraulic mechanism for brakes and as applied to suspension in unison.

Few have asked about, or even *know* of Pierre Cayla. Citroënistes know of Voisin, but what of the partially obscured Pierre Cayla? Certainly he should be recognized as another 'father' figure in the Voisin-Citroën story.

GERIN'S 'AERODYNE' – THE MISSING LINK?

Another Voisin pupil was Jacques Gerin. He was an often forgotten genius of vision, and notably created a one-piece pod of an aerodynamic car, an 'aerodyne', between 1923 and 1926. It was a stunning piece of design, and could be construed as that 'missing link' between the early experimental years 1910–25, and the Art Deco streamliner movement of the 1930s and later works such as the Burnley Streamliner and beyond.

Jacques Jean-Marie Jules Gerin (1898–1973) came from Dijon, and his family had no known engineering connections or training. His education was interrupted by the Great War of 1914–18; he was drafted for pilot training, and ended up at Voisin's early aviation school.

By 1923 Gerin had designed a propeller-driven car, with an independent suspension mechanism consisting of springs encased in oil-filled, sealed shock-absorbing cylinders – long before Citroën developed its 1950s oil-based system. Gerin's prop-driven car, or 'Helice', was the subject of a patent application on 8 June 1923; this was granted on 1 December 1923 as French patent 567,154, for his 'vehicule propulse pour helice aerienne'.

Gerin had created a suspension system that placed the springs inside an oil-filled sealed metal bath or reservoir, perhaps the precursor of later developments of the idea. He went on to design aerodynamic devices, safety systems that included an early form of crumple zone and safety cell, and other inventions.

For 1924, Gerin moved to Seine, Paris, to be at the centre of the action, and set up an office in the buildings owned by the Paulin-Ratier aeronautical and automobile company – helice builders, and who also worked with André Citroën. Before long Gerin had patented his design for an advanced, ellipsoid, low-slung aerodynamic car with a revolutionary form and

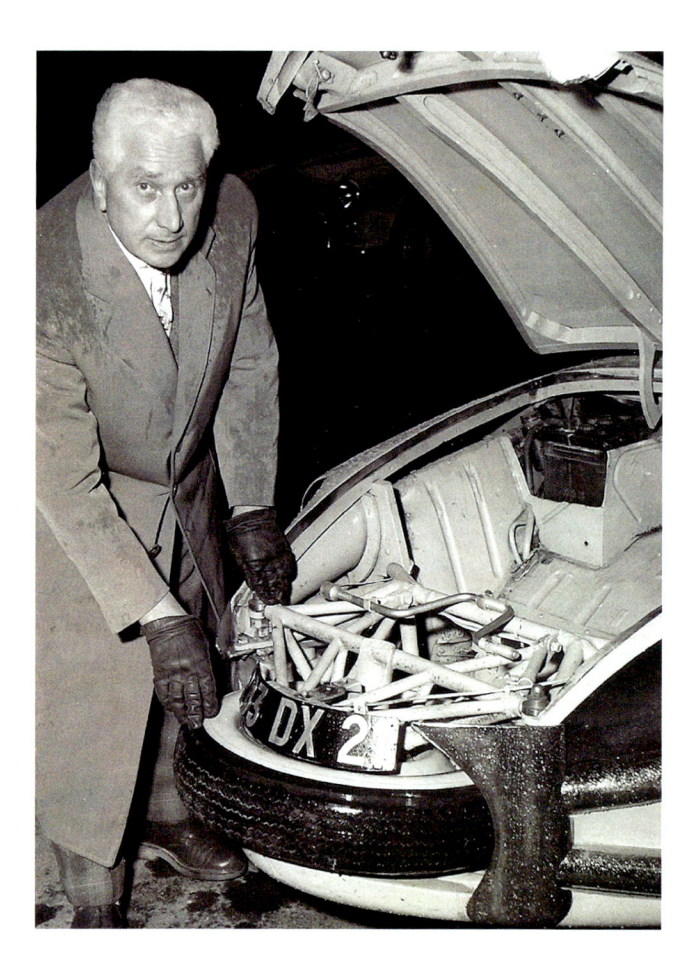

Jacques Gerin, another obscured genius of the Voisin arena, and designer of a remarkable Aerodyne and numerous safety devices.

GENESIS OF AN ETHOS: LEFEBVRE UNDER VOISIN AND BEYOND

ABOVE: **Gerin's Aerodyne seen unclad.**

RIGHT: **Gerin's one-piece single pod elliptical shape was of massive significance to car design.**

function – it was an aviation-style, fuselage-built car, with a stressed spaceframe skeleton of duralumin hoops tied to an aluminium undertray.

Gerin's design had features decades ahead of its time: flush fittings, a small frontal area, an elliptical profile and cross-section, allied to an alloy engine, advanced brake system design, an infinitely variable transmission, and suspended by lever-arm springs from oil-sealed spring casings. Many other cars subsequently used its themes, but no car used Gerin's ideas before his Aerodyne. In its low slung design it presaged the Citroën Traction Avant, while in its podded shape it predicted the DS.

Jacques Gerin moved on from his Aerodyne in 1929. He designed a system for increasing the area of aircraft wings in flight – an early form of flap design that added lift at low speed. This was his 'Varivol' experiment, with advanced wing area and surface control – an early form of 'slat and flap' to create a 'parasol' wing. He also created an idea for a trans-Atlantic airliner, giving it advanced canard-type wings and a variable wing shape (long before Barnes Wallis).

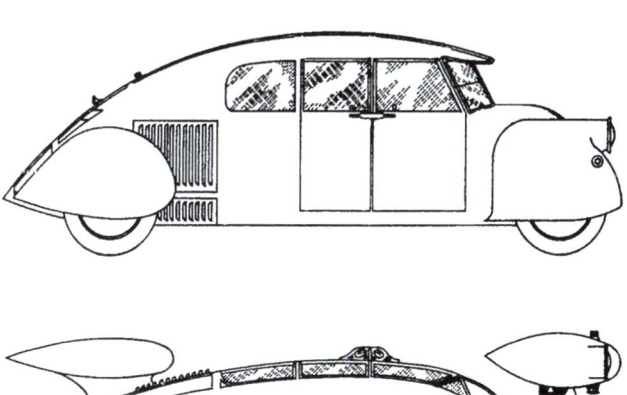

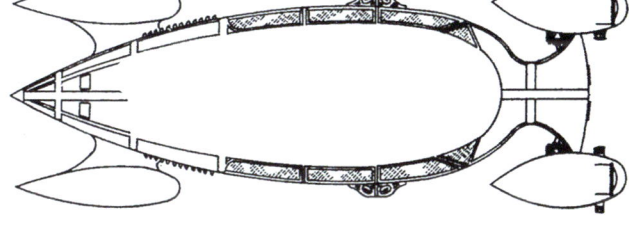

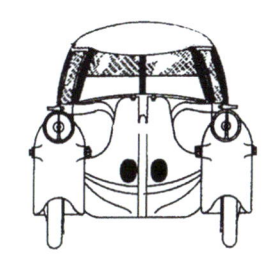

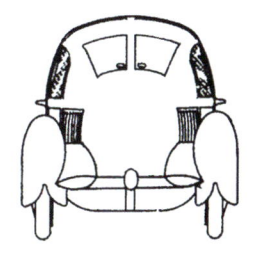

GENESIS OF AN ETHOS: LEFEBVRE UNDER VOISIN AND BEYOND

OPPOSITE PAGE:
TOP: **By 1929 some aspects of international styling trends were evident in the all-steel-bodied Citroën line-up. This is a formal style of Citroën.**

BOTTOM: **A wonderfully evocative Citroën C6 Berline dashboard design moment, and the beginnings of styling motifs. Even the Pope ordered one.**

THIS PAGE:
The interior salon was comfortable and spacious.

Plastique Fantastique

Perhaps even more spectacularly, post-World War II Gerin created not just a composite plastics process, but a composite blend that mixed glassfibre plastics technology with a blend of alloy fabrication and in-built metal supporting structures; this was a predecessor to the 'sandwich' composite plastics and metal now seen in airframe construction using a composite mix known as 'Glare' – a woven skin with a composite/alloy blended core. Only Lefebvre (with whom Gerin liaised) was a greater exponent of the new material, and as early as 1947 Gerin was experimenting with such advanced moulding technology – way ahead of the simple, floppy glassfibre one-piece mouldings that were to become so light and so dangerous in cars. Yet the Gerin Aerodyne disappeared from automotive consciousness and became a forgotten leyline in the automotive history map.

Gerin had immersed his suspension springs in an oil bath in the 1920s; by the 1960s he was developing reactive hydraulic suspension systems – reducing roll angles through controlling suspension resistance and introducing regulated roll rate interaction – and it is perhaps significant that Citroën's own 'active' system was to mimic such thoughts.

In the late 1960s, Gerin concentrated on improving car safety in terms of crashworthiness through clever structural design. He designed impact-absorbing 'crumple zones', and built two modified production cars in the 1950s and 1960s: first the Renault Dauphin, the other his Citroën DS 'Antishock'. To both cars he added his tubular 'crush can' impact-absorbing front structure, where the spare wheel was mounted near-horizontally at the front of the car to absorb impact. Crash tests included driving into a tree at 50km/h (30mph). The Gerin DS also featured pedestrian-friendly shock-absorbing plastic frontal bodywork cladding to reduce head and body injuries to impacting pedestrians – another instance of highly advanced thinking, and one that has only recently been featured in car safety design and on the 2005 Citroën C6.

Gerin died in obscurity, a man perhaps eclipsed by Citroën's output of ideas, which were so similar to his own. Surely Gerin must be now cited as an influence upon the DS: indeed, it defies design logic to do otherwise. Jacques Gerin was truly a man whose mind was ahead of its time: he is the forgotten hero of aerodynamics, structures and car safety.

LE CORBUSIER AND A CITROËN HOUSE

Perhaps we can cite the astonishing visionary architect Charles Edouard Jenneret 'Le Corbusier' as another of the French design movement heroes who did not care for the constraints of convention and closed minds. Le Corbusier drove a Voisin, and featured Voisin cars in his publicity photographs for his constructions. He also knew and admired André Citroën – indeed in 1921 he built a house that he called 'Maison Citrohan'[8], a play on the name of Citroën, and in concept a 'machine à habiter' – a machine for living in. But the house was squared and cubic, not curved – as both Corbusier and Citroën design *later* became. The house was 'like a car', said the architect, an early Citroën car; in fact it resembled the juxtaposition of the bonnet and the upright windscreen.

Le Corbusier knew Voisin, Citroën, Peugeot and Michelin: he consulted them, and even planned a major industrial complex of glass skyscrapers to be built in Paris just north of the Seine, *Le Plan Voisin*. In such a plan, Voisin reflected a socio-cultural thinking and status perhaps not unlike that which Citroën itself would achieve across the decades. Le Corbusier and his manager Monsieur Mongermon had sought funding from André Citroën in order to create new towns that reflected their new cars and the effects of them on life. In his *La Ville Radieuse*, Le Corbusier designed a town that would solve the traffic problems he anticipated the age of the car would bring – but it was too vast an idea for anyone to support. His designs featured high speed roads with an emphasis on aerodynamic cars of a type that he knew Voisin, Lefebvre and Citroën could and would produce.

For Le Corbusier, Voisin, Lefebvre and Bertoni, design ideology was to suggest the creation of a functional object with elegance and proportion, yet devoid of ornament (just as the DS or CX and others became so many years later). It is also interesting to speculate whether La Corbusier's design for a small car presaged the 2CV in the mind of another arts and architecture expert – Boulanger. And Lefebvre would have been aware of Le Corbusier's small call plans, as they were created with Voisin while Lefebvre was present. So there may indeed be a Le Corbusier link to the 2CV design concept.

L'Esprit Nouveau

Citroën design, its engineering and its ethos cannot have been immune to what was going on in Paris in this era. L'esprit nouveau – the spirit of the new, of daring to design to be different – was the essential motivation of the designers, architects, aeronauts and automobile men who were part of, or who created these movements.

It was as early as March 1916 that André Lefebvre entered the story as an employee of Voisin. And there can be no doubt that without the thinking and output of Voisin, Lefebvre would not have been trained as he was, he would not have been ingrained with the incredible engineering vision he latterly demonstrated for Citroën. Any observer in doubt of such a claim should perhaps look no further than Voisin's C6 Course 'Laboratoire' cars, or the later C25–28 cars, and most obviously, the 1936 'Aerosport', to see the influence not only of Lefebvre, but through these cars, the influence of Voisin upon Citroën itself. It was the great Gabriel Voisin who called André Citroën 'This astonishing man'[9].

For Citroënistes, the obvious questions are, how did the equally astonishing Citroën car company become the home of exotic engineering and advanced aerodynamics? And how did these qualities become the essential ingredients of Citroën – the soul of its being? The answers all lie in the DNA of Citroën, a DNA with many ancestors but which in part began with the input of several aeronautical engineers with an interest in art and architecture, notably Voisin and Lefebvre.

AERONAUTIQUE – AUTOMOBILE – MECANIQUE

So began the incredible story of Citroën. Through the amalgamation of chance and certainty, through the aggregation of

THE CORE ELEMENTS OF CITROËN CAR DESIGN PHILOSOPHY

- Low aerodynamic drag coefficient (Cd. /Cx.) established in smooth teardrop-shaped bodywork with attention to sealing and excrescences. Open flow of air over and around the turret of the car to minimize airflow bubbling and detachment. Attention to pressure, lift and stability factors through applied design, mathematical calculus and wind tunnel work
- Small frontal area and low cross-sectional drag coefficient (Cd.a /Cx.s); Reynolds number defined
- Definition of the critical separation point to define rear drag wake off the rear of the car
- Wake tuning of base drag and lift
- Centre of aerodynamic pressure defined and tuned
- Movement of polar inertia known and adjusted
- Light weight
- Low centre of gravity (cg), and the centre of gravity forward biased within the wheelbase
- Stiff chassis/body points at suspension mountings to ensure good handling
- Low suspension mass with inboard brakes to reduce roll centres and cg
- Front driven with the mass of the engine within the wheelbase to avoid pendulum or swing effect
- High speed from low power with engine/combustion process efficiency
- Predictable handling characteristics from advanced suspension expertise and tuning, creating 'active' safety qualities
- Front biased braking force
- Use of advanced techniques and synthetic materials to reduce weight
- Structural ingenuity
- Potential use of organic/sculptural styling elements

---

design evolution and revolution, it all came together. France was the centre of the industrial design world – indeed we might say that France invented industrial design, and that André Citroën drove the process.

Others, men such as Louis Renault (a long-time astringent to André Citroën's thoughts) maintained a more conventional, fiscally 'prudent' mindset towards engineering and design. After all, too much aeronautically derived quality in car design could ruin its maker. It seems that the Renault company of that time was typical of the corporate sclerosis that stifles so many engineers and designers trapped in lumbering corporate structures. But even Renault later had to embrace front-wheel drive, and the concept of the 2CV to its Renault 4, even if it took years for the company to throw off the idea of rear-engined and upright contraptions.

As regards Peugeot, this esteemed family-owned company had occasional design extravagances, such as the Andreau-penned Peugeot 402 of 1936 – a lovely 'Aerodyne' attempt of the era, and one obscured by others. Peugeot also pioneered the 'Eclipse' metal folding roof, and created a lineage – yet it would be the 1960s before it found a more secure design language, an engineering and marketing niche of its own – and ironically, a time when it would ultimately own Citroën itself.

THE REASON WHY – CASTING THE MOULD OF CITROËNISM

Citroën's engineering and design rationale encompassed key themes whose roots lay in marine and aeronautical experiments of about 1890 to 1920, and which became applicable to car design via early competition car knowledge.

Voisin and Lefebvre established these engineering themes long before their rivals, and when Lefebvre joined Citroën the knowledge transfer from aviation to automotive and from Voisin cars to Citroën cars was obvious. Throw in the scientific influence of Pierre Boulanger, and the resulting outcomes were the DNA of Citroën design.

Carrosserie Aérodynamique – a Sort of Aeromancy

The effects of a shape, form or body moving through smooth (non-viscous) water and air were long investigated, but these were the free-flowing effects of a form suspended in a single smooth element. What happened to airflow when it was forced to travel not only over or around and across a body shape, but when it was subjected to the effects of a road being close under that form or shape – in turbulent (viscous) air? This was the new science of road vehicle aerodynamics.

Furthermore, what were the effects of rotating wheels in wheel arches or panels, and of the protruding items on a car, such as wipers, mirrors and window seals or gutters? What was the point of a smooth clean shape if it produced lift that made the car dangerous – particularly extreme front or rear lift? And would pitching of the car by its suspension and braking forces, or its side-slip or yaw, make it aerodynamically unstable? From such issues stemmed the science of road vehicle aerodynamics and the Citroën obsession with it.

It might be argued by some that the French Art Deco *carrosserie aérodynamique* was intuitive rather than completely scientific, and that German research was more accurate; but the other side of the coin is that before Stuttgart claimed the plaudits, Paris and its auto-aeronauts were years ahead in their aerodynamic design research thinking. Through the early French researchers, the key elements affecting the creation of turbulence or 'drag' over a car, and its tuning to reduce drag, were revealed to be as follows:

- **Form drag** – expressed as a coefficient of drag as a *CD* or more accessibly a 'Cd.' figure (Cx in French), created by the shape of the body itself as air passes over and off it (as base/wake and also as cross-sectional drag as *CDA* or Cd.a.). Likely according to generalized rules to account for approximately 60 (+/) per cent of total drag – and needs to reference the shape's cross-sectional area expressed as *S*
- **Induced drag** – expressed as a *CDi* or Cd.i and resulting from the actions/effects of the body's actions in airflow. Likely to account for approximately 10–20 (+/–) per cent of total drag
- **Interference drag** – as a resulting action of parts of the car's shape on other aspects of the form in localized areas on the car. Likely to account for 10–15 (+/–) per cent of total drag
- **Internal flow drag** – the effects of under-bonnet and cabin airflow resistance patterns and expelled air behaviour. Likely to account for 10–12 per cent (+/–) of total drag
- **Pressure effects, boundary layer and airflow separation point** – such effects resulted from the actions that front grilles, windscreens, side panel and windscreen and roof profiles created close to the car's body skin, and in the lee or downwash of localized effects such as that of a side force (*YA*), or bonnet and grille leading edge in front of an angled front windscreen and cabin turret or canopy. Positive

or negative pressures (*CP*), notably the effect of unwanted or lift coefficient (*CL*) and its force (*LA*) allied to underbody effects, were vital issues and had significant effects on car performance

Key facts were knowing the centre of gravity (cg), also the side-slip or yaw effects, finding the car's movement of polar inertia, and studying where and how the airflow separated off the car as a critical separation point as vorticity patterns (CSP/SP). While all this is obvious today, it was unheard of in mass-market car design in the 1920s – but Voisin and Lefebvre were research pioneers in this field, and Citroën cars, starting with the Traction Avant, were the earliest road-going, mass-market cars to benefit from this knowledge before other car makers (notably Lancia) focused upon such issues.

Elemental Citroënism

On his own, André Citroën may well have emerged as an industrialist and car maker, and clearly he was a great man, but his works have a wider list of credits – he had that 'dream team' who created the Citroën engineering elements of expertise, elements not common amongst car makers: most car makers did not think like this in 1934.

In the essential Citroën elements we see the proof and the foundations of why Citroën design is evidently far more complex and multi-disciplinary than has previously been explained. And if Lefebvre's at times 'wild' futurism was reined in a touch by Boulanger's mathematical mind, even that circumstance was framed by Boulanger's creation of a design research practice at Citroën where science amidst Descartes-inspired psychology and free-thinking exploration constituted the foundations of Citroënism.

This was a unique set of circumstances leading to a unique process and a unique outcome – that of Citroën itself. And from such heady days, Citroën and its *modus operandi* evolved. Therein lies the explanation of the afterwards and the before of Citroën, and its first steps into an undreamed of future, a journey to the edges of rational design thought that touched not just big cars, but small cars as well. Here lies the answer to the *why* of the soul of Citroën, its DNA and its practice. As 1934 dawned the world of car design was about to witness the birth of the astounding Traction Avant. This was a car that would never have existed without the story as told herein, of the little known and wider effect of the 1920s design explosion in France and *all* the men who were a part of it.

So became Citroën as we know it, not least as producer of the world's most aerodynamic mass production cars.

CHAPTER THREE

TRACTION AVANT

THE FRONT-WHEEL-DRIVE PIONEER

TRACTION AVANT | THE FRONT-WHEEL-DRIVE PIONEER

SOME SAY THAT the Traction Avant was the world's first front-driven car, but this is not so, as Nicolas-Joseph Cugnot created a plan for a front-driven (and transverse aligned) vehicle in 1769. Alvis, Cord, DKW and the French engineers Jean-Albert Grégoire and Pierre Fenaille had also dabbled in front-drive thinking. Others say the Traction Avant was the world's first monocoque (chassis-less, self-supporting single shell) car, but it would be fairer to call it the world's first *mass production* monocoque car. Despite these small historical caveats, the Traction Avant was a major moment in global car design.

With its unique, low-slung stance and smooth styling, it also marked a moment of design signature – a defining hallmark not just of Citroënism, but of a new design era. The singular philosophy of approach that typified the 'design research' culture of the French created the Traction Avant, and was responsible for its massive advance. It was an advance that was timeless, and as late as July 2009, 1,000 examples of the Traction Avant met in Arras for the car's seventy-fifth anniversary meeting, a celebration that lasted for seventy-five hours. In the town's 'Grand Place', thousands of Citroënistes gathered to mark the most revolutionary mass production car of the twentieth century.

In terms of the Traction's success, the aforementioned Jean-Albert Grégoire should not go unmentioned, for with Pierre Fenaille, he designed a new type of front-wheel-drive joint, or 'Tracta' tractive coupling that pre-dated the constant velocity (CV) joint now so familiar. Grégoire also created the 'Tracta Gephi', a prototype for a small front-drive car in 1926.

For Citroën, after a decade of making cars and taking steps towards a brand identity of its own, the Traction Avant embodied the moment when the true ethos of Citroënism was born. Suddenly out of the automotive sky there came the most futuristic, most advanced car the world had yet seen. In the background, Peugeot reacted with ever-more aerodynamic devices and the elliptical styling themes of Jean Andréau (who would later assist Citroën). But André Citroën knew that if he designed a really advanced car, it would remain in production for years whilst the competition caught up.

TRACTION'S 'FIRSTS' WITHOUT EQUALS

Although some elements of the Traction Avant had been suggested in other cars, it was the combination of so many 'firsts' – the advances in *one* vehicle – that marked it out: front drive, torsion bar/wishbone independent suspension, a sleek,

Avant atmosphere. A wonderfully restored, 1939 British-built Traction Avant roadster seen hastening away in all its glory. Although powered by 4-cylinder engines, Paris was itching to produce a 6-cylinder powered Roadster and six or seven were built prior to 1940. In the 1980s, the British company Peacock Engineering built a 6-cylinder RHD Roadster. All the original Traction Roadsters had reinforced sills and bulkheads to make up for the loss of the monocoque's crucial roof.

low-slung body made in the new monocoque style, the special damped engine mountings, and a flat floored cabin, all created what can only be called a true advance. Within a short time, hydraulic brakes and the new rack-and-pinion type steering would also be included.

Speedily Designed

Also critical to the mix was the speed with which this new car was made. With no mathematical help or 'electrickery', and with minimal staff, the Traction Avant was designed in less time than today's car makers, with all their vast resources, might take to create a new car. Speed was of the essence – after all, how long would Citroën's money last? Money was once again of immediate issue, for by 1934 Citroën owed its bank a reputed FF200 million. There were indeed teething problems that affected Citroën's financial position, yet the car was so advanced that it would not need replacing for years, saving millions that would normally be spent on a replacement model under the usual industry production cycle.

The Traction Avant came together as a design project very quickly: there was no four-year-long design cogitation. If the car was going to be in production a long time, it would need to be advanced, ahead of the game at its inception in order not to date too quickly. This was the thinking behind the idea – egged on no doubt by Citroën's precarious financial position. Citroën had made a profit of over 100 million francs in 1925, and produced the commercially significant number of over 100,000 cars in 1929. Yet by 1932 the company was selling fewer than 50,000 cars, and recording losses. Citroën had a debt-to-equity ratio that was frightening – the company was reputed to be 125 million francs in debt – yet a potential lifeline came from Rosengart, for Citroën to co-produce a Franco-German car via a relationship between Rosengart and Adler: but Citroën rejected the offer and did what he had always done – gambled.

André Citroën remembered his time in America and in particular his adoption of Henry Ford's ethos, so he sent engineers to America to study the new metal monocoque bodybuilding process. At the Budd company, Citroën's Raoul Cuinet (body engineer) and assistant Pierre Franchiset worked long hours to help Budd create the master dies for the massive tooling presses that would be shipped to France. So advanced was this work that the Traction Avant's side-body pressing from A-pillar to rear panel was stamped as a one-piece pressing. This ensured a good fit and high torsional rigidity, with little lead filling required – as was the normal procedure in car making then.

With Maurice Julien concentrating on the independent suspension, Maurice Saniturat on the wet-liner, pushrod ohv engine (dispensing with side valves), and Roger Prud'homme as test engineer, the workshop group worked fast: there was nothing superfluous. Also working on the Traction's body engineering and weld points was Jean Danninos, who latterly went on to found *Forges et Ateliers de Construction Eur et Loir*, better known as FACEL, and renowned as the maker of exotic grand coupés. The Traction team included Pierre Lemaire and Paul d'Aubarede, who worked on the suspension. The Traction Avant was created and built in an amazing one year and one month.

The decision to make this revolutionary front-drive car was André Citroën's, and it was a conversation with Voisin in 1933 that brought the previous Voisin-based front-wheel-drive experience of Lefebvre to his attention. Lefebvre's *de facto* entry examination into his new job at Citroën was to engineer the car contained in André Citroën's idea and Flaminio Bertoni's styling genius. So the man behind this advanced car was André Lefebvre the visionary. Citroën also saw the rise of Flaminio Bertoni in the Traction Avant: Bertoni had come to France and been working as a designer for Sical, who were also carrosserie to Citroën – and it was via Carrosserie Sical that Bertoni had entered the halls of Citroën in the Rue de Théâtre.

The correct wooden dashboard and full array of instruments made such a difference to British-built Tractions. Note the cranked gear lever.

FLAMINIO BERTONI, AUTOMOTIVE SCULPTOR AND DESIGN PIONEER

Born in 1903 in Varese, Italy, Bertoni's father was a tailor. The young Flaminio started his career at the automotive carrozzeria company of Macchi – latterly associated with aircraft design. Drawing, woodworking and sculpting were his areas of focus. In 1922 Bertoni designed his first full car body, a monocoque inspired by aircraft fuselages. He also designed the World War I memorial in Varese.

Bertoni went to work for Macchi in 1919 as a young apprentice, and rose to be head draughtsman. He was head-hunted by a delegation of French engineers and as a result took up this first post in Paris in 1923; however, it was only for a brief period, and he returned to Italy soon after. But perhaps stifled by Macchi and corporate life, Bertoni set up his own design house in 1929; clients included Carrozzeria Varesina and Carrozzeria Barottio. Yet by 1931, with his wife-to-be in tow, he decamped to Paris. There he went to work for Sical, the coachbuilding carrosserie that supplied Citroën. Through contact with André Citroën, Bertoni joined the Citroën firm in 1932 and walked straight into the chance to re-style the Citroën Rosalie range, and then the Traction Avant: he seems to have led a charmed life in design terms.

Bertoni was a hands-on man – although he sketched, he also preferred to translate his ideas straight from mental concept into hard, sculpted model. Long before the brilliant 1970s' organic and animal-like shapes of Luigi Colani, Bertoni was inspired by animals – notably birds, fish and wild beasts of the tropics. He grasped the hydrodynamic and aerodynamic brilliance of nature's own forms. He also created 'space age' shapes and embraced technology.

For the Traction Avant, Bertoni created a new form, one that was not ellipsoid like his later DS, but a chamfered, smoothed, low-slung wind-cheating design that he formed with his own hands and fingers from clay and then plasticine in a matter of hours, working late into the night to tease out the definitive sculpture. All of this car's shape was harmonized and smoothly scaled, and it was the first car in the world to be created without a sketch: it came straight from Bertoni's mind's eye.

Then World War II intervened, and his Italian-French status proved difficult – yet it allowed him time to develop his passion for sculpture. After the war, Bertoni went straight back to Citroën, and the launch of the Très Petite Voiture (TPV) – or the 2CV as it had become. He re-worked the original from the 2CV prototype to the more angular, less organic 2CV production series.

Flaminio Bertoni, the Citroën sculptor and the man who shaped the Traction Avant (and the 2CV, DS and Ami) looks on over a model of a revised, more aerodynamic Traction Avant 'VGD' styling proposal. This was an early step before the DS was born.

Then came the sensational anthropomorphic DS and its advanced, 'space age', plastically moulded dashboard and sensuous single-spoke steering wheel.

Next came the delicate and characterful Ami 6 saloon with its reverse-angled rear windscreen – soon copied by others, notably Ford. The Ami (and its derivatives) also had an animal-like sculptural form, and a front grille that reminded the observer of a French woman's expressive mouth.

Bertoni brought intuitive genius for scale, stance, form, finish and presence to his cars and other designs; he understood surface tension and sculptural graphics, and translated them all into his cars. He worked quickly and impulsively – and his home was just a short distance from the Citroën studio, so he could work all night if he wanted to, and he would often go from mental concept to sculpted model in a few hours of activity with no sketching involved.

The Traction Avant was perfect in its balance and presence: nothing jarred, and every line 'worked'. It was functional yet not mundane. Later, the DS would be almost 'other worldly' beside a 2CV that was actually highly advanced in terms of its structural efficiency. Bertoni embraced aerodynamics, aeronautical engineering, and the new plastics technology that he and Lefebvre were so enthused about. Significantly in terms of his talent and his place in industrial design history, he produced designs of great smoothness that had none of the kind of excrescences and gargoyles that had for so long been expected and

TRACTION AVANT: THE FRONT-WHEEL-DRIVE PIONEER

ABOVE: **The Conservatoire Citroën's classic 1939 TA 11 Berline with original Bertoni curved bumper design.**

ABOVE RIGHT: **This is the original French specification cabin with the steel pressed dashboard and its simple but elegant functionality. Later British built cars had a 'wood effect' dashboard.**

LEFT: **Traction Avant design detail. Left-hand drive and simply stylish. Note the fuel level in actual amount of litres indicated.**

encouraged by car makers. Bertoni's shapes were organic and clean long before bigger names and larger car manufacturers 'discovered' smooth skinning and scaling and the aerodynamic benefits to be derived therefrom.

Similarly, any competent designer can make a shape cleaner, but Bertoni's shapes started out as clean, lithe and elegant – he would have hated some of today's heavily jowled, obese-panelled cars with their clumsy details and arrogant scale. If a large Lexus is an elephant of scale and shaping, then Bertoni's large cars were lithe dolphins or leaping gazelles.

Not all of Bertoni's work was for Citroën: he shaped cars for UNIC, the Adler-based Imperia TA9, and worked with the brilliant Jean Andreau (of 1936 Peugeot 402 Aerodyne fame) on the amazing 1940s, three-wheeler capsule-concept city car the Mathis 333 – the EVL or 'Économique Voiture Légère' (economical car lightweight). This was a futuristic ellipsoid flying seed or pod-shaped three-seater, and was designed to hit the the 3ltr per 100km fuel rating. It had an alloy body and a weight of 380kg (840lb).

Recently, parachutists have flown great distances in glide-ratio free-fall wearing 'flying wing' bodysuits with wing and leg panels, an aerodynamic profile and inflated sections to form an aerofoil. But how many of these men and women, or those watching, know that the flying-wing bodysuit they use was invented by Flaminio Bertoni in 1960?

In 1961 the French government made Bertoni a Master of Arts, and he also went on to win international art prizes. His work is celebrated today in France and Italy, and his son Leonardo[10] has created a lasting legacy and tribute to him.

Flaminio Bertoni must be one of the greatest industrial designers of all time, and he was undoubtedly the man who took Citroën to its defining forms.

Black Traction, blue H van, double chevrons. Two classic Citroëns of left-hand drive provenance and simply seething with Citroënism. The Yapp brothers' daily drivers wine company fleet make its own statement. André Citroën would surely have approved.

The interior of an early Traction Avant fixed-head coupé. French-built cars had a more spartan dashboard, as can be seen here.

STRUCTURE AND STYLE

In 1933 few car engineers were aware of the inherent strength of the self-supporting uni-body monocoque bodyshell – even racing-car designers had yet to see the benefits. The perceived wisdom of the time was that a stong central chassis with two 'rails' or beams of steel running down the centre of the car, then clad in a non-structural skin of the body, offered the best qualities of strength, torsional rigidity and crash protection. In fact this belief was a falsehood, for the 'battering ram' chassis failed to absorb any angled roof crush or side impact, and left the passengers sitting outside its central framework and thus vulnerable to the collapse of the weak, non-stressed bodies that formed the cabin and coachwork. Conventional chassis design was also subject to twist, which affected the dynamics of the suspension and steering.

Although not without merits for heavy vehicles, trucks and off-road types, the cars of the pre-monocoque era were notorious for peeling or splitting open in a crash, the wood, canvas or even steel coachbuilt panels offering little resistance to deformation and harmful cabin intrusion upon the occupants. Taking its cue from the Deperdussin monocoque airframe and the development of the self-supporting fuselage that the aircraft industry was slowly embracing by 1934, Citroën created the monocoque for the Traction Avant.

An early test car was dropped from a great height on to its nose to prove that this new idea offered superior protection to occupants because the body was a one-piece structure that allowed great stiffness in its 'hull', and each structural element supported the other, thus greatly increasing both local and overall rigidity. Early Tractions showed some problems with localized flexibility in their bodies, and extra welding and seams were added to strengthen the hull, thereby solving the issues. Other car makers such as Mercedes-Benz, Volvo and Saab might improve upon the idea in the 1950s, but Citroën's monocoque hull for the Traction Avant really was the true starting point for subsequent body design developments.

The body was low slung as it did not need to sit on top of traditional chassis rails, and nor did the engine. Instead, the engine was mounted low into the self-supporting body, and the hull was formed around the car's other components, such as the suspension and cabin fittings. This thinking, led by Lefebvre, allowed Bertoni to 'style' or sculpt the organic whole of the body – there was no need for 'add-on' design. The car still had externally mounted front 'wings' or mudguards in the fashion of the time, but everything else was faired in and in one piece. There were proper sills along each side of the cabin door apertures, and a smoothed-in tail.

The windscreen was narrow, but the side windows were much deeper and smoother than the prevailing fashion. The bonnet featured aircraft-style inspection panels. The windscreen pillars were gutterless and free of external seams, thus letting the airflow cleave around them. The underfloor was flat, and the car's frontal cross-sectional area lower than the norm.

Soufflerie Aerodynamique de Chalais Meudon

All this theory was born out by tests of the Traction Avant at the Soufflerie Aerodynamique de Châlais Meudon (the Châlais Meudon wind-tunnel) in 1934, when the car's drag factor and inherent wake were found to be lower than the then accepted 'barn door' standard of aerodynamics. A coefficient of drag of around Cd 0.45 has been reputed (where most family cars of the era were often Cd 0.60 and above). Without its freestanding front wings, a much lower figure for the Traction would have been likely, but in 1934 only racing protoypes had faired-in wing or fender panels.

But there was more to aerodynamics than just a total Cd: the centre of aerodynamic pressure and the flow down and across the car were just as vital, as was having a flat underfloor. These details were all known as key elements by Lefebvre from his Voisin 'Laboratoire' days. So despite its protruding front wing panels, the Traction Avant was, in 1934, a piece of advanced aerodynamic tailoring that employed such elements. Stability, flow, lift, turbulence and noise were all tuned for the Traction's body design. The Traction's cross-sectional drag coefficient was Cda.1.230 – a figure much better than any of its contemporaries (whose average Cda. was 2.000) – due to its low build.

Lefebvre and Bertoni's intuitive thinking and aeronautical legacy were proven, and it would be several more years before the exotic Alfa Romeo and the Battista 'Pinin' Farina-shaped Lancia Aprillia were created in wind-tunnels with their scarab-like tails. Before that happened, the new Citroën initiated the early consideration of such needs in the form of a mass-market saloon car. In the Traction Avant V8 22CV prototype Bertoni and Lefebvre were working towards Cd. 0.40 and Cda. 0.90 by smoothing and blending in the front wings, and reducing the metal area.

Integrated Styling and Engineering

Styled almost overnight from brainwave-to-clay sculpture (the first car to be shaped by such a technique), Traction Avant was Bertoni's impulsive, immediate work of balanced genius.

The Traction sported a chevron motif upon its rakishly set grille and frontal aspect – one that would create the 'face' or 'visage' of a Citroën in what car designers call the 'DRG', or down-the-road graphic. But above all there was Bertoni's hallmark: the actual stance of the car – the way it was set upon its wheels, the way in which its function was absorbed into form to create a design impression – an almost architectural or sculptural sense of occasion to the eye of the viewer. Here, for the first time, was 'integrated' styling for the mass market. Rakishly angled, smoothed, low set and stylish, the Traction Avant looked like an expensive piece of Art Deco design that had turned the mundane into the exotic.

UNDER THE SKIN

Front-driven it may have been, but the Traction Avant's engine was not transverse mounted, it was placed longitudinally and well back in the engine bay, with the gearbox mounted in front of the engine. This lengthways mounting of the drive train had the benefit of weight over the front wheels for added traction, but also of having the engine mass mounted low and further back, which improved the handling. The only quirk seemed to be the vertical mounting of the gear lever on the dashboard, resulting in some extra engineering being required to make sure it stayed in gear and did not 'drop' when selected at the top of the gate.

The low-slung stance of the car created a very low centre of gravity, so it started with an advantage – its inherent resistance to the then 'norm' of high roll-angles. Thus a radical low build – a car lower than any other mass production car – would reap massive road-holding advantages, and Lefebvre knew this, not least through the low-slung Voisin V12 'Myra' produced in 1930 in small numbers. He also knew that the front-driven handling would pull the car through bends – but also that the handling had to be stable: the front-biased understeer could not be allowed to perform a 'Jekyll and Hyde' transition to violent, rear oversteer. The lightweight rear of the car must not be allowed to react under throttle 'lift-off'. So the front and rear suspensions were also highly advanced.

One of the 22CV Traction Avant V8 prototypes, with revised aerodynamic styling on this cabriolet/roadster type.

MODEL DEVELOPMENT TRACTION AVANT RANGE

Model 7A: Launched April 1934 as a 1303cc 'Berline' model within the 7CV fiscal rating.
Model 7B: In June 1934 given a larger engine of 1529cc.
Model 7C: Production specification modifications in September 1934 resulted in a 1628cc engine and improved welding and construction tolerances.
Model 11 A/B: December 1934 revealed a 1911cc engine, available with standard original model bodywork légère and a longer wheelbase model with greater cabin room. Air vent louvre 'flaps' on the bonnets for 1937 and Michelin 'Pilot' wheels for 1938–39 were notable Traction features.
1935 Roadster: Built pre-war only, including twelve built in Denmark, this was the most stylish Traction – a true 'soft-top', two-door body that also lent itself to the very rakish, fast-backed Normale Coupé in late 1935. This was the Traction as a sleek, curved, faux-cabriolet.
V8 22CV: This period saw the stillborn V8 22CV proposal as a top of the range model. Several saloon and roadster/coupé bodies were built for the V8 engine, but none reached series production.
1938 Model 15/Six: 'La Reine de la Route', in May, with 2867cc – the first of the 'fifteen' CV-rated 6-cylinder cars in France.
Model Familiale: This was an eight or even nine-seater version with the long body '6-light' configuration.
Model Commercial: The extended length '6-light' window body, with a hatchback lift-up rear door and fold-down seats, made its debut as the Commercial model in 1939. Of note, the pre-war Commercial had a split tailgate, whereas on postwar resumption it did not.
Model Découvrable: This Traction was a pre-war conversion choice for independent carrosserie, who cut away the rear roof yet left the rear doors and a thin perimeter frame to allow a roll-back canvas open-top conversion on 2CV principals.
The last of the early variant 'Normale' models in 1939: Wartime disruption stifled development, but in 1947 the long-wheelbase models were again available with the larger engines.

In 1947 the shorter wheelbase models continued, notably in Britain as the 'Light Fifteen' and with the long wheelbase

The 4-cylinder, Slough-built British 'Light' specification still in original condition circa 2013.

'Big Fifteen' which used the original smaller 11-litre engine and due to differing tax ratings, caused great confusion between British and French 15 and 'Fifteen' engine specifications – which differed, being based on the French Model 11 yet entitled 'Fifteen' in British Slough-built specification.

More confusion stemmed from the French Model 15 (CV) 6-cylinder cars being tagged in Britain as 'Big Six', which referred to their 6-cylinder engines. British market cars were fitted with leather seat trim, a wooden dashboard, and some with a delightful sliding sunroof.

Tractions saw service in the French Army, as commandered cars for the Wehrmacht, with the Free French, the Resistance and with numerous criminals including 'le Fou Traction gang'.
Berline Légère Roadster was a Citroën idea which also saw post-war conversion by independent carrosserie. Of note circa 1951, the Swiss company Langenthal built fifty of these roadsters, but added extra chassis bracing, which made the car more rigid but heavier.

TRACTION AVANT: THE FRONT-WHEEL-DRIVE PIONEER

1952: Revised styling with larger 'box' boot added.
1953: Commercial II post-war as an intriguing, long-body modification with extra length via revised C pillars and 'six-light' window styling allied to a full height hatchback tailgate.
1954: Citroën created the ultimate Traction Avant, one born from the test development period started in 1949, and continued after Boulanger's death in 1950 at the wheel of a development Traction Avant. In a special series known as the 15H, an early version of the Citroën hydro-pneumatic suspension system was fitted to the rear wheels only of the Traction.

This 6-cylinder, rear self-levelling, top-of-the-range car was the last of the line that had started in spring 1934.
1957: Traction Avant production ends after 759,111 had been constructed in France, Belgium, Britain (with 20,000 made and some exported to Australia and the Far East colonies), Denmark and Germany, and including the few Dublin-built cars.

Short-tailed, clean-lined and low-slung, the 1934 design still looked contemporary in 1954. Seen here with its owner, the Revd. Mike Johnson, this Traction defines a usable classic.

Most cars of the era used ancient medieval leaf springs, often both front and rear via longitudinal or transverse mounting, and at the rear, hubs or axles were located with simple linkages. In the Traction Avant, the front wheels were independently sprung via a wishbone configuration; this gave individual absorption and a low centre of gravity and low roll centre. At the rear, a beam axle located by trailing arms and with a torsion bar providing bounce absorption allied to a rod created a set-up that offered smooth ride, low roll and light weight. The suspension loads were designed to be fed into the monocoque at specific points to preserve rigidity and handling response, another design innovation and one often overlooked.

Equipped with such advanced suspension and resultant handling, and with sensitive steering that had a light yet positive feel and tuned castor angles, the Traction Avant boasted a new level of driver engagement for a saloon car. It could be hurried along, scything through bends with minimal roll or reaction.

Fitting the car with a larger and heavier engine, ultimately a 6-cylinder unit, would perhaps reduce the 'feel' of the communicative and lithe early Traction experience: but whatever the engine, the car still steered, rode and reacted in a manner that was a significant advance for the 1930s. This was a car with tangible 'turn-in' steering behaviour and predictable handling, even if the early engines were low-powered and the gear-change a touch ponderous. The rigid body transformed the behaviour of the suspension components mounted to it.

The Traction was lighter than contemporary saloons, so not only did it handle differently, it was also faster and more economical – 30mpg (8ltr/100km) was attainable in the smaller 7CV engine variant. Despite the separate front wings and the spectre of aerodynamically induced lift, the smooth monocoque and flat floor created some level of speed enhancement. In its earliest form, the Traction could quickly reach 60mph (80km/h) and be punted along with verve.

TRACTION NOTES

- If the British could build Tractions in Slough, could the Irish build Tractions in Dublin? The answer was yes, and with parts shipped in from Slough, five very high-quality Tractions were created by the Irish for their local market. Subject to inspection by a team from Paris, they all passed with high marks. The white Traction Avant seen here is one of the rare Dublin-built cars
- Pre-war Tractions of 1938–39 had Michelin *Pilote* wheels, which are now very rare and highly coveted amongst the Traction élite
- Presidential 'Specials': Citroën's long history of creating specially bodied cars for France's presidents did not begin with Henri Chapron – it started with Citroën's

ABOVE: **The Traction Avant was also built in Britain and Ireland; this is one of the five Dublin-built cars, recently restored.**

LEFT: **A Roadster in action at the Prescott Hill Climb in 2012. Note the Michelin Pilot wheels and open doors in the bonnet side panel.**

60

TRACTION AVANT: THE FRONT-WHEEL-DRIVE PIONEER

The mythical Traction 22CV existed as a few prototypes, and the artwork for the advertisements for a car that was never produced. French Citroën enthusiasts closely guard the claimed last resting place of what they say is the reality of a survivor…

own VIP specification cars and President Coty's long-wheelbase one-off 15H six
- A Franay-bodied Traction 15 would serve as the presidential car in the 1950s
- François Lecot drove his Traction Avant from Paris to Monte Carlo every day for a year covering 400,000km (250,000 miles) in his heavily sponsored and liveried car.
- Large numbers of Traction Avants were exported from France to the French colonies in Africa and Asia, and by Citroën Slough to Britain's colonies in the same regions, and to Australia where they were arrogantly marketed as the 'British Citroën'.
- An exotic example of Traction Avant being modified was the car created on Traction 11B underpinnings by Charles Deutsch and René Bonnet. Deutsch was an engineer fascinated by aerodynamics and Bonnet an engine and drivetrain expert. The pair created a dramatic and advanced body for their first car project, which was the Traction-based DB1 of 1938. By 1947 the duo had created their own 'DB' company and used Citroen mechanical parts within their own designs of glassfibre low drag bodywork. They would soon switch to Panhard as parts supplier and create a famous niche.

Carrosserie Options

Traction Avant received attention from a number of specialist coachbuilders and modifiers up to the 1950s. Significant contributors included the Spaniard Jean Antem, who built his own modified body design on a Citroën Traction Avant underpinnings. Similarly the carrosserier Henri Esclassan built a smoothed-over, longer-bodied special with his Traction Avant 6-cylinder-based 'Splendilux'.

Marius Renard was an independent carrossier, and he built several special Citroën bodies to his own 'MR' designs; his advertising proclaimed him to be *Créateur de la transfomation MR spécialiste en coques Citroën*. He added length to the Traction by extending the front bonnet and *jambon* monocoque legs. He then added chrome fillets to the front wings and a Talbotesque grille, revised lamps and an ornate bumper, and extended the rear of the car into a streamlined tail of baroque feel.

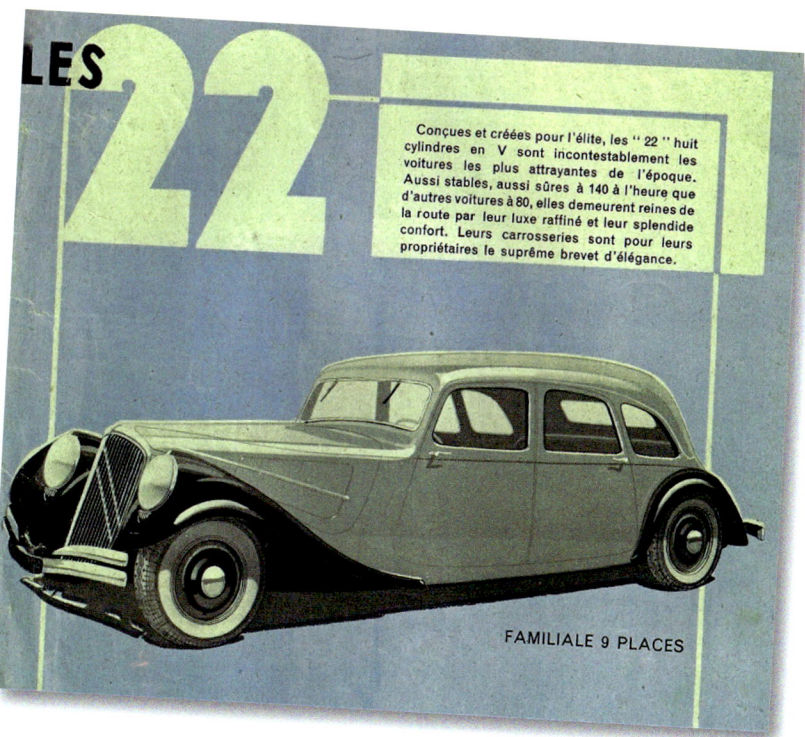

Specialist carrosserie who modified Traction Avants to varying degrees included the following:

ACB	Graber
AEAT	Joanny et Breal
Antem	Langenthal
Bernath	Leon Laisne
Beutler Bruder	Licorne
C. D. Waters	L. Mitre
Clabot	Marius Renard
Delage	Monceau et Truchot
Duchemin	MEP (Maurice Pezous)
Durand	Renard et Bec
Duriez	Rosengart
Emile Tonneline	Saura
Figoni et Falaschi	TTT
Georges Irat	Worfblaufen
Georges Ricard	

Traction numbers: In total, including the cars built in Forest and Slough, 759,111 are listed as constructed; over 1,000 Tractions are currently in road-going condition.

TRACTION AVANT: THE FRONT-WHEEL-DRIVE PIONEER

Elegance personified, as a Traction drives off into legend.

SPECIFICATIONS

TRACTION AVANT
7CV/11CV/15CV/LIGHT 15/BIG FIFTEEN/BIG SIX

Production
1934–1955

Body
4-door and 2-door all-steel monocoque. Lightweight 'Légère', coupé, cabriolet and long-wheelbase variants of which 'Familiale' has extra seats and 'Commercial' has opening rear hatchback. Numerous revisions to rear body/boot styling details.

Engines
Front-wheel-drive in-line 4-cylinder and 6-cylinder 1303cc; 1529cc; 1628cc; 1911cc; 2867cc (22CV rated V8 not launched).

Transmission
Three-speed manual column change.

Brakes
Drums of hydraulic operation on all wheels.

Suspension
Sprung torsion bars longitudinal at front, transverse at rear; later, hydro-pneumatic on rear.

Dimensions

Length	175.2in/4,450mm original model; 195.2in/4,960mm long wheelbase/15.
Width	63.8in/1,620mm original model: 70.5in/1,790mm.
Wheelbase	115in/2,910mm original model. 122in/3,090mm Normale, and 15 model 129in/3,270mm long wheelbase and limousine.
Weight	2,260lb/1,025kg to 2,600lb/1,170kg, depending on variant. (*unladen*)

CHAPTER FOUR

2CV

*NOT BASIC
AT ALL*

2CV | NOT BASIC AT ALL

SOME PEOPLE SAY that the 2CV is a basic, agriculturally engineered device, but nothing could be further from the truth. The 2CV was in fact a typical example of advanced Citroën intellectualism. In its austere functionalism it may have reflected architectural themes, but its graphically advanced body was a timeless stepping stone between the old and the new, though interrupted by a decade lost to World War II and its effects.

Inside Citroën and the Bureau were Lefebvre, Bertoni, Becchia, Sainturant, Franchiset, and before long, hidden in the engineering office, Mages. Boulanger worked well with these men, and it was he who in 1936 began to channel their talents into the very small car – or 'Très Petite Voiture' (TPD) idea that became the 2CV. The small car was Boulanger's inspiration, but it is often forgotten that the idea had also previously been thought about by Le Corbusier, Voisin, Lefebvre and Bertoni – but it was Boulanger who made it happen at Citroën. Voisin and Lefebvre would continue to tinker with the TPD idea for decades in the form of the *Biscooter* and *Cocinelle* respectively.

Boulanger lived in the Clermont-Ferrand area of Lemdpes, and there, as a keen fisherman and gastronome, he observed how local farmers and suppliers struggled to transport and unload their wares on market day. From this came the idea for a rural hold-all – which became the 2CV.

Framed by the French fiscal 'Système Chevaux', the 'Two Horses' tag soon became TPD's *de facto* name: 2CV – not as a fiscal rating, though over time it has erroneously become written as if it was. Some insist on 2cv, and many prefer 'Deudeuche' as a name. The 2CV was basic but advanced – that ultimate Citroën paradox. In its creation and construction, boundaries of engineering technique were explored. This was no agricultural dinosaur, as so many mistakenly thought: the 2CV was the result of cutting edge thinking of positively architectural origin.

The 2CV's suspension was the first interlinked suspension design – via its centrally mounted, leading/trailing torsion bars – recognized as a patented (November 1938) device. With a new engine, new body and new suspension defining a new concept, the 2CV was revolutionary in the late 1930s, and far from the agricultural device so often portrayed. By creating new solutions to old problems and inventing a concept, the 2CV was in fact something truly new. Only in its terrible aerodynamics and appalling drag coefficient of Cd. 0.53 did the 2CV eschew Citroën thinking – but then, at the rural speeds the 2CV was designed for (about 35mph/56km/h), aerodynamic considerations were secondary. Cabin utility, ride and petrol economy were paramount.

Under Pierre Boulanger's new lead and Lefebvre's brilliance, the Citroën team began to craft the new device in 1935. History does not solve the riddle of the possibility of the car having any reference to the Le Corbusier small car design concept which had been entered in the Société des Ingénieurs de l'Auto design competition. Lefebvre knew Le Corbusier well from his Voisin days – but whatever the inspiration, the new small Citroën began to take shape from 1936.

Flaminio Bertoni's styling buck for the production 2CV (post-World War II) is seen on p.66, and it clearly shows the distinctive and new form that Bertoni carved for the car. Unseen for decades, this styling buck shows how the original, more curved shape was evolved from its 1939 form into a production model. Bertoni's sketching shows a car with three headlamps 'cyclops' style, and with sharper features; the third headlamp was soon dispensed with, and under Boulanger's insistence the whole thing was toned down and made simpler and cheaper to make.

The pre-war prototype *circa* late 1938 featured a ribbed bonnet panel and much more curved styling than the post-war production model.

2CV: NOT BASIC AT ALL

Compared with the production car, the prototype feels closer to Art Deco and Le Corbusier architecture than the 2CV as manufactured.

The car's first iteration was in 1937, a sort of small tractor with a half cab and a twin-railed braced chassis with subframes. By late 1938 a proper saloon car type prototype had been constructed under Lefebvre's lead, with Roger Prud'homme managing the actual construction of the car; Maurice Broglie was lead engineer. A new, air-cooled twin-cylinder engine was designed by Edmond Moyet; Alphonse Forceau created the three-speed gearbox. Marcel Chinon worked on the suspension with Pierre Mercier, and Jean Muratet worked on the body. The car was tested extensively by Pierre Terrason as the chief test driver and engineering department development man. Citroën's La Ferté-Vidame test centre provided an ideal location for tuning the suspension and dynamics over many months by the team. The car weighed under 992lb (450kg). By late 1938, thirty-four prototypes had been built.

DURALINOX DESIGN

Lefebvre's search for aviation style, strength and lightness led him to the expensive new alloy 'Duralinox' (an aluminium/magnesium dense alloy) for the major body panels, while lightweight sheet steel was stamped out for extremities such as the front wings.

The car was built up round a twist-resistant, steel sandwich floor 'punt' of H-frame type, with aircraft-style tubular reinforcing members, into which suspension forces were channelled. Mounted above this were the body members, formed principally by the bulkhead and rear wheel-arch pressings. Roof supports were minimal, and Bertoni added a touch of tension to many panels, not just for design reasons, but also to increase rigidity and deflect vibrational harmonics. The 2-cylinder engine was highly advanced, and a great deal of work went into the cylinder head and combustion efficiency process. For a basic car this was unheard of.

Special welding techniques, magnesium alloys and a waxed canvas boot-lid panel to save weight, were just some of the previously unthought of engineering delights of the car. Forty-seven pre-production prototypes were constructed, and a planned run of 250 cars in late 1939 was begun, though not fully achieved. During World War II the prototypes were hidden in various locations, and some were destroyed. The TPV, or 2CV to be, was put into a long, cold hibernation.

When it emerged in 1945 it was revised into something slightly different, and it would be 1945 before Walter Becchia produced the definitive 2CV's 375cc air-cooled, twin-cylinder engine built in light alloy, yet still using a starting handle for rural reliability – though it was soon replaced with a starter motor. In 1946 Paul Mages and Leon Renault worked on an oleo-pneumatic suspension for possible use on the 2CV – but its concept was too advanced for the basic car. The advanced alloys and plastic inherent were replaced with materials that were easier to manufacture, and cheaper. Some of the philosophical intelligence of the original concept was diluted – though paradoxically, the production 2CV became more normal!

Key advanced design features were as follows:

- Front-wheel drive
- Advanced engine and four-speed gearbox design
- Lightweight body of great structural efficiency
- Bolt-on outer panels
- Inboard brakes and low centre of gravity
- Open-top roof of fabric construction to allow large loads
- Removable seats and practical fittings

2CV: NOT BASIC AT ALL

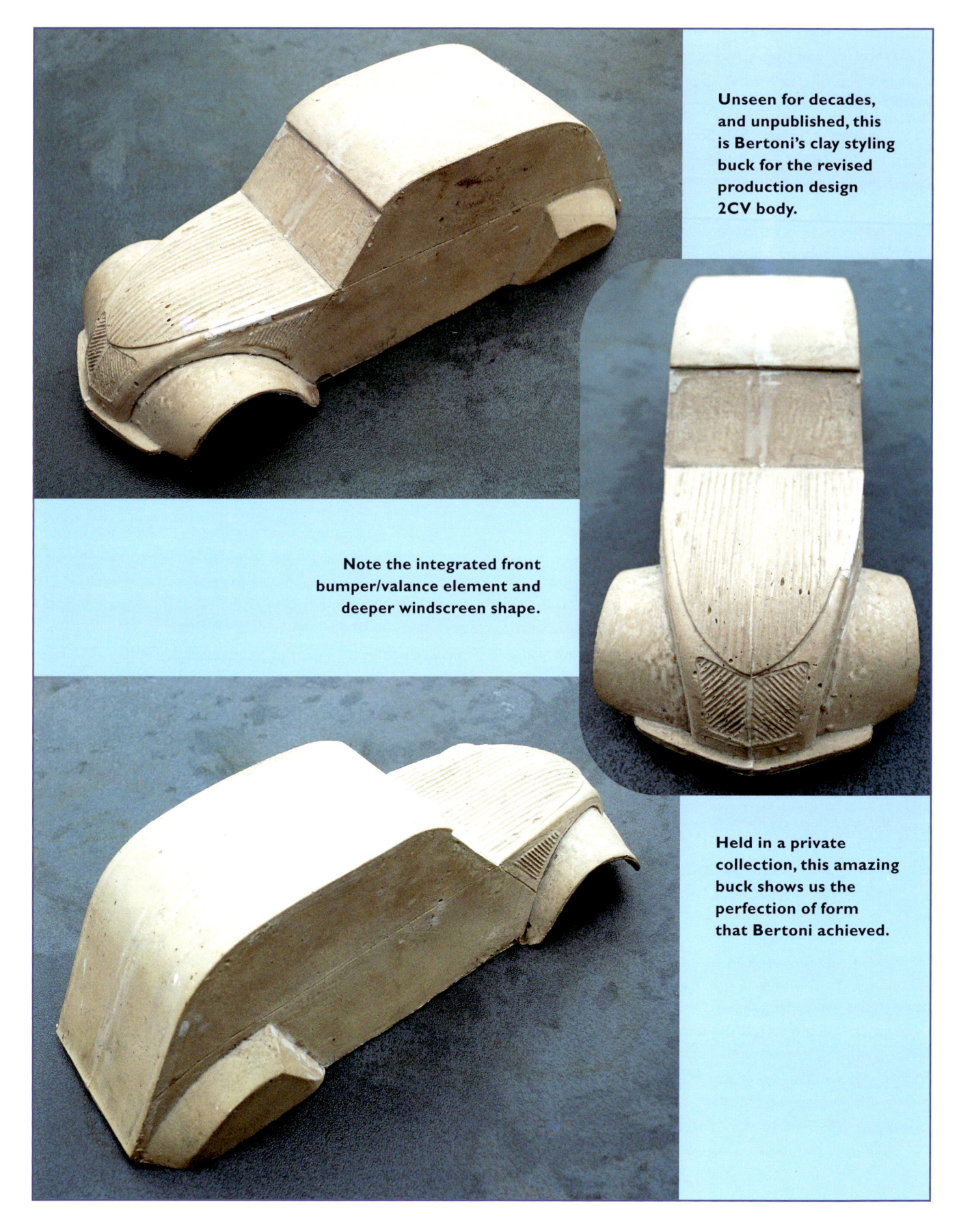

Unseen for decades, and unpublished, this is Bertoni's clay styling buck for the revised production design 2CV body.

Note the integrated front bumper/valance element and deeper windscreen shape.

Held in a private collection, this amazing buck shows us the perfection of form that Bertoni achieved.

PIERRE JULES AUGUSTE BOULANGER ('PJB'): A PHILOSOPHY OF DESIGN ALLIED TO BUSINESS DISCIPLINE

A product of the late 1800s, Boulanger led an interesting early life that must have helped create the open-minded and innovative thinking that latterly characterized his car design and engineering beliefs. Of note, like so many of the key players in Citroën, Boulanger had studied fine art and architecture before embarking on a more practical course. He was yet another product of the grand art schools of Paris. He was also exposed to military discipline at an early age, and the realities of war.

Boulanger served in the military from 1906–08, where the need for project management may have made its first mark upon him. He also met a member of the Michelin family, with whom he forged a friendship at this time. In an unusual move, Boulanger then spent several years in America in various jobs, including, it is reputed, as a ranch hand or cowboy; he then worked in architectural practices in Seattle, and also in Canada. Boulanger's first foray into business was his building and design company that he founded in Canada.

At the beginning of World War I, Boulanger re-entered the military and took to the air as a navigator and photographer. Here he encountered the products of early aviation and of Gabriel Voisin. Commissioned during the war, the officer Boulanger became a decorated man and holder of the Légion d'Honneur. Upon the establishment of peace, he found his way to his old friends at Michelin, and entered the security of their employ. By 1922 he had risen to Board membership, and by 1938 was co-director of Michelin.

During these years, Boulanger had worked with cars and aircraft during the development of Michelin tyres, and the technology needed to serve these two expanding markets and engineering fields. It was in Clermont-Ferrand at Michelin that Boulanger developed his techniques of creating and managing research into product design and engineering needs, all wrapped up in a commercially viable management process. Boulanger *was* an ideas man, a design engineering thinker, but unlike some of his colleagues, he also framed a more practical style. This *may* have limited the scope of design experimentation by the men of the Bureau in one sense – we can ask if the DS was too advanced to have been a Boulanger concept, but we know that the *type* of car was a Boulanger idea. Boulanger adhered to an almost scientific

Pierre Jules Boulanger – 'PJB' – seen pointing towards the 2CV at its Paris launch in 1948.

mechanism of philosophy of discovery, but it is clear that he was neither constrained nor conceited by received or perceived practices.

Boulanger's abilities meant that he could identify market needs and grasp the essentials of product design. After Citroën's bankruptcy, André's death and the Michelin company take-over of Citroën in 1934, under Pierre Michelin, Boulanger became not just a corporate director of Citroën, but also the engineering and design leader. Safety was one of his key passions. He also saw the Traction Avant through its 1934 birth pains. And without Boulanger's encouragement the Sensaud de Lavaud rotary engine prototype would never have been built. Some observers feel that Michelin and Boulanger were hard on Citroën, its staff and departments when they absorbed the bankrupt company, but it seems that Michelin and Boulanger had to apply tough business logic.

As president of Citroën after Pierre Michelin's untimely death, Boulanger drove his ideas and those of his design team. In 1938 Boulanger's lead gave birth to the Traction 15/Six, and soon after that he framed the team's thoughts for a bigger, more modern car: the 'VGD', or 'Voiture de Grand Diffusion'. Boulanger also cut costs and cancelled the Traction Avant 22CV. During the war he was forced to run Citroën by the German military, but he took several measures to undermine production for their war machine.

Continued overleaf

PIERRE JULES AUGUSTE BOULANGER ('PJB'): A PHILOSOPHY OF DESIGN ALLIED TO BUSINESS DISCIPLINE

Boulanger can be seen as the guiding hand behind the secrets of the Bureau d'Études and its stars; he encouraged the team to think the impossible, beyond convention, and when he learned of Paul Mages' suspension work, he seized him from his basic draughting role and placed him and his ideas for Citroën into the Bureau d'Études and ensured that the system was first tested on a 2CV prototype, and seen in production terms on a late model Traction Avant.

Boulanger's home in Lemdpes is now the Town Hall, and in 2005 the architectural firm of Bresson, Combes and Odet dedicated a new community building in Lemdpes in Boulanger's name.

A keen driver, Boulanger made the regular journeys from the Michelin base to Paris and back in his personal Traction Avant 6-cylinder, a tweaked development car. In 1950 he tragically died at the wheel of this car. He never lived to see the 'VGD' arrive as the DS, but the men of the Bureau d'Études, and the men of Citroën who rose through its ranks, such as Pierre Bercot and Robert Puiseux, would carry the flame.

Contrary to the more recent perceptions of some people, the 2CV design was highly advanced: in fact it was the leading edge of thinking. Originally created before World War II, it would be 1948 before the car took to the road. Its subsequent longevity and production up to the 1990s are evidence that the original concept was sound and highly advanced. And the driving force behind the 2CV as a project, not just as a design, was a 'thinker': Monsieur Boulanger and his men.

LA FERTÉ-VIDAME: CITROËN'S SECRET SPACE

As early as 1938 Citroën had built itself a test and development centre for new models. The specially built road circuit allowed high speed handling and performance testing, as well as providing examples of differing road surfaces to test suspension designs. The test track was built in the grounds of a château originally purchased by André Citroën in 1924, situated 60 miles (100km) from Paris in rural Normandy. Numerous sheds and buildings and a management centre were constructed but most importantly, Citroën built a 7ft (2m 15cm) high wall around the entire 7-mile (11km) complex to keep out prying eyes and competitors spies.

In a link to Citroën's own past, the site was previously used for farming and early aviation. All Citroën's cars up until the late 1970s were developed at La Ferté-Vidame, and when Peugeot took over Citroën, it continued to be a test and development centre for both marques. The three original 2CV prototypes were hidden in the attic of a barn at Le Ferté-Vidame, where they survived the war and German occupation.

In the early 2CV years, La Ferté-Vidame was managed by a Monsieur Clerc, and a Monsieur Terrason was the senior test driver for the 2CV development team. A wind tunnel was latterly built at La Ferté-Vidame, and this was run by a Monsieur Girardeau. Development was concealed during the war years, and the 2CV's actual concept was kept hidden from the occupying forces; however, Citroën did continue work on the 2CV during the war, somehow convincing the German authorities that they were working on a military vehicle. By 1945 the team, now with Walter Becchia on hand, got to work to finish and actually revise the original 1939 2CV design concept.

By 1947 this weird yet wonderful piece of advanced engineering thinking was nearly ready, and those who dismissed it because of its appearance would soon regret their judgement.

THE 2CV DESIGN AND DEVELOPMENT MEN

Walter Becchia	André Lefebvre
Maurice Broglie	Jacques Leonzi
Jean-Claude Bouquet	Pierre Mercier
Pierre Boulanger	M. Meunier
M. Caneau	Edmond Moyet
M. Chataigner	Jean Muratet
Marcel Chinon	Maurice Norroy
Jacques Duclos	Roger Prud'homme
Alphonse Forceau	Georges Sallat
M. Geel	M. Steck
Lucien Girard	Pierre Terrason
Pierre Ingeneau	

2CV: NOT BASIC AT ALL

Clever Suspension

Some changes were made to the 2CV's suspension in its early life. Originally its front and rear bell crank lever arms pivoted to create a vertical axis, and springs each side of the car linked the suspension longitudinally via the lever arms. This springing unit consisted of two opposing springs contained within a cylinder at each side of the car (underfloor mountings). At the 2CV's launch the springs were pre-loaded under compression, but by 1954 the system was altered so that the action of the springs worked under tension as the lever arms worked as tie-rods. Extra volute-type springs were loaded into each cylinder. The 2CV's ability to roll to high angles without inverting itself was down to the very low roll centre formed by the low-mounted wheel hub/carrier link to the suspension, which avoided vertically aligned loading up.

2CV MODEL DEVELOPMENT

1937–39: Prototypes and early build series cars.
1947: Revised body design.
1948: Launch of definitive 2CV with 375cc engine at Paris Salon.
1949: June. First full production: 971 cars made in 1949.
1950–51: First 3,000 cars built.
1951: 2CV AU Fourgonette van with 550lb (250kg) payload announced with smaller 375cc engine but lower final-drive ratio of 7:3:1 and larger 135 × 40 section tyres; AU van latterly with glazed panels option.
1953: First British Slough-built cars with specification changes and metal boot-lid. First British 2CV vans. Latterly followed in 1957 by British-built pick-up variant.
1954: Larger 425cc engine introduced, and twin tail lamps. AZ designation. Light grey paint.
1954–55: Centrifugal 'Traffi-Clutch' option.
1955: Changes to design of suspension mountings.
1957: AZL and AZM designations for saloon.
1955: AU series vans are given larger 425cc engines and new AZU designation.
1957: Metal boot-lid replaces fabric on all French 2CV Ss.
1960: 'Blue Glacier' paint offered in France; British 2CV production stops.
1960: Twin-engined 4×4 Sahara using Voisin-type mechanicals introduced.
1964: Front-hinged doors deleted and rear-hinged doors introduced for 1965 model year.
1965: 'Six-light' windows with rear side windows added to C-pillar.
1968: Ugraded 'Berline' model; 'Commercial' model.
1969: 602cc engine fitted.
1970–75: Numerous trim, colour and specification changes. Different headlamps.
1972: Paris-Kabul 2CV Rally. Launch of first 2CV Cross events.
1976: 2CV *Spot* edition.
1977: AK 400 van production ends; the Dyane Acadiane replaces it.
1978–86: Special Editions launched, culminating in *Boat France 3, Bamboo, Beachcomber, Dolly* and latterly the 2CV 6 *Charleston* of 1980, *James Bond* in 1982, *Dolly, France 3, Cocorico*.
1990: Production ceases in Portugal after just under 4 million cars have been built.

2CV Spot special edition and an Ami Super show off their Bertoni lines.

LEFT: **James Bond Special Edition 2CVs from 1981.**

BELOW LEFT: **Many designers have attempted to recreate the 2CV. Following previous design experience and working on a PSA project, this is the author's 1994 anti-retro design idea for a 'new' 2CV; it was featured in the motoring press.**

BELOW RIGHT: **The author's 2CV design featured flying buttress C-pillar and wheel spats, but was not a retro-pastiche.**

ARGENTINIAN 2CVS

The first 2CVs imported into South America arrived as early as 1958. These were imported by Staudt and company, yet by 1959 Citroën Argentina S.A. was in existence. Early cars were CKD, but by 1962, local toolings and pressings created the true Argentinian-built 2CV from Buenos Aires. Production also took place in Venezuela.

The first Argentinian 2CV range consisted of saloon and the rare van/pick-up variants. These cars were tagged 2CV AZU/AZL, and had the 12.5bhp 425cc engine. For late 1963 a 14bhp version with better breathing boosted sales in 1964 to over 5,500 cars. It is reputed that the Argentinian cars received the third-light rear window very early in the 1960s, before many other markets. In 1965 more power at 18bhp and revised interiors updated the Argentine range – as did the addition of changes to the clutch mechanism. For 1966–67 van production was increased. Production ceased in 1972.

In 1967 opening rear windows in the rear doors of saloons were added. Also local van production started: the 2CV Azam was made until the end of 1971, and the 2CV AZM until March 1972, when production ceased permanently after an amazing 64,644 cars had been produced with various badges and names.

Special one-off body conversions based on the saloon and van bodies were produced for the Argentine market, and these are now highly prized. The complex and rare Argentinian 2CV trim and variants included the 2CV, 3CV, AZU, and Fourgon.

2CV STATESIDE?

Citroën toyed with the idea of importing the 2CV into America, and a small number were sent over in the mid-1960s for evaluation. But the mindset of the American car-buying public resisted the 2CV's charms, though a few were tempted. But in 1970 Citroën gave up any hope and abandoned its US dealer stock. It is believed that up to 900 2CV s made it to America *circa* 1964–70. The remaining US stock was crushed by Citroën in America in order to save the costs of repatriation to the motherland!

SPECIAL 2CVS

Not only were special versions of the 2CV built around the world: a series of self-build cars that even have their own 'Citroën Specials Club' now exists. The 2CV basics, minus the body, seem to provide an enduring base for many interpretations.

Leading 2CV special-bodied cars include Lomax, Pembleton, Hoffman, Le Patron, Burton, Azelle, Charou, Alveras, Tripacer, BRA, Falcon and Deauville. Some use 2CV parts, others Dyane, Mehari, and even GS components. The popular Lomax comes in either two- or four-wheel variants. Most of the specialist marques use glassfibre for their bodywork, although alloy-fabricated bodies have been produced. The Hoffman-bodied variant uses 2CV body panels in a cut-down two-door convertible shell. The Burton special apes the Deutsche and Bonnet aerodynamic styling as seen on the one-off 1930s Traction Avant aerodynamic study.

ABOVE LEFT: **Leather-lined 2CV interior – the Hermes collection special edition 2CV.**

ABOVE RIGHT: **2CV interior sumptuously done out in leather.**

RIGHT: **'Mildly modified' might begin to explain this 2CV mud-plugger.**

2CV: NOT BASIC AT ALL

LEFT: **The Citroën Specials Club caters for the glassfibre and rarer steel-built 'kit' cars based on 2CV underpinnings and engines.**

BELOW: **2CV Cross** – a wonderful sport.

Variations on a Theme

- Jean Dagonet created modified and tuned 2CVs as early as 1953, and by 1954–55 he had re-bodied a 2CV with an amazing, curved, low-drag body of lozenge-shaped, Bertoni-esque elegance
- In 1954 the racing car fanatic and car designer Phillipe Charbonneaux created his own take on the 2CV as a 'pontoon' type design
- In 1953 Pierre Bardot produced the first tuned and modified 2CV for racing
- 1955 the 2CV 'Bicéphale' was used as a fire brigade 'Pompier' lightweight hold-all-type van with modified steering to allow manoeuvring off road
- In 1956, Henri Chapron tackles the 2CV with a modified bodyshell with an estate car-type rear end as a 2CV 'Break'
- By 1959 Citroën's Chilean factory is producing the Citroëneta – itself a three-box, booted 2CV. For 1963 Argentian-built 'La Rana' 2CV s with bodywork changes were produced
- For 1960 the Citroën produced the 2CV 'Sahara': it has 4×4 via two engines and two gearboxes mounted front and rear. Less than 700 are built, and in 2013 a rare survivor once owned by the Dupont family sold for over $140,000 in America
- In the 1970s, the 2CV-based 'Africar' project blended 2CV mechanicals and a composite and wood body in an attempt to realize a dream of low-cost travel in the developing world. Despite its brilliance, Africar failed
- The 2CV Contessa was a 1970s Spanish-built re-bodied four-light window version using the standard 2CV mechanicals and platform
- The Citroën Mehari was a 2CV/Dyane-based plastic-bodied derivative; there were also glassfibre and steel-bodied versions built as the Tangara, Pony, Baby Brouse and other iterations
- As late as 1988 a 2CV 4×4 concept-derived car known as the Katar was built in France by SIFTT as an all-terrain vehicle with the enlarged 652cc twin-pot engine from the Visa.
- In 1989 the 2CV 6 Charleston special edition was imported into America by Michel Fournet. It is reputed that he circumvented US Type Approval regulations by transferring the new cars' bodies and engines into a refurbished, previously registered 2CV base.

2CV: NOT BASIC AT ALL

High speed 2CVs tackle the Prescott Hill climb at La Vie en Bleu.

Some owners go to great lengths to smooth down and lighten their steeds.

2CV in 'Charleston' graphics.

73

2CV: NOT BASIC AT ALL

SPECIFICATIONS	2CV/2CV4/2CV6/VAN VARIANTS 1948–90

Body
Lightweight alloy/steel body panels mounted over steel base unit platform. Four- and six-window designs. Fabric roll-back roof. Numerous changes to roof, bonnet and boot-lid designs

Engine
375cc air-cooled twin-cylinder: 425cc, 435cc, 602cc. Front-wheel drive

Transmission
Four-speed manual

Suspension
Horizontally mounted friction dampers and shock-absorbing system with interconnectivity

Brakes
Drums/front inboard mounted, hydraulic operation

Dimensions
Length 152in/3,860mm
Width 58.5in/1,480mm
Height 63in/1,600mm
Wheelbase 94.5in/2,400mm
Weight 1,235lb/560kg *(unladen)*

DAGONET, UMAP AND THE 2CV

In the early 1950s, French engine tuner, after-market specialist and rally driver Jean Dagonet came up with an idea for a re-bodied 2CV using a decidedly Bertoni-esque, teardrop-shaped, low-slung five-door iteration of a coupé style moulded in glass fibre. This was mounted on a 2CV platform and using a tuned 2CV engine. Several were manufactured, and this led Dagonet to the idea for a less radical, two-door coupé on the same underpinnings. In 1956 Dagonet began to make a master body for a mould.

The very rare UMAP glassfibre-bodied 2CV two-door project. Only two or three road-going survivors are known, and the location of the moulds is not known.

2CV: NOT BASIC AT ALL

The ensuing events are clouded by a lack of records, but basically, a small company, known as l'Usine d'Moderne Applications Plastiques, run by Camille Martin in Bernon, France, created their 'take' on the standard 2CV. This was a two-door coupé-type glassfibre car on a standard base platform. The idea was to clothe it in an elegant glassfibre body that belied the humble origins and low capacity engine hidden under the Franco-Italianate style of the body.

It is an oft debated question as to who shaped the car – was it Monsieur Martin or Jean Dagonet? Several references credit Jean Dagonet with the original project, and cite a subsequent completion and separate production by UMAP. This could be because after manufacturing his teardrop-shaped, re-bodied 2CV, Dagonet embarked on building a two-door body that the UMAP resembled, to some extent. There was also a Jean Gessalin who was consulted on the car's construction process, so maybe all three men had a hand in the shape. The car was deemed attractive by many, and more sporting (but actually less aerodynamic) than the later British-based 2CV Bijou of similar idea.

From 1957, a small local production run of the UMAP-branded '425' and '500' models of this two-door, two-box coupé body were made, the 500 featuring a bore-out twin-pot engine of 499cc from the original engine capacity. The dashboard featured parts from various Citroën cars and commercials, but it is not known where the windscreen and windows were taken from – unless they were commissioned items, and Renault parts may be apparent. UMAP's body design was neither *avant garde* nor particularly aerodynamic, but it was smart, had shades of Simca and Renault Caravelle in its lines, and was therefore entirely contemporary.

Citroën did not officially support the car, nor did it supply new parts direct. The list price was high, approaching that of an ID, and the car briefly appeared at the 1957 Paris Salon. Production records are not available, and the much touted build run of 100 cars is a claim that seems unfulfilled – experts say that forty-seven cars may have been built. Two UMAP 500s took part in the 1958 Liège-Brescia-Liège rally. Today, only two UMAP cars are roadworthy, and the location of the moulds is unknown.

MÉHARI: PLASTIC DROMEDARY

Often cited as a 2CV derivative that might ape the 2CV 4×4, the Méhari (so named after a Sahara Desert camel or dromedary, and also cited as the French Army Africa regiment who were

ABOVE: **The ABS-bodied Méhari used many stock items, yet managed to look individual.**

LEFT: **In its element, Méhari flies through the mud.**

camel-mounted and thus 'Méhariste) was closer to Panhard and the Dyane. The very first technical references to the car cited it as a Dyane-Méhari.

Based on the platform of the Dyane 6, the Méhari used acrylonitrile butadene styrene (ABS) plastics moulding technology in its open-top body, which composed of only eleven or thirteen actual mouldings, depending on the variant. Underneath the ABS formed body was a Dyane platform and engine caged by tubular steel support structures. Of significance, the Argentinian market (Uruguay-built) Méharis and certain others used the glassfibre resin body technique because it was much cheaper to manufacture – thereby removing the need for ABS moulding costs. Early development of the idea in 1966 is credited to a Roland de la Poype.

With the 2CV/Ami twin-pot engine's 28bhp on tap (and latterly 30bhp), the car's light weight of 1,300lb (570kg) created a 'go-anywhere' animal that was limited only by its small torque – which the fitment of a reduction gear in the 4×4 variant slightly ameliorated from 1979 to 1983, late in the Méhari's production life. With the long travel, loping suspension of the 2CV, narrow tyres, low centre of gravity and light weight, the Méhari was a camel- or maybe even goat-like adventure vehicle ideal for military, agricultural, adventure and leisure use. Over 145,000 Méharis were built.

An American market version was sold as a truck to circumnavigate the US Type Approval regulations. Because it was required to fit bumpers and raise the headlamps to meet local rules, a new front valance moulding had to be created – yet

Here, the moulded chassis-less 'punt' reveals the core of the Méhari prior to its eleven main body panels being fitted.

Handbuilt at the factory, a Méhari with full roof kit is nearly complete.

2CV: NOT BASIC AT ALL

RIGHT: **The rare Méhari Azur in blue and white trim.**

BELOW: **The Méhari derivatives were often made in cheaper glass fibre or basic steel panelling. This is the 'Pony' variant seen in yellow paint.**

only 214 Méharis were sold in America. The car hire company Budget sourced Méharis for hire to tourists in Florida and Hawaii. Most Méharis were beige, but later 1970s colours included orange, yellow and green. A rare Méhari 'Azure' edition was blue and white and had deckchair-style striped seats instead of plastic coverings.

The Méhari went rallying in the 1969 Liège-Dakar rally, the 1970 Paris-Kabul-Paris rally, and then the 1971 Paris-Persepolis rally; a single Méhari was used as a support vehicle in the 1980 Paris-Dakar Rally. The French army ordered many Méharis and converted them to 24-volt specification. The Irish military also purchased a small number (ten to twelve) of Méharis, finished appropriately in green. The Méhari 4×4 had a four-speed gearbox with a three-speed reduction/transfer box. From 1979 to 1982 the 4×4 version received various trim and specification upgrades from the 2CV and Dyane parts bins.

A Méhari-based 'Bedouin' – shades of 'Africar', perhaps.

Steel-bodied versions of the Méhari were licence built, and a 'Baby Brouse' variant was built (up to 30,000 were made) in Africa and in Vietnam as the 'Dalat' for Asian markets. A 'Pony' variant was known in Greece and Turkey. A 'Tangara' variant was also created, comprising the amalgamation of 2CV, Dyane and Méhari components and often crudely built in local steel. Citroën even reverse engineered its own steel-bodied version, known as the FAF.

The Méhari was never officially imported into Great Britain, but instead was made available via official Citroën dealers as their own imported stock. Over 100 Méharis were sold in Great Britain, and approximately thirty-five remain known as running, but records are inaccurate and the name 'Méhari' does not appear on registration documents ('Citroën Two-Seater Utility' being the usual description).

Although without either safety belts or impact protection, the Méhari proved hugely popular and today has a growing following and rising values.

MÉHARI DETAILS

Launched 1968. Withdrawn 1988 (France)
602cc, two-wheel, front driven
Later 4×4 variant launched in 1979 with approx. 1,275 built
Open top, canvas roof (later plastic roof option)

CITROËN IN BRITAIN

Citroën's early agents in Great Britain were Gaston Ltd of Larden Road, Acton, West London. A showroom in Great Portland Street was a rather grand tangent, but Gaston also had a city centre Piccadilly outlet. Citroën appointed Harrods as their agents, and Harrods soon had a fleet of Citroën vans.

The link with Slough, just west of London and not far from the end of Heathrow Airport's main runway, came about from a demonstration of an autochenille tracked vehicle at the site of the then Slough munitions site, which soon developed into an industrial and engineering facility. By 1924 Citroën in France had decided to take over the operations of its British agency outlet, as the Gaston company was struggling. Citroën's first 'official' showroom and base was in Hammersmith. Within two years, and allied to a new British import tax, the logic of making Citroën cars in Great Britain became obvious.

On 18 February 1926 André Citroën opened the marque's new British base on the Slough trading estate. A major coup was to usurp Renault as suppliers of London taxis. Latterly, British-built Traction Avants were converted to 12-volt function and had British trim options, including differing dashboards and seat trims; they were even sold across the British Empire as the 'British-built Citroën'. Many Lucas parts were also used to increase the local British content. British 2CVs were pitched at a British customer base, but sales failed to take off in the early days. Slough-built 2CV vans were also produced, and 231 were sold.

Citroën GB's Nigel Somerset-Leake, with approval from boss Louis Garbe, created the idea of an agricultural version of the 2CV: a pick-up. Along with his managing of the Bijou

ABOVE LEFT: **2CV van showing off all the elements that make the design what it is. Pure and utter Citroën.**

ABOVE: **The interior of the van reeks of utilitarian functionality.**

LEFT: **Air-cooled engineering as originally intended.**

project, Somerset-Leake seems to have been an inspired ideas and marketing man. The special 2CV pick-up truck was built for a Ministry of Defence contract, and featured a handbuilt, locally engineered rear cab tooled up by metal bashing a 'master' over a concrete mould and using H van components. The mechanical guru of Citroën GB, chief engineer Ken Smith, worked on this project, which also took place as the factory was being rebuilt for British DS production. The 2CV pick-up sold sixty-five units to the public, and approximately sixty-five were also sold to the Royal Navy.

The 2CV was produced as a Slough-built car with modifications for local tastes that included a metal boot-lid and a revised roof in a more durable 'Everflex' material that allowed

ABOVE: **Timeless and beyond iconic, only the badging dates the modern build date of this car.**

LEFT: **2CV owners are individualistic, and this one has well and truly 'tripped the light fantastic'.**

a larger rear windscreen; it was also fitted was a wonderful Art Deco-style bonnet badge. Lucas semaphore trafficator arms were retro-fitted, as were folding rear side-window mechanisms. Chrome bumpers and over-riders were added to the British cars, of which 1,034 were built between 1953 and 1960 (672 saloons, 231 vans and 131 pick-ups).

A 'High-Roof' 2CV

As early as 1953, Citroën in Slough also produced a one-off 2CV with taller roof pressing and larger windscreen for a British customer of great height, a Major Wanliss, who could not fit into the standard car with its generous headroom. This car was chassis number 8530102, and at one time bore the registration number STJ 113.

British DS production began in 1956, and again, many local trim variations were made, including the British-style wooden dashboard, and numerous technical and styling tweaks. Early DS/ID19 production also relied on SKD base units being shipped in via the boat train until the expanded Slough factory could ramp up to full production. Between 1956 and 1964, 8,000 DS cars were British-built, with a further 500 SKD kits added. But at this stage, Citroën ended British production, closing a four decades long chapter in its relationship with British production. The company would remain at Slough until further PSA rationalization in recent years.

BRITISH BIJOU

The apparent early failure of the 2CV in the British market place led to an interesting idea – that of a more upmarket, more middle-class sort of faux coupé based on 2CV mechanicals. A better looking, more conventional car would, it was suggested, appeal to the more conservative British buyer. Pricing was also an issue: at £560 a new 2CV, even Slough-built, was not cheap in comparison to other small cars of the day, which retailed for around £400 to £450.

Citroën-Slough's sales manager Mr Nigel Somerset-Leake is credited with progressing the idea of reshelling the 2CV with a glassfibre two-door body – and often unmentioned is British Citroën director Louis Garbe, who is reputed to have suggested the idea. Garbe was also the man who happily sanctioned 'improvements' to British-built 2CVs long before such items were specified in Levallois-built 2CVs. Citroën Slough's chief engineer Ken Smith was also involved, though his main remit at the time was organizing the start of British DS production.

Glassfibre, or 'grp', was a new plastics-based material that had stemmed from wartime technology: it was much cheaper to manufacture curves in grp than in metal. Unlike other grp pioneers, the Bijou, as it was named, did not have a single one-piece moulded shell draped over its chassis: instead, Peter Kirwan-Taylor – who was a 'petrol head' and a design enthusiast with a clever eye for detail – created a separate section, multiple moulding grp monocoque of much higher strength

The Bijou was an elegant and aerodynamic car that surely should have become a fully available Citroën product across Europe.

Sheer elegance from a British-designed Citroën.

than a one-piece moulding. With a grp central tub and separate grp outer panels, this car had a strong cabin cell and was much safer than a normal one-piece grp body: it ensured that frontal impact was better absorbed, with less chance of the body shattering around the cabin structure's apertures, as is often the case with the alternative one-piece moulding.

Often cited as the Bijou's designer, Kirwan-Taylor was a businessman by profession, with a passion for cars and motor sport, which led him to be a key player within the corporate hierarchy of Colin Chapman's emergent Lotus brand. However, we can only speculate as to the role that Kirwan-Taylor's associates, the designer Ron Hickman (once of Ford) and the aerodynamics guru Frank Costin, might have played in shaping and engineering both the Lotus Élite and the Citroën Bijou.

The Bijou was devised with a similarly constructed body to that first used by Lotus on the grp monocoque of the Élite, but the construction costs were high, and Lotus soon switched to a cheaper, but structurally less advantageous one-piece single moulded shell mounted to a central chassis spine for all subsequent Lotus grp cars.

Bijou was a masterpiece of integrated styling, with shades of Bristol about its cabin and glasswork. It remains an often forgotten highlight of early grp car design. Due to its multiple-section moulded hull (and metal platform underneath), it was not as light as a single-skin grp-shelled car would normally be, and this affected the gears' performance until aerodynamically relevant speeds were reached.

Kirwan-Taylor must have had access to a great deal of aerodynamics knowledge, and not only gave the little Bijou hints of DS style, but also excellent wind-cheating shape and details, thereby offering very low drag with a resultant cruising economy of almost 60mpg (4.7ltr/100km). Unsurprisingly, Citroën GB endorsed the car and sold it through Citroën dealers. At £695 it was not cheap, but it was stylish and economical, and was linked to a national dealer network. We can only wonder why Citroën did not do a deal to secure the car's rights for European marketing in a left-hand-drive version.

Built between 1959 and 1964 at the Slough factory (with two attempts at securing a moulding supplier after early moulding issues), Bijou was never made in left-hand-drive form and never sold abroad – although six were exported to Australia. Of the 203 claimed production Bijous (and at least two prototypes that featured differing front styling), less than twenty remain. The engine was the 2CV's 425cc twin-pot with a 'Traffi-Clutch' mechanism as standard. The car used Lucas electrics, and parts from the Citroën DS, Citroën Traction Avant, and Morris and Standard-Triumph ancillary fittings: the facia design was particularly clever for its era.

The car was produced in low numbers for just over four years, and the final production figure is cited as an indeterminate 205 to 211 units – which must surely count as a success for a private idea, endorsed by a car maker and up against stiff competition in a new market. Today, the Bijou is a coveted example of a uniquely British Citroën design.

CHAPTER FIVE

THE MAN WITH A VAN

COMMERCIALS

THE MAN WITH A VAN | *COMMERCIALS*

THE FIRST CAMIONS

CITROËN PRODUCED COMMERCIAL vehicles in the early 1920s, vehicles that came before the more famous vans but which are often forgotten. As early as 1919 the A-Type cars had offered a Voiture Livraison: essentially a two-seat pick-up truck with a canvas roof. A longer bodied, half-timbered B2 of 1921 was possibly the first estate car or 'Break', and was given the variant name 'Normandie'. B- and C-Type chassis were all used for small trucks, ambulances, haulage vehicles and fire engines.

The larger-engined C-Type chassis allowed the creation of the first Citroën bus and coaches, with many special bodies also created by specialist carrosserie suppliers. By 1931 André Citroën had set up a completely separate commercial transport company named 'Société Anonyme des Transport Citroën'. The company did not just manufacture buses and coaches, it also operated them across many regional routes: there were 800 Citroën buses in service by 1933. By the mid-1930s, Citroën had sold nearly 10,000 buses and coaches or 'Autocars', and was offering diesel engines. Many of the Citroën chassis were delivered to the new industrial or utility coach-building carrosserie that had sprung up to provide specialist bodywork for these new and very popular commercial vehicles.

The defining model that started the new commercial series was the Type 23, which in various incarnations was built from 1923 to 1969; an indirect injection diesel engine was on offer as early as 1936. From 1937–65 there followed a bizarre model numbering system that quite illogically identified vehicles as Type 29, Type 45, Type 32, through to Types 46 to 48, and 60. Type 45 was the first big Citroën truck to have an engine that was not derived from a Citroën car.

Flamino Bertoni's truck designs for Citroën carried into the1960s and beyond his death. The 300, 400, 600, 700 and 800 series trucks with their distinctive windscreen shapes and styling motifs defined a whole era of Citroën commercial vehicles – even Robert Opron sketched out a 1960s Citroën truck.

ABOVE: **Sacré Bleu indeed. A well known British-based H van shouts Citroën design from its face.**

RIGHT: **Classic styling for the Types 55 and 60 launched from 1953, and the 4×4 as seen here.**

A Small Van?

As the 1930s progressed, the idea of a useful small utility vehicle came to permeate the minds of the men at the newly formalized Bureau d'Études, not least in the thinking of Pierre Franchiset, Jean Cadiou and a M. Ingeneau.

By 1940, and forced by Nazi occupation to manufacture vehicles during the war, Citroën turned to agricultural vehicle and implement production in an attempt to diversify. In 1942 the company started to produce the Citroën 'Brouette' wheelbarrow, and it also began exploring tractor production. Another Citroën agricultural machine was the Type T 'Terrassier' earth-breaking implement of 1943. These developments still originated from the Bureau d'Études, although it had moved to the safety of a new location at Niort in western France, where Jean Cadiou continued as patron of the Bureau.

Early Thoughts

Prior to the war, the idea of creating something more than a car-derived utility vehicle was beginning to take formal shape within Citroën; but with Bertoni busy on the Traction Avant and then utterly focused on the 2CV, scant extra resources were available. Jean Cadiou had also been wondering what might be next after the Traction and 2CV. But inside Citroën were Pierre Franchiset and M. Ingeneau, who created a project for a utility vehicle – a small van for commercial use.

TUB to TUC From 'Le Cube Utile' to 'Traction Utilitaire Série C'

Prior to 1936, all Citroën commercials had been based on passenger car chassis, but the developing theme for a dedicated small van design for industrial, commercial and agricultural use got the go ahead: and so was born the concept of a small trade vehicle with a 1,100–1,650lb (500–750kg) carrying capacity. Thoughts of adapting the vehicle to higher weights of 1,875lb (850kg) or even 2,200lb (1,000kg) were also considered. Lefebvre and Boulanger were keen to create the world's first front-wheel-drive commercial van.

Vital considerations were that the cargo bay should be square, tall, and easy to load through side and rear doors. The driver and his mate should be perched high over the front engine, which should also be easy to access for maintenance. By late 1937, the TUB prototype was ready. TUB had a smoothly contoured front with curved leading edge to the roof, tapering back into the boxed cargo section. Use of the Traction's double chevron grille motif gave it a distinct identity. Some called the TUB ugly – others soon realized it was ideal.

With Boulanger driving the project and Franchiset working on the design under Cadiou's direction, TUB was a clever and utterly pure Citroën concept that was intended to open up a new and vitally lucrative market for Citroën. But Michelin's management would hold the TUB back from launch whilst the Traction Avant's teething problems were sorted out, and it was not until the spring of 1939 that the small TUB van was

The Citroën tractor; the company also made earth tillers and wheelbarrows during the war.

The emotional appeal of the chevron-faced TUB from 1941.

launched. Once the van's true qualities began to be appreciated, especially by small business operators, sales took off despite its unusual and futuristic styling.

TUB was front-wheel drive with a 1,764lb (800kg) capacity; it had a three-speed gearbox and advanced rack-and-pinion steering, as opposed to the worm-and-roller mechanism that might have been expected. With hydraulic brakes, torsion bar suspension and an easily accessible cargo bay, it had all the essential elements of success. Of significance, it was the first van in the world to have a sliding cargo-bay side door – another essential ingredient in any van today.

TUB had a simple steel structure with body side cargo panels part-formed of canvas tightened with aviation practice 'doping' techniques to produce a cheap, durable, lightweight solution. Plastic window panels could be set into this side panel. The whole thing was an ingenious idea. Using the Traction's 1628cc 4-cylinder, water-cooled engine and placing it and the driver and crew directly over and just in front of the driving wheels gave superb access, great traction, and a fully flat load bay with minimal suspension intrusion. So was set the formula for every van ever since by many manufacturers.

TUB was front heavy, however, and with simple rear suspension and rear drum brakes, could be somewhat skittish when unladen. It went on sale in June 1939 and was priced at FF36,000. By 1940 a developed version using the Traction Avant's larger 1911cc engine of 11CV rating emerged. Load capacity was the same, at 2,250lb (1,020kg), but numerous trim upgrades and minor metalwork changes were carried out; this included a proper front bumper, and the addition of a second windscreen wiper for the passenger side of the split windscreen. This was the Mk2 or 'C' variant, or TUC: Citroën's records show that 1,749 vans were sold and the majority of those were the TUB version. The outbreak of World War II was a premature restriction for TUB/TUC and Citroën light commercial vehicle development.

Curiously, the company of Fenwick had had a long relationship with Citroën (at one stage they were potential investors), and they built an early electric, battery-powered version of the TUB. With limited range and the weight of the batteries affecting TUB's excellent power-to-weight ratio, the Fenwick vans (an unlikely 100 such conversions have been claimed) were of limited use, even when converted to ambulance configuration in 1942.

The H Van

Thoughts of a re-born van bubbled away throughout the war, and André Lefebvre laid plans for another van, something bigger than TUB, as early as 1943. With resources in short supply, formal work on the project could not really start until the end of the war. Yet incredibly the first prototype for the new van emerged in the summer of 1946, with the second being completed in September and used for extensive testing. By this time carrying capacity was intended at 2,205lb (1,000kg) and then by 1947, 2,650lb (1,200kg). So was born Type H.

TYPE G?

There were thoughts of a little brother to the H van, the Type G, which would have been closer to the original TUB concept, but these were sadly abandoned to allow the development of the 2CV-derived van. Type G would surely have been the Berlingo van of its day, and would have secured massive sales. Instead a 2CV van was created.

In an early piece of parts-bin engineering, Type H van used many components off the Citroën shelf, which massively reduced design and tooling costs. Items were also 'borrowed' from the Traction Avant (including the front hubs, door handles and window winders), 2CV and latterly from the Ami and DS.

Type H was a monocoque, yet reinforced by stiffened panels and strategically placed struts. A subframe carried the front engine and suspension loads, and the whole unit was held in by just four bolts for simplicity.

Monsieur Franchiset and Monsieur Ingeneau worked on the body design, and it was Franchiset who invented the special 'clasp' door hinges that were devoid of the normal pin rods. The H van had a high roof and flat floor and was the first commercial van to offer the now commonplace 'walk-through' interior. Geroges Leroy was also instrumental in the H van's engineering and worked on the Bureau d'Études own motorhome or camping car H-van idea as early as 1953.

Observers often claim that the Type H van owed its ribbed steel panel work to the use of such technique in the German Junkers aircraft 52. This is a myth that has been repeated so often that it has become folklore. The use of pressed ribs in steel panels may have become publicly obvious by its appearance on the JU 52, but the technique of locally stiffening flat steel panels had been around since the early days of metal-hulled ship building. By 'ribbing' the panel, great torsional rigidity is added at little cost and a floppy panel becomes pre-stressed and more resistant to twist. Early ships and aircraft deployed the technique to reduce aero-elastic 'panting' of panels under vibration, twist and load stresses.

Numerous claims to inventing the technique are known, and all Citroën did was use the idea to add vital strength to the new van it planned for the post-war boom. In fact Citroën had already deployed the use of a ribbed-steel panel in the bonnet of the original 1939 2CV, so we should cite the 2CV prototype for the inspiration for the Type H's ribbed steel, and not a Junkers 52.

With all the weight saving, there is enough power from the 1628cc or 1911cc engine to provide a load capacity between 1,875 and 3,530lb (850 and 1,600kg), depending on the model.

The H van, as it became forever tagged, was launched at the Paris Salon, and was immediately catapulted into French folklore, where incredibly it stayed as a production item until 1981, in direct descent of the original engineering concept and tooling. Production would take place in Javel, Aulnay and Forest, and in CKD form in Amsterdam, The Netherlands. Later Belgian-built vans had front-hinged doors, but French-built H vans had rear-hinged 'suicide' doors for many years.

The last H vans were manufactured in December 1981, and sales lingered into 1982. After that Citroën promoted the C35 van, which had been launched before the decline of the H van. By the 1980s, the C35 had been developed, and a C25 range created as a joint production stemming from the Citroën-Fiat partnership which although dissolved, continued to create badge-engineered light commercial vans – and does so to date.

Building the H van. Underneath the ribbed steel there lies a complex panel-work construction.

SUMMARY OF TYPE H DEVELOPMENTS

1947: Launch of Type H.
1949: Revised HZ with increased payload.
1958: HY with 3,307lb (1,500kg) payload.
1961: HYD diesel with British Perkins diesel engines 1621cc and 42bhp within 7CV rating. All vans were 12 volt after a change from the 6-volt system.
1963: HY and HZ 70/2 series with petrol engine of 1628cc.
1964: Spilt windscreen discontinued and new one-piece windscreen across all variants. In October 1964 there is a change of design of chevrons.

1964: HY-IN/HZ-IN with Perkins diesel engine replaced with Indenor 1816cc unit of 50bhp.
1966: HY and HZ 78 series with 1911cc and 58bhp engine. Increased payload to 2,205lb (1,000kg).
1969: HX IN2/HW IN2 with 6,350–7,060lb (3,100–3,200kg) payload and revised styling.
1972: Option of hydro-pneumatic suspension at rear with ambulance body variant only.
1973–81: On-going minor trim and specification changes. Belgian production 1949–63.

Classic H-van moment as Mr Sobey's camper-van conversion rattles along in all its glory.

THE MAN WITH A VAN: COMMERCIALS

SPECIAL BODIED TYPES

The H van engendered a mass following in the world of conversions and special use bodies. The vehicle was very popular as a mobile grocery, butchery or bakery, yet also served as a mobile laboratory, ambulance, horse box, cattle truck, low-loader, and builder's wagon. The French police used the H van, but so too did others, notably the Dutch police force. So from postman to painters, H van became the symbol of both French small and big business enterprise.

Today the H van is extremely popular as a mobile home or camping car, and is fashionable as a mobile catering outlet; with a carrying capacity of 1,875–3,530lb (850–1,600kg), its abilities cover a wide arena of use. With side windows added it becomes a Fourgonnette, as a farm animal transporter it is a Bétaillère, and as a pick-up truck a Plateau. The H van was the mainstay

ABOVE: **In a scene straight out of the 1950s but actually depicting the Yapp company's British registered H van in 2013, the fundamental brilliance of the device and its design is obvious. Note the boxed cargo area and curved cab roof. Simple but very effective, long before Ford thought of the Transit!**

RIGHT: **Classic ribbed construction for H van *en bleu*. This is the Yapp wine company's wonderfully original H van that is still in original condition and in daily use around Mere in Somerset in late 2013 delivering French wine.**

Still going, a baker's van in Brittany.

- Heuliez built an H-van hearse. H vans were also used as Tour de France support vehicles, and provided mobile advertising platforms for many major brands and small businesses.

The British H Van

The idea of a right-hand-drive conversion for the H van was suggested in the early 1960s. Citroën created a right-hand-drive prototype in 1964, but decided not to proceed. This left Citroën GB in Slough with the task of engineering a conversion. Between 1965 and 1966, Citroën Slough re-engineered the H van to right-hand drive but encountered problems with the steering column and rack and offset engine position. Ken Smith as chief engineer and the team worked hard to create a viable conversion package, but the costs of significant changes to the cab inhibited the project. The rhd prototype featured sliding doors on both sides and had split windscreens.

Of the British prototypes, one rotted away, but its right-hand-drive parts were rescued and used in a private conversion; another passed into private hands and was recently seen at the British ICCR international Citroën club meeting of 2012.

John Sobey, British H-van enthusiast and club H-van section expert, whose own vehicle appears in these pages, says of the H Type's unique appeals:

> *First you climb up into a seat, which is higher than any other van. The view is wonderful! You can see over all the fences and hedges and spot all the things you didn't know were there. This has the added advantage of seeing when the cars in front are stopping and will allow you to start slowing in good time, because even with the brakes in good order they are only 'adequate'. The engine starts easily with a short stab at the red button and idles smoothly. First and second gears are soon finished with using the long shift, and the motor pulls well from low speed in top. Steering is light and accurate once moving, and the handling is excellent – just watch you don't hurl the crockery off the shelf! Top speed is about 100km/h, but motorway cruising is usually in the range 75–95km/h.*

of the French local and regional police and fire services, and many department or regional administrations used them as ambulances and transporters. Some still remain in service in rural France, even as minibuses. In Britain the H van is at the centre of a fashionable mobile catering cult, and restored H vans are now *de riguer* on the catering and events hospitality circuit.

Carrosserie Options

- Carrosserie Le Bastard created an extended body H-van conversion from 1951; designed by Georges Han
- Carrosserie Currs made H-van camper vans and minibuses, including a school bus, from the late 1950s onwards
- Carrosserie Sagis built H van-based ambulances and buses, as well as a mobile laboratory version
- Carrosserie Leffondrie created mobile shop and butchers/fishmonger H-van conversions, and an ultra-long wheelbase version

2CV Van Years

The 2CV became a useful van in 1952. It had plastic-covered seats, and a few were available in black paint. As the 2CV AT and then the AU Fourgonnette van with 550lb (250kg) payload, it became available with the smaller 375cc engine, lower final drive ratio of 7:3:1, and larger 135 × 40 section tyres. 2CV van production also occurred at the old Talbot Lago factory

THE MAN WITH A VAN: COMMERCIALS

ABOVE: **For the 1960s the Bertoni- and Opron-styled truck series were the last big camions of Citroën.**

RIGHT: **Ranged across 350, 450, 480, 600, 700, 800, 850 and Berliet K series, the distinctive cab design became a famous sight across France.**

in Suresnes before 1954, but by 1956 it was also at the former Panhard factory at Ivry. Latterly, an AU van with a glazed panels option was hugely popular. But by 1977, 2CV AK 400 van production ended, and the Dyane Acadiane replaced it.

The quintessential imagery of the 2CV van years is that of a French postal van or a farmer rattling along in a haze of exhaust fumes, cigarette smoke and various animals' emanations. Incredibly the 2CV van boasted better aerodynamics than the saloon, this was due to a smoother roof and side panels and a defined rear bodywork cut-off point that aped Kamm principals – but not at below 35mph (56km/h)!

Recent Commercials

Citroën's position as a provider of small and medium-class light commercial vans grew in the 1980s and 1990s. Before Type-H production stopped, Citroën had already created a joint production van with Fiat, and this became the C35 van which emerged in the 1975 model year and was evolved into the C25 as PSA/FIAT joint venture in 1982. A significant factor in this growth was the use of the famous 1.9D and 1.9DT XUD diesel engines across the PSA brands.

Visa – Vantastique!

The Visa van range in XUD diesel form sold in huge numbers and created a wide buyer base beyond the expected French loyalists. As the C15 and as the 'Vin Rouge' and 'Vin Blanc' special editions, Visa was hugely popular in Great Britain. The first Visa van was a standard Visa bodyshell named 'Enterprise' with the rear doors welded up and with the option of rear side-window blanking plates fitted. However, by 1985 Citroën had created a proper 'box back' van of massive cubic capacity (2.6m sq) – it had widened sides that overhung the sill rails. It was tagged 'C' for cargo and became the C15. Originally it came with both petrol and diesel engines, including the strange idea of a 1.0ltr powered van carrying up to 1,050lb (475kg).

The C15 was offered with 1124cc and 1360cc petrol engines, and a range of diesel units of 1905cc, and the venerable 1.7 XUD engine. Payload went up in the later diesel version to 1,325lb (600kg) and then 1,685lb (765kg) – near to 1,765lb (800kg). Across Europe a whole range of body options was offered, from refrigerated to the rare pick-up truck style. Long wheelbase and six-wheel versions were also built in France. In Britain, from 1986 the Visa van was the basis for a camping car or motorhome with a fixed or flexible roof option from the 'Romahome' brand. It was possible to have side windows fitted to one or both sides of the Visa van, and this gave rise to a French market family utility 'Fourgonnette', which also had the rare option of rear bench seat conversion. This was true back-to-basics 2CV style motoring, and none the worse for it.

Production of the C15 lasted until 2006, and even continued as a low-powered diesel base model using the engine from the new Berlingo van range. In total, 1,181,471 Visa vans were produced – making it a million seller and huge earner for Citroën.

From the Visa C series van came the 1996 launch of the best selling Berlingo van range, its Multispace derivatives and the current Berlingo range. The 1994 creation of a PSA/Fiat-branded mid-sized van and its Citroën Jumpy ('Dispatch' in UK) variant also provided the Evasion MPV – re-branded as the Synergy in the UK market. The medium-size van market was also catered for by a joint production PSA/FIAT range of vehicles that successfully challenged Ford's Transit range. Perhaps the most bizarre Citroën commercial vehicles were the six- and eight-wheeled CX estate long-body conversions used by newspaper and courier companies for high-speed overnight delivery runs around Europe in the 1980s.

Light and mid-range commercial vehicle production remains a core element of Citroën's existence, and the company is recognized as the leader in light van design and production.

Lars Taubert's sketch for a twenty-first century H-van filled Citroënistes with hope for an H-van reinvention on the scale of the VW van legend.

CHAPTER SIX

DS

*THE WORLD'S MOST
ADVANCED CAR?*

DS | THE WORLD'S MOST ADVANCED CAR?

CLAIMS TO FUTURISM are often boldly made. 'Show' specials allow the design department to create design or styling themes that can point the way to future models but which are far too expensive for most car manufacturers to incorporate singly, let alone all at once, in one new car design. The halls of the Paris, Geneva and Turin motor shows are often filled with advanced styling fantasies that might trickle down, in diluted fashion, to a car in three or five years time.

But what if a car maker were to present a car so advanced not just in shape but also in structure, which was not a 'design special' but a new car, ready for sale? In the 1955 Citroën DS, this is what Citroën did: it threw everything at the DS, and its impact was seismic. At the Paris Motor Show there was a near riot as people jostled to see this car – only once before had Paris witnessed such scenes at a launch, when Stravinsky's *The Rite of Spring* was performed for the first time in 1913, and the shock caused panic in the theatre.

Was the DS launch an almost theological moment in car design? In one day, the rules of perceived wisdom were destroyed, burned up in the wake of a car that truly defined the beginning of what we might call Citroën's 'spaceship' years. It has long been argued just how much the DS touched other car makers – some say that as no one 'copied' it, its effect was less than claimed, but this is a flawed argument, because the effect of the DS on car design was long term, and one that would emerge through various strands of automotive DNA.

A bespectacled Pierre Bercot (*right*) shows off the DS at the sensation of its Paris Salon launch. The crowds are delighted.

An ancient Citroën in daily family use *circa* 2013. Pure Citroënism from a Slough-built car, driven by Citroën restorer Darrin Brownhill.

Amsterdam Zuid. Bertoni's stunning design for the DS still looks as if the aliens have landed.

In its launch form and revised variants, here was a car that was not just aerodynamic, it was a completely new design statement, one that was beyond fashion and utterly timeless.

BERTONI'S ELLIPSOID GODDESS

Of great note, the DS was curved, lozenge-shaped, ellipsoid in form, stemming from the triangular shapes and curved parabolas of car design between 1920 and 1940. Bertoni's 1930s styling work for Adler also gives us often ignored clues to his later inspiration for the DS. During this period, aerodynamic drag had been reduced because of the ellipsoid forms used, but by the mid-1950s, the car had become square-rigged with ungainly cabins or turrets in a rectangular planform. Some cars would soon even have forward-leaning fronts or noses (as in the BMW) and 'stick on' features and swages that interrupted the airflow.

Suddenly, aerodynamic drag coefficients for cars began to go *up* – reversing the previous streamlining trend. This was a bizarre paradox that many major car manufacturers embraced – increasing drag just as knowledge about how to decrease drag was being expanded: it was a crazy fashion that many embraced. For the big car makers, angles, ridges, protruding headlamps and styling elements that looked as if they were designed to create drag, were larded on to cars *circa* 1955 and beyond.

But for the DS, Citroën stayed with its learning. The animal-like DS was not actually shaped in a wind tunnel but was formed by Bertoni's intuitive hand – but a hand that by 1954 was steeped in the theories of Lefebvre and the forensic analysis techniques of Boulanger. Like Sason at Saab, Bertoni shaped his cars himself, but when actually tested in a wind tunnel, the intuitive hand was found to be accurate and almost mathematically correct when flow was analysed, with only minor alterations being required.

In the blending of its two asymmetrical part-elliptical lobes – these varied and tapered towards the rear, and thereby preserved local airflow velocity, thus delaying airflow stagnation and separation – the DS used ideas and theories that at the time were solely the preserve of a few advanced high speed supercars, and which would take another three decades to become normal practice in the design of mass-market saloon cars. Like the Saab 92-96, the DS approached the ideal minimum drag shape later defined by 1970s research.

The DS was also built *not* as a pure monocoque but as a subframe and sub-chassis with an outer skin of simple unstressed bolt-on panels. The bonnet was aluminium over a light steel perimeter frame. The roof was plastic (latterly alloy), the steering wheel a revolutionary single spoke. After two wheel testing on the Traction Avant 15H, the suspension scored a first in its use of the oleo or hydro-pneumatic pumped, 'live' pressurized system on all four wheels. Alloys were used in the structure,

DS: THE WORLD'S MOST ADVANCED CAR?

DS DESIGN AND DEVELOPMENT MEN 1950–72

M. Aligé	André Lefebvre
M. Allera	Michel Lefebvre
Paul Baert	Paul Mages
Flaminio Bertoni	M. Maignan
Walter Becchia	André Martin
M. Bouzinac	M. Meunier
Jean Cadiou	M. Michel
M. Caneau	Jacques Né
André Colin	Raoul Henrique Raba
Henri Dargent	M. Poillot
Louis Delgarde	Roger Prudhomme
M. Doré	Alain Paget
André Estaque	Claude Puech
Pierre Franchiset	R. Ravenel
Antione Hermet	Georges Sallot
Pierre Ingeneau	Hubert Seznec
M. Lachaize	

and front disc brakes were powered – along with the steering, and of course eventually the gearbox.

By 1967 Citroën's DS was the most aerodynamic production car with a Cd of 0.37 (having been latterly improved by Opron's chiselled front-end restyle). It also steered and rode like no other car in the world. The seats were massive armchairs with 'Dunlopillo' cushions, and the 'feel' of the philosophy within the car was tangible. Settling into a DS was a previously unheard-of sensation. The car encapsulated the Citroën ethos and has never aged, nor lost its allure since.

Was this car not the boldest statement of automotive industrial design for the mass car market ever seen?

The launch of the DS at the 1955 Paris Salon caused a sensation, and the car continued to do so right through the 1960s when Press and PR were handled by Jean Paul Cardinal and then Jacques Wolgensinger. Only the engines really remained as 'standard' in terms of their ethos and engineering. But surely Citroën would attend to that in time?

DS DETAILS OF DESIGN

The idea of a larger, more modern Citroën, one with appeal from mid-range to the top of the range, was long thought of. Citroën needed a top-of-the-range model, but it also needed a car with a wider appeal across the French marketplace. Little did it realize that it would create a car that defined its own international marketing niche and model sector.

Early studies for a new car began in 1938. The Traction Avant was only four years old, but the ever-active minds at the Bureau d'Études wanted to build a bigger Citroën: the code name was VGD or the 'Voiture à Grande Diffusion', and it would be a car for the new, fast roads of France. With André Citroën dead, Pierre Boulanger and Michelin were the key proponents of this larger, faster car, which would be able to cruise as a VGD 125 – that is, at 78mph (125km/h); perhaps an even higher cruising speed could be achieved with an even bigger engine.

To achieve this, Citroën would have to be radical. Perhaps Boulanger and Lefebvre were at their best in co-operation, for Lefebvre was always way ahead, and now Boulanger had to be too in order to look at every conceivable design and engineering possibility to secure yet another advance for Citroën. The Voisin legacy would again touch Citroën as the idea for a long wheelbase, aerodynamic car became seeded in the thinking for the new car.

Inside a DS engine bay. Citroën also made a V4 two-stroke supercharged prototype engine for the DS.

Walter Becchia's Brillance, Lucien Girard's Tuning

There was speculation as to the engine that would be used: would it be four or six cylinders – maybe even eight? And should it be in-line, or V-angled, or rotary? By 1941 there was an ex-Fiat and former Talbot engine designer who had also worked in England, now working at Citroën. His name was Walter Becchia, and as an Italian he soon forged a friendship with Flaminio Bertoni at the Bureau d'Études. By 1943 Becchia was joined at Citroën by his old Talbot colleague Lucien Girard, who was an expert in fuel/air carburation and cylinder head combustion research, and brought much Talbot experience with him.

Becchia had been head-hunted by Boulanger before the outbreak of World War II, not least due to his fame from designing a more efficient 'hemi' head design that improved engine combustion and compression by optimizing the processes within the cylinder head. The intervention of the war years slowed progress at Citroën, so both the 2CV and large 'VGD' car were held up; it was not until late 1946 that Citroën was able to restart the design process for the production of both a small car and a big one.

There were three main issues for the big 'VGD' car: its shape, its engine, and its suspension.

Why 'DS'?

Many experts claim that 'DS' does not indicate anything at all to do with déesse (goddess), or any grand intellectual nomenclature. Instead, DS simply derives from the following two points: the D comes from the basic inherited Traction Avant 11D engine type, while the 'S' derives from the 'hemi' (hemispherical) design of the cylinder head as expressed in French as 'culasse Spéciale'. '19' indicates the cubic capacity rounded down from 1911cc to 1900cc. The 'ID' was a simplified, more basic trim and specification designation for a cheaper model DS.

Styling

Bertoni envisaged a teardrop *grande routière* in true *gouette d'eau* style, and he got there in stages by drawing up a more rounded, smoother version of the Traction Avant. He also thought of a forward-biased or 'cab-forward' concept that was decades ahead of a wider use of that concept. Saab's Ursaab 92.001 prototype of 1947 and its resultant Saab 92 production car of December 1949 must have raised the stakes, and Bertoni quickly moved on from a smoothed 'three-box' style to the aerofoil or teardrop style that led to the DS.

By 1948 Bertoni had transformed the teardrop ideas into a shape that had a full breasted, 'cab-forward' stance and a narrowing tail section. It retained a somewhat bulbous frontal shape and a rounded rump, and some called it the 'hippopotamus'. From that idea Bertoni evolved a sleeker, more aerodynamic form, or should we say a more hydrodynamic form because there was a shark-like imagery to the later shapes, and Bertoni himself made verbal references to the influence of birds and fish to his styling choices. After all, nature knew all about the ellipse, smooth skins, and tapered tails. So there were two distinct

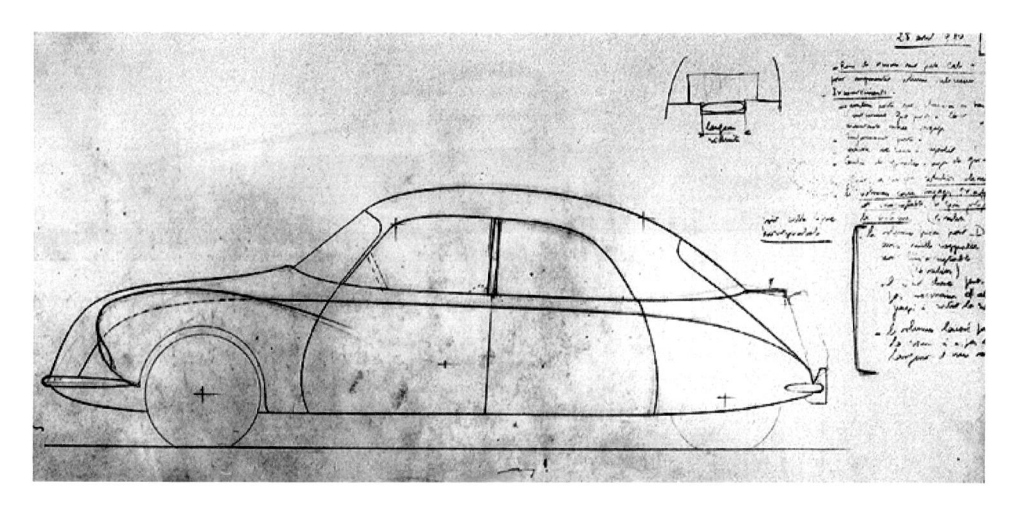

ABOVE: **Bertoni was sketching large, sleek ellipsoid shapes for the 'VGD' spec in the mid-1930s.**

LEFT: **A Bertoni stepping-stone concept from Traction to VGD which led to the 'Hippopotamus', and thence to the DS itself.**

early attempts at the 'VGD' car, before Bertoni settled on the DS's form.

One benefit of this anthropomorphic approach was that the front-biased shape with a tapered tail also met Lefebvre's scientific calculations relating to the aerodynamic centre of pressure needed for such a large car. Step by step Bertoni evolved the DS's shape through various 'four-light' and 'six-light' side window combinations – but there was to be a twist in the tail over the shape of the rear of the car, relating to headroom, appearance and design trends.

Bertoni's shape for the DS had numerous highly advanced aerodynamic features, including a scooped frontal air intake instead of the expected radiator grille, and an in-built spoiler treatment that altered pressure patterns according to velocity under the front of the car. There was an 'open' air flow across the wings and scuttle region, and a curved windscreen to reduce turbulence and drag around and along the car, also concealed windscreen wipers that lay under a flicked-up trailing edge to the bonnet, and smoothed and sculpted rear panels that narrowed inwards at the rear. There was a defined airflow separation ridge at the top of the rear windscreen. Attention was also paid to the under-body flow and the vortices emanating from wheel arches.

The accuracy of Lefebvre's and Bertoni's work was proven across the decades, in that here was a car that was aerodynamically stable, kept its windows clean, suffered minimal buffeting, and had low lift levels at the rear. Only two issues marred the DS's aerodynamic performance: one related to the latter 1970s fitting of some very unCitroën-like 'barn-door' rear-view mirrors on the front doors, and the other was the effect of a sunroof and radio aerial on airflow separation off the roof; both factors pushing the Cd figure higher than quoted.

With its domed roof and sharply defined, aerodynamic, critical separation-point ridge at the rear edge of the roof above the rear windscreen, the airflow should have remained attached along the roof to this point and then neatly separated to leave the rear window and boot in a reducing airflow envelope of wake drag. However, smoke tests in the leading French wind tunnel at the Office National d'Études et des Recherches Aérospatiales (ONERA) revealed some degree of premature airflow separation upstream of the roof's trailing edge, triggered by the fitment of a sunroof or badly angled roof-mounted aerial. The further addition of heavy chrome trim at the top of the front windscreen created an airflow disturbance – a 'peak' just at the point where such effect should be reduced.

Many DS owners and restorers have closed up panel gaps in the bodies and reduced chromework and embellishments to lower their cars Cd. and retain smoother roof and side flow.

How Aerodynamic in Numbers?

Much has been made of the DS's aerodynamic prowess. Although various drag coefficients have been cited, and some have suggested the car is not as aerodynamic as claimed, one thing is accepted by automotive experts, and that is, that Citroën's wind-tunnel claims in terms of Cd. figures for all its cars have always been legitimate and are unlikely to be exaggerated. In 1955, only the Saab 92/93 as mass production cars had a better Cd. – that being Cd.0.35. In Britain the 1948 Jowett Javelin, a strange blend of pre-war wind tunnel styling from the Lancia (also aping the Lincoln Zephyr), managed Cd.041. So the DS was way ahead in terms of its drag coefficient.

The early DS/ID shape with upright headlamps sitting atop the front wings was improved upon in airflow terms by Opron's 1967 slant-eyed and chamfered restyle, but nothing else was changed. However, wider wheels, more chrome trim and the later large area, rear-view mirrors would not have improved the Cd. It is reputed that airflow over the roof can be upset by a fabric sunroof if one is fitted, but perhaps the DS's only real aerodynamic question mark was its large frontal cross-sectional area, which meant that its Cd.a (or Cx.s) figure was a little high for its size – but at least it tapered towards the rear to reduce such effects.

CITROËN'S COEFFICIENT OF DRAG FIGURES CITED AS CD. FOR THE DS

Citroën wooden scale model, design-study test body minus trim and mirrors*:	Cd. 0.326.
Citroën 1955 production car with standard wheel size and trim:	Cd. 0.382.
MIRA/*Autocar* 1982 later post-1967 slant-front car with standard trim:	Cd. 0.371.
Citroën 1970s D Spécial frontal cross-sectional coefficient:	Cd.a 0.817.

* Scale effects and lack of production trim account for a lower Cd. figure at the ONERA wind tunnel.

A Last-Minute Change

Few people beyond the Citroën cognoscenti know that in late 1954, just months before the launch of the first 'spaceship', the Citroën DS, its designer Flaminio Bertoni was asked to alter

DS: THE WORLD'S MOST ADVANCED CAR?

Different DS? How different the low-roofed original idea would have looked.

The original fastback low-roofed DS styling proposal model, which was modified at the last minute on the orders of senior management.

the rear styling from the roof and rear window backwards. Two reasons are reputed to exist for this significant and expensive alteration: first, the international fashion was changing from fast-backed cars to a 'notched' or 'three-box' saloon-shape fashion, where a car had a bonnet, cabin 'turret' and a stepped rear boot line – therefore three boxes of shapes in total. Bertoni was aware of these stylistic changes in the general marketplace.

The second reason cited for the DS re-design was that the men of Citroën had identified a similarity between the DS, its stance, its look, and the look of a supposed new car from a major European manufacturer – a car not then announced. There were obvious questions regarding how Citroën could know about the still-secret shape of a new car from a major maker, but the story centres around a possible German car maker who had styled an aerodynamic four-door coupé, to whose rear-end shape the DS's was said to be similar. Clearly if this were true, it would detract from the DS's impact upon its launch. It is often stated that Pierre Bercot, Citroën's head, drove the issue and told Bertoni to revise his DS body design at the very last minute – no easy task.

Yet there are no obvious records of a car that could have been similar. Some say it was Ford who were about to launch a fast-backed car of such design, others that DKW were creating a car with a wrap-around rear screen and fast-backed sloping rear aspect – but it was a car in a different class to the DS.

However, subsequent claims and physical evidence suggest that it is a strong possibility that the revised styling of the forthcoming Saab 96 – a variant of the pre-existing Saab 92/93 – may well have been the car in question. Although not produced as a four-door design, nor a 'six-light' window design, the Saab 93 and the 96's domed roof and revised rear aspect closely resembled the original DS drawings. Not only that, but for the Saab 93, its designer Sixten Sason had by 1955 already created a further derivative – the 96 (with a four-door variant, though this was never manufactured): this had a new wrap-around rear windscreen that had been sketched up by Sason in 1955, long before it went into production in the early 1960s.

Saab's design man Sason was not just a huge fan of all things Italian and French, he had actually trained in Paris in the mid-1930s as a sculptor and artist at the same time as Bertoni was

99

DS: THE WORLD'S MOST ADVANCED CAR?

LEFT: **The US specification cars lost the glazed headlamps, but this one still looks great outside the not irrelevant legend of the Holland Amerika Line offices.**

BELOW: **The rare plastic, coloured, rear roof lamp trims.**

RIGHT: **British-built dashboard and space-age styling. Note the single spoke, white plastic steering wheel.**

100

there doing the same thing: Sason had close links with the Italian design houses. Did he and Bertoni talk and resolve certain issues or share ideas?

In order to better define the DS, Bertoni added the two top corner cone-shaped lights, and a higher roof, with light fittings at the top of the DS's new roof. These created a distinct motif and had an aerodynamic advantage in terms of creating two beneficial airflow separation points off the roof and side panels. The new plastic roof – higher than Bertoni's original – meant that the angle between the roof and rear windscreen and tail was too steep for the airflow to remain attached. What was needed was a critical separation point for the airflow so that it did not spill uncontrolled down the car's rump and create massive wake turbulence. So the shape of the revised roof shape had a sharp 'edge' or razor slice to it, just as Michelotti would use the same technique on his car designs.

The DS, with its smooth panelling, open curved windscreen profile, domed roof and sculpted undertray, met most of the rules of road vehicle aerodynamics design that had been explored in France and Germany between 1925 and 1939. But DS *redefined* what was possible in car design amidst a world of swage lines, fins, bulbous wings, podded headlamps and American-inspired 'space age' styling that looked contemporary with 1950s culture, yet which was in fact dramatically unaerodynamic, and contaminated with excrescences and adornment in car body shaping.

The DS also used a modern take on the chassis-based, clad body construction method, eschewing the increasing use of the monocoque, and taking a very surprising and maybe even inexplicable step backwards from the Traction Avant's earlier use of the monocoque. Money may have been behind the switch, as the DS used an underframe/skeletal body construction that was much cheaper than tooling for, and welding up, a complex monocoque.

For the interior design, Bertoni created a massive one-piece synthetic moulding for the dashboard – a nylon-based piece of space age sculpture. Of interest, the ellipsoid door armrests were as if one with the car, yet were designed not by Bertoni, but a Monsieur Michel.

MEN OF THE BODY DESIGN AND FABRICATION TEAM

Bertoni is associated with the styling of the DS, but there were others in the body design and fabrication team at Citroën who were influential in making the DS. Raymond Ravenel was the project's technical director and did much to sort out the hydraulic issues (he managed men such as André Paget, who worked on the DS launch under PR chief Claude Puech) and the service recovery programme due to the car's teething problems; and in terms of design, men such as Pierre Franchiset and André Estaque were clearly influential. Estaque had joined the company in 1944 and was the design specialist who rose to senior level in the Bureau d'Études, while Franchiset was the body engineer who came up with so many of the DS's advanced solutions, from plastics to window design. Franchiset also engineered the idea of the DS estate, and solved many of the DS's design issues in his role as body engineer.

During the later DS years, an important role was also played by Michel Harmand, a French car designer with a training in Fine Art, who was at Citroën from 1964 to 1987, before a spell with the Peugeot studio. He specialized in interior and ergonomic design, creating innovative designs for the revised DS, the interiors and dashboards of the GS and CX, and the 'satellite' controls for the Visa, the GSA and the BX. Harmand also influenced body shapes.

Raoul Henriques Raba worked for the Bureau d'Études from 1959 to 1963. Born near Paris in 1930, he was an artist and another sculptor in the team. He had won the *Prix de Rome* sculpture prize in 1955, a launching point for a higher profile. He contributed a series of ideas to the development of the DS, and notably in 1961 sketched a revised headlamp and frontal design motif for the DS that may well have reflected

Later DS revisions saw a 1970s design iteration. Note the elliptical interior door-handle motif.

ABOVE: **Pure DS delight: 'cats' eyes' DS in metallic blue on the move.**

RIGHT: **Unsung hero. Henri Dargent at work in the studio of the Bureau d'Études. Dargent had a big influence on Citroën design, yet is not well known beyond the cognoscenti.**

Bertoni's own ideas for such changes – the same ideas that inspired Opron's final 'cat's-eyes' treatment for the slant-front DS. Citroën had this slant-front DS restyle on the books for some time before using it on the restyled, relaunched DS of 1967. Raba also worked on the roof of the revised 2CV and the Dyane.

Henri Dargent: Master Craftsman of Style

Bertoni may have been the star designer, but Henri Dargent was for many years Bertoni's assistant at the Bureau d'Études, and as a young man took a significant part in the DS development days. Dargent was a model maker, an expert in plaster and clay, and as we know, Bertoni often went straight from the sketch in his mind's eye to model, bypassing the sketch and rendering stages of car design. Bertoni often said that he and his team were principally sculptors, not sketchers. Dargent worked with Bertoni in the vital years from 1957 to 1964, a decade in which the DS and the cute Ami emerged alongside other themes. He first worked on the last iteration of the Traction15H, and designed the dashboard for the Dyane and Ami 6.

In fact Dargent rose from the factory floor after joining Citroën in 1945 via an André Citroën scholarship; he then attended a school for model makers at the Académie Grande Chaumière in Paris. He joined the design office as a junior in 1953, and then became Bertoni's assistant in late 1957. It was an association that would prove very fruitful.

Like Bertoni, Dargent in the early days had to sculpt in a gypsum-based plaster which was difficult to 'work', and had

Colour can change a car's graphics: here a crimson DS basks as if beamed down to earth from afar.

nowhere near the ease of moulding made possible by self-setting clay and plasticine compounds in later years. By building large-scale styling models of plaster over a wooden- and wire-based skeleton, Bertoni and Dargent learned to sculpt and to scale, and to judge how light and shaping affected the look of a car from many angles. Out of these difficult plaster scraping and sanding techniques came the clear, open contours of the DS and other Citroëns, which were then handed down to the 1970s and beyond.

Dargent led the work on the DS presidential cars, and contributed to the Ami, the SM and onwards towards the BX, prior to his retirement; clearly he should be credited as a major contributor to Citroën design. Incredibly Dargent worked on the Traction, the DS19–23, the Ami 6, Dyane, GS, SM, CX and the Visa. One of his non-production projects was the little Citroën city car of the 1970s, which looks for all the world like a precursor to today's branded eco-cars.

After an incredible four decades-long career at Citroën, ending in the 1980s, Dargent retired to the south of France.

Paul Mages

The 'father' of the Citroën hydropneumatic suspension was Paul Mages, who had been working on the idea since the late 1930s. His early experiments were a brake-force distribution valve that he wanted to apply to the early commercial vehicles *circa* 1937. Whether or not he was inspired by the Cayla-Lefebvre-Gerin ideas dating from the late 1920s is not known. Mages' main idea was to drive all such supplementary systems that could be hydraulically driven from an engine-driven pump.

For Mages it was a short mental hop to the idea of a suspension – or was it levitating a car – using a blend of pressurized air and oil. The oleo-pneumatic as a suspension medium had indeed been hinted at before by the likes of Cayla and Gerin, but here was a cohesive, engineered, fully handed mechanism.

By 1938 Mages had built a Traction Avant with hydraulic mechanisms for gears, and by late 1954 you could buy a hydro-pneumatic rear suspension Traction Avant 15H. This had been preceded by a 2CV with inter-connected hydro-pneumatic suspension. Paul Mages went on to 'tune' the suspension of the hydro-pneumatic, and those Citroëns with springs and torsion bars. Even as late as 1970 he was Citroën's 'Mages the magician' when it came to making cars like the SM handle and ride.

Mages was also a pioneer of a science now assumed and expected in car design: 'NVH', the art of designing out noise, vibration and harshness. The DS was the first car to do that in a new way. Those who worked with Mages included Messrs Maignan, Descotte, Chinon, Renault, Barron and Boullay.

OLEO-PNEUMATIC HYDRAULIC SUSPENSION: BRAVE NEW WORLD

Citroën is not alone in having a pressurized, oil-based suspension system, but it was the pioneer of such systems and retained a unique mechanism and action. What was the point of this expensive engineering solution, with its pumps, accumulators, spheres, pipes and its paint-scarring, red (latterly green) 'life blood' fluid? The answer lies in the issue of frequency of suspension-related ride oscillations acting upon the car to which any suspension is attached. This frequency of ride rate factor is the motion frequency of the car's sprung mass in free movement or oscillation.

The modern mass-market car possesses a ride-oscillation suspension frequency in the order of sixty-five to eighty such events or cycles per minute under average conditions. This gives rise to a characteristic of ride quality that, give or take a small amount, represents a common behavioural feature across most suspension set-ups as fitted to many cars.

From such base dynamic numerical range are taken the perceived reactions and comfort levels of modern cars – only recently more affected by tyre and wheel aspect ratio and 'sport' shock-absorber settings. Clearly a car on low-profile tyres attached to large alloy wheels and with 'sports' suspension settings is going to have a different number of reactive suspension movement frequencies to a more deeply shod wheel and tyre with softer spring and damper rates. A short-wheelbase car with very soft or very hard suspension will also possess differing frequency patterns.

Clearly, the more the frequencies, the less settled and less comfortable is the car's ride – with all the resultant effects upon the occupants in terms of reduced comfort and higher stress. And the spectre of vibration and structural shake being set off by road conditions is amplified by today's fashion for harsh ride and almost rubberless tyres on wide alloy wheels.

The Citroën system of having an adaptable, 'thinking', self-monitoring, independently reactive suspension that features no springs and no mechanical linkage to the car body, results in far lower rates or frequencies of movements or oscillations. These frequencies can be as low as forty cycles per minute, half the standard rate of most cars in the 1950s and 1960s when the system was at its most unique.

This lower (or slower) level of reactive frequency of movement smoothes out the car's ride quality, and as a result of having no mechanical metal-reactive spring rate connection to the car's structure, creates the unique and uncanny sensation associated with the Citroën's hydraulically suspended ride quality.

The Citroën system's fluid-connection based ride is smooth, with minimal pitching and no steel-to-steel rebound to reverberate around the car's structure and into the cabin. The car is predictable and has high limits of adhesion (given the correct tyres), with the long wheelbase in tune with the suspension, damping out uneven surfaces. The key advantage is that of the car becoming self-levelling and self-reacting to achieve maximum ride comfort, and in having a constant ride attitude which enhances aerodynamic effects. Smoothing out not just undulations but also serious surface irregularities is the vital capability. Even the seat foam and springs were tuned to soften the ride – fitting non standard, after-market seats to a hydro-pneumatic Citroën will soon reveal issues of comfort and ride

For the DS and subsequent hydro-pneumatically sprung cars, the Citroën system is best briefly explained by stating that a set of pressurized metal spheres containing a mix of gas and fluid, are actuated from an engine-driven pump. This system has a 'brain' and is self-monitoring and self-adjusting. The mechanism – the actual working of the act of suspension – is defined by pre-set values and pre-set reactions from the mediums of the suspension itself in an act of hydro-pneumatic interaction.

The springing and damping of the car is created by the action of a fluid on a gas within individual spheres sited at each wheel, which are themselves controlled by a central pressure regulator and a 'mother' sphere as the core of the system (further control spheres and electro-mechanical controls were added in recent years). Because gas will, under compression, harden or become denser – essentially stiffening – but fluid will not, this results in a transmission or transfer of energy to a more malleable element (the gas). Special vents, ports and channels allow the system to be kept 'wet' even when it is not running. The DS was the only car in the world which had its suspension arms mounted on tapered roller bearings, and not on cheap synthetic bushes.

From the central control mechanism, a myriad of pipes run off around the car principally to feed the suspension, and then the brakes, steering and gearbox, although some ID/DS models did not have all these other systems powered by the oleo-pneumatic hydraulic unit after it had pressurized the suspension. Certain Slough-built DSs of the 1960s were made with mechanical gearboxes as opposed to being hydraulically actuated.

The main DS suspension pump is fed by a fluid tank which feeds the accumulator or 'heart' of the system. From that point the nitrogen-charged main gas sphere reaches a working pressure that was at launch set at 2,490psi, and at that pressure effectively 'pumps' the other spheres via the network of piping, and then recirculates the central sphere pressure back to the main fluid bath or reservoir.

A drop in pressure below a pre-set level (2,090psi) allows the main pump to re-engage and re-pressurize the system.

The 'caisson'. Note the massive safety sills and thick lower chassis members that are in contrast to the very thin pillars, and their external, 'floating', non-monocoque construction. The revised design's roof extensions to the rear C-pillar are also obvious.

SAFETY

In terms of active, or driver safety, the DS offered much. Here was a car that could survive a high-speed blow-out without skidding or crashing, and could be driven on three wheels. The DS with its low cg, in-board brakes, and brilliant new technology Michelin X tyres, had huge reserves of handling and grip despite its dramatic roll angles. Yes it understeered, but predictably so. The brakes were powerful, the car's aerodynamic stability superb. Thin pillars – *very* thin pillars – gave good visibility. The driver was kept comfortable and alert by excellent seating, and long distances could be covered with minimal fatigue even if the rather noisy engine and its block protruded back into the cabin.

The interior was padded and the cabin sealing excellent – noise vibration and harshness were kept to unprecedentedly low levels, although the engines were a touch 'rattly'. But there was much to commend in terms of design and safety.

In the context of its time, when many cars were still built on the 'horseless carriage' coachwork and frame, the DS was a safe car, in that although it was not a monocoque design, it was strong. But just like a Land Rover, for example, the DS was strong deep down in the *centre* of the car and below the engine bay, but not *around* the car and its occupants. Unlike the Traction Avant, the DS had a non-monocoque construction. Monocoque cars require expensive toolings, pressing machinery and welding facilities, and Citroën may have saved money by not having to create such mechanisms for the 'bolted together' DS. The DS's construction actually aped that of the last Voisin car, the grand C30 saloon which pioneered the clad platform construction idea, with major structures and panels being made to 'float' externally to the base unit.

This method meant that the body panels were neither stressed, nor self-supporting, nor continuously welded into a hull or shell. Instead, the DS used an underframe construction that had elements of the old-fashioned chassis techniques; therein the basic unit was 'flocked' or added to by structural members that provided localized strength yet were not linked to each other. In fact the DS's underfloor punt was very strong indeed and had big reinforcing members, but on top of this underframe, the lightweight outer body panels were simply bolted on individually.

HENRI CHAPRON

Running deep in the stream of Voisin and Citroën thinking was Henri Chapron. Born in 1886, Chapron finished his military service in 1920 and purchased some military surplus Ford Model T cars. In a workshop at Neuilly-sur-Seine, Paris, he fashioned a torpedo-tailed body on the Ford chassis, and he went on to design bodies for Chenard et Walcker, and for the Delahaye 135M – a car of outstanding proportional balance. It would be years before Chapron would re-body a Citroën, and he had the temerity to reshape the DS. Citroën had refused him a 'free' DS to work on, but after the 1958 Paris Salon, where Chapron's re-worked DS convertible roofed design wowed the crowds, Citroën realized that it would be better off cultivating Chapron. By 1961, 300 Chapron DS conversions were sold, and by 1974, 1,800 had been made.

Chapron's DS enthusiasm, fired up by freelance designer Carlo Delaisse, led to the elegance of his DS convertible and coupé modified body designs: *Caddy, Concorde, Croisette, Dandy, Leman, Lorraine, Majesty and Palm Beach*. A re-roofed, long-wheelbase, 5,865lb (2,660kg) behemoth of a DS *Presidentielle* for President de Gaulle was perhaps the highlight prior to the SM conversions of the 1970s.

Short-bodied specials were also constructed, not least the elegant Frua-styled Bosseart DS (see photo) and the two-door André Ricou cars.

MODEL DEVELOPMENT AND SPECIAL CARS

1955: Launch car with first frontal air vent/bumper/valance design.
1956: DS19 launched; made until 1967.
1957: Minor trim and front valance changes.
1959: ID19 model with lower specification introduced with manual gearbox, no power steering and 63bhp engine. Estate car body launched as five-seat brake and for 1960 seven-seat Familiale. Branded as 'Safari' in the UK.
1960: Specially built DS convertible launched.
1961: Trim revisions and changes to estate car paint and roof schemes.
1963: Second version of revised frontal design and radiator aerodynamics.
1964: Trim changes and new dashboard design: first 'Pallas' iteration.
1966: DS21 launched and made until 1972. 2175cc engine of 109bhp until 1968, then 115bhp carburettor unit. From 1970 with Bosch D Jetronic fuel injection giving 139bhp.
1967: Third version with new 'cat's eyes' headlamp design and self-steer lamps. Revised dashboard design.
1969: DS20 with enlarged engine; ID20 1969 model year only. IDs have black dashboard treatment; fuel injection on D21 as production first.
1970: D Super launched to replace the ID20.
1972: D Super 5 uses DS21's 2175cc engine and five-speed gearbox. New dashboard and steering wheel for power-steering cars. Highlights of the 'Pallas' 'Injection Electronique' years; fabric sunroof often fitted.
1973: DS21 replaced by DS23 with engine of 2347cc with 124bhp in carburettor or 141bhp in fuel injection specification.
1975: Final cars and production ceases.

DS estate or 'Break'. This, too, was a groundbreaking car that set a new fashion followed by other car manufacturers. This is the seven-seat version. The roof rack did not lower drag!

AUSTRALIAN DS

Australian DS production created unique variants of the model. The cars were built in the 1960s at Heidelberg, Victoria, and were given special, local market name tags – the ID19 *Parisienne* and the *D Spécial Deluxe*. Although right-hand drive and aping Slough-built specifications, there were many local market differences which were not seen in Europe.

The Australian Citroën plant built 1,400 cars up until 1966. Locally sourced seat trims and an alloy roof panel, as well as local 'duco' or paint, were the key Australian-made ingredients. More welds and better dust sealing dealt with the demands of outback motoring. Latterly an oil-bath air cleaner helped 'up-country' cars keep going.

These cars were different from the British spec, Slough-built cars, but the DS estates or Brakes (not 'Safaris') seen in

DS: THE WORLD'S MOST ADVANCED CAR?

DS *décapotable* elegance in rare repose.

Chapron DS two-door hardtop with a very different design language.

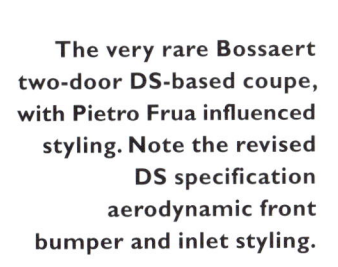

The very rare Bossaert two-door DS-based coupe, with Pietro Frua influenced styling. Note the revised DS specification aerodynamic front bumper and inlet styling.

Australia were Slough built. Various manual and hydraulic gearbox specification DSs were created in Australia.

The DS became a French import to Australia when the West Heidelberg factory closed in 1966, and DS sales continued up until 1975, although the larger 2175cc cars were not imported despite the five-speed gearbox being available in Australia on the 1985cc D Super. A total of just over 4,000 examples of the various DS models were sold in Australia.

The DS was also subject to local manufacture in Britain, Rhodesia (Zimbabwe) and other countries.

THE DS AND A SECRET LIFE UNDER THE SUN

> *The DS Prestige of the last King of Laos, Savang Vatthana, overthrown by the Communists in 1975, is still resting peacefully in the sealed-off garage of the former royal palace of the old capital of Luang-Prabang. An old mechanic in Vientiane seems to be wondering whether he will one day be able to restore one of his two DS, the only ones he knows of in the capital he says. I don't know if I should encourage him...*
>
> Pierre Jammes
> writing at www.DSinAsia.com

The DS gained fame on the world stage as not just a revolutionary car, but as something more than a moment in industrial design history: for the DS was a social icon. But that iconography was not just European, because DS also found itself earning friends in Africa, Asia and other parts of the world.

It is in Asia that an unknown legacy of DS remains, alive and with a dedicated following. Like the British, the French had former colonial interests, and at the time of the DS's launch, the French still had colonies in the East and in Africa. In Asia the DS was used by diplomats, businessmen, government leaders and local people such as engineers or doctors, who were attracted to its qualities of superb ride over poor roads and that sense of occasion that marks a great car out from the herd.

Now, there is an enduring subculture, that of DS in Asia, which itself is framed by the work of Pierre Jammes, a Frenchman who has charted the life and times of the DS in that part of the world, and the surviving cars in his web-based history, DSinAsia.com Pierre owns a D Special in France, but from his base in Thailand he charts the survivors of the DS in Asia.

At his amazing web site can be found Pierre's documented research history into how various models of the DS were used and maintained, and how they are now being restored across the region. We might expect the affluent of Hong Kong or Singapore to have a DS 23ie Pallas as a classic car in their inventory, but what is more astounding is the affection for the DS to be found in towns and villages across the Asian rim. Hidden in garages, resting under shacks and trees in yards, or just sweating life out beside a quiet road, DS in Asia astounds with the sheer number of these cars.

Travelling through Asia, Pierre-fellow DSinAsia hunters photograph the remaining DS and interview their owners to preserve their stories of life with this unique car. From Japan to Malaysia, and through all points down to Indonesia and even the island of Bali, DS (and other Citroëns) can be found being loved and cared for, or awaiting rescue. It seems that the affection for the DS in the region touches everyone from local villagers and garagistes, to classic car enthusiasts and active club members.

For example, a DS21 is the mascot of the Citroën Club Indonesia Jakarta. Over in Bali, Dutchman Peter van den Hoek Ostende is even restoring an SM – an SM on Bali! As for the sight of his DS in the rice paddies, we can only wonder what Lefebvre and Bertoni would have thought. Peter is a true car and aircraft fanatic and a true Citroëniste. Across the island can be seen a DS, GS and a Méhari in a rust-free classic car time-warp.

Pierre tells the story of a Mr Wong and his beloved DS in Malaysia:

> *Mr Wong has seen the first DS arrive in Malaysia, and he maintained them. He kept one for himself, too, a 1974 DS23 Pallas, almost new. We visited Mr Wong one foggy day in July 2007, in his workshop in the suburbs of Kuala Lumpur. At seventy-five years old, this is the place he feels good in, hands full of grease. He nevertheless paused to recall his beginnings as a mechanic: 'It was in the fifties, I was a young man, and I found my way inside the British Air Army base, where they maintained their cars during the weekends. That's where I learnt my trade.'*
>
> *Mr Wong remembers the Tractions existing in what was called then the Malaya State (before independence in 1957), and the first DS. Very early on he catches the Citroën virus, and specializes himself in their maintenance: 'There used to be perhaps as many as thirty DS in Malaysia, in the seventies. Several belonged to government people, at least six or seven as far as I can remember. The French embassy also had one, a wagon version, the only one in the country.'*
>
> *Mr Wong treasured one of these DS, a 1974 DS23 Pallas he purchased that same year from the family of the then Deputy Minister for Transport. He kindly accepted to start it for us, a smile on his face as soon as the engine purred – and quickly returned to where he belongs: in his workshop, hands full of grease.*

DS: THE WORLD'S MOST ADVANCED CAR?

From Sri Lanka, where Ray Welaratna, a classic car collector is restoring two DS (one being the former car of the French ambassador in Colombo), to Iran, India and beyond, DS lie sleeping or being awakened. In Pakistan in early 2009, a young classic car enthusiast, Agha Ahmed Husain, found a US-export DS21 in a Karachi garage. He says it gave him 'goosebumps'.

In the former French-influenced areas, Citroëns in the form of Traction Avant and DS are more numerous. Cambodia may still have 'barn finds' awaiting discovery, and in southern Vietnam DS are sometimes spotted. As Pierre writes in his DSinAsia history: 'A man in Saigon named Do Van Chanh does not have one DS, he has three of them. He took them over about ten years ago, when nobody knew what to do with them. If you ask him why he did that, he'll tell you "Why, because they deserve it!" '

In Thailand, the DS had a relatively big following, and many remain in use or resting. A garage named 'SP Cars Service',

RIGHT: **DS in Japan, where the car remains a legend.**

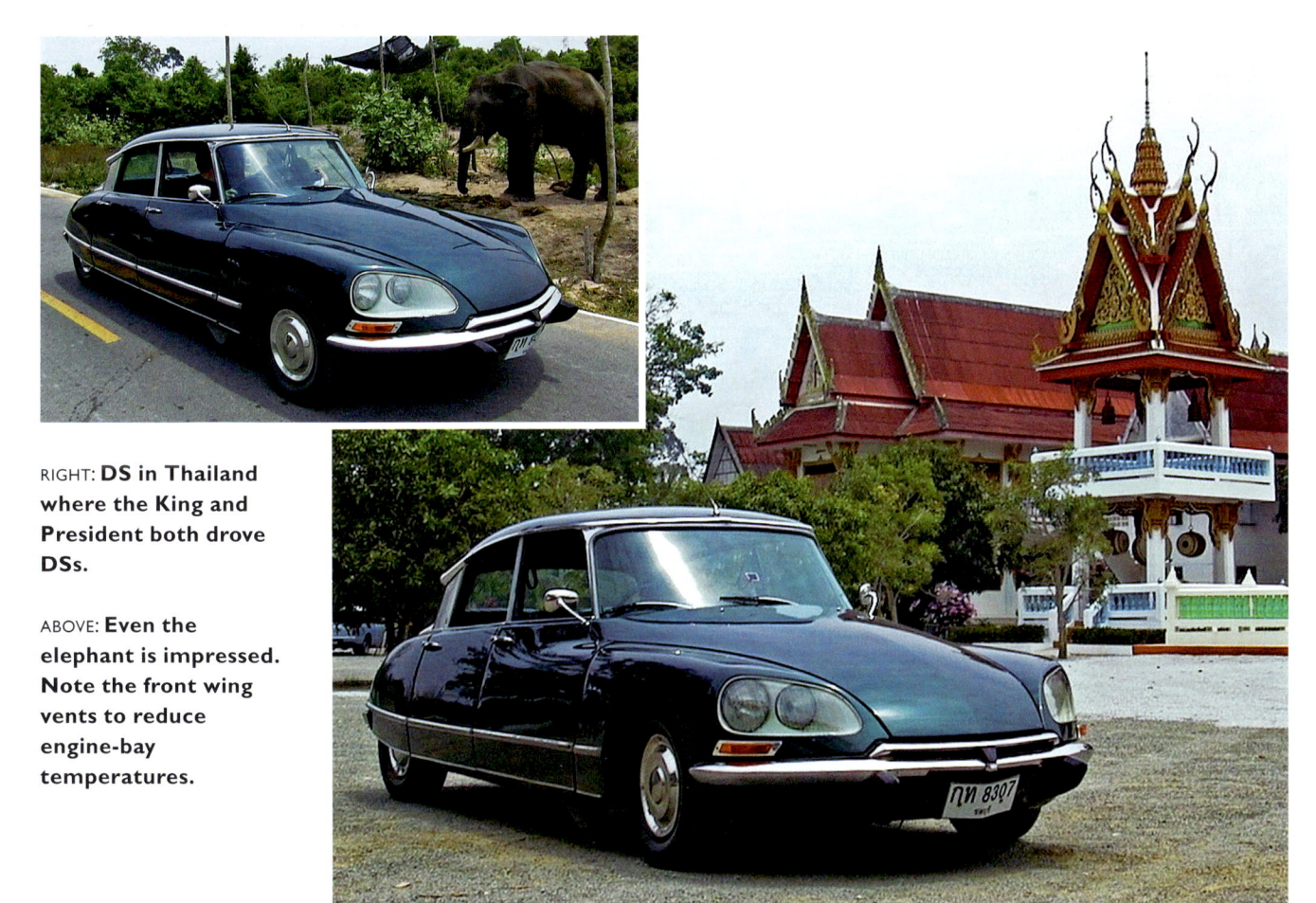

RIGHT: **DS in Thailand where the King and President both drove DSs.**

ABOVE: **Even the elephant is impressed. Note the front wing vents to reduce engine-bay temperatures.**

109

AN OWNER'S PERSPECTIVE

DS owner Christopher Wilson talks about his DS, why he bought it, and its design.

My father, a lover of British cars and working for Jaguar cars, often spoke of an experience he had in the 1960s when he was in Paris. A Citroën DS taxi drove at frightening speed up those long cobbled boulevards of Paris, straight across the ultra-busy roundabout that is the Arc de Triomphe and onwards. The road holding was apparently remarkable, and my father was in love with the DS from that day forth.

As a result we could never pass a DS without stopping for father to enthuse about the advanced engineering and the beautiful lines. I inherited that strong interest, and learned of the intricacies of the design and the history many years before I acquired a DS for myself. For me, the appeal emanates from the remarkable vision of the design team that looked so far into the future and incorporated the very latest technology such as GRP, plastics and highly curved glass. It is said that when Citroën approached the St Gobain Glass company with designs for the front and rear screens, they initially declined since the curvature was far too extreme for contemporary manufacture. The compromise was a very wide tolerance of +/−5mm, resulting in a most original fixing solution.

Today, any one of the above initiatives would be considered an unacceptable commercial risk, and would have been turned down by the management. I was tantalized by the concept of high pressure hydraulics, and how that pressure was applied to so many functions, including that wonderfully imaginative hydraulic gearbox.

The whole car shouts aerodynamics. Where is the radiator grille, the focus of most cars now, and then? The sleek, smooth nose flows beautifully not onto, but into the doors – doors that have frameless glass, doors that close on to, rather than into the main body. The A pillars are wonderfully slim, resulting in a glass-house cockpit. The rear wheels are encased by the rear wings, and the elegant C pillars, with their polished metal panels, also lie next to shining metal finishers that turn out to be the boot hinges.

You look through the window at a space-ship design of flowing lines. The large arm-rests on the door cards are an integral part of the seating design, rather than an afterthought. Everywhere is covered with fitted carpet, soft leather or velour. Together with its airy and light atmosphere, the interior has the ambience of a hotel lounge rather than a car.

In every corner, every aspect, every view, outside and in, this vehicle pushes all others into the background. It was a world leader, a world beater, a fashion icon, an item of pure beauty. And all this was achieved by a small team in those early post-war years of recession and dreariness. This car and its story have captivated me entirely. So I set my sights on a right-hand-drive version of one of the final models, the DS23 with Bosch fuel injection, with luxurious Pallas trim, that tantalizing hydraulic gearbox and a Webasto sunroof.

My son phoned with information on an eBay DS sale, and I contacted the owner who was mystified at my removing the rear wings under a street light while he held the umbrella. While all panels had serious rust, there was no corrosion to be seen on the caisson. There were no puddles, green, amber or clear. All electrics functioned correctly, and the car drove really well and sprightly. It had a recent MoT, and was in daily use. A price was agreed and money handed over.

As intended, I drove the car for a year to gain experience and learn of its foibles. I decided on a complete restoration, ending up with a quality re-spray and interior re-trim. Then fate stepped in as I reversed out of the garage: the open driver's door hit the support pillar and concertinaed. The bottom was rotten and the door was now unrepairable.

Christopher Wilson at the wheel of his treasured DS.

Time for the restoration: the engine was very good and backed by documentation, while the fuel injection system, as used in my VWs, was familiar to me. I left well alone. All panels were removed, together with the roof. The interior, with glass and dashboard, was stripped out together with all cover panels. The rain channels above the rear wheels were rotten, as were panels behind the rear wheels, known as epaulettes. There were small holes in both outer and inner C pillars. That was it – so out with the welder and add new metal. All areas of surface rust were then cleaned with a grinder brush, treated with rust remover, rust converted, etch primed, painted and sprayed with Waxoyl.

I now had a 100 per cent sound carcass – or caisson, as Citroën call it. I turned to the panels that were all in very good condition with little attention required. We agonized over the colour and considered Porsche's metallic 'Yachting Blue'. This was certainly the colour for our lithe and beautiful car. On its return from the paint shop all panels were assembled and added to the car, which was again waxoyled from stem to stern.

Next stop the trim shop, where cream leather seats and door cards toned well with fawn carpets. It was fascinating to see those wonderfully comfortable seats stripped down to reveal their complex construction. While the original car design is good, that would not preclude my adding improvements. High-level brake lights, LED indicators, rear fog light, air horns, multi-pin connectors, oil and voltage gauges and a leather-covered lower dashboard were added.

After eighteen months work we have that dream car in the garage to drive and enjoy. It was never my idea to own a museum piece where every item was polished and unused as on the day it was first sold. I wanted to enjoy owning, driving and showing off this beautiful car, and explaining its complex and advanced engineering to our friends. I own a BMW 5-Series that is quieter, faster and more economical than my DS 'Cydnee' – but it is the DS that provides the greatest pleasure.

close to the Rawai beach on the Phuket island, runs a fleet of DS. And Fabrice Mattei, a Frenchman living in Bangkok, is a true Citroën fanatic, and has an impressive collection, which currently includes a Traction Avant, a pair of 2CVs, and a DS. And no ordinary DS: she is a beauty.

As DS values and their restoration costs in Europe go up, surely there is something wonderful about the legacy of the DS in Asia, and how a car is still touching the lives of ordinary people. And without the web, and the work of Pierre Jammes in preserving the DS in Asia story for immortality, another chapter in this amazing car's history would have gone unrecorded.

DS RALLYING?

The DS was, despite its size, a strong rally car, and under René Cotton's management the official DS rally cars competed in everything from the Monte Carlo Rally (winning in 1959) to the London Sydney Rally, and the RAC Rally. A DS won the 1961 and 1963 Tour de Corse, and the 1,000 Lakes Rally in 1962. And a DS won the 1966 Monte Carlo Rally, though in strange circumstances, as they 'inherited' the win after the British Minis were disqualified. Much argument followed, which was bad publicity for Citroën, who then withdrew from FISA events.

Björn Waldegaard at the wheel of the two-door DS sport short-wheelbase car. Note the 'RR' type wheels.

The DS rally team had P. Toivonen as its star, and other DS conductors were Paul Frère, and René Trautman, Lucien Bianchi and Paul Coltelloni. Privateer and dealer-supported DSs competed in events in Europe, Africa and Asia, Jean-Pierre Bugnot being the leading name. Michele Charles was the leading DS rally driver at regional level between 1969–72.

DS in Monte Carlo Rally moment.

THE DS EFFECT?

Should the DS define Citroën as a marque? Many argue that it should, and does, and has done so for decades, yet this is a singular view which may detract from the achievements of Citroën's wider design work and its range of cars. But in terms of design bravery, design inspiration and design purity, is any rival obvious? DS was not without fault, but its achievement and its effect was, and remains, realized upon a global scale.

As a product design and as a piece of social science within a corporate and a national psyche, the DS was, and is, unique. It was surely the height of design and marketing, and the consequent effect of a product defining a brand, rather than a brand defining a product. For a while, alongside Concorde, the DS defined both a national and a European identity. If only today's standards of build quality could have prevented the tarnishing of the jewel that was the DS, if only it had been built as well as Concorde. Despite the caveat, the DS can only be called a magnificent event in automotive history. And it *still* looks as if it has come from some future visionary film.

SPECIFICATIONS — 1959 DS19

Body
Non-monocoque, non stressed, clad subframe base unit; plastic roof panel

Engine
Type — 1911cc 4-cylinder in-line longitudinal inclined pushrod with alloy 'hemi'-head unit
Bore and stroke — 78 × 100mm
Compression ratio — 7:5:1
Solex single carburettor
Max power — 66bhp (SAE) 4,500rpm
Max torque — 97.6lb/ft 2,500rpm
Max speed — 82.6mph (132.9km/h)

Transmission
Four-speed manual via single dry plate clutch

Brakes
Type — Hydro-pneumatic
Front — Inboard discs of 11.8in diameter
Rear — Outboard drums

Suspension:
Front — Twin leading arms, self-levelling hydro-pneumatic; anti-roll bar
Rear — Trailing arms self-levelling hydro-pneumatic; anti-roll bar

Tyres
Michelin 'X' design with differing (lesser) width to rear

Dimensions:
Track — (front) 59in (1,499mm)
(rear) 51in (1,295mm)
Wheelbase — 123in (3,124mm)
Length — 15ft 9in (4,801mm)
Width — 5ft 10.5in (1,791mm)
Weight — 24.22cwt (1,230kg) (*unladen*)

Total number of factory built DS/ID: 1,330,755

CHAPTER SEVEN

BRAVE SIBLINGS

AMI AND DYANE

BRAVE SIBLINGS | AMI AND DYANE

IF THE DS was Citroën's new hallmark, its international legend, what could it offer the more traditional car buyer? And how could it target the new emerging market of female car drivers? With so much emphasis on its new DS spaceship, Citroën was in danger of being perceived as having gone upmarket and of leaving its core buyer base, notably its French audience, way behind. And could a new, smaller car capture buyers across Europe, even in Great Britain, or even more daring, in the USA?

Everyone wanted a DS in one form or another, but not everyone could afford one, or even the basic, stripped-out ID austerity model which the company soon came up with in 1957. But would Citroën create a new 'half-way-house' type of car, something bigger and better than a 2CV, yet below the DS's market sector? Given French fiscal tax ratings – hence 2CV, 7CV and so on, the car was thought of and spoken of internally as the '3CV' in reflection of its intended engine tax rating size.

However, wouldn't such a new size of car require an expensive new body, suspension, floorpan and range of engines? And surely all this would take at least five years to develop, never mind the funding issues or factory capacity required from an already over-stretched Citroën. In 1959, nearly five years into the life of the DS, and just as the first revisions to its front bodywork and mechanical and trim specifications were being enacted, the men of the Bureau d'Études were given the go-ahead to start sketching out ideas for a new small saloon. As for the floorpan, engine, tooling and specifications, it was decided that these could wait, because first it had to be styled to be different and new – not a mini DS, but something in its own right.

STYLING – BERTONI'S LAST GREAT FLASH OF GENIUS?

Enter maestro Bertoni and his gypsum, clay and sculptural skills. After the success of his DS styling, Flaminio Bertoni's stock was high. By now he had also been joined by the talented Henri Dargent and R. Henrique Raba, and André Estaque. A Monsieur Lattay was the man who assisted Dargent with the early Ami styling models.

The 'Ami', as it became named, was again a car body design teased out by Bertoni's hands, but unlike the Traction Avant, early ideas were committed to paper, and a definite feel of the 1960s soon became apparent. The reverse raked rear window had already been seen by 1957 in America on the Mercury *Turnpike* design, and had been tried on various Packard and Lincoln design studies. But its use in a small saloon was a new approach. The Ami may have lacked 'fins' in the idiom of the day, but with its tailored rear design, long rear boot deck, four round, chrome-rimmed rear lamps and deep body side swages pressed into the steel from the front wings through to the rear, the car had a glitz or glamour no one was expecting. It was a great piece of integrated, Franco-Italian styling, with some of the glitter of the new age thrown in.

Only at the front was Bertoni frustrated: he wanted a sharply dipping frontal aspect, a 'face' for the car which would have had an aerodynamic scoop for a grille bordered by two subtle wing lines with headlamps recessed into each side. However, the constraints of tooling, the height of the engine block and the need for under-bonnet venting for the air-cooled engine, all contributed to robbing Bertoni of his radical and futuristic plunging frontal style.

Despite this, the Ami was a pioneer of the use of squared, shaped headlamps, and these were set in chromed housings; Bertoni also managed to incorporate a hint of his original front apron and low bonnet idea by giving the car a strong visual scoop in a concaved and compound curved bonnet pressing that must have given the toolmakers consternation – but it made it to production.

Observers often miss the subtle ribs pressed into the steel of the front wing behind the wheelarch: were these a 'faux' suggestion of air vents, or an expensive piece of design? They

The Henri Dargent rendering of an idea for a three-door car of Ami derivation, dated April 1962.

were deleted in the 1968 body changes. Across the car's front below the headlamps were two parallel trim strips that were smoothly chamfered into the front apron, with the turn indicator lenses designed to sit between them. Again it was stunning, simple, pure design – though it was soon removed in the cost-cutting days that lay ahead.

Inside lay a 'space-age' dashboard, and seats that could be removed for outdoor use. It seems that Bertoni put all he knew and intuitively felt, into this wonderfully designed car.

With its domed roof ending in a sharp, Kamm-type ridge and with the rear boot deck acting as a *de facto* spoiler, the Ami was a blend of style and science allied to an anthropomorphic style of sculpted integrity. The original Ami 6 Berline is a long-forgotten piece of singular design excellence; sadly it has perhaps been shrouded by its simpler, more 'normal' derivatives of the late 1960s.

Much as Bertoni adored the DS, it was a modified shape, whereas in the Ami 6 Berline it was his own pure shape that had won through (minus only his scooped airflowed front end): it is reputed that this car was Flaminio Bertoni's favourite piece of design work. Looked at from the present day, it is indeed a stunning blend of science, future fashion and elegance, which

RIGHT: **The incredible dashboard built on DS themes.**

BELOW: **Ami Berline with classic rear screen angles and pure Bertoni style. No wonder it was his reputed favourite design.**

Building the Ami. Note the triangulated footwell reinforcement pressings and strong bulkhead. The sill gauge remains somewhat thin.

may also look more French than just about anything else of similar stature. Is this one of the most original, individual, elegant, organic car shapes ever seen and often forgotten for its excellence? There are no excrescences, no gimmicks, just wonderful 1950 to 1960s 'space age' styling moulded into a quintessentially French form.

Under the Skin

As the styling team thought about the new car's shape, Citroën's management took the decision to use the underpinnings of the existing 2CV for the car that would become the Ami. The rear inner wing panels, floorpan and other existing 2CV metal pressings were amalgamated into a new body to which a much stronger front cabin tooling was added. Given the lightness of the 2CV's front cabin construction, Citroën's engineers created a strong, one-piece pressing for the A-pillar and windscreen aperture panel. This was welded to a strong bulkhead that featured triangulated footwell sections at each side; these also provided an early form of anti-intrusion device behind the wheel-arch area. The roof was attached to a rigid perimeter frame.

In the fashion of the time (and of the DS), the main vertical B-pillars were thin and the floor flat. The car used box-section sills, which were somewhat light in gauge. At the rear, a capacious boot projected behind the reverse-angled rear windscreen. Up front, lightweight external front wing panels and a deep frontal cross-member bodywork section gave the car a softer nose. Although a new design, the carry-over of previous components and the blending of techniques meant that the Ami was a sort of semi-monocoque, platform-based car.

The 2CV's leading/trailing arm long travel suspension with torsion-bar damping and independent function gave the car superb ride quality and a 'loping' feel that could eat up distances; however, the high roll angles persisted – but so too did tenacious grip and typical front-drive understeer. In a strange and typically Citroën paradox, we can see that the original Ami was a 'Berline': a saloon car with a boot, yet it later became a fastbacked saloon and a true estate.

Citroën's managing director Pierre Bercot had authorized the study of a flat-four engine of around 1.0 litre, but neither that idea nor a Panhard small engine of approximately 850cc were deemed suitable. So Citroën simply bored out the existing 2CV twin-pot of 425cc (itself uprated from its original 375cc), and created the 602cc version found in the first Ami 6 Berline with its 22bhp.

The Ami 6 Berline stayed in production from 1961 to 1968. Thereafter it was subjected to some degree of 'normalization' – perhaps a contradiction to the Citroën purist, but certainly a rationalization to increase sales and decrease costs.

For the 1962 model year upgrades were made to the Ami 6, notably changes to the rear window opening function to make them slide. Various trim and specification changes took place in the 1960s, including some wonderful two-tone colour combinations. The reality was, even with the Ami 6 advertising and specifications aimed at female buyers, the car lagged well

BRAVE SIBLINGS: AMI AND DYANE

behind the 2CV and its enduring minimalist appeal – even in 1963, the 2CV was outselling the Ami 6 by a ratio of nearly two to one. The Ami 6 was over one third more expensive to purchase than a 2CV, yet it had the same engine as the larger capacity 2CV models. It was a case of another Citroën paradox: however, the Ami would come into its own.

Citroën's idea for a mid-range car had slowed at the altar of engine power and body practicality. The answer was to fit

ABOVE: **Front and rear views of the Ami 8 in contrast to the car's 2CV ancestor seen in 'Spot' special edition mode.**

BELOW: **Triangulated rear side windows were a design theme at Citroën long before the GS and CX.**

117

BRAVE SIBLINGS: AMI AND DYANE

bigger engines and add a pretty fastbacked body and a proper estate-car variant. Heuliez suggested the first Ami estate or 'Break', and kept the existing rear side doors; but Citroën rejected this and created a more radical re-tooling for the eventual estate bodyshell.

So were born the Ami 8 and ultimately the Ami Super, a car with nearly 60bhp – nearly three times the horsepower of the Ami 6 Berline of 1961, and almost twice that of the Ami 8. With added sound proofing, better trim, less bare metal in the cabin and the GS-type 1015cc engine, not to mention a floor-mounted gear shift, the Ami Super more than lived up to its name in comfort and in its peppy performance and overtaking

ABOVE: **For the 1970s, a plastic interior was fitted.**

LEFT: **Bright blue Ami Super hot hatch!**

BELOW: **Saloon and estate seen together capture the Citroën atmosphere.**

118

ability. The British loved the Ami Super and its power-in-a-light-body theory of an early 'hot hatch' capable of 87mph (140km/h) – or even 95mph (153km/h) downhill with a tailwind!

The rare Ami 8 van and the Super service van ought really to have a cult following, but few examples remain of this stealthy Citroën. Even rarer are the North American Ami. A few Berline cars were imported into North America from 1963 to 1965, with a very few later Ami Breaks rumoured in 1968.

MODEL DEVELOPMENTS

1961: Ami 6 Berline launched.
Autumn 1961–1962: Model year cars with revisions, notably opening rear windows.

ABOVE: **Ami fanatics!**

BELOW: **Under the bonnet, the forward-biased engine location is obvious.**

1968: Ami 6 Berline terminated. One bodyshell used for M35 engine and suspension development.
1968: Ami 8 saloon launched, featuring new front styling and completely new rear end with sloping rear windscreen and triangulated rear side windows as 'six-light' styling. Vertically tailed, 'Brake' or estate version also soon launched (1969), both cars with larger 32bhp engine. Front disc brakes installed.
1973: Ami 'Super' launched with much larger 1015cc flat-four 'boxer' engine, revised plastic-moulded facia and fittings. Significant under-bonnet tooling changes were required for the fitment of the horizontally opposed engine taken from the lower-powered Citroën GS range. Gearbox and gearshift actuation changes were also specific to this larger-engined car. The Super and the Break used wider-section tyres of 135 15 ZX ratio, compared to the Ami 8 saloon which retained the 125/15 ratio. Trim levels were Luxe, Confort and Club. Difference in seat type and trim were the most obvious trim variations. Club models had individually reclining seats.
1974: Thicker rear anti-roll bars to reduce roll; fog lamps fitted; use of vinyl side stripes for some markets.
1976–78: Continuing trim changes and 'run-out' specifications, including vinyl stripes and seat trim changes. Production of Ami Super ceases in 1979.

America: In 1963 low numbers were exported to the North American market; these featured added chromework, bumper bars and turn indicators to meet legislation.

Spain: The Ami 6 and Ami 8 were also built by Citroën Hispania in Vigo, Spain, as the 3CV and C8 (not the Ami) from 1967 to 1978. The name 'Familiar' and C-8 were used in Spain, not 'Ami'.

Argentina: The Ami 8 was manufactured in Argentina until 1978. The estate version was exported to Uruguay and Paraguay, and to Chile as a CKD kit (see below)

Chile: The Ami estate was built up at a CKD assembly plant in Arica, Chile, from late 1975 to 1978, when, amazingly, the complex CX was built from CKD kits as a prestige Chilean market offering.

Vans

Ami service vans were rare; even rarer was the glazed 'Vitre'.

Total production of the Ami models (except the M35) reached 1,840,121 units, of which 722,000 were the Ami Super, according to Citroën figures.

'OPERATION M 35': A SINGLE ROTOR FASTBACK AMI

Fascination with Felix Wankel's rotary-cycle engine had been around for decades. Unlike a normal piston-cycle engine where the intake, compression, combustion and exhaust all take place within the same space, the Wankel offers separate chambers for such functions and provides a continuously functioning, gas-flowed path in the cycle from chamber to chamber. The cycle is of a rotating or radial action rotor (as a piston) that passes around a main housing containing the relevant chambers, and allows separate efficiencies, as compared to a standard cylinder head and piston design where everything takes place separately and in the same space. In the rotary engine the piston action process is continuously driven.

People talk of the 'turbine smoothness' of the Wankel engine, but this is a misnomer as the Wankel is not related to the *jet* turbine because it is an internally driven combustion engine, not an external one like the jet turbine function. It does function as in the gas-flowed sense of the gas turbine, but not with blades: with the conventional engine's pistons replaced by rotors in chambers, the Wankel is much smoother in its function and power/torque delivery, and lacks chattering valves and shafts.

The claim is often made that Citroën's first investigations into rotary-cycle engine technology were in the 1960s, but this is incorrect because in 1938 Citroën sponsored the building of an orbital rotary-cycle engine to a patented design by Dimitri Sensaud de Lavaud, who designed a five-lobe outer rotor that possessed an inner hypocycloid motion allied to an inner rotor of six lobes with a 5:6 reduction ration. This single prototype engine was built by Ateliers de Batignolles under the French Air Ministry from 1939 onwards, but was abandoned in 1941 due to a number of issues and war-time perspectives.

Post-World War II, investigations into numerous engine cycle ideas led to the further development of the Wankel engine in Germany, Japan and in America, notably at NSU, Mercedes, Mazda, Suzuki and Curtiss-Wright/GM. With impending emissions, safety and other legislation, it was deemed that the Wankel engine had a future. Of interest, the Wankel engine is much smaller and lighter than a normal piston-cycle engine, and offers the engineer and designer the chance to build a car with a lower centre of gravity to benefit handling, and a lower frontal styling line to benefit aerodynamics and visibility.

These were the reasons Citroën became interested in the Wankel engine in the early 1960s. After preliminary talks in 1962–63, in 1964, at the primary instigation of its lead engineer at the time, Jacques Nougarou, Citroën entered into a partnership with the main Wankel design development licence holder of Neckarsulmer Stricken Union (NSU) in Germany; the result was the Société d'Étude Comotor company in June 1964, which was a joint project to study a small, rotating Wankel cycle engine.

BRAVE SIBLINGS: AMI AND DYANE

The rear side window design is a precursor to that for the GS and CX, and surely weakens the claims made by some about the influence of the Pininfarina Aerodinamica cars on the GS and CX styling?

By March 1965 the joint venture began as Comotor Société Anonyme, with a capitalization of $300,000 US dollars. In May 1967 this had resulted in the Compagnie Européenne de Construction de Moteurs Automobiles (Comotor SA), capitalized at $1,000,000 US dollars (registered in Luxembourg) for the *production* of a smaller, single rotor engine for use in a Citroën 'M 35' car. Comotor was housed in a small factory in West Germany. Citroën created its own laboratory, headed by Michel Audinet, which led to the single and bi-rotor Citroëns. The chief engineer across all Citroën engine development at this time was André de Bladis. The engine was to be manufactured by Audi-NSU/VW and transported to France for installation in the car. On start-up in 1970, Comotor was funded to the tune of $4,040,000 US dollars.

Developed from 1967 through to launch in 1969, NSU and Citroën created an engine that was actually more advanced than the engine in the NSU R0 80. (Of interest, the new Citroën engine replaced chrome in its working surfaces with a nickel-silicon alloy.) In order to cure cracking around the sparking plug portal, a copper housing around the plug was designed. Stronger tip seals than those used in the RO 80 or Prinz cured the tip seal issues that affected those cars' engines, and achieved a significant reduction in engine working temperature.

Citroën and NSU were at the leading edge of Wankel developments[11], and the news that General Motors had paid Audi-NSU/VW 50,000,000 US dollars in 1970 to buy Wankel licences shows just how advanced the Wankel idea had travelled. Citroën's investment was looking like a wise move if GM were considering a range of Wankel-powered cars. The Toyo Kogyo Matsuda-owned company – Mazda – were also racing ahead with Wankel engine development (and still are to this day).

In a move that encapsulated the Citroën thinking of the time (SM, GS and CX were all in their complicated developments in this period), Citroën decided to build up to 500 specially bodied cars based on the Ami, and to let chosen special customers in France buy them (at nearly the cost of a DS) as officially sanctioned public research vehicles via the official dealer network. In a strange paradox, Citroën effectively 'sold' a non-production model that in theory was never mass produced nor offered 'for sale' in the traditional sense. As an engineering research exercise it seems a bizarre and costly affair, and yet was one that gave us the now revered M 35.

Using an Ami floorpan and front under-skin structure, M 35 had a special lozenge-shaped, fastback body with triangulated rear side windows that were a precursor to such shapes in the GS and CX. Styled by Opron's team and significantly Giret and Harmand, the M 35 was a two-door small coupé of immense appeal to the younger Citroëniste, and many think that even if fitted with the GS flat-four engine as used in the Ami Super, as opposed to the Wankel unit, the car would have sold very well for Citroën in the early 1970s. Because the engine needed to be placed well forward, the front body metal was elongated in a hand-built nose cone, and is not a standard Ami pressing.

Heuliez were part of the car's original design and development in body engineering terms, and they built the car up as a full body and then shipped it to Rennes la Janais in Brittany for engine and drivetrain installation and trimming by Citroën. Heuliez chairman Henri Heuliez drove an M 35 for years, and travelled over 50,000 miles (80,000km) in his specially painted, blue M 35.

Some writers claim that the M 35 was pure Ami in structural terms ahead of the B-pillars, but this is incorrect as M 35 had a faster-raked windscreen and A-pillars of greater length (with resultant modifications to the bulkhead metal), and this required a new, larger windscreen of greater height; glass was specially made in low numbers for the project.

The leather-trimmed front seats pre-dated the similar SM seat design by incorporating a reclining backrest that pivoted not at its base, but at the lumbar region. Many of the trim items came from the DS.

The Ami front end was extended and a specially fabricated nose cone built for each car.

Citroën planned to build 500, but the numbering system and odd and even number usage has led to confusion. Were 473, as numbered, built? The answer is no, 473 were not built even if the inaccurate wing-mounted number on the final car is '473'. And where are they now? The biggest M 35 enthusiasts remain the Dutch and many are owned in the Netherlands – one garage has stored over twenty M 35s. The records state that Citroën built 267 M 35s, well short of the advertised 500. The first M 35s were built in 1969, 212 were built in 1970, and forty-nine in 1971, with the last car numbered as 473 being sold on 12 March 1971. Today it is believed that fewer than eighty cars survive.

Like the Ami, the gearshift was a facia-mounted device of convoluted design. However, three cars were built with the later Ami Super-type floor-mounted gearshift – these cars were painted in a metallic blue rather than the sable grey metallic of the other M 35s. One of these cars was reputedly fitted with the GS-type 'Convertisser' automatic transmission; the only known 'blue' car was no. 39, which resided in the Heuliez collection until the entire collection was sold off in 2012.

Of particular note, the M 35 used the DS-style hydropneumatic suspension system, but in modified form. This meant that M 35 had its suspension spheres placed not above the wheel as *de facto* strut length, but as a horizontally linked trailing/leading arm connected to a more centrally mounted hydropneumatic springing system. Despite the nose-heavy engine mounting, understeer is not excessive and the super-smooth ride and sleek bodywork give the car a real coupé air.

The single rotor engine had smooth power from below 2,000rpm. Noise from the engine and specially modified GS gearbox was minimal, and other niceties included aerodynamically vented, inboard-mounted, powered disc brakes at the front. The test mule for the 35 single-rotor engine was an Ami 6 Berline, which was fitted with the Wankel unit in 1968 and extensively run at Montlhéry. In the M 35 a rev-limiter warning buzzer went off at 7,000rpm to warn the driver to ease off or change gear, but even with this, some engines expired at low mileages. A tachometer was wisely added in the cabin as a 'stick on' item on the facia. Problems with the spark plugs (two) were soon solved, and any M 35 driver who got stuck with his plugs could always borrow some from an NSU Spider or Prinz!

Clearly, with its upgraded engineering, specially designed and built body, luxury cabin trim, and build run of the intended 500 units, M 35 was an expensive and questionable way of conducting research. If the 1970s economic crisis had not struck, Citroën may have actually mass produced a version of the M 35 – with or without the Wankel engine. If only even a flat-four GS engine from the Ami Super could have been used in the M 35, Citroën enthusiasts would have had yet another wonderful 1970s Citroën to saviour. But it was not to be in any sense, and today M 35 represents both a lost 'moment' and a true classic car. It also paved the way for the twin rotor Wankel engine in the equally abortive GS 'Birotor' project, and the early work on a triple rotor engine that was abandoned. In 2011 one M 35 owner did indeed fit a GS engine to an M 35, and others may do likewise – at the risk of offending M 35 purists.

M 35 Today

What happened to the M 35s that were let out into arranged ownership? Given the fragility of the rotor tip seals and the special 'prototype' bodies, Citroën tried to get them back from the public test customers and the dealers who had taken them, but in France and the Netherlands, many M 35s 'escaped' and remain in private hands to this day; they are perhaps one of the rarest of all Citroëns.

Citroën had entitled the M 35 project 'Operation M 35'. Today as M 35 fanatics search out the remaining cars, a Dutch collector and his associates have brought many of them together (plus or minus twenty-three cars) and launched a new

SPECIFICATIONS 1970 YEAR CITROËN M 35

Body construction
Platform frame with semi-monocoque welded bodyshell

Engine
Type	Wankel single rotor
Chamber displacement	30.03 cubic inches (497.5cc)
Equivalent total displacement	60.6 cubic inches (995cc)
Compression ratio	9:1
Power	49bhp at 5,500rpm (55bhp claimed in some references)
Torque	50.6ft/lbs at 2,745 rpm
Carburation	One two-barrel Solex 18/32 HHD
Ignition	Coil
Cooling	Water
Clutch	Single dry plate

Transmission
Type	Four-speed manual

Suspension and steering
Suspension	Front single leading arm on each side, with hydro-pneumatic sphere springing with anti-roll bar. Rear suspension trailing arms on each side with hydro-pneumatic sphere springing with anti-roll bar
Steering	Rack-and-pinion type

Brakes
Power assisted. Inboard discs at front of 10.65in diameter: rear drums of 7.12in diameter

Tyres
Specially adapted Michelin X 135-15 radials with finer-mesh belting and differing compound

Dimensions
Wheelbase	94.5in (2,400mm)
Front track	49.6in (1,260mm)
Rear track	48.03in (1,220mm)
Overall length	159in (4,039mm)
Width	61.25in (1,556mm)
Height	53.25in (1,353mm)

Performance
0–50mph	12sec
0–60mph	16sec
Top speed	89.5mph (144km/h) (fourth gear)
Fuel consumption	24.5mpg (11.5ltr/100km) (average)

Operation M 35 – 'La Nouvelle Operation M 35'. Sander Aalderink is the man at Eenden Garage in Womer, the Netherlands, who fronts the wonderful M 35 'rescue' programme. It has now been decided to allow the sale of some of the M 35s in the collection. Sander's records show that there are even M 35s that made it as far as Texas, Canada and Australia.

All these years on, for some Citroënistes (the author included), the Wankel-powered M 35 coupé provides a tantalizing example of pure Citroën intelligence on a scale so typical of the men of the Bureau d'Études. M 35 is a wonderful yet forgotten example of the essence of Citroën.

DYANE – THE DELIGHT

When Renault finally grasped the front-wheel-drive concept and produced the Renault 4 in 1961, it was a compliment to the 2CV idea that the Renault 4 mimicked it. However, the Renault 4 was far more than just a copy of a 2CV: it was an updated, more modern, slightly more comfortable car far more in tune with the 1960s than the austere and abstract 2CV. As such, the Renault 4 created stiff competition for the 2CV, and Pierre Bercot at Citroën immediately realized that the 2CV might be in trouble. Could Citroën reverse engineer the Renault idea into an upgraded Citroën 2CV?

Yet with Citroën just about to launch the Ami, had that not in some context been achieved? In reality, however, there was

LEFT: **So smart: note the rear bootlid airflow management pressings. Even if it had been fitted with a GS engine, surely this would have made a stunning 1970s Citroën coupé? What a waste...**

BELOW: **A blue Dyane 6 hastens through rural Brittany: original and in daily use, this is a Dyane that kept going.**

124

Dyane delight on the move. Another lovely Dyane shows off the integrated elegance of its cute early 'eco' car design credentials. Note the concave side panel sculpture and its resultant tension and clean lined form.

still a gap between the Ami and the 2CV, and the Ami was bigger than the Renault 4. From these events stemmed the idea of updating the 2CV, yet retaining the essential basic appeal of the concept. But the Ami was a saloon (at that stage), whereas the Dyane was a proper hatchback.

Dyane Design

Citroën at this time was hard pressed for resources and capacity, as the revisions to the DS, and new projects, were stretching it to the full. Of relevance, Citroën had since 1953 had a close hand on Panhard, purchasing 25 per cent of the marque in 1955 and the remaining share in 1964. It was obvious that Panhard could add to the resources needed to create a modernized version of the 2CV.

So it was that Panhard and its designer Louis Bionier were asked to create the new idea – the car that would become the Dyane. Behind Bionier's headlined name there lay the now forgotten and uncredited work of the designer René Ducassou-Pehau, from Basque country. Much of the design development work and themes for the Panhard-Citroën that became the Dyane stemmed from René Ducassou-Pehau, and also from assistant designer André Jouan. In 1961 Ducassou-Pehau also created a design for a floating, non-rotating steering hub containing essential driver information and aids; such an idea appeared on the 2004 Citroën C4. René Ducassou, as he is sometimes known, was also a key part of the design of the Panhard range before the company closed.

By 1965 Panhard had presented its sketches and models of the proposed car, with some changes being made by Citroën at Bercot's request. In the Bureau d'Études Henri Dargent was by now established, and it was he who suggested themes for the new car's interior (re-used in the later revised Ami range). Jacques Charreton, who contributed to the revisions to the exterior as well as Dargent, wanted modern square headlamps, but the cost-cutters at Citroën put 2CV round headlamps in chromed, square housings – which must have been just as expensive as plain square lamps on their own!

Despite having several fathers, the styling of the Dyane was taught, elegant and utterly original, and not as easily dated as the 2CV's abstract form. Some say the taught, concave door skins came from Bertoni's mind prior to his death in 1964; others attribute them to Panhard's men.

Possibly originally planned as a separate Panhard-Citroën creation with its own chassis or monocoque, and originally presented in prototype form with a Panhard grille and badging, the Dyane was soon to be based on the existing 2CV platform and components – a huge saving in time and money for Citroën, even if it did not lead to the car as originally suggested.

Running Gear

Dyane used the 2CV's 425cc engine and then the 435cc version, but by late 1968 it was a Dyane 6 with the 602cc-type air-cooled twin-pot engine with its higher compression and forced induction system. The Dyane could also have the 'Traffi-Clutch' (also fitted to the Bijou), which was an early form of centrifugal slip device to reduce wear in urban use.

The suspension was the long travel, independent, interconnected torsion-bar system from the 2CV, which gave the expected ride quality via the linked bars and arms on each (lengthways) side of the car. The Dyane boasted its own body structure and interior, as well as dedicated trim items; only in engine and floor punt was it a 2CV derivative.

The Dyane 435cc had a top speed of 68mph (109km/h), but it could be coaxed to 70mph (113km/h) quite easily, especially if well maintained and not suffering from worn spark plugs or a carbon-clogged head. The Dyane 6 claimed a top speed of 75mph (120km/h), but Sir Douglas Bader said his Dyane 6 (with tyres over inflated) could 'Easily get to eighty, old boy' – though he may have used high octane fuel, and he certainly turned his door mirrors inwards to reduce drag.

The name 'Dyane' is said to have stemmed from Panhard's internal code name (their cars had had a DY prefix), yet some people claim that the use of a 'D' prefix stemmed from Citroën's marketing men, who wanted to link the new small car to the DS and its Greek goddess derivations. Given the 1967 launch of the revised 'slant-eyes' DS and the 1967 launch of the Dyane 4, the marketing men may well have been correct.

Using the 2CV chassis platform, 2CV engines and a myriad of fittings, the Dyane was cost effective and appealing to customers young and old.

The Dyane was indeed an economy car, yet an elegant one, and with smoother style and more practicality than a 2CV it should have eclipsed the venerable 2CV – yet strangely it did not, and the 2CV outlived the Dyane. Yet the Dyane was a delight to drive – a 'peppy' little car with 'point and shoot' steering, a great ride and handling ability, and the combination of a useful hatchback, a roll-back sunroof, and 50mpg (5.6ltr/100km) economy. The Dyane was well finished and comfortable, and only in terms of performance and passive safety was it of its time – and otherwise, wasn't it a precursor of today's 'eco' car?

The Dyane 4, Dyane 6 and the Acadiene van (and Fourgonnettes) racked up sales figures of over 1 million, at 1,444,583 units sold from 1967 to 1987 (van production continued for nearly three more years after the late 1983 cessation of the standard bodyshell).

DYANE DETAILS

1967–69: Dyane 4 with 425cc, 21bhp at 5,500rpm, and 435cc, 28bhp at 6,750rpm. Top speed: 64mph (103km/h).
1969–84: Dyane 6 with 602cc, 28bhp, then 32bhp at 5,570rpm. Top speed: 75mph (120km/h)
1970: Six-light body with extra side windows in the C-pillars.
1978: Dyane Acadiane replace the 2CV-based AK400 as Citroën's light van, with the old AK400 rear body mated to the Dyane at the B-pillars. In production until summer 1987.
Overseas production: Dyane production took place in Argentina, Iran (as the Jiane), Spain, and in Slovenia (then Yugoslavia) by the then Tomos company.

Several Special Editions were created, the most numerous being the 1,500 examples of the Dyane *Cabane*, the 600 Dyane *Capra*, and 750 *Edelweiss* that were built in Spain. *Edelweiss* had blue paintwork, front and rear bull bars, and wind-down windows. The Dyane Weekend was widely popular across northern Europe.

Late model Dyane in rare metallic paint looking very stylish indeed.

CHAPTER EIGHT

THE SM

**THE WORLD'S FIRST
HYPER CAR**

THE SM | THE WORLD'S FIRST HYPER CAR

The Citroën SM has four wheels
Like other cars.
That is the only way it is like
Other cars

CITROËN USA ADVERTISEMENT 1973

'WHAT CRAZED IMAGINATION created this monster?' So asked an American observer of the SM, but the comment stems from deductive logic, not from the abductive. Maybe you had to be French to 'get' the SM. And yet the SM went on to sell well in America, and it was no monster, either – it was more intelligent than that. In 1970 as the auto industry lay in a torpor of short-term fashion, the American magazine *Road and Track* said that the SM proved that 'progress of a revolutionary nature may still be possible.'

Today a hyper car is a super car with everything thrown at it in design terms: a boundary-changing car. The SM was perhaps the first car to have all that within it from scratch – so it was surely the world's first hyper car. Certainly in 1971 it was the world's most advanced act of engineering. The SM created a new fashion in its own context: GT – Grand Tourers – had existed before, but not like this car.

The SM also answered the structural issues of the DS, and took Citroën into supercar territory. With Talbot, Bugatti, Delahaye, Delage and the grand names gone, and with Facel Vega a dying minority item, France had lacked a national symbol. True, Concorde was on its way, but the DS was old, so something special, a new, grand, super coupé for France was needed.

In the SM, France delivered a supercar to match the bubble of 1970s supercars that Italy, Germany and Britain would produce. Thankfully, SM was quintessentially French – and when you consider the Jaguar XJS, Alfa Romeo Montreal, Mercedes Benz 450SLC, BMW CSi, and the Aston Martin V8, none of these were of the SM's seismic design impact. Perhaps the Maserati Ghibli or Ferrari Daytona 365 GTB were of equally stunning presence and ability, but they remained utterly traditional in every aspect of the engineering, whereas SM did not. Even the wonderful style of the low volume and so stupidly dismissed Toyota 2000GT coupé, the first Japanese supercar, was eclipsed by the form and function of the SM.

Somewhere deep inside Citroën a decision was taken to create a new type of car, a decision that was the result of discussion between several people. It is thought unlikely that the overall project was driven by one man or one personality, but maybe Robert Opron should be given credit for creating a GT car, and not letting himself be pushed into making a two-seat sportster with race or rally pretensions at the sacrifice of everything else. Opron and Bercot are reputed to be the two people who held out for the SM to be a grand touring car of advanced design and engineering content: so were they the lead players in establishing the SM's 'GT' formula against rumoured internal corporate opposition which favoured a two-seat lightweight sports car?

By 1966 Bertoni was dead, Lefebvre was long gone, and the likes of Robert Opron and a design director named Albert Grosseau were in the ascendant under Chairman Pierre Bercot. They knew that Citroën needed a flagship, a car that transcended even the DS and its '*haut de gamme*' Pallas version, which would at last soon have *injection electronique*. And yet the DS had never been re-engined as it should have been, but still used creaky old 4-cylinder engines that had been around for decades – in spite of several attempts, the V6 or flat-six idea for a DS never became a production reality. But those who say a flat-six was never built were wrong, for at least one such engine was built and sighted by witnesses as it lay hidden in a corner of the Bureau d'Études in the 1960s.

Citroën was the purveyor of the 2CV, Ami, Dyane and the DS range, but where was its symbol of, and for, the future? Voisin and Lefebvre would surely have seen the SM as a true legacy of their thinking, for it was a grand aerosport coupé in

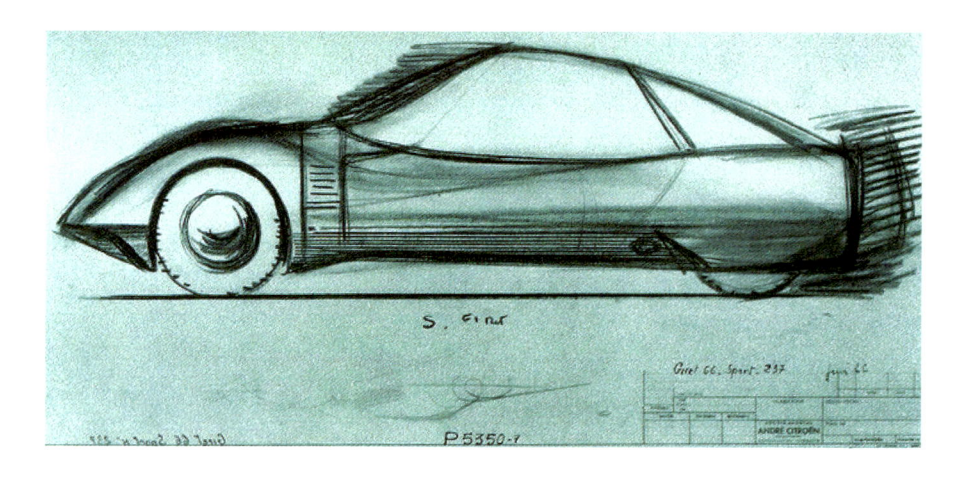

A 1966 design sketch for a coupé by Jean Giret.

every sense. The men of Citroën's Bureau d'Études had been sketching such a car from around 1961. Bertoni had left sketches of a large coupé, and Dargent and Giret had created their own sketches as well.

Chief engineer Jacques Né had held many informal meetings about a bigger, better engine – and the car to go with it. But he was thinking of a two-seater sportscar – perhaps a sort of Mercedes SL competitor?

FROM DS TO SM

So it was Albert Grosseau who led the SM project, and Jacques Né who sanctioned the building of two DS coupé bodies, and even placed an altered Panhard 24 two-door bodyshell over an extended DS base unit as an early experiment; perhaps this car was the moment of the true genesis of the SM? By 1965 the go-ahead for a really big Citroën had been given, perhaps as if by corporate and engineering osmosis. It was christened 'Type S' – or 'Special' or 'Sport'. Soon with an Italian Maserati engine, 'S' would become Sport/Maserati or 'SM'.

Robert Opron (and the newly hired Jean Giret), Dargent, Jacques Charreton and others (see below) all presented sketches for their ideas as to how this new car might look. Henri Lauve de Segur, who had led a design team at Buick, joined the SM development team and contributed several ideas, including work on the facia and automatic gearshift handle. Team member Regis Gromik also drew a stunning ellipsoid rendering of a grand tourer idea for SM, and Jacques Charreton took an often uncited role in the shaping of the SM.

In Bertoni's time there was fifteen people working in the styling and modelling department of the Bureau d'Études – by the 1970s there was 150. From 1948 to 1962, direct translation of an idea from thought to clay often took place without interim styling sketches; under Bertoni, car shapes were often first realized in clay. Soon after joining Citroën in 1961, and as Bertoni was ageing, it was Opron who began sketching, and then sculpting, small-scale models of a sports car that would not be a DS derivative but a truly new car – this was the beginning of what eventually became the SM.

Henri Dargent made early sketches for the SM's facia, and Jean Giret and he worked together to realize the final form, with Michel Harmand and Regis Gromik also closely involved. The unusual oval shape to the instruments and the steering hub motif stemmed from the appreciation felt by these men with regard to the ovaloid aerodynamic forms used on the exterior. The aerofoil-shaped sculpture of the entire facia seems to have pre-dated current design trends in the field by decades.

What is particularly striking about the team's individual exterior proposals is that they all contained a Bertoni theme – that of a wider frontal lobe aspect giving way to a tapered, narrower rear sculpture, with a flowing roof turret or glasshouse. The influence of birds or fish was still evident, despite the rise of the 'folded paper' school of car design at this time. Detachable rear wheel spats as seen on the SM became a post-1960s Citroën hallmark.

The new car would have to possess lower aerodynamic drag than the DS, and would also have to address the structural safety issues of the DS. More sporting handling would be required, as would a level of trim to take this car into the upper echelons of *haute couture*. The cabin, and not just the exterior, would have to be out of this world.

Opron concentrated on the frontal aspect of the design and how to meet the aerodynamic issues. He thought about the effects of licence or registration plates on frontal styling and aerodynamics; the effect of headlamps had also been a part of his creation of the revised DS frontal design, so this was another key consideration. After weeks of work and wind-tunnel research, the SM gained its frontal visage: an unusual glazed display, a sort of 'showcase' containing six headlamps and a licence plate, and which provided excellent leading edge airflow penetration as well as under-car and under-bonnet flow. The key to its form was the two-dimensional ovaloid shaping – the aerodynamic ideal.

For the side profile, Opron boldly created the flowing and rearward fuselage tip shape with its drooping action line (something we see on the more recent C6). This line gave dynamism to the car, helping it to look lithe and purposeful. The kinked shape at the C-pillar and rear side window was a masterpiece in that it preserved the fluid look, yet strengthened the lines of the glazed rear deck and tied in the side panels very neatly; Opron used a similar trick on the later Renault Fuego which he is credited with, although the contribution of Michel Jardin to the car's styling cannot go unmentioned.

Similarly, the SM contribution of Michel Harmand – not just as an interior designer but also as an exterior designer – cannot go unstated in the SM story, for in the Citroën archives are Harmand's mid-1960s sketches for a car design with a

A 'DS Sport' project coupé sketch from the mid-1960s Bureau d'Études: SM genesis?

SM in gold and displaying the effectiveness of the frontal design by Opron.

kinked-up, angled rear side window rising into a triangulated C-pillar and rear glazing. So while SM was Opron's, his team and the likes of Harmand offered significant contributions.

The rear end of the SM presented a problem. Aerodynamic considerations meant that blade or corner angles needed to be preserved to control flow separation, vortex turbulence and side-wind stability, and to tune the lift and pressures over, under and off the back of the car. Panel joints, welds and flanges all had to be hidden. The mildly American feel to the squared meter of chromework used is of interest in its departure from the frontal design motifs, and highly distinctive. The rear-end design was, suggested Opron, one of the more challenging parts of the design process.

DEVELOPMENT WORK AND AN UNSUNG HERO – JEAN NICOLAS

One of the less well known names of the SM's development at the Bureau d'Études was that of Jean Nicolas. Nicolas was one of the 'behind the scenes' men who worked on a diverse aspect of prototype development. He studied at the school for industrial design in the late 1940s, and secured a place at the Citroën-sponsored training academy. There he specialized in toolmaking and making pre-production items and 'one-off' prototypes.

Nicolas trained under Citroën's head of sheet metal and tooling design, a Monsieur Cassiat. Then came liaison with the team that made the plaster models of Bertoni's design and styling ideas, whereby the body dies and presses were created; this provided Nicolas with an entry into the world of prototyping and the sphere of Roger Prud'homme's workshop, and the secrets of the DS developments. Bertoni saw some of Nicolas's design and styling sketches, and soon had him working in the research department of the Bureau d'Études. This included wind-tunnel work at the *Soufflerie Aerodynamique Gustave Eiffel*, and drivetrain and packaging issues. After the DS's launch, Nicolas worked on the new frontal styling, dashboard designs, and the development of the DS estate body, and the re-engineering needed for the roof panel.

Of interest, in the later DS programme Jean Nicolas experimented with making the idea of headlamps concealed under a glazed, leading-edge frontal design, as used on the SM. He had previously worked on the structrual and aerodynamic effects of concealed and glazed headlamps by creating the four, centrally mounted headlamp set-up seen under a revised DS development 'mule'. This was long before the Opron-designed, 'slant-eyed' DS re-style for 1967.

Nicolas had worked under Bertoni, Estaque, Cadiou and Leonzi. The study team had worked on the sporty, shortened DS 'mules' that were a precursor to the exploration of Project S. As is well charted, some of the team wanted a smaller, two-seat car with overt competition potential, while others wanted to create a larger, four-seat GT car.

Jean Nicolas had also studied the structural and handling issues that were essential Citroën ingredients – low centre of gravity, aerodynamics and drivetrain behaviour. As Chausson were subcontracted to build the DS development mules and early SM structure, Jean Nicolas worked closely with Chausson. One of the SM's advances was its windscreen design, and he

ROBERT OPRON – MASTER OF STYLE, SCALE, ENERGY AND LIGHT

'The dolphin, the leopard, the swift, they each move at a speed consistent with their environment, each using a minimum of energy. What a great lesson for a stylist!' So said Robert Opron.

Robert Opron may be pictured by Citroën enthusiasts as the leading Citroën designer of the 1960s to 1970s era, but the fact is that he also designed cars for Renault, Fiat, Alfa Romeo and Ligier, and other products, too. He began his motor industry career at Simca. Like Voisin, Lefebvre and Bertoni, Opron had also studied architecture and had an early aviation interest. This meant that he was able not only to style and design, and not just to sculpt in steel, but also to consider structures and aerodynamics at a time when many designer-stylists knew little of this art.

All Opron's car designs have an organic wholeness as if they have been grown or shaped by the forces of wind, light, scale and structure. Many agree that one of the signatures of an Opron design is the way it will catch the light, and that it has a dynamic graphical element – movement being intrinsic in its shape even at rest. We can cite the Citroën SM and Renault Alpine A310 as prime examples. But not all his work was svelte and swept – the brutish yet finessed Alfa Romeo SZ proves that point.

Although his cars had scale and at times a grand stance, Opron's shapes were never flabby or excessive – they were taught and lithe, just as the great car styling of the years 1930 to 1950 had been. Nowhere can we find an Opron design that is superfluous or bloated, as are so many cars today. Opron, in the same way as Bertoni, Sason, Fioravanti and Sergio Pininfarina, brought the brilliance of artistic scale and sculpture to car design. His shapes have action and also peace, and surfaces and textures are all explored yet harmoniously integrated. In the mastery of such techniques, surely Opron's designs can only be compared with the quality of the 'greats' of the leading carrosseries or carrozzeria.

Again, like the aero-autonauts of Paris in the 1920s, Opron was a product of the Grand École system, having trained at the École des Beaux-Arts, studying architecture, painting and also sculpture. He then worked for Arthur Martin Design and learned his interior and product design trade in the expanding world of 1950s modernism. By the mid-1950s he was at Simca, where at a very young age he styled the lead themes in two cars, notably the important 1100. From there it was a single step to Bertoni's domain at Citroën, where within four years he took the lead as Citroën chef du style.

The maestro himself. Master of design, one of the world's top car designers.
PHOTO: MARTIJN VAN WELL

Opron's first meeting with Bertoni is reputed not to have been easy: Opron recalls that it was a stormy and explosive event – yet Bertoni recruited him soon afterwards, and the two men clearly shared a belief in natural forms, and took inspiration from mammals, the sea and sky creatures. Both, of course, had studied architecture and sculpture. After Bertoni's death, Opron led on the SM, GS, CX and commercial vehicles, and, of huge importance, so wonderfully re-styled the front of an existing icon – the DS – at some professional risk, yet it was a massive success. The 'face' or visage of the revised 1967 Opron slant-eyed DS has to be cited as one of *the* great masterpieces of design, even if it was a bit-part and not a whole car. SM, CX, and the smaller and harder-to-style GS, are complete car design achievements.

Opron remained at Citroën until 1975, and the effects of the State intervention and Peugeot takeover saw him depart to Renault. There he penned the later A310, the humble yet stylish Renault 9, and the clever Fuego.

From Renault, Opron went to Fiat, and after that he set up his own design company and consultancy. A celebration of his work, *OPRON Cinquante Ans du Style*, was held in 2002, in his seventieth year. He was one of the twenty-five designers cited for the 'Designer of the Century' award in 1999.

For Citroënistes, Opron, the stylish man with the look of a jazz musician or theatrical star, ranks as the high priest of modern Citroën design. Furthermore beyond the Citroën enclave he is an internationally respected figure, and without any doubt, one of the greatest shapers of the automobile in its history.

studied airflow across and around the windscreen – this led to the flush-glazing technique used on the production car.

The SM took less than three years, from 1967–70, to reach fruition, but the desire for a smaller sports car remained within the Bureau d'Études. There, just after SM's launch, the older, senior men of Allera, Mages and others, quietly created an ultra short-wheelbase two-seater using SM pressings and components. This little known car, largely created by Jean Nicolas, was hand-built in a dusty corner of the old buildings of the Bureau d'Études on the Rue de Théâtre. However, it has to be said that Nicolas's short-backed SM two-door design with a concave C-pillar did not sit well on the SM pressings.

This led to a re-think, and the creation of the so-called 'Bandama' rally car, or the SM 'breadvan', with its Kamm-tailed sliced rear canopy and 2in (500mm) shorter wheelbase. It seems that the little known name of Jean Nicolas was the rally driver and technical driving force behind this 'one-off' rally and race special SM[12].

STYLE SET BUT AN ENGINE NEEDED

By early 1968 the styling scenery of the new car was established, yet the problem of the engine remained, and Citroën did not have the resources or time to create a new large capacity engine to power what would effectively become a 1970s 'supercar'. Pierre Bercot looked around and had a conversation with people he knew: the Orsi family, who owned Maserati of Italy, a company famed for its mellifluous alloy-constructed engines and somewhat fragile lightweight 'leggera' bodywork. Were Bercot's thoughts to commission an engine, or did he envisage buying the Maserati company from the start? Whatever his thinking, the outcome of talks at the 1967 Salon d'Geneve was that Citroën SA purchased a large shareholding in Maserati.

At the beginning of 1968, Citroën's Bercot and his chosen man Guy Malleret were running Maserati, even if the Orsi family retained a titular role. In 1968 Citroën gave Maserati six months to suggest an engine design, and it had to concur with the perennial problem of French taxation laws, so 3-litre capacity or above was out – besides which Citroën set a limit of 2.8 litres. So was born the idea of a smooth, V-configured 2.7-litre engine.

Maserati had already done the groundwork, as they had a V-8 and a V-12 engine on the books. But surely there was more to this than simply slicing up one or the other?

V-angled engines require careful balancing and firing orders, and there are also temperature issues within the engine. The wider the V-angle, the more room between the head banks for associated gear, so two factors stand out in such engine design: the actual angle of the V and the water/oil cooling system, and the associated engine-bay airflow. Maserati had already built a 90 degree-angle V-8 – of note, not a 56-degree or 60-degree V as favoured by so many other engine designers. For the V8-derived V6 in the SM, Guilio Alfieri – responsible for Maserati engine design – added a balancer shaft and jackshaft drive to the hydro-pneumatics and chains that ran between the cylinders; contrary to some claims, the SM's engine was not 'half' an engine at all (it would have to have been a V12!). And does the SM's C114 Maserati engine result from removing two cylinders from a 3560cc V8 engine and creating a 2670cc engine with a bore and stroke of 87 × 75mm, or does it stem – as some say – from a cut-down 3856cc engine of 85 × 85mm bore and stroke and 2892cc, then reduced?

The resultant SM engine was alloy built and machined from a single alloy billet. So was born the Citroën-Maserati quad-cam V-6/C1114 coded engine with its low weight of 306lb (140kg), a very low centre of gravity (reducing roll), interchangeable cross-flowed alloy heads, and an early lean-burn hemispherical head design with sculpted piston heads that tuned the combustion flow. The engine came in rated at 2670cc or 2.7 litres, and an early variant had triple carburettors. But 170bhp seemed low for a supercar, and SM was going to be heavily built, too.

With a mid-range compression ratio of 9.0:1, and 170bhp (DIN) at 5,500rpm, the engine was short, low, light, and responsive in manner. Top speed was quoted at 139mph (220km/h) – no doubt assisted by the aerodynamics – but plenty of people have hit 140mph (224km/h) and above in their SMs. The SM could reach nearly 140mph using about half the power that a conventionally engineered large sportscar of the 1970s would use to reach such speed. How? The answer lay in the SM's exquisite Citroën aerodynamics, and in its equally exotic engine design and drivetrain efficiency.

The cooling issue was aided by a water-cooled, free-flowing jacket, two thermo-controlled fans, and the addition of an oil intercooler thrown in. Air scoops under the front valance ensured that cooling air flowed through the engine bay and driveshaft/brake systems. A great sign of success was that the engine's torque output of 172lb at 4,000rpm was higher than its bhp and achieved at much lower revs. These two parameters were indicators of a well designed engine with minimal losses in its function and rated energy at the flywheel.

The only note of caution at the time was cited as the length of the timing chain, and the demands that would be put on Citroën's single hydraulic pump to drive the brakes, steering and suspension system. And carburettors would eventually give way to the evocative *injection électronique*.

Other design highlights were that the engine and its weight sat well back in the car. The gearbox was an in-house Citroën design derived from the five-speed unit created for the 1970 DS.

THE SM: THE WORLD'S FIRST HYPER CAR

Alphonse Forceau was the man who led on SM gearbox design – no easy task, given the long-throw gear linkage down towards the front of the engine bay – but a smooth gear-change was achieved, and one that 'clicked' or 'clacked' as you stirred the alloy-gated *levier de changement de vitesse* (gear lever).

Overnight Citroën was the producer of the fastest front-wheel-drive car ever made, and one with a creamy-smooth Maserati engine that had that rare feature of both smooth, low rpm pick-up from about 2,700rpm, and a high-revving, high-speed ability. The engine breathed beautifully and ran smoothly. Overhead camshafts could mean a certain 'peakiness' to the power delivery, but not in Alfieri's sweet-running motor and its tenor-pitched 'bark' with a hint of induction howl and a touch of 'rasp' and 'throb' from the exhaust flow according to rpm.

Despite all this engineering excellence, despite the alloy engine and straight-line stability and efficient traction with no RWD drivetrain losses, here was a huge risk for the 1970s: a front-wheel-drive car of high power and great size. Would it eat driveshafts? Would it run hot and have huge warranty claims? Would the front tyres be shredded in under 5,000 miles (8,000km)? And could there be suspension and handling issues? The answers were that these issues had been dispensed with by the Citroën-Maserati fusion.

In Britain, Michael Scarlett, technical editor of *Autocar* and consumate thinker of 1970s technical editors, discussed the SM at length in rave reviews. Latterly Ray Hutton, *Autocar*'s editor, would praise the SM and drive one in a rally. SM, despite or because of its technicality that worked, won over many sceptical motoring noters, even in America.

SPORTING SUSPENSION

To exceed the DS saloon handling qualities, SM needed changes to its suspension. So pressure rates in the system were altered, mounting angles changed, and roll centres lowered. The ride was stiffer but the roll less noticeable than in the DS, and given the correct technique, the car could be steered and pointed as a fast sporting car with higher abilities than the DS-derived suspension might suggest.

With all-round independent suspension within a typical Citroën hydro-pneumatic set-up the SM had the expected leading arms up front (but with rally-inspired trailing pivot arms), and DS-type trailing arms to the rear. There were reinforcements to metal gauges where suspension components were mounted to ensure torsional rigidity and handling consistency – the hull did not flex and upset the handling. Internal pressures in the spheres were raised, and a notable difference in front and rear tyre pressures – 32psi and 29psi respectively – meant that the SM's handling was excellent and predictable – once you had learned how to drive it. There was no 'snap' understeer-oversteer reaction or transition, nor 'tailwagging' when pushed. Lift off the power mid bend, and the SM would tuck in.

The fully powered steering design was called Direction à Rappel Asservi – 'DIRAVI' – or latterly in Britain, branded in capitals as 'VARIPOWER'. This was the DS-derived super-sensitive steering with just two turns of the steering wheel across the lock, which meant that those not used to it would lurch all over the road. The system gave full assistance at low speeds, and leaned off the assistance at higher speeds. A monitoring of a gearbox shaft speed was used to calibrate the system 'live'. At rest with the engine running, a driver could be 'hands off' the wheel and the car would steer itself straight. Jean-Claude Pajot was a lead technician in creating SM's steering system, and worked with Marcel Le Breton (who had worked for Panhard) on the project. Jean-Claude Janes worked on the SM's complex electrical system and dashboard, and an engineer by the name of M. Joly, working with Chausson, was consulted.

All this is commonplace now, but in 1970 it was sensational. For a glider or fighter pilot, the minimal steering inputs required

SM on the road: Italian, Milano-registered SM gets going during the 2013 European SM Club tour.

133

were normal, while everyone else had to learn how to steer and brake the sensitive SM; but once mastered, rapid, sweeping progress could be made with the greatest of ease. Only the strange 'button'-type brake pedal really needed continuous vigilance, but this was Citroënism in the pure – and after all, you didn't *have* to buy one...

CITROËN, NASA AND MICHELIN – WHEEL TO WHEEL

At this time in the 1970s NASA was at the height of its moon work and had devised a composite fibre moon rover vehicle of ultra-light weight. Somehow the idea of Citroën and Michelin creating a lightweight, composite resin fibre wheel using space technology for the SM, became a funded design project. Opron sketched the wheel, and after many attempts to get the correct carbon-fibre composite 'cure', and expensive durability trials, the option of an 'RR'- (*roues en résine*) branded composite fibre wheel became a reality on a car – the SM. The current cost of purchasing four SM resin wheels approaches 10,000 Euros.

CHASSIS AND SAFETY

Although there were aspects of the DS 'platforme' chassis design in the car, much was improved. The front leading-arm chassis legs were moved further out into the wings to provide better crash protection and impact catchment zones. There was a proper reinforced scuttle and transverse bulkhead. The doors, roof and pillars were integrated into a welded semi-fuselage unit that was adapted to the underframe chassis technique. Deep sills and reinforced A-pillars were close-welded into the punt or platform, but the key thing was that the other body members did not 'float' in structural isolation as they had with the DS. Side-impact protection was built in, and the fuel tank was plastic. The car was also tested to the offset frontal impact standard long before it became a legislative requirement.

In SM, Citroën had learned its lessons – and these were also applied to the super-strong GS, designed at the same time. The SM was incredibly strong, and very few people have ever been seriously injured in an SM.

AERODYNAMICS

Citroën really went to town with the SM body in the new wind tunnel, and every vital aerodynamic parameter was studied and tuned. Just as with the Lefebvre-Voisin cars of the 1920s, the car was tuned to have a controlled centre of aerodynamic pressure. Side-wind stability was studied, and the body sides, the rear panel or blades were specially shaped to ensure consistently good aerodynamic performance.

The SM was subjected to the highest level of intense aerodynamic study and mathematical calculus then seen at Citroën. Particular attention was paid to creating a body shape that did not react in cross winds or yaw angle in airflow. The careful shaping of the front and side profiles meant that the measurements for drag and lift were as stable as possible with minimal divergences. Axle/body-related lift and lift 'curves' on graphs and flow patterns were studied between prototype shapes at vast expense – as they also were for the concurrently developed GS range. SM had excellent longitudinal trim stability, just as a well designed aircraft has; this work gave the car superb directional stability. The windscreen wipers were shielded by the trailing

---

KEY SM PEOPLE

Claude-Alain Serre – senior Citroën project manager
Jacques Né – senior engineering director
Albert Grosseau – Bureau d'Études director
Robert Opron – designer-in-chief
Jean Giret – senior designer, styling details
Henri Dargent – senior designer
Jacques Charreton – senior designer
Bernard Derreumaux – engineer
André Estaque – lead project engineer
Alphonse Forceau – gearbox engineer
Jean-Claude Janes – systems/electrics engineer
Jean-Claude Pajot – steering system engineer
Marcel Le Breton – systems engineer
Paul Mages – lead oleopneumatics engineer
Guy Malleret – Maserati engine department
Guilio Alfieri – Maserati engine design
Hubert Allera – designer
M. Albertus – designer
Michel Harmand – interior designer
Regis Gromik – designer
Henri Lauve de Segur – design consultant
Jean Nicolas – development design engineer
M. Lattay – modeller
M. Truillet – body engineer
M. Delassus – Citroën wind-tunnel manager

edge of the bonnet, and the windscreen itself was sculpted to ease flow off and around it along the car's sides and over its roof. Was this the first flush-glazed glass technique? Special low drag, side door mirrors were created (in contrast to the peculiarly large mirrors on other Citroëns).

At the front, SM saw the first use of a glass-shrouded, full-width leading edge to the bumper and bonnet area – under which lay the headlamps. These were ventilated by ram-air to avoid condensation build-up. Although the car had a long front, it was low and narrow so the Cd.a (Cx.s) cross-sectional drag coefficient was much lower than appearances might suggest. The rear glass hatch flowed smooth air down to a Kamm-type separation ridge, beyond which turbulence was tuned to reduce wake drag and keep the rear lamps clean.

The SM was the first car to be developed in Citroën's new wind tunnel (managed at that time by a M. Delassus), and every aspect of its airflow was honed. Boundary layer smoothness was studied to the point of re-shaping the car's side panels and tumblehome. Detachment or bubbling of the airflow was tuned out. Window seals were refined, brake disc airflow and underside flow all tested. The rear spats gained a massive effect of base-drag reduction. With a test body Cd. (Cx.) of 0.33 and low wind noise with no buffeting, SM was smoothness made near-perfect. Longer cars are easier to make sleek, but there were plenty of other cars longer than 16ft (5m) that were aerodynamic nightmares as opposed to SM's airflowed excellence. Production car drag figures are likely to be *circa* Cd. 0.34–0.36, dependent on specification.

CABIN DESIGN

The crew of the old Bureau d'Études, Messrs Opron, Giret, Dargent, Harman, Allera and the team, created an equally exquisite interior for the SM. Harmand made an early mark on the motifs. The sculpting of the facia or tableau de bord was something entirely new and fresh. The mouldings, trims and appliqué were of the highest quality. The cabin was a circle of sculpture and fine colours. The centre console was finished in an alloy-type effect, and the plastics for the facia had an expensive feel to them. The small ovaloid steering wheel was a design never seen before on any car, and was adjustable in two axes. Its shape was aped by the instrument dials' oval form. Like the later interiors of Paul Bracq, this car was a sculpture show inside, as well as out.

The front seats reclined via an unusual mid-point lumbar region hinge, rather than via the base of the seat back. Seat trims were offered in leather or a rich cloth. In tan leather the laterally pleated seats looked large and stylish, whereas if trimmed in black leather, they and the interior seemed to lose a touch of its *avant garde* feel. Vinyl was also available – strangely.

Citroën built several pre-production 'mules' to test the SM's components, but it only built one fully finalized pre-production tooling car. Strangely it was a dull white and had a nasty black vinyl roof that tended to corrupt the styling graphics. But by late 1969, the SM was shaped, specified, pressed, and primed for lift off. The factory presses were to take a little longer to finish. The SM was announced, but not production-launched at the 40th

SM: AERO DETAILS

Model	Cd. (Cx)	Cd.a (Cx.s/m^2)
SM test body	0.339	0.662
Estimated production*	0.345/0.360	

*USA Spec has a higher drag coefficient due to the lack of nose cone and the fitting of sealed beam lamps in open valance, with resultant higher CD.

The above figures should be noted in comparison to that of the DS (*below*). Note the SM's much lower Cd. and the lower cross-sectional Cd.a

D Spécial	0.382	0.817

Cool green leather was a rare SM seat colour choice.

THE SM: THE WORLD'S FIRST HYPER CAR

LEFT: **Under the bonnet lies what can only be described as an intimidating sight for the uninitiated.**

BELOW: **SM's classic black leather hyper car interior with its shapes that reflected the car's frontal lobe and parabolic styling graphics in side profile.**

The seat design stemmed from work on the M 35 and is pure Citroënism.

Geneva motor show, where it caused a sensation in March 1970; but it would be several months until the sales-ready SM was premiered at the Paris motor show of the same year. Wisely, Citroën would soon have the car on sale in Britain and America in 1971 and 1972 respectively.

SM also boasted an early form of self-regulating windscreen wiper mechanism, where an electric motor had a resistance-sensing capability that measured the amount of electrical current needed to move the wiper arm. A dry windscreen would require more current so the sensor would reduce its power cycle and thus reduce wiper-arm activation as the surface drag of the blade increased.

THE SM LAUNCH

The SM was launched in the south of France. Under Citroën press chief Wolgensinger's lead, André Piquet prepared the press cars with a team of men including Messrs Paul, Touret and Minaud. A range of colours was used for the press launch cars, but Wolgensinger drove a bright orange SM, just as he would with the later CX. In Great Britain, Citroën had a PR man named Graham Rafael who promoted the SM to the media and most notably, placed a pale metallic blue SM with the 1970s television series *The Protectors*, in which the SM's lithe and elegant form was cast alongside that of an equally elegant actress named Nyree Dawn Porter.

Numerous celebrities owned SMs, including James Bond music composer John Barry. French diplomats favoured the SM, including the French Ambassador to Germany with a modified car (see below). SM sales in Germany were very strong, and today over 400 SMs remain in Germany, with 250 actually registered and roadworthy and forming the world' largest nucleus of SMs. In Britain, the SM Club's chairman, Brian Cass, knows of approximately 140 remaining British cars in various states of repair. In France up to 200 remain in use.

MODEL DEVELOPMENT

The first French market SMs of the 1971 model year were priced F300 francs short of FF 50,000 – including air conditioning, although the SM could be bought without such an essential option. Across Europe, the SM was priced within a few units of the local currency of its nearest supercar competitor – DM32,000 would buy an SM or a Mercedes Benz 280. In Britain a Jaguar E-Type was cheaper, but an Aston Martin V8 was also nearly £5,000 – as was the SM. It was a huge sum.

Some very early cars were available in two rare colours – grey and red, with their roofs painted in contrasting colours of grey or black respectively. Thankfully the 1970s fashion for a vinyl-clad roof missed most SMs. Plans for the production of a right-hand-drive SM never materialized, although a handful were converted by private outfits such as Chapel Engineering for the

Australian market where SM had a big following, and in Britain, Middleton Ltd for Citroën Slough – who reputedly financed the conversion of just three right-hand-drive cars by Roy Middleton. The reversed dashboard on these cars was a mirror moulding formed in fibreglass with a specially textured applied surface.

1971: French initial cars, then main launch year worldwide; sole badging and trim description as 'SM' with no other descriptions. Note the rare optional Michelin composite wheels available from 1971 to 1974.

1972: USA launch and sales in Japan: All 2.7 litre cars with manual or auto transmission except US and Pacific specification. Revisions to timing chain on all models. Fuel injection introduced in Europe in autumn 1972 as C114/3 engine variant. 'Injection électronique' badging and changes to 'SM' badges. 2.7-litre carburettor cars March 1970 until November 1972: 7,808 manufactured.

1973: Larger 3.0-litre branded engine for US (and Pacific) markets as C114 /11, with Borg Warner three-speed auto transmission. 3.0-litre engine retains carburettors.

1974: 2.7-litre manual on sale in Europe, and matched by 3.0-litre-engined automatic models for the European model year. Note Ligier factory contract based production late 1974–1975.

1975: Debut of Citroën CX and rationalization of Citroën under Peugeot ownership. Liquidation of Citroën-owned Maserati. The last months of SM production saw no trim changes other than new model-year colours, and a hike in British and European prices. Production-line building of SMs stopped in July prior to the French national holiday month of August, but some cars were hand-completed in September as a final production run.

Due to France's former colonial role, SMs had been exported to Africa, the French Caribbean and to Pacific Oceania – meaning that today, tropical 'barn-find' SMs may be awaiting discovery. The SM was also sold in Japan and Australia.

American Specification SM

After an SM pre-production car was shown at the 1970 New York Auto Show, the New York-based Citroën America introduced the car in late 1971 for early 1972 delivery, at US$11,500. Due to lighting/headlamp legislation, American cars were not allowed to have European-style glazed-in or flush headlamps. For the SM this resulted in the most unfortunate frontal surgery, which removed the six rectangular headlamps and the aerodynamic glazed shroud over them.

As a result, USA-bound SM cars were retro-fitted with four ungainly, sealed-beam round headlamps that sat in scooped out housings each side of a glazed central valance. Latterly the full-width aerodynamic glazing was privately fitted by some owners over the round lamp set-up, but early cars had an unaerodynamic frontal visage that increased the Cd.

The emissions rules of the USA in the 1970s meant that the SM had to have significant alterations. This included an injection pump.

Other American legislative requirements meant that the SM's elegant front and rear wings (fenders) were defaced with

THE SM: THE WORLD'S FIRST HYPER CAR

OPPOSITE PAGE:
Blue and gold duo. Are these the best colours to show off the SM's lines? Some say so, others disagree.

THIS PAGE:
ABOVE: **Whatever your view on colour the passing of an SM leaves its mark on the senses.**

RIGHT: **American specification headlamps were forced on Citroën by legislation, as were side repeater flashers. This smart example rests in architectural contrast.**

add-on side repeater flashers and changes to lamp lens colours. Chrome side-rubbing strips also marked the car's elegantly sculpted side panels. For the USA, the SM began to look fussy. The rise of US 5mph (8km/h) bumper lays required the bumper to remain at a set height – which was impossible for any hydro-pneumatically activated Citroën!

Ultimately, increasing (California-led) emissions rules saw the 2670cc engine being upgraded for the American market in 1973 to 2965cc and 180bp (DIN). Performance went up, but fuel economy remained poor at below 20mpg (14ltr/100km). By this time European specification cars had lost the carburettor set-up and switched to fuel injection for cleaner running, at the cost of some torque graph changes. For 1975, as Citroën ramped up SM prices in Europe, American stocks of SM could be bought for 1974 prices as 'clearance' bargains. It was a sad end to America's affair with the SM.

There is, however, a riddle in the sands of the SM's American existence, because none other than General Motors purchased an SM and tested out both it and its ideas. GM's senior engineering managers all took turns to sample the SM and study its incredibly expensive design and manufacturing reality. So there was an SM on the GM test fleet for years, a car that stunned the American engineers with its front-wheel-drive excellence.

The final commercial production figure was a high 12,290, the pre-production single SM and the single V8 SM prototype giving a reputed hull total of 12,292.

Good as the Alfieri engine was, it gained a reputation for being temperamental later in life at higher mileages – particularly in the area of the primary timing chain and supplementary chains. The sodium-treated valves could develop fatigue. But the worst issue was that the timing chains could not be tensioned, and in time they slackened off. Also the oil pump had to work hard, and the alloy engine head might warp under sustained high temperature use. As SMs aged, these inherent problems began to manifest themselves, and the car's reputation began to suffer. Even today restorers must modify the engine.

Brodie, Lowdell, Daunat, *et al*

The recognized lead SM restoration experts are in Britain, Europe, America and Australia. Andrew Brodie was the British SM guru; now retired, he competes in his privateer rally-spec SM, with Robert Lowdell as co-driver. The now unconnected Brodie Engineering still fettles Citroëns. Barry and Robert Lowdell and their BL Motors are leading British SM specialists and can call on Andrew Brodie as appropriate. Tony Stokoe at Semantics also forged a niche as an SM expert. In the USA, Jerry and Sylvia Hathaway can be found at SM World in Los Angeles, and David Hume at Excelsior Motors in Lexington Kentucky: all are respected SM experts, as are the Australians Peter MacLeod and Warren Hatherley (who makes right-hand-drive SM conversions). In Germany, Dirk Walter runs Oltimer Technik as an SM specialist of expertise. There remains in France the revered SM expert Frédéric Daunat, and Patrick Regembeau in Crèches sur Saone; in the 1970s it was Patrick's father George who became the first SM 'guru'.

George Regembeau re-engineered the V6 engine with revised alloy hardness for the head, revised crankshaft, new main bearings, better quality piston liners and new valves. Crucially he changed the main timing chain design to have better lubrication, and he added automatic tensioners to the secondary drives – these having to run the alternator, air conditioning and the hydropneumatic system.

Regembeau also added louvred slats to the front glazed apron to allow more air under the bonnet. He reduced the peak torque by 1,000rpm, and fitted a six-speed gearbox to his other conversion. Carburettor cars could be tuned up to about 240bhp (DIN); with lower revving, lower temperatures and a longer final drive ratio of 56km/h/1,000rpm, these Regembeau SMs could do 160km/h (100mph) at under 3,000rpm and simply loved driving.

SPECIAL CARS

Jean Nicolas and the SM Short-Bodied 'Mule'

Soon after the SM's launch, the 'old guard' within the Bureau d'Études secreted themselves away in a dusty corner of the oldest part of the building. There, under SM development engineer Jean Nicolas, a strange looking, concave-backed, two-door SM 'sport' was created as a one-off special. With its short back and long SM nose, its styling did not work and this one-off was abandoned; but it did lead directly to the creation of the Kamm-backed Bandama rally car version of the SM – itself using a shortened wheelbase. Monsieur Bertrand Havel also built a part-glassfibre-bodied SM rally car that was 300kg lighter than the standard car.

The Ligier Racing Car

Because of Citroën's connection with Ligier, an SM engine was used in Guy Ligier's own design of racing car. Named after a deceased friend of Ligier's, the JS2 used a tuned version of the Citroën-Maserati V6 in a delicate lightweight glassfibre body. Ultimately the car was not a competition success, but it did lead to Citroën investment in Ligier, and a contract to build what turned out to be the last of the SMs in 1974–75.

An SM V8?

Maserati were working on a new lightweight V8 engine, one developed from enlarging the V6 that Citroën had used. With some modification to the firewall, this slightly longer 4100cc, 4-Weber carburettor V8 'one-off' was installed in an SM. After several months and many kilometers of hard-driven testing, the car was scrapped.

The SM V8 Specification
Engine: 4100cc V8, DOHC per bank, 4 Weber 42DCNF carburettors
Power: 260bhp at 5,500rpm
Transmission: Five-speed manual, front-wheel drive
Top speed: 150mph (240km/h); 0-60mph in 7.8sec

The V8 engine was bought by the Panini family of cheese fame, then sold to Hermann Postert in Germany, and thence to Philip Kantor; he had it fitted into a re-creation of the SM V8 by the renowned SM restorer Frédéric Daunat in 2010.

The Heuliez T-Bar

Citroën had a relationship with the ancient coachbuilding firm of Heuliez, which had begun life making carriages for horse transport. Based in Cerizay in western France, the firm became famous in the 1930s and 1940s for building buses and Art Deco-styled coaches or 'autocars'.

Heuliez was known to Robert Opron and to Citroën not least through his former employer Simca, and the Citroën contracts that Heuliez had in the 1960s. Heuliez had also built the Ami-based, M35 Wankel-engined Citroën prototypes – to very high standards. It was therefore natural that as the SM became the subject of re-styling attention, Heuliez should suggest their own revision to the SM. This took the form of

RIGHT: **The Heuliez SM Espace T-bar roof cars. Two were built, both with electrically actuated roof slats. Sadly the design did not reach production.**

BELOW: **SMs in red are rare, and this one even more so due to its owner's modifications. Some may not approve, but others love it. Note Heuliez SM Espace-type roof slats.**

an open-top SM convertible design that was modern and safe, and likely to pass the increasingly stringent US safety rules for open cars. The T-bar reinforcement idea having originally been conceived in America in the 1950s, it was adapted by Heuliez – and so the T-bar targa-type SM was born.

Heuliez called their SM an 'Espace', and it was designed under the watchful eye of Opron by a young stylist at Heuliez named Yves Dubernard, who would make a mark creating numerous Heuliez specials.

Heuliez took the T-bar targa roof concept and modernized it by replacing the lift-out targa roof panels with motor-driven folding 'feathers' or louvres each side of the central T-bar spine. The conversion was so expert that it did not add to the car's weight. The roof's *feuilles*, or leaves, were like aircraft flaps and were electrically retracted and deployed, and therefore needed no separate panel storage bag that would take up luggage space. It was a brilliant idea, and Opron and Citroën approved. Inside the car, a cockpit-like overhead console with rocker switches added to the aviation theme: Dubernard's design was made reality by an engineer named Pierre Thierry.

Two such SM Espace cars were made; one of these was a glitzy show special with rather too much chrome adornment, a rear window blind and unsubtle purple paint, and was on show at the 1971 Paris Motor Show – here its purple paintwork, tan leather and aquamarine suede interior were set off by a scantily clad, tanned, tall blonde woman draped over the car.

This Belgian SM in blue makes its own statement. Grand designs indeed.

The second T-bar SM was better looking in its standard trim and tan leather interior, and was shown at the 1972 Brussels Motor Show. Reaction was strongly in favour, and Citroën thought about putting the car into limited production. But the world fuel crisis and Citroën's own fiscal situation killed off the chances of the Heuliez SM in late 1972. It was left in its stunning blue paint at the Heuliez factory, and was auctioned off in 2012.

Henri Chapron's Mylord Convertible

Having learned his trade on DS conversions, there was an inevitability to Henri Chapron's outfit taking the knife to the SM. As De Gaulle had ridden in a DS, so President Pompidou would ride in an opened-up SM.

Chapron's 1971 open-top SM was called 'Mylord', and featured massive side and floor reinforcements to replace the torsional rigidity lost from removing the roof. An elegant folding convertible hood was engineered. The bodies were constructed by Citroën's contractor Chausson, with the engines fitted by Citroën in a rather tortuous transport process. The cars were somewhat defaced by typically excess Chapron chromework additions, notably wheel-arch embellishers that were even stuck to the rear spats. Composite wheels were also part of the specification. Seven such cars were constructed, and today are regarded by some *aficionados* as the holy grail of SM enthusiasm.

Chapron would also build the two presidential four-door SM state carriages or landaulettes, which featured an extended wheelbase, a folding rear roof, and a transverse brace across the top of the retained B-pillars. President Georges Pompidou made full use of these dark grey, tan leather-trimmed beasts, the French flag flying proudly upon the cars' prow.

In late 1972 the controversial four-door Chapron SM named 'Opera' appeared. This was an SM based on an extended wheelbase but with the roof left in place, and steel C-pillars grafted on to create a three-box, booted shape that used the bootlid from the Mylord. It was not exactly elegant, but had a certain style; eight were made and sold.

Chausson's Scale Model

Chausson – constructors of the Chapron cars – would also build a four-door SM design study in model form for Citroën. Opron and the design team were reputedly not so keen on the styling of the Chapron four-door cars, and gave thought to creating their own in-house four-door SM. Citroën funded the creation of a large-scale model from Chausson, featuring

THE SM: THE WORLD'S FIRST HYPER CAR

ABOVE: **The very rare Chapron Mylord convertible seen in all its glory.**

RIGHT: **One of seven Chausson–Chapron-built Mylord cars from the 1971 launch. It is still in use.**

an elegant and somewhat Saabesque concave rear deck styling aspect. The car was still-born, yet aspects of it may have been adopted by Maserati for its parallel development of the hydro-pneumatic Quattroporte Mk II.

Would a Citroën-produced SM four-door have worked? Perhaps not, as the original coupé was so pure and the four-door, even with Opron styling, seemed an uncertain animal.

Frua-bodied SM

Pietro Frua was an Italian stylist with a deft and light hand who produced a series of beautiful car-body designs for major Italian manufacturers, and Frua-bodied cars on non-Italian cars. He had penned the Bosseart DS two-door with great success. Using the 1971 SM as a base, Frua created his own delicate version of the SM's motifs. The lines were low but more angular,

THE SM: THE WORLD'S FIRST HYPER CAR

Comparing the SM and SM Opera saloon reveals the differences. Opera used the Mylord-style bootlid pressing.

with touches of Lamborghini or later De Tomaso elements, and an interesting C-pillar blade buttress defined the styling. Only the single prototype was constructed upon SM underpinnings, yet in it perhaps we saw the smaller, sportier thoughts that some had originally had for SM.

Gendarmerie Cars

Were these police car engines really tuned to 201bhp (DIN), as later seen in the Maserati V6 used in the Merak and Quattroporte? Many say they were. The five police-spec SMs built used steel wheels and had minor interior modifications. Sensibly the French police avoided fitting un-aerodynamic square rooftop lamps to their cars, and just had a small, round blue lamp above the windscreen; only the addition of a tall VHF radio aerial marred the car's appearance. It must have been tough having to drive a Citroën Maserati at 140mph (224km/h) on the autoroute every day and get paid for doing it.

The SM Pick-up or Ute

Amongst the world's leading SM experts and restorers are Jerry and Sylvia Hathaway, who run SM World, in Los Angeles. They have created a Bonneville competing SM, and the famous SM pick-up or ute. With a rebuilt and tuned version of the Maserati V6 engine equipped with twin turbos, a terminal velocity of 202mph (323km/h) has been achieved.

Diplomatic Cars

Russian President Leonid Brezhnev took a shine to the SM, and ordered one in light metallic green, as seen in the photograph of the car as recently restored by Jan Paul Klijntun (p.145). Similarly impressed was the former French Cabinet Minister Jean Sauvagnargues, French Ambassador to Germany in 1971: he ordered a specially equipped SM where the front passenger seat was removed, and in its place a fold-up table and television mounted in the front footwell, so the Ambassador could work from the rear seat. The car, built by Citroën and finished in black, is now being restored by German SM expert Dirk Walter, who owns nine SMs at his Old Timer Technik SM facility. At least one SM was used by French diplomats in Asia and today lies rusting in a back street garage in Bangkok; another is under restoration in Bali by Peter van der Hoek Ostende.

RALLY AND RACE – THE SM GOES OFF PISTE

With Jacques Né and Marlene Cotton within Citroën, both keen competition drivers and advocates of rallying, it was no surprise that a car as big as the SM should receive the budget to be modified for rally use. As early as 1971 the SM rally-spec car saw action in the Morocco rally, with two of the three SMs entered taking first and third places – first outing, first victory. The SMs were driven by Bjorn Waldegard/Fergus Sayer in Group 2, and Jean Deschaseaux/Jean Plassard, and Rauno

THE SM: THE WORLD'S FIRST HYPER CAR

LEFT: **President Brezhnev's SM** seen in 2013 after restoration by its Dutch owner. The glazed frontal aspect is a unique design hallmark.

BELOW: **SMs say it all.** No other car ever had a tail like this, not even a Ferrari.

145

Aaltonen in Group 1, respectively. A third car was entered, driven by Jean Vinatier and Pierre Thimonier, but withdrew with gearbox problems.

The rally SM was fitted with a modified exhaust that added a handful of bhp. The interior was stripped of its luxury fittings and a heavy-duty roll-cage added. The car was a Group 4 rally device that was lighter than the production model. For the Monte Carlo Rally of 1972 an SM was entered in the rally series. The car also competed again in the Morocco Rally of the same year, crewed by Björn Waldegaard and Fergus Sager, but did not win – although a DS driven by Robert Netret did. A support or supplementary SM entry is also cited in the records for this rally.

Citroën added a heavy-duty full cabin roll-cage frame inside the 'factory' rally SM, but some SMs were rallied without the addition of roll cages. Citroën also included some seam welding, and replaced four of the six headlamps under the frontal glazed shroud with circular *Cibie* rally lamps. The glazing itself was protected by wire mesh cladding to prevent stone damage. Finished in an unusual pale blue as opposed to French racing blue, the car latterly received a modified bonnet to incorporate an engine-bay vent and increased clearances. Final weight of the rally-spec SM rose from a standard production trim weight of 3,200lb (1,450kg) to 3,700lb (1,680kg).

1973 was the last factory-supported SM rally season featuring the re-styled 'breadvan' Kamm-back short-wheelbase SM with a 250bhp tuned engine and lightweight glass-fibre panelled body, with a total car weight of 2,760lb (1,250kg), a project created by Jean Nicholas. The car finished third overall and won its class in the 1972 TAP Portugal Rally. In the Bandama Rally this SM finished fifth. Jacques Né and Monsieur Cotton played a major role in creating these special SM-series cars.

The well known competition driver Guy Verrier wanted to enter an SM in the 1972 Le Mans, but Citroën were concerned about the new car's image and any reliability issues that might result from a twenty-four-hour exposure, not least because in the 1971 24 hours Spa Francochamps production car class, two SMs had entered, driven by Lucien Bianchi and Roland de Jambline respectively, and suffered engine failure.

But according to the Automobile Club de l'Ouest, one SM, driven by Guy Verrier, was entered in the 1972 Le Mans event. A second SM was also cited as a private entry, though its status is not clear. The Club's records show that the Verrier car had the bored-out 2.9-litre Ligier-tuned engine and weighed 154lb (70kg) less than a production SM.

For the 1972 Spa Francorchamps, one SM was entered by a J. Bigrat. A further entry that is reputed to have been withdrawn or retired was an SM driven by R. van der Schrieck with J. Hendrickx.

Records also indicate that an SM was entered in the 1974 Spa Francorchamps by Ligier with G. Chausseuil and F. Magault as the crew, but the car retired due to an accident.

A standard specification SM is said to have competed in the 1972 Tour de France Auto driven by G. Verrier and M. Martin. An SM was entered in the 1972 Monte Carlo Rally in Class One, driven by René Trautman and Jean-Pierre Hanrioud.

André Costa was a famous French motoring magazine editor who was able to secure from Citroën and Jacques Wolgensinger loan cars for various purposes. One of these ideas was to drive an SM (as a private entry) from Paris, across the Sahara Desert to Chad and back – over 16,000 miles (10,000km) in a rally or raid as the 1972 'Paris au Lac Tchad'. The pale blue SM, named 'Coralie', was entirely standard apart from a sump guard, and despite the extreme temperatures did not suffer any of the mechanical troubles later associated with the SM. Costa's co-driver was a M. Le Prince.

In the 1972 Rallye du Bandama, the two 'breadvan' short-chassis SMs with composite wheels finished fifth and sixth, driven by Verier/Umbricht and Neyert/Terramorsi respectively.

The SM 'Breadvan' or short-body rally spec car.

SM Privateers

How many people know of the SM campaigned in national class rallying in Australia? There, alongside rally car CX, GS (including a CX-engined GS) there were private owners who rallied the SM. The best known of these was Joe Caudo, whose SM saw action on both sides of the Australian divide. Jean-Pierre Bugnot also campaigned the SM in France.

Another SM privateer was the British Mike Beckwith, who in 1972, with support from the Eurocars London dealership, entered a white SM registered JYT 250K at Snetterton racing circuit in a Castrol production saloon car class.[13] Beckwith's SM (built in November 1971) also appeared at Thruxton, at Mallory Park and at Brands Hatch. It featured a roll-cage and revised rear exhaust box. Ray Hutton, *Autocar* editor, co-drove an SM during the Avon Tour of Britain in 1973. More recently Thierry Quignard has raced a private SM in the French National Historic series, and Andrew Brodie and Robert Lowdell have co-driven Brodie's rally-spec SM as privateers.

SM PERSPECTIVE

Plans for a four-door V8 SM, and versions with a more economical engine, as well as a rotary engine, came to nothing. Yet in the XM and the C6 and beyond, the legacy of SM (and its four-door prototypes) is very obvious. Was SM killed solely by the 1970s economic crisis? Perhaps, but we might also consider Citroën's own failings, and some of the development issues of the SM, as contributory factors.

Today over 1,500 SMs remain in use in Europe alone, according to figures from the SM Club of Europe. Others reside in Australia, America, and even Bangkok and Bali.

The car's design, inside as well as out, has to rank as one of the last century's greatest art works, and the blend of style, skills and sheer Franco-Italianate engineering excellence has to rate as one of the highlights of car design and driving. This was a unique hyper-car that ticked all the boxes, and was truly the result of unblinkered thinking – and unless you have driven one, you cannot know how close to a different form of travel an SM was, or is.

SPECIFICATIONS SM 1971 MODEL

Body

Two-door shell with glazed rear boot area in semi-monocoque unit frame, blended with reinforced mono-body cabin cell, mounted on to sub-punt platform with chassis-type engine bearers and load bearers/impact beams. Over-large side sills with anti-intrusion members; plastic fuel tank mounted over rear axle

Highly advanced wind tunnel-tuned aerodynamic body with flush glazing and pressure/lift and vortex-tuning device. Under-bonnet/brake-duct airflow control. Cd. 0.339

Engine

Type	Maserati-type C114-1 6 cylinders, V engine set at 90 degrees
Construction	Alloy bloc-engine
	Alloy head with hemispherical chambers
	2 overhead valves per cylinder positioned at 90 degrees; four chain-driven overhead camshafts
	Forged iron crankshaft with four bearings. Length: 402mm
Bore	87mm
Stroke	75mm
Capacity	2670cc
Compression ratio	9.1.00 94 Octane minimum
Power	170hp DIN or 125Kw at 5,550rev/min
Torque	174lb/sq ft, 23.5m/kg/230.5m/n (DIN) at 4,000rpm

NOTES:

Chain-driven relief or 'jack shaft' runs along V centreline, driving overhead camshafts. Jackshaft-driven from crank, with camshafts driven by supplementary chain drive from jackshaft. Mechanism must be inspected/modified to 'Brodie' spec.

2.7-litre Bosch fuel injection engine and a 3.0 litre engine latterly offered.

Dimensions:

Length	193in (4,890mm)
Width	72in (1,836mm)
Height	52in (1,324mm)
Wheelbase	116in (2,950mm)
Weight	3,197lb (1,450kg)

SM on ice – a different SM memory.

SM – THE AUTHOR'S PERSONAL EXPERIENCE

I first saw an SM in 1975 and was a boy rendered speechless, gawping at its blue-painted elegance and tan-leathered capsule. For me, the SM was the design climax of several decades, the first hyper-car. The SM was unlike anything else, ever. In its overall package it was far more advanced than even the DS, not least as the SM had the engine specification that the DS had lost out on – even if it was not a Citroën engine.

The body design is just so accomplished, so pure, so utterly brilliant that I often simply sit and stare, watching the way the light falls upon the curves, tensions, scaling and emotion of this great sculptural artwork. The men who created this car with Robert Opron – outside and inside – surely all deserve the highest awards.

My favourite journey in the SM that was briefly under my tenure, was heading south from St Malo with a Breton brunette named Amandine. We drove off Brittany Ferries' wonderful Pont Aven flagship, and stormed down a route nationale to Rennes, then took the by-ways to Guer through the remains of a great forest that is packed with remnants of Arthurian legend. A gendarme smiled as we shot past at high speed, waving us on. The SM simply traversed the tarmac, dismissing all behind: some drivers waved, and we responded with flashing headlamps, a blast on the twin-toned horn and a wave from behind the tinted glass amid the richness of brown leather.

The SM, Amandine and I rocketed further south. We parked the SM in the square at Guer and sat in a café, watching the French young and old, who gathered to stare at their forgotten finest. Then it was the fast, open, beautifully cambered bends of the road to Malestroit. There, in the medieval square we left the SM settling down on its hydro-pneumatics as the hot engine ticked loudly and a shimmer of heat vented from the chevron-shaped flue on the bonnet. As we lunched outside, beside SM's incredible elegance, the light dancing upon its bronzed flanks, did we hear Raymond Blanc muttering 'Oh, là là!'? We think we did.

My memories of that day in Brittany will live long, recalling how the car cleaved through its element like a racing yacht riding the sea. There was that bark from the Maserati engine, and the swoosh of Citroën-sculpted aeromancy across its hull; soon I forgot all my fantasies about other cars, for the SM trounced them all with its mental, emotional and physical exoticism. The exquisite sensitivity of the steering, and the need to place the car perfectly and to concentrate on creating the desired effect, was utterly compelling. On blue days, the SM offered the drive of your life, sweeping along in a detached yet involved moment.

Driving a 'proper' (pre-electric steering) two-wheel-drive Porsche 911 (993 series) through the twisting roads of eastern Germany's forests has always been one of my seminal, visceral motoring experiences, but driving an SM cross-country on French main roads was beyond comparison: not even driving a Ferrari 365 Daytona or a Maserati Khamsin in the hills of the Var gave me what the SM offered.

The SM has to be one of the greatest products man has ever created for himself. A non-perfect icon, an amazing amalgamation of intellect and knowledge: a car and yet something else – and one that captivates and endures to this day.

The SM has to be the ultimate French design couture achievement, a 'Concorde' moment. I often wonder if any Air France Concorde pilots are SM owners. Imagine for a moment if you will, amid some kind of narcissistic, ego-driven late 1970s fantasy, descending from the narrow confines of Concorde's flight deck, removing your gold-braided captain's epaullettes, walking to your SM, throwing your flight bag on the passenger seat, lighting a cigar and speeding home to whatever awaited…

If I am to die in car, let it be at 140mph in an SM in France on a blue afternoon as the pine trees zoom past and the cicadas smile at the SM bolide as it erupts off the D road and enters the woods and disintegrates, for then, I won't mind if the chevrons of Citroën pierce my heart.

CHAPTER NINE

GS

GENIUS

GS | *GENIUS*

IF ANY CAR in the modern era captures the combination of the elements of Citroën, it must be the GS: it is the jewel in the crown of a more modern Citroënism. For here in this 1970s car was true futurism, an alchemy of themes, legacies and design motifs that came together in a piece of engineering that rivalled anything from the Citroën past. As the modified GSA, the GS even lived on into a new, reincarnated 1980s existence. Yet today, only a select band of GS enthusiasts have realized just how important the achievement of the GS and GSA was. They may have suffered from rust, but it is time they were accepted as truly classic Citroëns by a wider audience.

GS was designed by the men who gave us the SM and the M 35, and these three models certainly had more development money spent on them than many other Citroëns. Everything about the GS was entirely new,:

- Advanced aerodynamics with low drag and low cross-sectional drag; use of tuned polar, pressure and lift behaviours across the car to create stable performance parameters; first use in the mass market of an integrated front spoiler under the leading edge of the car
- Smooth airflow off the rear end, with Kamm-type separation ridge beyond the base of the rear windscreen
- Low centre of gravity via the use of flat or 'boxer' engine design, in-board brakes, and attention to c.g. design details
- Integrated oleopneumatic suspension with double wishbones and stiff subframes, giving class-leading handling and ride combination
- Economical engines that achieve high speed from low bhp and low drag
- Four-wheel, powered disc brakes
- Advanced body hull design with efficient and strong structure and class-leading crash-test performances in frontal and side impacts

We should remember that when Citroën was designing the GS, Ford, Opel, Austin, Morris and others were churning out dinosaurs of cars whose roots lay firmly in the 1950s era of antediluvian car design – often with rear-wheel drive, leaf springs, live axles, wheezing cast-iron 'square' engines, unaerodynamic styling and minimally padded cabins, and much flatter roofed: a square-rigged 'basic' car design. These cars appealed to a mainstream mindset in that they were developments of existing practices, but soon to be wrapped in the faux modernity of 1970s styling.

Renault might have been about to launch the hatchback Renault 16, but even that car was built and trimmed up in the old-fashioned, chrome-laden, baroque manner. BMC/BL aped the Renault with the Austin Maxi – a rare bright light of design potential, yet one whose final form and fittings were still wrapped in the brown paper austerity thinking of a typically British myopia. Indeed, the British had had their chance to seize a golden future of car design through the amazing and advanced aero-weapon Pininfarina 'Aerodinamica' concept cars that the Italian carrozzeria offered the British car leviathan.

Europe's auto makers slumbered on in their torpor of conceit – their expressions of so-called modernity masking a malaise of the mundane. Car buyers were offered what car manufacturers thought they could least get away with, and this was why so many of the cars of the 1970s were little more than window dressing for an industry that did almost nothing to advance safety, aerodynamics or true design integrity– until it *had* to be dragged into the reality of new thinking.

Such blinkers and such cynicism did not, however, apply to the creators of the GS at Citroën.

GS – GENUINE GENIUS

Even in the 1980s, when Citroën's years of aerodynamic excellence were suddenly usurped by the Ford marketing machine and the paradox of the slippery yet agriculturally engineered Ford Sierra, advance was slow. Before then, before the 1980s, we can perhaps single out two cars that were not just 'designed', they were created and conceived by bold and clever thinking, yet they were not risky or mad, they were simply the *real* state-of-the art of the possible – if a car maker dared to show you what was really in their mind, what really lay hidden behind the wire fences of design centres.

These two shining lights of design were the Citroën GS and the Alfa Romeo AlfaSud. Both had an advanced body shape, a flat-four engine, superb handling, a chopped Kamm-type tail, and a cabin that had been thought about, rather than just thrown together using existing parts-bin thinking. Argument has long raged over which car was the most advanced, which of this pair marked a 1970s milestone that opened the doors of perception for mainstream car buyers.

The Rudolf Hruska-engineered, Guigario-influenced Alfasud may have had more sporting handling, but it was in its suspension and its fittings that it was more conventional than the GS's avant-garde psychology. Therefore it was the GS, with its in-board brakes, hydro-pneumatic suspension, low c.g, sleeker bodywork and smoother detailing, that was the more advanced car in terms not just of its total design package, but also in its overall driving experience. And if the GS slowly rusted, the Alfasud simply flaked away in months.

In the GS, Citroën produced a real driver's car, yet one that cosseted its passengers. Its aerodynamics were so exquisite that

The essential correctness of the GS body design in all its scaling is clear in this shot of the low-drag car on the move. The lobed front and Kamm-tail define good aerodynamics.

it offered speed advantages, significant fuel savings, a quiet cabin, and good cross-wind characteristics. The efficient horizontally-opposed engine delivered a good torque curve, decent compression and a sound to remember. The GS was tuned to deliver fast cruising and deft nimbleness on country roads.

The only real issue was the small engine size forced upon the early GS range by French fiscal engine-capacity tax rules, and the legacy of the 'Système Chevaux'. Citroën attended to the matter with a larger engine that still retained the air-cooled and sweet-revving nature of the flat-four engine, an engine with an oddly sporting character that might have been expected of a Saab, perhaps?

Inspiration

But for the want of some proper rust-proofing and better build quality, the GS could have further shaken the world of mid-market car buying and owning. As it was, however, a reputation for rust latterly began to dent the GS's halo. Despite this, it sold very well: it gave 'normal' car buyers something almost revolutionary, a completely new revelation of what a mid-range car could be.

So the GS rode like a limousine, cleaved the air like an aircraft, and had that great sense of occasion that marks successful cars. The cabin was comfortable, and its fittings far more modern and safety padded than those in rival cars. The GS had thick, reinforced doors with great depth to absorb side impact, and in the 30mph (50km/h) head-on crash test it performed well, with minimal roof, A-pillar and sill deformation. Even in the offset frontal crash test – at the time unlegislated – the GS performed well.

The 1970s motoring press loved the GS, and even today top motoring writers wax lyrical about its attributes. After winning 'Car of the Year', the GS also took the *Style Auto* car design award. More recently a huge GS/GSA fanaticism lurks, bubbling away with sheer enthusiasm for what must be one of the most 'complete' organic and homogeneous pieces of industrial design engineering. Keeping the GS/GSA family on the road is the task of several independent Citroën specialists, and the British company, Chevronics, run by Rob Moss, is well known for its GS enthusiasm.

Any reader in any doubt about the GS's legacy to the car industry and the car buyer need look no further than the Ford Focus of the late 1990s. For the Focus seemed to be a re-born GS/GSA. In an incredible paradox, Ford took the essential elements not just of GS styling and design, but also its total consumer package, and turned these themes into a properly sorted Ford. With its Kamm tail, curving roof, trapeziodal front and rear lamp cluster shapes and other motifs, the stance of the cabin turret and rear side window designs, not to mention its dashboard, the Focus Mk1 was seemingly an unintended part-pastiche on the GS, and deservedly a highly successful one.

GENESIS OF THE GS

Project C

The DS spanned more than one market sector by being developed into a range of engine and trim options, from basic ID to Pallas 2.3 injection. But the bodyshell remained the same – big. In Citroën's stable there was the 2CV, and then the delightfully bizarre Ami with its Bertoni sculpting, reverse-raked rear windscreen, and the embellished yet still agricultural fixtures and fittings. But Citroën had a huge gap in its model range, and it was a gap that was costing it sales and therefore money. Renault would soon step in to seize the opportunity with a car that boasted some aspects of advanced design, yet was still thoroughly traditional in its underpinnings – the Renault 16.

But before Renault tried to steal the show, Citroën developed in 1960 what some frame as a 'super-Ami' in the form of the Project C or C60. This was a car that seemed to blend the front of the DS with the back of the Ami 6 in what may have been Citroën's (and Bertoni's) most anthropomorphic styling yet seen. Was it a halibut or a pumped-up sole? A scarab beetle or a squashed tortoise? Whichever, with a reverse-angled rear windscreen and smoothed bodywork, the prototype was oddly attractive and far sleeker than the chrome-laden galleons that comprised the competition from other car makers.

Two engine options were suggested – 1100cc and 1400cc. Hydro-pneumatic suspension was also an expense deemed possible.

But due to protracted development and rising costs, and some unease that the car was not 'mainstream' enough in a wide market sector, Project C was cancelled. By late 1963 this led Citroën straight into Project F, and a controversy unresolved to this day.

Project F

Again Citroën conceived a mid-range family car that could be offered with various engines and trims to appeal across its sector. The idea was that as Citroën had spent money investigating the Wankel-cycle engine, a top-of-the-range variant would have a Wankel engine, powered hydro-pneumatic suspension brakes, gears and steering, and be luxurious. A lesser 'family' version would use an air-cooled 1100cc engine of flat or 'boxer' design.

The styling was less Bertoni and more modern, with early contribution from the recently employed Robert Opron in that it was smooth but less organic, less animalistic and more contemporary, with the trend in car styling that the mid-to-late 1960s would signal for the 1970s. Although smoothly panelled, the car had a more upright stance and clear indications of a capacious, hatchback-type rear end. Of note, four square headlamps were cited behind a glass shroud, as would later be seen on the exquisite SM.

The advanced prototype Project F – or in France, *Projet F* – was built, and full toolings and costings for the body drawn up. The car had the look of contemporary success, and was the most angular Citroën yet. It had the essence of a family hold-all and a mid-range business car for middle-class professionals.

Despite massive financial investment, the car was abandoned for two principal reasons: firstly, despite the development of the M 35 Wankel-powered Citroën Ami derivative, problems and costs with the Wankel power plant were growing. And secondly, Renault suddenly revealed its early plans for the Renault 16, which looked to present a major problem because the similarity between the Renault 16 and Citroën's Project F was astounding. The Renault had the same proportions and stance, the rear hatchback seemed near-identical, even the new tooling process for the roof that Citroën claimed was theirs had appeared – or so it was all alleged.

The rare stepping-stone concept design from Ami to GS dimensions. It is elegant, but perhaps not modern enough for the task – which the GS certainly was.

GS: GENIUS

Had industrial espionage been at work? Were secret early details of the Citroën leaked? Or did Renault reach its own interpretation of the future on its own merits? The answer lies buried in the past, but the combination of the engine issues and the launch of the Renault 16 led Citroën to waste more money in abandoning Project F and starting the third search for a mid-range car concept: this time it would lead to the GS of late 1970.

Continuing Development for the GS

From 1967 to 1969, Citroën developed the GS, and it would later have a range of engines from 1000cc + to 1200cc +, and a basic-to-luxury trim range, these features matching the original 1960s Project C idea. Amazingly the hatchback disappeared for the GS – a reaction to the Renault 16 perhaps, although the GS-derived GSA did have a hatchback grafted into the existing GS-sourced bodyshell.

Citroën developed its new series of flat horizontally opposed engines for the new G-series, and also spent large amounts of money in the wind tunnel creating a small yet highly aerodynamic shape that gave significant fuel savings.

With its plunging, sculpted form, 'three-light' triangulated rear side windows, chopped Kamm-type tail and trapezoidal headlamps, GS presented a strong design graphic and new 1970s 'face' for Citroën's corporate branding. Such themes would look even sleeker in the 1974 CX model, a stretched, more lithe iteration of Opron's GS themology.

By 1971, the Opron-styled, ultra-sleek GS had been voted Car of the Year and astounded other manufacturers with its blend of style, aerodynamics, handling and cabin design – not

ABOVE: **A GS and its big brother CX show off their elegant and sculptural designs. Both possess total design integrity and perfection of form.**

RIGHT: **Classic GS design shown off by this quintessential 1970s orange ténéré (paint code AC329) hued GS estate. The car also has the rare orange interior and was exhibited in the GS 40th anniversary event at the museum at Thenay, France. The expensively shaped and glazed headlamps were a signature design motif later refined on the CX.**

GS: GENIUS

to mention its 'Rolls-Royce' ride quality, as the British called it. The GS had very rigid axle mounting points via subframes and a stiff hull, allied to its unique suspension these factors gave the car great stability and handling consistency.

With increases in power and a newly designed four-speed gearbox, the mid-1970s GS could hit 100mph (160km/h) on just over 50bhp – though the engine had to be revved hard and the gearbox stoked to extract such performance. Citroën's three-speed C-Matic semi-automatic transmission was available as an alternative to the manual gearbox, but ran at high revs, causing some increase in cabin heat and noise (poor ventilation and heating being a GS issue caused by its sleek aerodynamics), and a decline in mpg.

The rear end design of the **GS** was carried over to the **GSA** estate. Seen here in original **GS** estate variant, the expensive-to-manufacture rear windscreen with its roll-top curvature performs a vital aerodynamic 'air-wiper' function without resorting to a more conventional kamm-type ridge.

AERODYNAMIC ARGUMENT

It has often been argued that the Citroën CX and GS 'copied', or were greatly influenced by, the Pininfarina 'Aerodinamica' Berlina design prototypes originally created for British Motor Corporation (BMC) – latterly British Leyland. While it would be brave to deny that there is no similarity between the CX, GS and these one-off design specials from Pininfarina, a balanced

The **GS** boasted interior design that was a big improvement on the vinyl and tinplate trappings of late 1960s cars.

The seats' springing was tuned to the suspension rates: weird, but true. Fitting a non-standard seat ruins the seat/ride comfort interaction.

GS MEN

Alain Roche – project manager
Robert Opron – lead body design
Henri Dargent – body design details
Jean Giret – body design
Jacques Charreton – body design
Paul Mages – suspension design
André de Bladis – chief engineer/engine designer
Pierre Cordier – engine design
M. Dupin – engine design
M. Hondet – engine design
M. Albertus – designer
Michel Harmand – interior designer
M. Maillou – design details
M. Nozati – design details
Regis Gromik – design details
M. Quinn – design details
M. Delassus – Citroën wind-tunnel manager

analysis clearly reveals significant differences in the shaping, sculpting, dimensions and major styling details (such as the front and rear panels) of the Citroën cars in comparison to the Pininfarina cars. Indeed, one might as well argue that if the Citroën shapes are so-called 'copies', then what about the Lancia Gamma, Rover SD1, and the AlfaSud? For these cars also contained some very similar styling elements to the two Pininfarina BMC Aerodinamica cars.

Back in 1964, the British were designing the excellently engineered, Issigonis-penned Austin 1800 that was a simple expansion of the Mini philosophy. However, Austin was a long-standing Pininfarina client, and Sergio Pininfarina was keen to make his mark upon his father's legacy. Pininfarina was exploring the art of aerodynamics, and via its rising star of Leonardo Fioravanti as a young stylist, Italian minds were capable of lateral and disruptive thinking which was likely to shock the closed world of BMC's corporate conceit and its certainties. Fioravanti would go on to lead Pininfarina design, and became a well known name in car design.

Also credited with a role, notably in the smaller of the two Aerodinamica shapes, was a young Paolo Martin who joined Pininfarina in 1968 from Bertone, and went on to become a significant name in design. Martin shaped the elegant little Peugeot 104 that became, by default, the Citroën LN and the basis of the Visa.

But BMC rejected the 'exotic' Italian styling – it was clearly too much for those blinkered minds trained in the arrogance of the British motor industry and all that involved. Pininfarina separated itself from the BMC/BL axis as fast as was possible, and who could blame them.

As 1969 turned into the 1970s, Pininfarina's second, smaller Aerodinamica concept, the Austin 1100-based car, wowed those in the closed world of the car industry. But was the newly launched Citroën GS a so-called 'copy'? Was the 1971 AlfaSud similarly accused? In both cases the answer has to be a qualified 'no' – but surely laced with the caveat that the GS did agree with some of the Pininfarina 1100s themes.

Citroën have always denied that they saw or 'copied ' the Italian design study, and the manner in which Robert Opron, Jean Giret, Jacques Charreton, Michel Harmand and the Citroën styling team scaled and sculpted the GS (and the later CX) shows distinct and very clear differences in panel shapes, window graphics and detailing. Only perhaps around the dimensions and angles of the rear side doors and windows at the C-pillar zone is a likeness between the GS and the Pininfarina car more obvious. Certainly the rear end of the GS – its sloping roof and tail – *are* differently shaped to the Pininfarina design concept, lacking channels and troughs either side of the rear windscreen. The frontal motifs also differed (Rover's SD1 was far closer to the Aerodinamica cars in its design cues).

The Citroën archives show a DS revision styling model being worked on by Opron and Michel Harmand. In this, Opron was adding a sleek tail and Kamm-back to the DS, and the rear side windows, roof, and tail design for this DS revision categorically signal the rear end shapes Opron used in the GS and CX. This revised tail for the DS was the subject of a drawing as early as 1967 by Michel Harmand, and it may have been drawn and built *before* the Pininfarina Aerodinamica was publicly shown. It was also a GS precursor, and might be cited as evidence that Citroën reached the GS/CX rear-end design at its own hand. Jean Giret was also styling a car that was a GS precursor, and this also featured the shaping and detailing that were close to the later Citroën and Pininfarina shapes.

Flaminio Bertoni's archives also clearly depict a small model of a GS-like car (with hints of Alfa Sud) that was intended as a 2CV replacement. This sleek car had strong shades of the Pininfarina Aerodinamica shapes, yet predated them by many years. So did such a design exist within Citroën *before* the Italian output that has for so long been claimed to have inspired the GS?

It is also true to observe that the GS in its proportions and in its rear cabin architecture closely mimicked the abandoned, earlier 1960s styling models of Citroën's Project F – the car that Renault's subsequent 16 model also mirrored (with claims of industrial espionage). So perhaps the GS's graphics were achieved separately, and were quite independent from

155

the Pininfarina concepts? Opron would also work on a large fastbacked saloon shape for Citroën as 'Project L' – the antecedent to the CX.

Similarly, a glance at the Opron and Heuliez-styled Ami-based M35 will clearly reveal the triangulated rear side window design and sloping rear roof line that were so closely aped by the GS – and the M35 was shaped independently.

Decades later, it is impossible to find a definitive answer from those involved, and there are claims and counter claims, but the evidence is that Citroën did indeed 'do its own thing' and create the GS look early on, on its own. Whatever the opinions and the truths, the fact is that the GS achieved something perhaps even more important than the easier-to-style larger dimensions of the CX: the GS made a smaller car look sleek, smooth and balanced, and created the first real mass-production, four-door, small coupé style in a saloon body of very low aerodynamic drag.

There was a further riddle to the story, for FIAT and Citroën were partners, and even after the relationship had been dissolved, were jointly developing a large flagship saloon car with hydro-pneumatics. It was stillborn, but its remains surfaced as the Lancia Gamma saloon – itself another 'take' on the Pininfarina Aerodinamica ideas.

GS/GSA DRAG FIGURES

In the GS/GSA and CX, Citroën built on its DS knowledge. For the GS, the key aerodynamic areas to be tuned would deal with the core factors in road vehicle aerodynamics as form or body drag, induced drag from the body shape, interference drag, and internal flow drag. These were the key elements to creating a slippery and stable car in aerodynamic terms.

As with all hydro-pneumatic Citroëns, the GS/GSA self-levelling capability ensured consistent angles of attack in the horizontal axis, and minimal pitch-related airflow changes – another unique advantage of the constant level suspension design. In the 1970s a German car magazine questioned the veracity of Citroën's claims for the GS's aerodynamics, as German 'experts' did not believe such a low Cd. – an incredible 0.318 – could be achieved in such a short car. Citroën volunteered all its aerodynamics test data, and the magazine had to withdraw its claim, with some embarrassment.

The drag of the Citroën GSA X3 was even lower than the GSA X1, being reduced by the addition of an under-bumper, forward-angled spoiler which changed flow and pressure under the car, and also of a sharp, moulded, plastic rear lip ridge-spoiler beneath the rear window, which reduced drag by modifying the critical separation point and the consequent lift characteristics, and through specifying new low-drag door mirrors. The new front spoiler improved the Cd.a by 2.7 per cent, and the new razor-edged device at the rear improved the Cd. by 7.4 per cent. Such improvements lowered the GSA's coefficient of drag to the order of 10 per cent, and reduced petrol consumption by 7.5 per cent at 75mph (120km/h).

The Cd. figures for the 1970s GS and 1980s GSA are stunning, because for a small and short-length family production car to achieve such figures at this time was a major achievement in car design. But it is worth noting that if another, less aerodynamically revered car company than Citroën had produced a Cd. such as the GS's in a small car at that time, motoring writers would have hailed the figure as a massive advance –

TYPICAL CITROËN DRAG COEFFICIENTS 1950s TO 1980s

Note that the Cd. as expressed in French becomes Cx. Therefore the Cd.a becomes the Cx.s as the cross-sectional drag coefficient to a value S that defines the area (m²) and reveals the vital sectional drag. It can be seen the similarly sized DS and CX models show that the CX car has a lower Cd. and a lower Cd.a (Cx./Cx.s) cross-sectional figure, and thus has lower drag than the DS, with the GS lower still.

Cd./Cx: = drag coefficient
Cd.a/Cx.s: = cross-sectional drag coefficients frontal area via form measurement as S(m²)

Model	Cd. (Cx)	Cd.a (Cx.s/m2)
D Spécial	0.382	0.817
CX	0.369	0.709
CX Gti 2	0.332	0.709
SM	0.339	0.662
Visa Super	0.391	0.677
Visa Club	0.378	0.660
BX (Base)	0.342	0.634
GS /GSA*		
GS 1220 Club	0.361	0.653
GSA Club	0.345	0.624
GS X3	0.332	0.600
GSA X3	0.318	0.575

* Measured at Aerotechnical Institute Saint-Cyr l'Ecole

GS: GENIUS

but Citroën's GS Cd. achievement was only noted by the technically competent: somehow it was *expected* of Citroën. Of interest, the later GSA competitor, the similarly sized Lancia Delta, had a Cd. of 0.46 – a very poor drag coefficient for a post-GS, 1980s car.

ENGINES

Initially constrained by French tax rules on engine capacity, the GS soon received the developed, larger, free-revving, air-cooled engines that were to become its audible hallmark. The engine history was as follows:

1015cc flat 4
1129cc flat 4
1220cc flat 4 from 1972
1299cc flat 4 from 1978
1301cc for the Italian market only
2 × rotor 497.5cc Wankel-cycle engine (Birotor) 1973–74

The GS's boxer engines used alloy construction and were light and low mounted to lessen the c.g. effects in the roll and pitch axes.

The lead supporting names in developing Citroën's and 1960s engines were André de Bladis as chief engineer, Michel Audinet, and Messrs Cordier Dupin, Gautier, Hondet and Foucher. Gautier and Foucher went on to develop two versions of the proposed 4-cylinder unit, one with a capacity of 950cc and the other with 1130cc, which in turn led to the GS engine size. Audinet went on to develop the Citroën single rotor and birotor engine projects.

For the GS, the engine team produced low stress, air-cooled engines devoid of all the ancillary complications of water pumps and jackets. The engine did, however, have fine tolerances and required quality lubrication; for example, a rash of camshaft problems was traced to the suggested use of lower quality oil by garages servicing the GS in its first eighteen months of production. This episode was soon resolved, and no long-term issue resulted.

The GS X2 of 1978 used an enlarged 1299cc engine – although one curious event prior to the introduction of the GSA was the use of a claimed 1301cc version, to flout Italian road use legislation which stated that to be allowed on the motorway (*autostrada*) a car had to be of 1300cc minimum.

The GS power increased from 55bhp/41kW to 60bhp/45kW as the 4-cylinder engines were enlarged in capacity. For the GSA, the final-drive ratio was changed to reduce revs, improve economy and increase top speed. The gear/speed drive ratio went from per 1,000rpm from 14.3mph (23km/h) to 15.3mph (24.5km/h). The larger-engined cars reached 65bhp, and in 1975 the GSX and then the GS X2 developed 65bhp and had a top speed of 98mph (157km/h). Both were launched with revised trims and high-backed sports seats. Black anodized bumpers and a rear lip spoiler were part of the package. Ultimately a GSA X3 emerged. GS X cars could for a short period be ordered with long or short final-drive ratio gearboxes (400 GS X1s were sold in Great Britain).

GS AND GSA MODEL DEVELOPMENT

1970: GS Series One announced: voted Car of the Year 1971 in launch year.
1976: GS Series Two with styling and specification revisions.
1979: GSA derivative with longer rear body and hatchback takes over: GSA estate retains GS estate rear body.

The GSA with its revised bumpers, trims and longer rear body looked very contemporary, as seen in this Russell Wallis artwork.

GS: GENIUS

1986: French production ends but overseas production continues until 1991 in Indonesia.

The GS range began with the GS as launched in late 1970 and produced to 1979 as 'Club' 'Comfort' (badged 'Confort') and in 1974 the DS-style trimmed 'Pallas' then 'Cmatic Pallas' and then the lesser trimmed 'Special'. The principal derivations were tagged as the GS 'Berline' or saloon, and the five-door estate 'Break'. Latterly the automatic was entitled 'Convertisseur'.

A GS three-door service van, also made with the side window conversion, was available in Europe and briefly in the UK, but a three-door GS estate variant was not sold in the UK.

In late 1976 the GS Series Two arrived for the second chapter in the GS story. Citroën lightly revised the GS with new rear lamps, revised trims, new colours and more powerful engines allied to the option of a five-speed gearbox.

The GSA hatchback and GS-bodyshell-based estate were launched in 1979 and produced until 1986. The GSA replaced

RIGHT: **The GSA van was a special GS estate shell with both rear side doors and outer skin panels removed and replaced by this smooth-looking van design.**

ABOVE LEFT: **Classic GS X 2 in 1970s orange paint and special wheel trims.**

ABOVE RIGHT: **Note the rear lip spoiler to enhance the Kamm effect and increase downforce.**

LEFT: **GS X design delight.**

GS: GENIUS

LEFT: **Early GSs** used a 'cyclops eye'-type speedometer; later left-hand-drive cars received this **DS**-style cluster.

RIGHT: **Classic GS** interior with aerofoil motif instrument binnacle. Some early rhd **GSA** cars came with this **GS** dashboard prior to the new design's fitment.

LEFT: The **GSA's** revised 'TV screen' facia with Harmand-designed 'satellite' controls and improved ventilation.

159

the GS in 1979, and added a hatchback structure with new rear three-quarter side windows of greater length. Aerodynamic tweaks included revised front spoilers, smoother thermoplastic bumpers, under-car vortex fences, and a sharp airflow separation lip moulded in plastic applied to the trailing edge of the Kamm tail. New door handles, trim items, colours and badges complement what was a 'refresh' that also saw expensive structural changes to the rear of the body to create a hatchback configuration, as the GS had originally been designed for.

The left-hand-drive (lhd) market GS cars had had both a 2CV-type speedometer and an early iteration of the unique 'cyclops' eye-revolving drum speedometer as per the later CX model, but right-hand-drive (rhd) GS had the conventional dials set in a fake machined alloy appliqué panel that was first seen on the lhd launch GS cars. Some early rhd market GSA cars were equipped with the dials of the original GS; however, after a few hundred were produced, all such rhd GSA cars received the new TV display-type dashboard with control pods, satellite-type auxiliary functions, and the revolving drum instrument cluster.

Small improvements were made to the cabin ventilation for the GSA revision.

SPECIAL EDITIONS GS/GSA

GS *Basalte* 1977: A black GS with Pallas-spec chrome side mouldings and red vinyl stripes along each flank. A sunroof and tinted glass were also applied.

Two other GS specials also existed. Just after the car's launch several examples were painted up in flags of the world to coincide with the Munich Olympics, and some were sold off through the Citroën dealer network. Later on, in 1976, a French artist created an especially hued GSX2 featuring seventy-three colour zones laced with arrow motifs. This was the GS *Énergétique* by Jean-Pierre Lihou. After hundreds of hours of hand-painted effort, the Citroën-endorsed GS artwork made its debut in the Champs-Élysées showroom.

GSA *Tuner* 1982: Black with blue striping and trim; audio upgrades to Philips radio.

GSA *Cottage* 1983: Special metallic colours and trims for estate-only variant with an unfortunate name once translated into English.

GS Basalte special edition. A weird idea for stripes perhaps, but it worked.

GS: GENIUS

The GSA looked sleek and modern in the 1980s despite its 1970s origins. Note the front spoilers.

The British market saw 'SE specification cars with Pallas trim and added items such as alloy wheels, a sunroof and side stripes'.

GSA *Chic* 1985: Grey with red striping and trim upgrades with X3-type rear lip spoiler, different wheel-caps.

GS *Plus* 1983: Advertised in a bright green paint, this low volume dealer-special edition featured additions from the Citroën accessory catalogue, and some rather unfortunate chromework such as wheel trims and rubbing strips and a host of shiny badges.

GSA *Pallas SE*: The GSA Pallas SE (Special Edition) was a British market, Citroën Slough-specified car with a luxury velour seat trim, alloy wheels, and locally applied side stripes. It was sold in a smoke grey metallic or, more rarely, black paint finish.

GSA *Club Executive*: A Danish market dealer special that was reputedly briefly sold in 1981 with nothing more than extra badging, alloys, and audio upgrade.

GSA *Voilà*: A low-cost Dutch market special for 1985 with special badging and random additions from the Citroën accessory catalogue by a local dealer. The car was a marketing ruse to coincide with the major Dutch auto show and the run-down of GSA availability – a stock-shifter.

GS: GENIUS

Revision to lamp motifs and badges only added to the GS's modernity.

Overseas Production

As well as an export model-spec GS called the *Grand Exportation* (GE), there was also a Special GS GE version. This was a Rennes-produced GS for overseas markets. More widely recognized are the GS and GSA that were assembled as SKD and CKD 'knock down' production in various countries around the world. Indonesian and Bulgarian production were two of the last outposts of the GSA. Right-hand-drive GS were produced at Umtali Rhodesia/Mutare Zimbabwe, and many such cars can still be seen on Zimbabwe's roads today. Indonesian GS/GSA variants were still being made as late as 1990.

Numerous trim differences and engine variants were used in the overseas production specifications; the expensive trapezoidal headlamps were often replaced by twin circular bulbs per unit, giving a (Morette) four-headlamp set up.

The principal locations of non-French GS and GSA production were:

Australia	Mozambique
Bulgaria	Portugal
Chile*	Spain
Indonesia – last known	South Africa
GS/GSA variant	Thailand
production was in	Slovenia
1991 by PT Alun Indah	Zimbabwe

*The GS was a firm favourite in South America, and available in Uruguay, Argentina and Bolivia as well as in Chile, where locally built 'SKD' cars were assembled, with 2,500 GS being claimed between 1979 and 1982.

The total number of GS and GSAs sold reached 2,466,757 cars, which seems an incredibly large number given just how few are left today.

American GS?

A small number, perhaps twelve GS cars, were imported into America in 1971 by Citroën North America. Despite a huge showroom response and many orders, the GS never officially made it, due to Citroën's withdrawal from the country, because of increasingly expensive legislative requirements. The dealer

Pumped up – proof of the hydro-pneumatic three-wheel ability.

162

stock was sold off privately. In the early 1980s, a handful of GSAs were also privately imported to America. Up to thirty GS/GSA are reputed to remain in the USA and Canada.

The GS 1299cc engine was used in an upmarket American vehicle project known as the *Trihawk*, the idea for which was a three-wheeled aerodynamic motorcycle crossed with a car; it was constructed in 1984, and Citroën may have assisted in engineering terms. 150 such *Trihawks* were built, and the idea and stock were then purchased by Harley Davidson.

The GS Birotor

A twin-rotor GS was launched in 1973. Entitled the Citroën GS Birotor, it featured a Wankel birotor produced by the joint NSU-Citroën Comotor company that emerged from the Ami-based M 35 experiments. The rotors were hollowed out with oil transfer trenches inside them, which was an exquisite engineering solution. Michel Audinet was Citroën's lead birotor engine man.

GS Birotor was more than just a Wankel-cycle engine shoehorned into the GS engine bay: it was an upgraded car with many additional technical and trim specification changes. So it was about more than just new badges and a 'drop-in' engine transplant.

The bronze-hued Birotors differed from the normal GS, having front wheelarch flares to accommodate the wider track/wheel spec, and five-lug (not three-lug) 14in rims mounted on 165-type tyres. GS Birotor lost its in-board mounted Brakes due to lack of space, but it gained thicker anti-roll bars. The car was a torque converter automatic only – which dealt well with the Wankel's (adjusted) displacement of 1990cc, and with 107 (DIN) horsepower at 6,500rpm – and with 101lb/ft, the Wankel GS had great performance and that serene 'waftability' that might be associated with an SM or a Rolls-Royce.

The performance figures really underlined the brilliance of Wankel-cycle capabilities: 0–60mph in under 12sec, a top speed of 110mph (177km/h), and a rev limit at a wonderful 7,000rpm.

GS Birotor was expensive – nearly as much as top of the range DS in 1974 – FF 24, 952 – or FF25,000 Francs and that was without options. A top of the range standard engine GS was FF10,000 cheaper to buy. Birotor fuel consumption was heavy – worse than a DS23 EFI – and while the turbine-smooth power may have been amazing, the servicing bills and fuel costs mounted just as the French Government invoked a new lower motorway speed limit that would constrain the Birotor in its ideal high speed element.

In a question long unanswered, the official tally of Birotors is often quoted at 800, though some cite 847 and 873, others 900. What is fact is that between 1973 and 1975, the GS Birotor existed and was sold in nearly one thousand units. Citroën

---

GS AFFECTION

Former Royal Navy submariner, Commander Eoin Sloan is the British GS enthusiast best known for his GS rallying exploits and GS Birotor ownership. Eoin's GS Birotor is the former Andrew Brodie car and represents the ultimate incarnation of the GS genius.

Eoin owned GS and GSA from new but bought a GS1220 in 2005 to take part in the London–Taj Mahal (Himalaya) Rally. Although the rally was cancelled, the Sloan GS, with Group 2 Spec to include roll cage and upgraded suspension, competed in several Tour Autos, France Tours and Rallye de Paris and always finished. Historic rallies in Germany were also undertaken. Eoin's co-drivers who he describes as 'a dedicated lot' included Andrew Sloan, Mark Stone, David Newton and David Gilhooley.

Although used by many rally privateers in Europe and Africa, the GS was too underpowered for the UK rally scene, and despite the fact of a GSA entering the ParisDakar rally in the 1980s, the GS failed to rival other more conventional rally cars. Of note, F1 driver Patrick Depailler drove a GS in a 1970s rally. The Sloan GS is now a regular sight at Citroen Car Club events.

bought as many of them back as possible, but perhaps 100 escaped. At least two cars made it to Australia. The only legacy was a fuel-injected twin-rotor experimental engine that died along with so much else at the hand of Citroën's 1970s fiscal crisis, when Citroën lost $80 million in 1970. Just two years into the launch of the GS, Citroën had made a $5 million profit – a stunning turnaround – but had good GS sales figures masked high operating costs that still lay hidden below the surface? Only time would tell.

The GS Bertone Camargue and Ligier GS Coupé

In the early seventies Citroën did some research on a GS Coupé, and Michel Harmand, the interiors specialist, penned a pretty GS Coupé exterior. But then Citroën commissioned two independent design specialists to also suggest ideas. The GS Camargue was shaped in 1972 by Nuccio Bertone's company (the name 'Camargue' was later sold to Rolls-Royce). The French carrosserie specialist Ligier also built a GS Coupé prototype. Neither concept made it beyond one-off prototype stage.

The GS 4×4 Military Vehicle

In 1973 the GS floorpan and engine was used to create the M7, a lightweight military vehicle for all-terrain purposes ('Voiture Légère Tout Terrain': VLTT). But this Heuliez-built, GS-based jeep lacked power and was abandoned in favour of a Peugeot-based offering. The sole remaining prototype was recently advertised for sale.

LEFT: **The 1973 GS Birotor featured flared wheel arches front and rear, special badging and trims. Michel Audinet was the Birotor project engineer.**

BELOW: **The Bertone coupé based on GS underpinings.**

AN OWNER'S VIEWPOINT: GS AND GSA OWNER GRAHAM H. WILSON

In early 2005 I bought a 1978 GS Pallas C-matic saloon. It is a technological marvel even today, with self-levelling suspension and amazing directional stability on motorways; it steers and brakes safely with a puncture; the three ride heights cope with uneven ground and jacking up the car; the four disc brakes are power operated (rather than servo) with inboard front discs; and it has superb halogen headlights – all in a car from the 1970s with a modern aerodynamic shape that assists high-speed cruising.

To put it in perspective, my 2011 model VW Golf 1.4 TSI automatic is a good car, but the GS is better to *travel* in (unless the weather is very hot!). You don't want to stop driving the GS because it is so comfortable, has much better all-round visibility, and makes very little tyre noise – the latter being a problem in so many modern cars.

The GS was bought from Rob Moss, owner of the Chevronic Centre. It had only done 18,600 miles by 2005, but needed new doors, wings, boot-lid and a respray. I bought my 1981 GSA Special hatchback in June 2007. I discovered it is the only 1129cc GSA known to be on the road: all the rest have 1300cc engines. I have now done 20,000 miles and the odometer reads 54,000 miles.

How do the two cars compare? Most important for me, the GSA has better heating and ventilation thanks to additional central air vents and a three-speed fan. The GSA's hatchback is easier to load than the GS boot, but both are very big. The GSA Special is very basic with no rev counter or clock, but it does have the ergonomic switch pods on each side of the steering wheel. I have fitted a modern stereo.

The GS has 60bhp going through a torque converter and does 0–60mph in about eighteen seconds, so it is not too slow. Both car engines have a sweet spot at 4,000 revs that gives 60mph in the GS top gear and 70mph in the GSA. The latter has 55bhp and is about three seconds quicker to 60mph with its manual gearbox. Both have official top speeds of around 95mph.

Perhaps the most memorable journey was in September 2010 when the GSA completed 1,946 miles in two weeks for a holiday up to the north coast of Scotland. It averaged 39.7mpg overall, and had no problems because a well maintained GS/A should be reliable. I drove several hundred miles on some days and never felt tired – and occasionally I got that 'magic carpet' feeling when the car seems stationary while the scenery moves past you. It is only when you complete such a journey that you really comprehend how competent a GS/A is on all roads.

I love the looks of my GS in particular; however, I am aware of the failings compared with a new car. Top of the list are heating/ventilation and 'passive safety' – there are no airbags. The GS/A has good 'active safety', and other design features make it safer than expected for a 1970s car. It is just a shame that the GS and GSA have a desire to rust, and an interior that needs protecting from strong sunlight. If you enjoy driving in comfort, try a GS or GSA if you can find one.

The MEP X27

Maurice Pezous was a Citroën dealer from Albi, whose experiments in the early 1960s included fitting the flat-twin Citroën and Panhard engine into lightweight tube-chassis single-seat racing cars for the junior formulas. His prototype MEP X27 of 1971 used a 1015cc GS boxer flat-four with increased compression ratio and tweaks to its breathing via a twin-choke Weber 40 carburettor. From such work nearly 80bhp (at 6,750rpm) was coaxed from the buzzy little flat four, and this led to twenty-five single-seat MEP racing cars using GS power (with a top speed of approximately 125mph/200km/h) being built and competed at privateer level in the Formula Blue series in France at regional circuits.

RALLYING THE GS

The GS had a significant rally history, which is often forgotten. Although seen on the British privateers rally circuit, most Brits eschewed the GS, yet the French, Germans, Italians and Australians all used it. In Australia, Citroën distributor Jim Reddiex rallied the GS from the mid-1970s onwards. Fitted with bull bars, a roll cage and modified panels, and with extra cooling and proper harnesses, a GS was a regular on the Australian rally scene. Reddiex went to some expense re-engineering the front of a GS to accept a CX 2400 engine in the 'Maxim Motors' GS rally car, which was based on an orange GS X1. Other Australian GS rally entrants included Ken Tubman, André Welinski, Ian Steel and Eddie Perkins, all in various GS, CX and DS cars.

GS: GENIUS

Citroën supported the GS at club and lower level French national rallies, including the 1977 Portugal Rally. In the 1977 Jarama Rally, Munoz and Zovita campaigned a GS, a GS competed in an early Paris-Dakar race, and Claude Laurent competed in several French national rallies in 1975 using a modified GS. Citroën sponsored a GS in the 1972 Chamonix Trial.

Incredibly the GS saw action in WRC class events, such as the 1976 Rally of Portugal when F. Romaozinh / J. Bernado competed. The 1975 RAC Rally of Great Britain witnessed the GS of J. Luc, and the earliest GS international event was the 1973 Rally of Morocco, with C. Laurent / J. Marche taking part. Sadly transmission and suspension issues precluded some GS entries finishing, but many class placings were achieved in rallies between 1973 and 1976, including the 1975 rallies of Portugal and Morocco. A GS finished eighth in the 1975 Rally of Finland with the crew of J. Luc and C. de Roux.

More recently, in Eire and Northern Ireland several GS rally cars were campaigned, with John O'Sullivan driving his in the 1986 Galway Rally.

The GS also rallied on snow. F1 ace Patrick Depailler drove a GS in the 1972 Chamonix Trail.

SPECIFICATIONS GS/GSA

Body
Aerodynamic four-door saloon and five-door estate. All steel monocoque. Later GSA has extended rear body as five-door hatchback with longer rear wide windows, but the GSA estate retains the GS estate rear body. Production 1971–86.

Engines
Types — Front-wheel-drive 4-cylinder horizontally opposed air-cooled 'boxer' or 'flat' type of: 1015cc, 1129cc, 1220cc, 1299cc, 1301cc. Output range: 55.5–65bhp.
Also limited production of twin-rotor Wankel with 106bhp.

Transmission
Four-speed and five-speed manuals; three-speed automatic.

Brakes
Discs/front inboard mounted.

Suspension
All-round hydro-pneumatic system with front wishbones and rear arms.

Dimensions
Length	166.5in (4,229mm) (*GSA hatchback*)
Width	65in (1,659mm)
Height	52in / 1,346mm)
Wheelbase	104.5in (2,654mm)
Weight	2,314lb (1,050kg) (*unladen*)

CHAPTER TEN

CX

COEFFICIENT OF EXCELLENT DESIGN

CX | COEFFICIENT OF EXCELLENT DESIGN

PERHAPS IF THE DS had not gone before, the CX would have stunned the car industry, but the truth is that people expected the DS replacement to do something no car could ever do – be more innovative than the DS itself. It was an impossible equation. For no matter how good the CX was, it was to be received in the wake of its illustrious forebear. And yet all these years later, we can see in the CX (and its GS forebear) shapes and styling that other, far more modern designs have mimicked. Quietly, the CX design would in fact prove to be more influential than any of the 'revolutionary' big Citroëns that had preceded it.

In the CX we see the first real mass-market large four-door coupé car; it is a style that, with the addition of the hatchback, has been copied across the world. In the CX body design we see the precursor of today's mainstream upper-sector coupé-saloon executive cars, a precursor that has even encompassed Jaguar. CX was also, of course, highly aerodynamic – long before the vogue for such design took hold in the mainstream market.

Underneath the CX was also advanced, as it used many DS engineering themes and provided a stepping stone to more recent technological standards. True, the early CXs had to soldier on with Citroën's heavily revised but still old, four-pot oversquare engines, but that was soon changed and the CX gained revvy, free-breathing powerplants. To build the CX Citroën spend millions on a new factory at Aulnay-sous-Bois, near Paris: this was not to be a Breton-built Citroën. Production started in September 1974. Less than three months later, in December 1974, Citroën and Peugeot were merged, the Citroën-owned remains of Panhard were absorbed, and the Citroën-owned Berliet was sold to Renault. Within two years, on 12 May 1976, the fully merged PSA group existed with the Citroën name a trading entity, but one under Peugeot Société Anonyme (PSA) control.

Meanwhile, the new CX not only had a stronger, integrated monocoque body, it had significant structural reinforcements and two extra chassis longerons under the cabin floor, which increased torsional rigidity and carried crash forces away from the front cabin. The car was tested to the then unofficial offset frontal crash test at a 60-degree angle. The C-pillars were reinforced to form a roll hoop, and the heavy foam padding was added to the door trims to absorb side impact.

The new car was popular and safe, and production reached just under 500 cars a day within months.

THE CX'S GS DESIGN CUES

Building on the GS styling and aerodynamics knowledge, and incorporating the SM's technical teaching, the CX had all the makings of a grand Citroën in the true mould. Again, the

The CX's frontal aspect was architectural in its elegance. The trapezoidal headlamp motif and integration with the grille and bonnet scaling and shapes were masterful. The windscreen shape was also of great elegance. This early gold CX seen from the front, somehow says it all about a great car design.

CX: COEFFICIENT OF EXCELLENT DESIGN

Pininfarina 'Aerodinamica' work is often cited as relevant to the CX style, but a glance at the styling sketches from the Bureau d'Études and the DS-derivative clay models created by Opron, Giret, Dargent, Gromik and others in the late 1960s as they sought to develop and then replace the DS, clearly evidence that the CX's shape stemmed from Citroën in-house thinking and motifs, however often the 1967 'Aerodinamica' studies have since been cited. The early large saloon proposal design renderings of Regis Gromik can be seen accompanying this text, and their architectural relevance to the big Citroën project are obvious.

Achieving a low drag coefficient and creating a four-door coupé with a Kamm tail and airflowed canopy details would inevitably lead to similarities in shape.

ABOVE: **CX Prestige seen with XM and C6 siblings. Now that CX is out from under the DS shadow, its importance is more obvious.**

LEFT: **An early 1970s design rendering by Regis Gromik for a DS replacement. Elements of CX architecture are evident.**

As a young design student in the early 1980s, the author penned this 'Cxi' updated CX idea based on architectural themes, having never seen the Gromik drawing.

169

CX: COEFFICIENT OF EXCELLENT DESIGN

Michel Harmand's fine arts and sculpture training was evident in the CX's ellipsoid interior design motifs. The 'flying saucer' instrument pod looked superb.

The men who had worked on the SM and GS were also the team for the CX. Robert Opron directed the body shape, with detail work supplied by team members. Jean Giret, Henri Dargent and Regis Gromik were there, and, of course, the interiors' maestro Michel Harmand, who played a significant part with his first 'satellite'-type 'piano key' idea in the CX control capsule design for the main instruments and controls. Harmand was a keen sculptor and painter, and carved the prototype instrument pod from wood when drafting the dashboard. He had also suggested several exterior styling themes.

André Estaque led on the body engineering, and the principal engineer was André Barthelemy. Pierre Cordier led the engine team for Citroën's first big front-wheel-drive engine laid across the car. The man who had run the SM project, Albert Grosseau, was also the CX project director.

The flying buttress, C-pillar and dynamic swage lines that give the shape life and action are captured here.

170

CX: COEFFICIENT OF EXCELLENT DESIGN

Particular highlights of the CX body design included the stance and scale of the car, and its cabin canopy or turret, the delightful shapes of the front and rear lamps with their cathedral-like architectural motifs, the concave rear windscreen – a world 'first' in design terms – the curvature of the car's side panels, and the elliptical and podded themes of the dashboard design and cabin fittings. Of interest, the shape of the windscreen was singularly distinctive, and observers have questioned whether it influenced Giorgetto Guigario in his own 1980s windscreen motif hallmark.

As with all Opron work, the car caught the light wonderfully and featured very subtle swage line pressings and the suggestion of the drooping 'dynamic' line towards the rear that he was so fond of. A great deal of time and money went into the design details – door handles, window trims, nameplates, wheels. The CX was thus overly designed but not overly done. It was lithe and dynamic – so different to the offerings of the other car makers. Such was CX's amazing style, yet one initially eclipsed by the legacy of the DS.

Here in the CX was a large coupé with the capabilities of a grand saloon, yet with no excesses in its shape and which seemed sculpted. Was this car the last true inheritance of Bertoni's influence, and yet also a stand-alone design statement of its own and its designer? Many think so.

A Unique Rear Window Design

Although the airflow could have been smoothly streamed down the rear of the car and made to separate at the tail or bootlid, Citroën created a rear end where the two D-pillars or rear roof buttresses provided guidance to the air so that it flowed correctly down and off the car via these two pillars that effectively functioned as blades. Then instead of fitting a smoothly raked rear windscreen, Citroën's aerodynamic experts created a localized airflow separation point off the top edge of the roof – this then 'tumbled' the airflow down on to a heavily concaved rear windscreen. This inward-curving glass shape made the air revolve and had a revolving or brushing effect on any water droplets on the glass; it also took place within the boundary layer and so cleaned the rear window without the need for a wiper – it was the world's first 'self-cleaning' rear windscreen.

With air vanes under the front of the car to direct cooling air into the brakes and engine bay, 'tumblehome' side glass shapes and a flat underfloor with spatted rear wheels of narrower track, Citroën threw the book of aerodynamic theory at the CX. Having had the SM and GS go beforehand, it was

ABOVE: **CX airflow was excellent, and the result of many hours in the wind tunnel.**

RIGHT: **An attempt was made to modernize the DS. Here in a late 1960s photo a new rear end is being modelled, and the CX rear side window line is very obvious as a Citroën creation.**

171

CX: COEFFICIENT OF EXCELLENT DESIGN

easy for the men of Citroën, and it would be years before anyone else even came close.

Excellent Drag Figures

The CX had a Cd. (Cx in French – hence CX model name) figure of just under Cd.0.36 in base model trim, rising to Cd.0.39 for the estate. Later Mk2 variants of the CX with smoother bumper panels, less chromework and a rear deck spoiler, achieved Cd 0.34.

Project L

The CX also built on the legacy of the Project L large car prototype that Opron and the team had created in the early 1970s. Project L was a one-off design study for a large car of two-box style yet a full-sized saloon. It looked very contemporary for 1971, but was a shape that may have dated quickly. It lacked the consequent CX's elements of stylistic definition, and yet it was still a car that might have been a more conventional, more marketable car for Citroën at that time. The elegant interior was somehow less than the CX's wildly futuristic salon. Project L seemed to blend GS, SM and some wider European design themes into a more mainstream iteration than CX eventually presented. It was the discarded precursor to the CX, and yet elements of its design were later reborn as the Renault 20/30 by Opron at Renault.

Unlike the DS, the CX had a transverse engine and a very low height to the front wing and scuttle line – perhaps stemming from an original idea that the car should be Wankel rotary-powered (rumours of a rotary-engined CX development 'mule' car persist).

The CX was designed with the full panoply of hydro-pneumatic functions of suspension, Breaks and steering, although a very few early, 1974 base model cars were built without the advanced 'DIRAVI'-type steering, and some were right-hand drive. With stiffened roll resistance, a lower c.g., and the wide-aspect ratio front tyre/track set-up, CX handled with tenacity, but, like all big Citroëns, demanded a certain technique to deliver its best. For the CX hydro-pneumatic application, the gas spheres for each wheel were interconnected at each location to a secondary mechanism within the pressurized system, giving an even more refined ride quality than in the DS.

The 'Old' Engine Issue

CX was launched in late 1974 using the revised version of the DS engine line-up. This was a decision that marred the early cars, but which was very quickly resolved. Launch engines were a 2.0-litre, and a 2.2-litre petrol engine with carburettor, and a 2.4-litre diesel. But within two years the CX would be given fuel injection, and soon after that, a new range of 1995cc engines.

The CX was a transverse engine design (Citroën's first), in contrast to the longitudinal mid-engine layout of the DS, so the CX was 8in (20cm) shorter than the DS. This led to a minor

French plates, black paint. It is a CX Prestige moment.

CX: COEFFICIENT OF EXCELLENT DESIGN

ABOVE: **Two CX Prestiges at rest capture the light and look timeless.**

RIGHT: **CX Prestige leather interior in Series 2 guise with fake wood door card inserts and revised centre console mouldings.**

limitation in rear legroom, though this particular problem was solved in 1976 by the longer wheelbase 'Prestige' model, which borrowed the CX estate car's extended floor pan to provide an extra 10in (25cm) between the wheels in the rear cabin. The 'Prestige' was also given an increased roof height that required a completely new roof panel tooling. Suddenly, the French presidents had a new, elegant limousine.

Launched in 1974, the new CX was fanfared across the media and met positive reaction. Some early cars lacked the full hydraulic kit, and certain CX 2000 models had manual steering, manual windows and basic steel wheels with small chrome centre caps. Further up the range, rather too much chrome trim was added around the windows. Highlight of the range for the late 1970s was the CX Gti – a 127mph (204km/h) car with less chrome, and some beautifully designed alloy wheels. A rare 1970s moment in the CX story was the production of the orange CX Gti cars for a limited period. Citroën's PR chief Jacques Wolgensinger (who married Marlene Cotton – the first female rally team manager ever) drove one with some style. Somehow an orange CX was a bizarre yet vital part of the early CX period. Over 180,000 CXs were sold in the first model years, despite the lack of totally new engines. The revisions to the old engine blocks kept the matter at bay for a while.

MODEL DETAILS AND DEVELOPMENTS 1974–1991

Model Range

Series One: 1974 to 1985
Series Two: 1986 to 1991

TOP: **CX Series One in metallic gold with brown interior – sheer French style,** *circa* 1974.

ABOVE: **A real four-door car, yet the first that worked as a coupé.**

INSET RIGHT: **Entering the salon, note the very rare dashboard moulding for the optional tray.**

CX: COEFFICIENT OF EXCELLENT DESIGN

Developments

1974: Launched as CX 2000 and CX 2200 in Super, Confort trims. Some lower spec UK cars without active steering were held by the manufacturer for British type approval use.

1975: Voted 'Car of the Year'; in the 1976 model year the *Prestige* version was launched, and also the long-wheelbase estate variant.

1976: 2200 diesel saloon and estate. Semi-automatic 'C-Matic' transmission introduced; also CX 2400 carburettor model. September: CX Familiale estate with seven seats.

1977: Gti variant with Bosh Jetronic injection and 128bhp/95KW; trim changes and specials steering wheel and seat trims/head restraints.

1978: CX 2400 Pallas Injection 'C-Matic' transmission and vari-power steering as standard. CX 2.5 diesel launched.

1979: *Reflex* and *Athena* trims launched to replace Super and 2000 Confort. New 1995cc engine; four-speed gearbox on Reflex, and five-speed gearbox on higher range Athena with better seat trim and specification.

1980: Full auto transmission option replaces original 'C-Matic' version. Long-wheelbase CX *Prestige* models complemented by diesel-powered *Limousine* models. Note the higher roof on the *Prestige* models as from 1978. CX 2400 engine receives mild work to increase torque. ZF automatic transmission option on the Pallas range.

1981: Launch of the 2000 Reflex Safari, 2000 Reflex Familiale, 2400 Reflex Safari and 2400 Reflex Familiale estates. New, wider lipped, wheel-arched front wings are introduced across the range to allow the fitment of Michelin TRX tyres. These tyres are standard to the CX Gti and optional on other trims. Further revision to brightwork, and black finish trim across the range.

1983: 2.5-litre diesel engine.

1984: Gti Turbo launched as Mk 1 in small numbers prior to Series 2 production.

CX Version 2

In July 1985, the CX's styling was revised, and became the Series Two. A rash of applied plastic was smeared across the CX's lithe flanks, and thicker, moulded plastic bumpers replaced the elegant metal of the original car. It was as if a super model had put on a touch of weight. The suspension pressure setting was revised in some models. The car retained the ellipsoid dashboard pod, but lost its revolving drum instruments and sported dials! A new central facia zone and revised ancillary controls tidied up the previous design. More aerodynamic mirrors

CX Turbo Series 2 looking elegant in silver as it glides serenely along. Note the plastic bumpers and more aerodynamic mirrors.

CX: COEFFICIENT OF EXCELLENT DESIGN

and plastic cladding over the rust-prone door bottoms and sills offered better corrosion protection, although hidden corrosion was to remain a CX issue, not just in the doors, but in the front floors, and in the front and rear inner wing seams.

Most illustrious of the CX Series Two was the inelegantly badged 'CX 25 Gti Turbo 2', which was a true performance car: with 2.5 litre fuel injection allied to a turbocharger, output was 168bhp at 5,000rpm. The vital 0–60mph time was just under

LEFT: **White was a popular choice for the CX in Series 1 and 2, and made the car look bigger.**

BELOW LEFT: **CX Turbo 2 control post.**

BELOW RIGHT: **CX Gti Turbo 2 rear wing increased downforce and tuned wake drag, but detracted from the looks.**

CX: COEFFICIENT OF EXCELLENT DESIGN

8sec. The top speed touched 140mph (225km/h), and ABS brakes provided excellent retardation.

1985–86 model year: Series Two was launched with steel bumpers replaced by plastic cladding and revised instrumentation, and window and lamp trims and motifs.

1984: CX Enterprise models as CX 20/25D Enterprise with only front seats fitted and the rear cargo deck rubber lined. The limited edition CX 20 Leader is launched. 700 units: the CX 25 Gti Turbo is introduced

1985: ABS braking becomes optional to the CX 25 Gti Turbo. July: Introduction of Series Two.

1986: Introduction of the 25 Gti Turbo 2, with new intercooler and improved performance.

1989: CX production at the Aulnay-sous-Bois factory ceases. All saloon models discontinued. Heuliez-built estates continued until 1991 as TGE/TGI/TGD trims.

1,170,645 CXs were sold from 1974 to 1991.

Heuliez

From 1978 Heuliez built the extended wheelbase CX estate or 'Break'. He designed and tooled an extended rear section with stepped roof and a large rear tailgate. 6in (16cm) was added to the rear side doors and floor pan to increase the wheelbase behind the B-pillars. Heuliez also built the CX Evasion and CX Corbillard two-door hearse. As late as 1988 he built an Evasion Familiale seven-seater with a leather- and wool-trimmed interior.

ABOVE: **The famous six-wheeled CX estate towing its Piper Comanche caravan! Pure Citroënitis.**

RIGHT: **CX made an elegant extended wheelbase estate via the usual Heuliez interpretation.**

CX Loadrunner or Bagagère

The CX was used as an ambulance and as a TV camera car, when the self-levelling suspension was especially valuable. A number of CX estates were elongated and retrofitted with a second rear axle; they were mostly used for high speed bulk transport such as carrying newspapers across Europe. They are known as the 'load-runner' variant. Most of them were prepared by the French company Tissier. Some were even given a third rear axle.

CX in America?

In 1978–84 the CX was also built in SKD form in Africa, Chile, and is still a regular sight. At one stage it was to be a Chinese-produced car as early as 1984. Although this did not in the end take place, it opened the door to the Dongfeng/PSA relationship, which today has reaped many rewards.

A small number of CXs were imported into America by the Netherlands-registered, but New Jersey-based CX Automotive (CXA) concern. 400 such re-badged CXs were sold, but minus the official Citroën name or branding.

A number of CXs including some diesels were privately imported into North America *circa* 1977–1982, Trend Imports and Yareb Hydraulics being the two main importers of the CX into California. As a diesel, the CX could side-step the stringent California State EPA emissions regulations. Expensive modifications to the glazed headlamps, and the addition of side-impact reinforcement struts in the doors, added to the task and the price. It is suggested by enthusiasts that approximately 150 CXs of all variants remain in North America, including Canada.

CX Special Editions and Special Series Cars

Leader: A 'budget' CX from 1984 with approx. 700 cars were produced at the end of the Mk1 production run, and re-introduced in the CX Mk2, with over 1,000 reputed as made. It featured metallic grey paint and some trim upgrades.

Concorde: In 1986 using a CX Gti Turbo specification, this was a re-trimmed car that copied the then Air France Concorde interior design using crimson leather seat trim in box pleat design, and white trim panels. Twelve of the cars were produced (five for Air France, five for Citroën VIP customers, and two held by the company).

Croisette: 1987 using a base model CX series 2, 22 TRS, with trim upgrades, alloy wheels and a turbocharged diesel offered. Up to 2,000 cars were reputed as sold.

Roland Garros: A 1985 Gti Turbo Series One base car used for transporting tennis stars and VIPs for the Paris-based tennis tournament – sole additions being vinyl decals. Not commercially produced so perhaps not a real special edition at all.

Enterprise: A CX estate van based on the 'Break' Mk1, with rubberized cargo loadbay and steel window blanks. Believed to be sold in Denmark, Belgium, the Netherlands, Germany, Eire and France only.

Orphée: A CX cabriolet (single unit) manufactured by Guy Deslandes.

Tissier: The French coachbuilder made several versions of CX basis, both Series One and Two, including van, ambulance, limousin and a platform or flat-bed rear body version.

Heuliez: Like Tissier, Heuliez made special versions, usually with more luxurious equipment, plus funeral vehicles.

Henri Chapron: Of 1978 Prestige basis, with more luxurious features including hardwood, mini bar, telephone. A Plexiglas roof version was built.

The rare special seat-trim option in crimson leather.

CITROËN IN AMERICA

Given André Citroën's love affair with all things American, and the often forgotten reality of his toying with General Motors, it was obvious that Citroën would sell its wares in the United States of America. As early as 1938 an agency in Los Angeles named Challenger Motors became Citroën's West Coast distributor.

A company known as Campbell Motors of Pasadena had also imported Traction Avants in the early years, though, as with many such imports, the records of what happened to the cars are not clear.

Citroën's early 1950s foray into the USA was as a result of an export programme for American tourists visiting France (and Europe), who could order a Citroën for delivery back in the USA. Clearly some form of support network would be needed for such cars in America, and from there grew the official import body of Citroën Cars in North America.

When in 1954 Citroën decided to set up an official import base in the USA, the company tried to trace the previous 'freelance' imports and many were identified.

Louis Garbe, who played a role in Citroën Slough and the creation of the Bijou, was involved with setting up Citroën in America as part of the Export Department with Michel Koundadze and Claude Alain Sarre, André Noel and Alfred Lucas. The aptly named M. Paradis was sent to California by Citroën to set up this palm-fringed Californian outpost. He enlisted the help of a M. Bonford who became sales manager. Armand Garnier was latterly the west coast director, with Claude Braux as chief engineer.

The man in charge of the 1954 start-up was Charles Buchet; Michel Rappellini was his technical manager. Citroën shared its head office location in New York with Air France, so the lunches must have been good: the New York showroom was on Park Avenue. In California, the official home for Citroën was on Wiltshire Boulevard in Los Angeles; imports of 2CVs originated from these two bases. Amis, Méharis, the DS family and the SM – Citroën's great last gasp in the USA before terminating its presence there in 1974.

In Canada, Citroën retains a dedicated following: an owners' club, Antonin Bouffard and Sons of Quebec, who were the leading Citroën garagistes for many years, and Gilles Bouffard, who remains a dedicated Citroëniste. Citroën's first official presence in Canada began in 1962, and the three dealer outposts in Canada were AutoFrance in Montreal, Jim Ferguson Motor Company in Toronto, and Docksteader Motors of Vancouver. By 1972 a network of dealers existed in Canada, with one of the best known being Ville Motors in Montreal.

The US and Canadian specification DS cars reflected local laws and legislation and featured a confusing blend of French, British, and other trims and specifications notably to headlamps, turn indicators, chromework, badges and cabin fittings.

A wind-down in operations and sales became obvious by late 1972, and by 1974 Citroën's official presence in North America would be over. Perhaps recent PSA – GM developments will once again see the chevrons cross the Atlantic.

After Citroën's 1974 withdrawal from the USA, numerous small specialists continued fettling and selling Citroëns. Leading lights of the Citroëniste garagistes in California were the Helig family. Patron Hank Helig had emigrated from the Netherlands to Canada; he had worked for Citroën Cars Canada, and was the first man qualified to work on the SM in North America. After owning his own Citroën dealership, Parthenon Motors of Vancouver, which was unfortunately timed with the closure of Citroën Canada (and the USA) in 1974, Helig moved south over the border, to run Riveria Motors in San Diego for many years – but he created a new brand identity in 1980 as Citroën Concours.

The 2CV was catered for by re-registered 'restored' cars, and for a short time was framed by the Escargot Motor Company as America's unofficial 2CV outlet.

Thanks to J. Sobey and Citroënet.

Protection: Prestige model with an underbody tray and reinforced doors and glass, with a 1,102lb (500kg) weight increase.

Gendarmerie: 1982 Gti to police specification as motorway pursuit cars: fourteen were built.

CX: COEFFICIENT OF EXCELLENT DESIGN

CX Pallas Diesel: Made by Citroën Spain with the carburettor 2400cc engine and the 2500 diesel.

CX Birotor: It is claimed that several pre-production 1973 year, Wankel-cycle CX prototypes were built – but were never seen outside the Citroën test facility.

CX RALLYING

The thought of campaigning such a large car was not a barrier to doing just that. Citroën created a CX rally team, entered the 1975 Morocco Rally and took the top places. Numerous privateers rallied the CX, and Paddy Hopkirk drove one in the 1977 London–Sydney Rally. Andrew Cowan rallied a CX in the 1979 Round Australia Rally, and several Australian privateers used the CX in national rally events – Jim Reddiex even rallied a CX-engined GS.

From 1976 to 1980 Citroën officially entered the CX in the following rallies: Acropolis, Finland, Great Britian (RAC), Monte Carlo, Morocco, Portugal, Sweden, Quebec. Apart from the early win and podium places in the Rally of Morocco, CX's best international (WRC class) rally result was eighth, twice, in the 1974 and 1975 Rally of Portugal.

The lead CX rally drivers/co-drivers were:

P. Alessandri	J. Deschaseaux	J. Luc
J. Bernardo	B. Dondoz	J. Marche
D. Brichot	M. Fouquet	J. Nicholas
B. Charbonnier	M. Hoepfner	M. Prud'homme
C. Dacremont	V. Laverne	F. Romaozinho
C. de Roux	C. Laurent	A. Warmbold

Paddy Hopkirk's CX rally car for the Singapore Airlines-sponsored London to Sydney 1977 Rally.

180

CX: COEFFICIENT OF EXCELLENT DESIGN

CX on the Moroccan Rally.

OWNER PROFILE: PATRICK RUGG, THE CX MAN

The most common question I get asked about CXs is, where did my CX obsession start? No different to most people, it began in my childhood, and to be precise when I was eleven years old and my parents owned a village filling station with cars for sale on the forecourt. My Dad had a Black CX Pallas for sale, for which I often 'obtained' the keys so that I could start it up and watch the rev counter rotate!

One day this super-cool guy came in, all dressed in black, and made a bee line for the car – neither looked right for this village filling station, as they were both way too cool. The guy bought the Pallas, and it transpired he was the lead guitarist for the legendary rock band *The Stranglers* – Jean Jacques Burnell. He became a family friend, and even gave us a signed copy of their hit Golden Brown inscribed 'Who would buy a used car off this man? I did!'

Of course CXs became more than just a family friend to me: they became part of my family, and for a long time a way of life. I have always craved things that are so different, so cool, and in many ways the unique CX is them all. What could be cooler for an eleven-year-old seeing an international rock star dressed all in black, driving off into the sunset in the coolest car, which was also dressed all in black. A superb style combination of both car and owner.

Roger Bradford

Years passed until I was in the motor trade myself, deciding that wholesale selling to the trade was to be my niche so contacts were important. This led to me being introduced to the late Roger Bradford, whom I can only ever describe as the 'CX guru'. He was keen to buy CXs, so I sourced them daily, to the point where he had so many that we decided to form a partnership, with me constantly finding the cars and him selling them. This was in the mid-eighties so there was no Internet, and not even *Auto Trader*, just the good old *Exchange and Mart* where we would regularly advertise twenty-plus CXs per week. I hate to think how many I have bought over the years, without doubt hundreds and possibly a thousand or more! I wish I had listed them all, just so I know – maybe I might even have kept the thousandth one!

One of the most bizarre deals I ever did with a CX was when I stopped to refuel the CX Gti Turbo I was driving. A chap stopped in his CX Gti Auto, finished in the very rare Cardamom Green (*Vert Cali*) – we got chatting, and half an hour later we drove home in each other's cars!

Continued overleaf

CX: COEFFICIENT OF EXCELLENT DESIGN

Continued from previous page

OWNER PROFILE: PATRICK RUGG, THE CX MAN

One of the wonderful things about a CX is that anybody can own one – from French presidents to rock stars. I also know of English MPs, funeral directors and taxi drivers who have owned them. It must be the most versatile car ever, with numerous records held, including the powerful and economical DTR model – a CX achieved third place in the London to Sydney 1977 Rally – and they were even used regularly by the BBC to film horse racing, due to the smooth ride. Amongst the most bizarre uses of a CX I know of includes a lady who bought a Safari as her husband could only travel lying down! It's a good job the car was white, as had it been black it may have caused other drivers to have a heart attack!

There was also, of course, the infamous CX 'Grand Designs' Camper driven on *Top Gear* by Jeremy Clarkson. – though probably the funniest in my personal experience was a Safari I bought off a chap who turned out to be a burglar! Half an hour after I bought it from him in the car park of a car auction the police came and took the car away for fingerprints – it had been used in a 'job' in Cambridge just two hours before! So there you have from president to thief, and most in between!

Prices of CXs have risen year on year for quite a few years now which is marvellous as it will encourage more owners to invest in their CXs. Many owners of DS models have also been buying a CX, as they can see the superb value compared with the DS.

Gti!

I get asked a lot what is my favourite CX…well, that's easy – it's a sold one! Without doubt in the eighties it would have been a Series 1 Gti Turbo, as I used to drive them, normally in anger, trying to get to the next CX I was trying to buy. They were, and still are, brilliant to drive, with superb comfort and smooth ride allied to the tremendously torquey engine. I have great memories of motorway 'burn-ups' with Merc Cosworths and the like, and just loved seeing the astounded faces of the Merc drivers when I came whistling past them!

Overall, though, nothing pleases me more than to see a well kept CX – the model is immaterial. It is just that I know that a good CX, which is well looked after, will survive to ensure a healthy turnout at our shows and a future for the marque. This is very important to me, and is my main objective as the current chairman of the CX section of the Citroën Car Club.

I get asked what I look for when judging the shows, which is an interesting question. Unlike most judges who seek the perfection of Concourse, it is far more important for me to see a CX that is loved, not just a bit, but really, *truly* loved.

These days I am particularly sweet on the very early cars – I suppose as you mature, comfort takes precedence over speed. The early cars do really seem so amazingly soft, and what about those rotating speedo and rev counters – which I guess is where it all began.

SPECIFICATIONS — CX SERIES ONE

Body
All-steel monocoque with reinforcing rails and strong points to safety cell.

Advanced aerodynamic body

Engines
Types	2.0, 2.2, 2.3, 2.4, 2.2 diesel/2.5 diesel
Transmission	Five-speed automatic, five-speed manual, four-speed automatic, five-speed semi-automatic

Suspension
Engine-driven, inter-connected hydro-pneumatic self-levelling system

Dimensions
Wheelbase	112in (2,845mm)
Length	184in (4,666mm)
Width	68in (1,730mm)
Height	54in (1,360mm)

NOTE: Prestige and estate car dimensions differ

Curb weight	2,789–3,351lb (1,265–1,520kg)

CHAPTER ELEVEN

BASIC TO BRILLIANT

VISA

FROM LN TO VISA

BASIC TO BRILLIANT
FROM LN TO VISA

THE VISA MAY have been a product of the Peugeot takeover of Citroën, yet two things stand out about the car: Visa was, despite its so-called humble 'parts-bin' origins, a properly designed, innovative car with the Citroën ethos contained within it. Visa was also a direct descendant of the 2CV, Dyane and Ami 8 in its offering. Hidden within the Visa story is that of the Oltcit or Axel, which some mistakenly think was a product of the Visa, which it was not – being instead a reverse-engineered, original Citroën small car design utterly devoid of subsequent Peugeot influence. Many Citroën purists are still dismissive about the Visa, but a tribe of Visa enthusiasts are keeping these wonderful little cars from fading. Visa values are already on the rise.

For so long dismissed by many, the Visa was not just another 1970s hatchback or small saloon in the mould of the Ford Fiesta, Austin Allegro or other such cars. Instead it was a modern and forward-looking piece of engineering that contained many advances in practice, yet it was a car obscured by circumstances and its rather unfortunate nose styling in early guise. The trend-setting, thermo-plastic, one-piece moulded nose was in fact a great piece of innovative design thinking, but it was just a little too organic for the mass marketplace beyond Citroën loyalists. But Visa was full of 1970s 'firsts' which had not been seen in other small cars (or large ones), and it is odd that the car should have become eclipsed, as it has. Citroën snobs will, of course, always decry the Visa, but that would be their loss.

VISA'S 'FIRSTS'

- First use (1978) of the tall body, chopped tail, mini people-carrier concept in small car design – latterly used by Guigario's Ital Design concepts of the 1980s, leading to tall cars like the Fiat Uno and others
- First achievement of sub-Cd.0.40 drag coefficient in a small, stubby car body
- First use of electronic ignition in the mass market small car
- First use of advanced ergonomic design in a small car via 'satellite' control function for the driver, supplemented by the innovative use of colour-coded plastics in cabin design and trims
- First use of large synthetic one-piece bumper/apron/grille panels in the mass market car – a fashion others would take a decade to adopt
- First car with external plastic protective cladding applied
- First car available with both air-cooled and water-cooled engines
- First use of 'Nicasil' bore liners in a small capacity engine – technology taken from Wankel rotary developments of NSU-Citroën-Comotor
- First small five-door hatchback to achieve rallying success

BEGINNINGS

In the late 1960s and early 1970s Citroën had undertaken several co-operative agreements with other car makers – before such practices became the industry-accepted norm. Citroën had purchased the rival French design innovator, Panhard, in 1965, and followed that up with Berliet in 1967, and then in its first Italian escapade, seized a major shareholding in Maserati in late 1968. It had also formed the Comotor Joint venture with NSU to build Wankel engines in 1967, which led to the M 35 and later GS Birotor – whose technology legacy would, incredibly, touch the ancient Citroën twin-pot engine's redesign in 1977.

The origins of the Visa lie in another Italian moment for Citroën via its relationship with FIAT, where Citroën, FIAT and Total formed a collaborative agreement known as the Participation et Dévelopement Industriel, or PARDEVI, with Michelin having sold a 49 per cent stake of Citroën to FIAT – hence the access to the 127 model platform for the planned new Citroën small car.

But as the 1970s economic crisis grew, Michelin were still Citroën's masters, and FIAT wanted rid of the Citroën investment. In the end, the French government drove through the Peugeot takeover of Citroën in what can only be called a politically expedient move for the national good. In 1974 Peugeot took 38 per cent of Citroën after FIAT had handed back their share, leaving Michelin carrying the can. By 1976, with French government intervention, Peugeot owned over 90 per cent of Citroën and absorbed it into PSA.

By the late 1970s the FIAT 127 was selling well across Europe, and the Renault 5 was making its iconic mark. Citroën's initial studies for a sub-GS sector car, yet one above the 2CV/Dyane/Ami, reflected FIAT's supermini 127, but it soon realized that the Visa would have to be less of a small hatchback and more of a family holdall.

Early development saw two projects, 'Y1' and 'Y2', and although these were stillborn design studies, it was through these that the Visa came about.

Following the creation of Peugeot-Citroën under the 'PSA' umbrella, Robert Opron left to join Renault, and André Estaque and Jean Giret directed the remains of the old Bureau d'Études in the difficult circumstance of the Bureau finding itself under the control of Peugeot's own styling centre and design/engineering control. Visa's lead designer was Jean Giret,

BASIC TO BRILLIANT: FROM LN TO VISA

LN AND LNA: HYBRID IN HASTE

The Peugeot 104-based LN/LNA was a good car but not really a Citroën. This is the van version.

Concurrent with this low-cost, parts-bin thinking, there lay the first real outcome of Peugeot's takeover of Citroën – a car that really was nothing more than a badge-engineered Peugeot 104. This was the 1976 Citroën LN, a quick fix for an economy model in the French marketplace model line-up. And while the 104 was a sharp-suited, trapezoidal headlamped, Paulo Martin design, its Citroën variant was ruined with round headlamps and ungainly grille, and rubber side strips grafted on to the LNA, strips that rarely lined up and created a visual anomaly.

With the 2CV, Dyane and Ami 8 as small car legends, did Citroën really need another loss-leader? And was not Visa soon to arrive? The truth is that the LN was a stop-gap car that was very cheap to create and was used to generate showroom traffic and tap into a more modern 2CV idiom in buyers' minds. All of France knew it was really a stripped-out Peugeot, but with some tinkering it became a wheelbarrow of a Citroën in true 2CV mould. As Citroën itself told the press at the LN's debut, the LN stemmed from: 'The need to supply customers and the network with a model to strengthen Citroën's position at the lower end of the market.' In other words they were desperate to shift steel.

The LN used the small, low-mounted twin-pot engine which, with its low c.g. and much lower weight, improved the handling and reduced the roll centre. But with only 32bhp to tap into, the benefit was small. Of note, LN had tiny 13in wheels as opposed to the Peugeot 104's larger 15in wheels, and this affected the drive ratio from the otherwise long-legged Citroën GS gearbox that was grafted into the drivetrain in place of the 2CV/Ami-type unit; LN was short-geared so its fuel economy was not as good as it could have been, however it could be stirred along quite quickly.

Incredibly, 'LN' is supposed to have been derived as a model name from Hélène (and LNA from Hélèna), in a bizarre attempt at continuing the tradition – first seen in the name DS – of referring to figures and goddesses of Greek legend. Quite how anyone, even after a three-hour French lunch, could construe the LN as 'goddess-like' is beyond rational conjecture. *Motor* magazine called LN the 'Hasty Hybrid'.

This car, offered with a transplant of the 602cc engine from the 2CV/Dyane, upgraded in 1978 to 652cc, sold very poorly, and in 1979 (after the Visa's launch) was also transplanted with the Peugeot 1124cc engine to create the LNA: this sold 223,772 examples across Europe. These low numbers reflected the weakness of the badge-engineering practice.

The LN/LNA dispensed with Peugeot's elegant headlamps and trim specifications and was turned into a base model of poverty spec. Yet many proved popular with rural customers, in true 2CV style. The LN was the *first* true badge-engineered Citroën, and *not* the last real Citroën just because it arrived at the period of the PSA takeover. As such it was indeed a hybrid of a car, but it was far from being a disaster, not least as the base car the 104 was, by the standards of the time, a robust and well equipped little buzz box that found many friends in the face of its asthmatic and aged competitors.

The interior of LN was a re-hash of existing Peugeot plastics and add-on Citroën items from across its cars. Peugeot's instructions were clear: change the badges, alter the seat trim material and a few 'stick on' items, and make the front and rear look basic. Thus was the LN and LNA – a hybrid hatch of stark proportions. Only now does the LN/LNA have a more enthusiastic sect of followers.

The LNA was restyled for 1982 with new lamps motifs and revised plastic bumpers that aped the Visa design. The 1124cc LNA also saw a special edition for the UK known as the *Inca*, based on the LNA 11E with the addition of alloy wheels, audio upgrade and a brown and cream trim combination and a split/folding rear seat. In Europe it was tagged the *Canelle*. A *Prisu*-tagged edition was also reputed.

Continued overleaf

BASIC TO BRILLIANT: FROM LN TO VISA

Continued from previous page

LN AND LNA: HYBRID IN HASTE

The final model range of LNA 11E, and LNA 11RE saw the fitment of luxury trim including tinted electric windows, headrests, alloy wheels, cigar lighter and side mouldings. These *de luxe* cars seemed to make a mockery of the whole point of the original idea of the LN – a basic sort of 2CV of a car with no frills. Cast alongside the Visa, the LN and LNA in 'bling' trim simply looked bizarre, especially with ill-matched plastic-type strips tacked down each side of the car in an often wavy line!

LNA Final Specification
1124cc, 4-cylinder, light alloy, water-cooled engine with overhead camshaft. Four-speed gearbox; electronic ignition; conventional strut and spring suspension system with front anti-roll bar; top speed of 87mph (140km/h). Best claimed mpg of 60.1mpg (4.7ltr/100km). Front disc brakes/rear drums.

LN /LNA Production Figures:
LN: 129, 611 to 1979
LNA: 223, 772 to 1986

who then retired after a long and illustrious career with the chevrons.

Citroën's own Y2 project was perceived as a threat to the Peugeot 104, which had been designed and launched just prior to the Peugeot takeover of Citroën. It can only be viewed that the pert, advanced Y2 was dumped to protect the solid but entirely normal 104 range. The subsequent creation of the LN from the 104 only added insult to injury for men such as Dargent, Giret and the team at the Bureau d'Études, who had long honed a 1970s small car jewel for Citroën.

VISA DESIGN DEVELOPMENT

From such ashes came the unfortunately named 'Project VD' ('Projet Voiture Diminuée') as an idea for a vital new small Citroën yet one that would use the Peugeot 104 floorpan and suspension parts. A bored-out version of the old 2CV engine rated at 652cc as a 2-cylinder or 'twin-pot' Visa base model would tackle the old 2CV/Dyane customer base, while a larger-engined version with a four-stroke cycle and better trim levels would attract Ami followers.

The strength and purity of the Visa styling remains obvious three decades on. Only the Mk1 grill/bumper moulding was deemed to warrant re-tooling in Visa Series 2.

BASIC TO BRILLIANT: FROM LN TO VISA

A very early Visa prototype styling buck, with shades of Fiat and Renault 5 perhaps.

Early styling models of the Visa show a car with definite hints of the contemporary Gaston Juchet-penned Renault 5 and perhaps touches of a Fiat theme. Even at this early prototype development stage, Michel Harmand's innovative ideas for the interior of a cheap, small car were showing through. The Visa was designed very quickly in just under two years and from the early styling model, emerged a car which provided the basis for the final form. Of curiosity in design terms, was the fact that the later Citroën Oltcit bore closer resemblance to the *earlier* Citroën styling prototype than did the production Visa. At least Citroën called the Visa its name and not 'VD' as in Voiture Diminue. A well known British motoring editor had the unfortunate task of telling Citroën's senior management over a Parisian lunch why they could not call their new car 'VD' in Britain. So Visa it became.

Peugeot's 104 floor pan was narrow, and it used transverse engines – something only the larger Citroën CX had used in the 1970s. Under the project management of Boris Gonzales, with André Estaque, Jean Giret and Henri Dargent, the team created a major feat of engineering by shaping and building a sleek, modern, highly aerodynamic body for the Visa. The car also had an avant-garde interior styled by Michel Harmand (fresh from his GS and CX successes), which featured the drum of a control module and a sliding selector panel, each being located either side of the steering wheel – known as the 'satellite' control function. This revolutionary idea really did mean that the driver did not have to remove their hands from the wheel, and could 'play' the control keys using their fingers to deploy 'zoned' functions. In Visa, the concept was vertically mounted behind the steering wheel, but the Axel used Harmand's *original* horizontally opposed twin-drum satellite control invention.

The interior trim also saw an early use of fully coloured dashboard and door card trim mouldings and a range of vivid seat-trim materials. Unlike the basic vinyls, brittle plastics and dull cabins of the Ford Fiesta, Toyota Starlet, and offerings from Fiat, Austin, Vauxhall/Opel and most other car makers, Visa offered an advanced exterior style and a trend-setting interior technique created by Michel Harmand, the man who would lead Citroën's interior design specialism to such huge effect.

Smart, clean, and not looking like a base model car design at all.

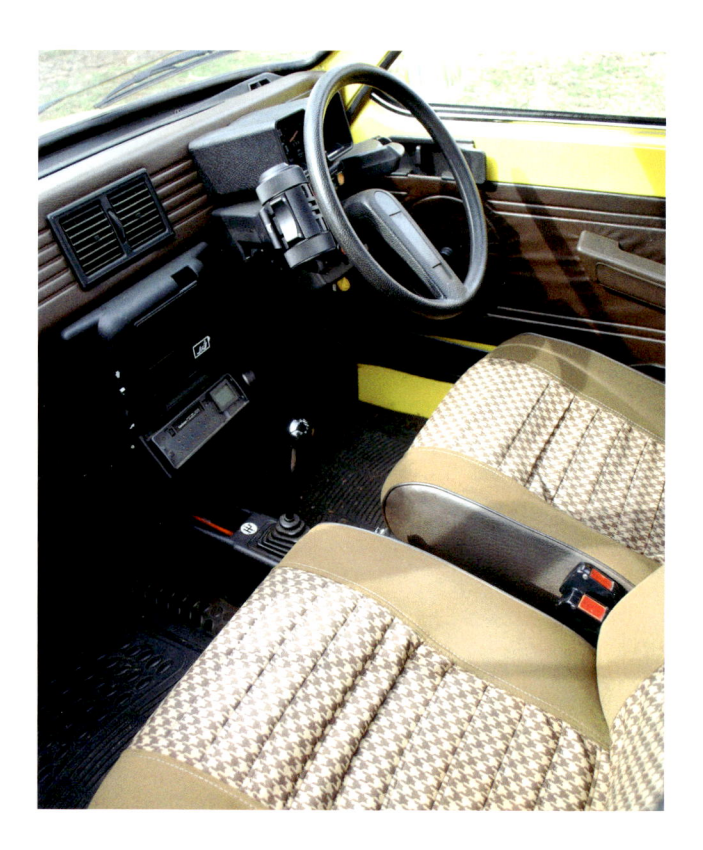

Visa used Harmand's interior design skills to the full, and was a radical departure from normal 1970s small car interior design.

Engineering Differences

Unusually the Visa was a car in which both air-cooled and water-cooled engines could be ordered. The Citroën twin-cylinder was a light unit that gave the Visa wonderful steering 'turn-in' and front-end handling, while the 4-cylinder Peugeot engine was free-revving and not too weighty. Only the addition of the 1.7-litre heavy block diesel changed the Visa's wonderful point-and-shoot handling and steering nature and also added more oversteer. The Visa diesel also needed plastic wheel-arch extensions to cover its wider track.

The availability of either a Citroën or Peugeot engine in the Visa range created some interesting technical anomalies. The air-cooled twin-pot cars had a Citroën steering rack as opposed to that on the 4-cylinder cars which was a higher-ratio Peugeot unit. The narrower-section tyres on the twin-pot allowed it a tighter turning circle of 30ft 6in (9.3m) as opposed to 31ft (9.4m) for the larger-engined car. There were also very small (non-structural) differences in wheelbase due to the differing engine mountings and driveshaft lay angles. In the Citroën-powered car, the engine is canted forwards ahead of the drivetrain/gearbox.

'Nicasil' Cylinder Liners – in 1978!

The adaptation of the 2CV's ancient engine involved dispensing with the bore liners and replacing them with alloy using a wear-resistant 'Nicasil' coating developed by the Citroën-Comotor group for the Wankel-cycle GS Birotor. (Jaguar and BMW would latterly use such coatings in similar manner!) This was advanced engineering and astounded some competitors: the bore was taken to 77mm with the iron liner removed, and so the cubic capacity and the compression ratio were both increased, and power was up by nearly 30 per cent: the torque figure at 38lb/ft was higher than the 36bhp – a sure sign of a great engine. There was also an unusual three-bearing crankshaft for a twin-pot engine. For Citroën's venerable 2CV engine to be treated to the very latest technology and 'Nicasil' liners was another example of the paradoxical delight of Citroën in the 1970s.

Transistorized Ignition

The Visa also boasted the first mass-market use of an entirely electronic ignition. It was developed by the French electronics company Thomson in collaboration with Citroën. The electronic ignition was designed to send timing pulses from a flywheel base to a computer, while a vacuum-sensing transducer within the inlet manifold evaluated engine load. Ignition advance (and retard) was sensed by two proximity detectors (at 10 and 45 degrees), and the computer calculated the spark rate impulse between the two opposing timing parameters and sent the information to the coil to convert into secondary electric output.

The system had no mechanical parts to wear out or jam, needed no adjustment, and delivered a constant advance timing curve which improved emissions and lowered fuel consumption.

The 4-cylinder 'Super' used the 4-cylinder light-alloy single overhead camshaft transverse engine and transmission of the Peugeot 104 – known as the 'Douvrin' made for PSA by the Société Française de Mécanique with modifications to gear ratios and the cooling pattern. However, the unit's old failing of gear-noise whine was never addressed, and transferred direct into the Visa. An adapted GS-type box was used in the twin-cylinder car, however[13].

Suspension was from the Peugeot 104's Citroën LN, with adapted rates and with longer strut reach and re-tuned dampers complimenting the MacPherson struts in front with an anti-roll bar and trailing arms behind. Brakes were LN drums at the back and an entirely new Citroën-designed disc at the front.

Sleek Style

Of interest in styling terms, this was a mid-1970s version of a small, short, upright car *before* Guigario's later 1980s ideas for such cars. The Visa had a very elegant front wing line that ran in a compound curve up its flanks and through into the A-pillar at the windscreen junction. This was a very unusual feature on so small a car, and gave the frontal aspect great elegance. Some designers were very impressed with this proper 'wing line' or hip joint, and the manner in which the bonnet, door and wing panel gaps were integrated into their shapes.

With a swept-back windscreen angle leading into a high roof, the Visa had the look of real design competence and knowledge of aerodynamic flow. The windscreen was curved and the transition to the sides of the car was both aerodynamically open and elegant.

At the front, the early Visa had an innovative bumper-less one piece moulding that blended the front apron, bumper and radiator grille function into a single thermoplastic item. Again this was an early use of such techniques, when most cars still sprouted steel/chrome and angle-iron bumper bars jutting out from the bodywork. Dargent and Estaque are reputed to have styled this clever frontal design graphic, but it was susceptible to colour fading of the plastic moulding and was later dispensed with in the revised Visa Mk 2 that was branded 'Visa II'.

At the rear, Visa was tall – as was the entire cabin itself in true Pierre Boulanger tradition where the cabin had to accommodate people wearing hats. A deep hatchback bay, folding seats, wipe-clean plastics, and room for luggage meant that the Visa was no cramped little economy box, but instead could offer proper accommodation.

Although the suspension was entirely conventional and non-hydro-pneumatic, Visa was given long travel struts, and at the front, very well tuned dampers; in Gti form it handled well, and with the fuel-injected Peugeot engine was extremely quick.

Aerodynamics

With its sleek, swept front, high cabin, partially covered rear wheel-arch shaping, and a very careful attention to the way in which the airflow separated off the top of the rear roof at its separation point, Visa, whatever its Peugeot base, offered not just Citroën aerodynamics, but the best aerodynamics package seen at that time or for years afterwards in a small, short car. Such cars are very difficult to style and to make aerodynamic, and drag factors of Cd.0.41–0.46 were quite normal in 1978 for small hatchbacks. The Visa Mk1 managed a stunning Cd. 0.378. This certainly helped its fuel economy and stability – Visa had excellent side wind/yaw angle performance. Of interest, the revised styling of the Visa Mk2 with its more angular frontal treatment and wider wheel/tyre specification, meant that the overall Cd. increased to Cd. 0.391.

Visa Mk1 Club, Cd. 0.378, Cd.a 0.660
Visa Mk2 Super, Cd. 0.391, Cd.a 0.677

The Visa also used computer-designed body panels, and was notable for the very strong windscreen pillars and scuttle frame member, which meant that the car passed the frontal crash test very well. Like many cars of the era, the Visa rusted, and was susceptible to corrosion in the sills and rear wheel arches.

Visa sheer simple elegance. Mk1 Visa twin-pot in a classic Citroën colour. Note the wing to hip joint and tall cabin turret as design hallmarks subsequently copied by others.

Just as the BX was rationalized into its Mk2 version – devoid of a few of its original ideas – so too was the Visa 'normalized' with a new, more conventional interior and the removal of its satellite controls. However, all was not lost, as the most paradoxical Visa was the luxurious 14TRS with its luxury specification upgrade and the BX's 1360cc engine, which made it a bit of a wolf in sheep's clothing. So too was the Visa GT, with the same engine offering 0–60mph in a stunning 10sec and a 104mph (167km/h) terminal velocity – but this was nothing in comparison to the Visa Gti 115 with its very low 1,962lb (890kg) bodyweight being pulled around by a 1.6 litre Peugeot 205 Gti engine. This was a true sub-10sec 0–60mph 'hot hatch' in the most bizarre of senses – a true Citroën, then.

A curiosity was the Heuliez-developed Visa cabriolet with the safety-related retention of its door frames and B-pillar roof supports, allied to a fold-down, roll-back roof and a proper boot. These cars were unusual, rare and very smart. Many were sold in the smart areas of Paris and Nice, not to mention West London. However, not even being handbuilt by Heuliez could stop the rot, and very few remain.

Electric Visa

Many years prior to the creation of the electric battery-cell-powered Saxo, a study for a battery-powered Visa was undertaken by Citroën in 1989. This was based on a Visa van, and several development prototypes were made. Bizarrely, in 2011 a Chilean-built solar panel and battery-equipped Visa was created by a company named Terra.

MODEL DEVELOPMENT

1978 Paris Show – the Visa was launched.

Visa Special 652cc twin-cylinder air-cooled base model.

Visa Club higher trim level variant.

Visa Super 1124cc water-cooled 4-cylinder. Fitted with plastic side rubbing strips.

Visa Super 'E' displaces the Super in 1981 as 'economy' trim.

Visa Super X 1219cc 4-cylinder; alloy wheels.

Spring 1981: Visa Mk2 launched with revised Heuliez-styled bumper/grille/lamps and colours/trims. Black paint applied to all window surrounds above Super trim level.

Visa II Special.

Visa II Club.

Visa II Super X 1219cc with sports trim. French market orientated.

Visa Trophée: Only 200 homologation cars for sale made by Heuliez as part of a Citroën brand rally promotion. Based on the Visa Super X 1.2 litre tuned to 100bhp and sold to privateers, including the Group B rally class.

This Visa Series 1 has the addition of a front spoiler and side stripes, alloy wheels and metallic paint in which it looks very smart.

BASIC TO BRILLIANT: FROM LN TO VISA

Visa II Chrono Rally-inspired special trim version with 1360cc engine of 93bhp in Chrono I and 81bhp in Chrono II. Revised trims and first deletion of satellite controls. Red and blue striping over white body with spoiler kit. Sold in two production batches in 1982, then 1983 with a total of 3,660.

Visa GT from late 1983: 1360cc engine with 80bhp, twin carburettor with special trim and special paint schemes. TRX tyres.

Visa II L 1.1-litre model between base and Super E trims. Special southern Europe market model with 954cc 4-cylinder engine to meet tax bands.

Visa Super E Convertible (Décapotable): A Heuliez-built car with folding roll-back roof, based on the Super E model.

Visa Enterprise: 1983 Visa with welded rear side doors and window blanks created a small commercial van.

Visa Van or C15 1984: A large, boxed, rear cargo bay including twin rear doors but no early side door. Pressings included window stamps for glazed versions. Fitted with petrol and diesel engines, and then only as a late model 1.7-litre diesel. Remained in production beyond the Visa car model life. Also available as a pick-up 'ute', extended wheelbase. Twin-axle cargo van, and as a base for a camping car/motorhome conversion.

Spring 1984: Changes to badges and trim names.

Visa Special becomes 'Visa'.

From the 1985 model year, all Visas are re-branded as 'E' or 'RE', displacing the previous Special, Club or Super variants. Revised dashboard removes the satellite controls.

Visa 11 E.

Visa 11 RE: Mid-range model with a rear hatchback spoiler.

Visa 11 Convertible based on 11 E. All production stopped in summer 1985.

Visa D Diesel from spring 1984 as '17D' and '17RD'. 1769cc diesel engine.

Visa 14 TRS/RS from summer 1984. 1.4-litre engine. New wheel trims and interior colours and materials. RS trim in selected northern European markets only.

Visa Gti from early 1985, fuel-injected 1588cc, 105bhp engine from Peugeot 205 Gti. Revised suspensions and anti-roll bars with wider alloy wheels. New trims and interior specification. Four round headlamps and front and rear spoiler kits and side

Four round headlamps really changed the face of the Visa in Gti form. The car looked great in red or white.

VISA SPECIAL EDITIONS

Carte Noire: 1979, based on Super E; 2,500 made. Black paint with gold striping, some export cars with red striping.

Sextant: Spring 1980, based on the Super, with 2,000 made for the French market. White paint with blue decals, white front bumper moulding.

Reflex: Special trim and engine size for southern markets in Greece, Turkey and Cyprus.

West End: Based on the Super E for the French market, and dealers in Paris and Nice areas. 1,000 made. Leather trim, sunroof, tinted glass and alloy wheels. Dark red paint.

Drapeau: British market only as twin or 4-cylinder with special stripes.

Platinum: British market only also for 1982. Alloy wheels, striping and decals, metallic paint.

World Cup: A series of twenty special editions, each named after a member of France's 1982 World Cup football team. Featured vinyl decals similar to Chrono. Spec includes sunroof. 1219cc engine. Navy blue interior and seat trim. Of note, special steel wheels not alloy. Each car numbered and named.

Champagne: British market only in 1983–84. Sunroof, alloy wheels, metallic beige paint.

Platine: 1984, based on 11RE; 2,000 made. Finished in very dark grey metallic with check interior. Alloy wheels.

Junior: French market driving school edition with bodykit.

Mille Pistes: Rally car 1984. Group B 200 unit homologation special. 1360cc engine of 112bhp; four-wheel-drive.

Visa 'Challenger' was one of the smartest special editions. Here the Visa Series 2 front styling changes are obvious.

The plastic strips framing the bonnet's leading edge and headlamps camouflaged the original Series One metal shapes and saved the cost of re-tooling.

Olympique: Spring 1984: Los Angeles Olympics special edition based on Visa 11E. Special wheel covers in fake alloy finish; unique paint schemes offered. Body decals. 3,000 built.

Tonic: 1983–84. Based on GT with bodykit addenda; 2,000 made. Export model.

Bi-Campeao: Portuguese market dealer special of 750 units to commemorate Visa rally success in Portugal 1984.

BASIC TO BRILLIANT: FROM LN TO VISA

Spirit: 1984 car as Netherlands dealer special with all-white paint and plaque on the dashboard. Based on the Visa Chrono, derived from unsold Chrono special edition cars in the Netherlands.

Stilo: Spanish dealer-based special edition based on the 14 and 17RD.

Challenger: 1985, based on the Visa 1.4 GT in white with red decals; 3,500 built. Special black and red-trimmed interior: known as the 14 'S' in northern Europe.

Leader: 1985 as Leader version 1. Made with 1.7 D or 1.1 engines. Special light grey pearl-effect paint with full wheel trims and headrests with special seat trim material in chequer pattern. A small number of cars made in very pale metallic blue. Leader version II in 1987 to same specification. 12,000 of both variants made.

Crystal: 1987; 1,000 cars for the German market as diesel in light blue with stripes.

Versailles: British market 1987 with new wheel trims, audio upgrade and special striping. Sunroof. Dealer special by Moto Baldet dealer.

The Visa Gti may have looked odd, but it went like a hot hatch should with 115bhp. Note the sill and wheel-arch extensions.

skirts and wheelarch changes. Visa Gti 115 re-rated to 115bhp with '115 ch' decal badges to proclaim such power rating on front doors.

Visa 11 Convertible based on the 11 E. All production stopped in summer 1985.

Visa D diesel from spring 1984 as '17D' and '17RD'. 1769cc diesel engine.

Visa 14 TRS /RS from summer 1984. 1.4-litre engine. New wheel trims and interior colours and materials. RS trim in selected northern European markets only.

193

STRANGE VISAS!

Visa Estate? With Heuliez input, an idea for a Visa estate car (Break) was developed in early 1982. Teaser shots were released by Citroën that contained the as-then unannounced styling for the Visa Mk2. But with limited production capacity, Citroën felt it could not launch the Visa estate, and the idea sadly died.

Visa II Mercure: A 1982 Heuliez device based on the Visa, with six wheels and a pick-up or 'ute' body as another Paris Salon 'show special' when Citroën had little else that was new to fanfare.

Visa Luxor: A Citroën idea of 1983 based on the Visa GT with special trim for that year's Paris Salon. Not produced.

Visa Funny Car: 1982 was a busy year for Visa; this 'Funny Car' idea had a special body and a weird and wonderful dragster-type injected 1100cc engine of 'Donovan' design fitted in a long-nosed dragster glass-fibre shell and claimed to give over 1,000bhp. This 'car' was built in 1982 under sponsorship by the French magazine *Auto Loisirs*. The aerodynamic dragster body was designed by Pascal Meslet and built by Yves Charles with support from Citroën, and the car was covered in Visa branding.

The Visa Funny Car dragster was launched in May 1982 and even latterly appeared at the British dragster meeting at Santa Pod. With its 1,500bhp channelled through a three-speed automatic transmission, this was a rear-wheel-drive Visa that could reach 190mph (300km/h). The crew for the Visa dragster included *Auto Loisirs* journalist Phillipe Danh, Dominique Dorigo, with Francis Lopez as crew chief. Kent Persson was the first driver of the car, and Phillipe Danh later drove it in events including a dragster meeting at Le Mans and Santa Pod, where the best performance on the quarter mile was 8.1sec at 181mph (291km/h)! Not bad for a Visa. Citroën used the car for dealer promotions, but in the end it was left in storage and ended its days on the dragster Funny Car circuit in America. The fate of the car is unknown since 1993.[14]

A Chinese Visa?

What would it take to make the Visa modern? If the Visa were launched today, the body style would still be fresh if slightly cleaned up. And only the need for thicker sills and a stronger side frame and floor would be needed to pass today's much more stringent crash-test legislation. Which engine type would suffice – surely the only possible answer would be a high tech, 3-cylinder, fuel-injected little gem of an engine that would 'thrum' away and beat its heart out?

Incredibly, we nearly got a Visa that was one step on the route to the realization of the above, for the Visa lived on in China where Citroën Visas in semi-knockdown form suddenly appeared. Had Citroën brokered a deal, or was this a third party piece of fun? The records are unclear.

But crates of Visa body pressings and trim materials arrived in China in 1990. A company called Wuling created a car that was a Citroën Visa in all but name and engine. The Wuling LZW 710 was a Chinese-built Visa, but one equipped with an independently sourced Daihatsu engine taken from the brilliant little Charade micro car. Supplied under licence build by the Tianjiin-Xiala Auto company, the Daihatsu engine was a peppy 3-cylinder unit that had minimal effects upon the Visa's engine bay tooling or its c.g.

Production began in 1991, and ended in early 1995 with just under 1,000 of the re-invented Visa being sold. The thought of the Visa with an advanced, high-technology 3-cylinder Japanese engine makes the missed opportunity of a re-invented Visa seem all the more poignant in the light of the lacklustre Citroën AX that replaced the French car.

VISA RALLY CAR MANIA

As early as 1981 the idea of a rally or circuit car from the Visa was suggested. Guy Verrier was in charge of Citroën's competition department, and had a small tuning firm called 'Poly-Tecnic' build a one-off tuned Visa with a centrally mounted mid-engine of 1955cc sitting in a heavily revised floor pan and engine cradle. It is believed that two further such cars were hand constructed at some expense – notably one fitted with a Lotus 2.2 engine. This included the 'Strakit'-tagged Visa rwd with 1955cc. The creation of the Visa 'Trophe' and its development to a 4×4 'Mille Pistes' rally car are the essentials of Visa's rallying record.

By 1982, Verrier was requesting proposals for a Visa rally car chassis from a number of small sub-contractors. This included developing the mid-engined idea. Six varying prototypes were created, and one led to the Visa 'Mille Pistes' experiment. From these ideas came an actual build in 1983 of three rally-car prototypes including a reputed 'twin-engined device – a bi-motor that led to a further version with a combined output of 280bhp (100bhp front/180bhp rear). A 2498cc Visa S with the 'Strakit' centrally mounted engine was driven by P. Wambergue and J. de Alexandris as car build number 205. Car number 204 was a Visa O with a 1397cc 'Ordinet' central engine, conducted by C. Rio and O. Tabeti. Car number 203 was a front-engined prototype driven by D. Breton and M. Chomat. Car number 202 was a Visa 4×4 with a 1457cc 'Mathiot' tuned front engine. In 1984 a car build number 206 with a 4×4 and 2200cc Mokricki-type engine was built. The final Visa 4×4 prototypes were cars 209 and 210:

BASIC TO BRILLIANT: FROM LN TO VISA

The Lotus-tuned Visa rally car with mid-engine.

car 209 used the 'Strakit' 2498cc engine driven by Pagani, and car 210 was the twin-engined (2× 1219cc) driven by M. Lacaze.

Visa was used all over France and Europe at 'Rallye' events for privateers and small teams. A 4×4 Visa was created in house, and a Visa 4x4 rally team was supported by Citroën and achieved many successes. The Citroën Visa rally team competed in the WRC series 1982–87.

Main Visa Rally Types

Visa 1000 (Mille) Pistes: 1982–88, 145bhp, four-wheel drive.
Visa Chrono: 1982–88, 145bhp front-wheel drive.
Visa Super: 1982–83, 210bhp, rear-wheel drive.

Visa WRC Rallies 1982–87

The Visa competed in the Monte Carlo Rally, Acropolis Rally, Finland Rally, Great Britain Rally, Portugal Rally, San Remo Rally, Swedish Rally, Tour de Course, and French national club group events.

Jean Claude Andruet finished seventh in the 1985 Monte Carlo Rally. Mark Lovell would make an early mark in the Visa Mille Pistes in the 1984 RAC Rally.

BELOW: **Citroën Team Sport supported Visa rally car in action, driven by X. Moine and J. Moine.**

OLTCIT – BIZARRE LAST GASP OF THE BUREAU D'ÉTUDES

What was the Olcit, or Axel as it was also known? Strangely, it was seen as an export market basic version of the Visa that bore a close resemblance to the prototypes for the Visa. But it was not actually a Visa derivative at all. Some thought it had some GS body parts thrown in – although the GSA dashboard was used. Under the long low front could be found GS engines of 1129cc and 1299cc. The 'styling' was a Citroën in-house affair and utterly in keeping with the motifs of the Visa and the GSA – indeed, was there not a touch of CX elegance to the elongated, low, front wing line?

The windscreen posts, the A-pillars, were not from the Visa, but were an extension of a styling shape used on the CX tooling, featuring a wider top leading down to a triangulated base. From some angles, Oltcit looked more like the love child of a GS and a CX than it did a Visa – and in doing so, did it not echo Citroën's stillborn past prototype 'projets'? Oltcit came with the lusty GS range, four-pot, 'boxer'-type engine; unlike the Visa it kept the Citroën torsion bar and wishbone suspension.

The often unrealized truth is that the Oltcit was a true product of the old, original team of the Citroën design bureau, and contained many Citroënesque themes and oddities. Here was their iteration of a 1970s new economy car for Citroën that was indeed a 'pure' Citroën. As such, Oltcit is far more important in design terms than many realize. With a 1.2-litre flat-four under the long bonnet, it also had a fair turn of speed in its light, three-door-only bodyshell.

The car was a joint venture between Citroën and Automobile Crajova of Romania, with official Romanian government backing. Confusingly, the little reframed Visa with the GS engine was the 'Axel' in some parts of Europe from 1984, and the 'Oltcit' in Eastern Europe. OltCit (Olt – Citroën) stemmed from the Automobile Craiova factory in Oltenia – the name of the town where the car was built (using 40 per cent local content). With its lighter weight, three-door body and GS engine, it went very well despite the roll angles encountered. Build quality standards were variable.

The Axel variant benefited from late 1979s Citroën branding in the 'E', 'R' and 'TRS' model badging. For a short period Citroën exported the Axel back to France and, it is reputed, to Canada. A van version with blanked windows was also tagged 'Enterprise', like the earlier Visa hatchback van version.

The Romanian agreement had also resulted in the Renault-Dacia project, where the Renault 12 was built in Romania and resulted in today's Dacia brand, and led to the Citroën – Romanian government set-up. This was a 36 per cent Citroën/64 per cent Romania ratio, with Citroën allowed to sell their own version of the car in Western Europe. The local Oltcit car would have to have 40 per cent local content. In December 1976, the

It looks like a modiifed Visa, but Oltcit was far from being that.

ABOVE: **This view shows the three-door car's long, low front and different A-pillar design from the Visa.**

BELOW: **Michel Harmand's original 'lunele' or satellite control design was horizontally opposed and first seen in the Oltcit before its vertically orientated use in Visa and GSA.**

agreement to build a joint-venture factory went ahead and turf was cut. Sadly it took five years for both the factory and the full production process to achieve reality. Dreams of selling 100,000 cars a year were simply that – dreams. In the end, the combined Oltcit/Axel total was 60,184 between 1984 and 1988.

The car was three-door only, had both twin-pot and four-pot engine options, and was given increased ground clearance, which gave the Citroën torsion bar and wishbone suspension an even better capability.

BASIC TO BRILLIANT: FROM LN TO VISA

Model Range

Oltcit Spécial with 652cc flat twin from the Visa base model.
Oltcit 11 R with 1129cc flat four from the GS range.
Oltcit 11RL with 1129cc and higher trim spec.
Oltcit Enterprise van with window blanks.
Axel 11 E/TR with 1129cc flat four.
Axel 12TRS with 1299cc GSA X-series tuned engine; upgraded seat trim and grey plastic exterior side panels, revised badging and motifs.

The joint Citroën production agreement commenced in late 1983 and ceased in 1989 when the corporate and political deal collapsed amidst Romania's growing problems under the Ceauçescu regime: Citroën stopped supplying parts after only 20,000 were sold in that year, but Oltcit did in fact move to a new Romanian brand name and a new factory, which saw a limited production run to around late 1995.

So the Oltcit did in fact briefly live on in several 1990s guises. In 1989, a locally created pick-up or ute truck version had been made, and even had a glass-fibre canopy option, and these sold well after the Citroën withdrawal. Several Oltcit bodyshells were manufacturer-converted to full open-top cabriolet status with just the A-pillar frame remaining – although what that did for torsional rigidity was anyone's guess, and the idea folded – just as the open-top Oltcit would have done. A five-door version aping the five-door Visa was also briefly shown.

As a result of the end to State or Party control in 1994, a further 'Oltena' incarnation of the Oltcit and a later joint venture between Korea's GM partner Daewoo and the Romanian government led to the 'Rodae' – another weird acronym of a brand name – and a 1.3-litre Dacia-powered variant that

The Oltcit cabin used a collection of Citroën parts.

SPECIFICATIONS — CITROËN OLTCIT/AXEL

Engine

Types	2 horizontally opposed air-cooled, 4 horizontally opposed air-cooled
Cubic capacity	652cc; 1,129cc; 1,299cc
Bore and stroke	77 × 70: 74 × 65.6: 79.4 × 65.6
Compression ratio	9.5:1/9:1/8.7:1
BHP per RPM	34.5 at 5,500rpm: 57.5 at 6,250rpm; 61.5 at 5,500rpm

Transmission

Gearbox	Four- or five-speed manual
Clutch	Single dry plate

Brakes

Front	Inboard discs of GS spec
Rear	Discs to Citroën design

Suspension

Front	Double wishbones with longitudinal torsion bars
Rear	Trailing arms with transverse torsion bars

Tyres

135 SR 13   145 SR 13   160/65 R

BASIC TO BRILLIANT: FROM LN TO VISA

The **Axel** version was plusher, with revised trims and plastic cladding and a new range of colours. It sold well in the northern European markets.

SPECIFICATIONS

VISA 0.652-LITRE TWIN-CYLINDER BASE MODEL

Body
All-steel monocoque five-door only. Plastic components for bumper aprons and front grille.
Cd 0.0378.

Engine
Cylinders	2
Displacement	652cm³
Power	26KW/36hp at 5,500rpm
Torque	37.6lb-ft at 3,500rpm/51Nm/3,500rpm
Fuel	Petrol, carburettor system

Performance
Top speed	77mph (124km/h)
Acceleration	0–62mph (0–100km/h) in 26.2sec

Transmission
Type	Front-wheel drive
Gearbox	Manual, four-peed Citroën GS type adapted

Brakes
Front	Discs
Rear	Drums

Tyres
Size	135SR13.

Dimensions
Length	145.3in (3,691mm)
Width	59.4in (1,509mm)
Height	55.5in (1,410mm)
Front/rear track	50.8/48.8in (1,290/1,240mm)
Wheelbase	95.7in (2,431mm)
Ground clearance	5.2in (132mm) (unladen)
Cargo volume	10.6cu ft (3cu m)
Weight	1,620.41lb (735kg) (unladen)

was stillborn. After that died, there was a brief affair in 1996 entitled SC Axa, when SA Craiova briefly produced a car with new nose styling, an add-on body kit of spoilers typical of the era, extended arches and thick sill panels in plastic mouldings.

There was even the suggestion that Chrysler might purchase the Romanian factory and upgrade the Oltcit for sale in America as a new ultra-compact eco car. Quite how it would pass the ever tougher emissions and safety legislation is not known. Given the way in which major European and American car makers swapped models, brand names and body designs to create weird and not-so-wonderful cars for the South American market, an American specification Oltcit born from a multi-parented mutation of a car might not have been as crazy as it sounds.

Today the Oltcit remains a rather rare curiosity, although the later Axel range is still seen on the roads of Belgium and the Netherlands, where it sold quite well and seemed to resist rot. The car has a fan base of admirers, not least because it was in fact the very last 'true' Citroën of the company's own design, in so far as it represents being the reverse-engineered, Project Y/Project TA - Visa prototype – a paradoxical last car from the older men of the original Bureau d'Études.

VISA ENTHUSIAST MIKE HARKER

After twenty four years of Citroën Visa ownership, it's often said that I am smitten with the model. The opportunity has presented itself to upgrade my Visa Gti to a ZX Volcane or a Saxo VTR, but I have never succumbed. My Visa initially was my company car, then a family car, and these days the two Visas I own are solely hobby cars.

It all started in 1989 when I was given a Visa Gti 115ch as my company car, the Gti being the last Visa model. That original Gti launched my enthusiast's journey, which is surprising, really, as I had never been interested in cars that way before. It was very fast for a small family car with good road handling, if a little heavy on the steering. It didn't have the good looks of its contemporaries, and sometimes it had a mind of its own, but I loved every minute in this ugly duckling, even on a bad day. It's ironic that the first Visas in 1978/79 were more typically in the quirky Citroën mould, with seventies' bright paint colours, heavily patterned interior fabric and a challenging dashboard. However, as the years went by the paint colours and fabrics became more pastel, the dashboard more conventional, and the soft Citroën ride became hard and low by the time the Gti was launched, influenced by the success of Visa rallying.

I currently own a white Visa Gti 115ch, bought from an enthusiast in 2000 with 34,000 miles on the clock. It was then used as our family car for five years and 36,000 fun miles, before being retired to become my first hobby car. Gtis of a certain age suffer from hot start problems, synchromesh wear and instrument cluster circuit-board problems, and my Gti was no exception.

I also own a mimosa yellow 1979 Mk1 Visa Club, which is chalk and cheese when compared to the Gti. Its 652cc air-cooled twin-cylinder engine generates only 35bhp; however, it has all those quirky Citroën features of the seventies. My search for a Mk1 model ended in 2007 when I bought my Visa Club from a 2CV GB Club enthusiast. The car had been in damp storage, but even so it only needed a minimal amount of welding, the brakes serviced and some new tyres before it was back on the road again. The two-cylinder models seldom suffer engine-related problems, apart from the occasional electronic ignition troubles. However, the earlier models did suffer more from rust, and the seat fabric was very prone to sunlight damage. Again, my Club is no exception and the seats, carpets and some body panels have had to be replaced.

In the early days we often went on family holidays to France in the Gti. It is not the most spacious and comfortable family car ride due to the bucket seats and sports suspension, but it always got us there and back without any problems. Three Gtis later and these days my Gti hobby car is still as fast and reliable as in days gone by. My image as a middle-aged boy racer has changed over the years to elderly boy racer but it still feels just as good in my 'hot hatch'. If age and image mattered, and elderly was the criterion, then my Visa Club would be the car for us. It is simple to maintain, comfortable and easy to drive, very economical, and reliable too. At 35bhp, acceleration alongside heavy goods vehicles can be interesting, but once it's up to speed it will cruise comfortably at 70mph. The quirky instrument satellite takes a little time to get used to with its non-cancelling indicators and switches instead of stalks, but that all adds to the quirky factor. The car is a pleasure to drive, and we attend many rallies in the UK and mainland Europe, where the Visa family is at its strongest.

CHAPTER TWELVE

BX

*THE CAR THAT
SAVED CITROËN*

BX | *THE CAR THAT SAVED CITROËN*

THE BX IS often ignored by certain marque purists and derided as common or too modern to be a true classic, except those fans who can see its worth. Yet BX was aerodynamic, hydro-pneumatic, used composite materials and had a unique identity, so it was a true Citroën – just a different *type* of Citroën.

Sometimes observers are blinded by their perceptions, and maybe this explains the fate of the BX in the minds of today? But things will change, and the BX must begin to rise from near the bottom of the Citroën pile, for the BX is the car that saved Citroën in the 1980s at a time of great fiscal crisis. Citroën was beset with debt from its SM, GS and CX forays into the future, and its manufacturing inefficiencies. The Peugeot masters had to rationalize things, but BX retained the essentials of Citroënism.

The BX sold very well and was packed full of Citroënology. Maybe because it was not curvy in the Bertoni or Opron mould, Citroënistes reacted to its late-1970s origami-esque design cues. These stemmed from the 'folded paper' school of car design at the hand of its designer – under Nuccio Bertone and Marcello Gandini at their Italian studio.

The BX ultimately expanded to twenty-three models in six trim lines with a power output ranging from 60bhp to 125bhp (DIN), and a four-wheel-drive option in hatchback and estate variants. In the ABS-equipped BX 19GTi, Citroën tapped into a late 1980s fashion and won many new 'conquest' customers to the marque. In France, Italy, Britain and even in Germany, the BX Mk2 was a top selling car. With rallying success and a mid-life refresh under Citroën's then *chef du style*, Carl Olsen, BX earned money for Citroën and took the idea of a mid-range car with character into a new era. In Britain the BX even became a corporate or 'company' car and a diesel economy favourite.

BX BEGINNINGS

Good though it was, the GSA was ready for retirement. So advanced had the GS been that the GSA derivative had held its own in an increasingly competitive marketplace packed with much more modern metal.

Along with the larger CX, it can be seen that the GSA was the last true post-war era Citroën of avant-garde design research, in that it was designed by, and with, the inheritance and the techniques that had created the wonderful Citroëns that had gone before it. For the 1980s a new Citroën was needed for a new age, and however hard it would be, the Citroën mindset and its products had to move on and step into a more mainstream market. If it did not, carrying financial debts, Citroën would die at its PSA master's hand.

In creating the BX, Citroën did move the ethos and the product on into a new era, yet it still packed the car with advanced Citroën design research thinking. The BX had to cover more ground in a wider market sector and win new converts to Citroën, not just rely on its dwindling band of loyal customers who would buy a Citroën whatever happened. That way led ruin, and PSA's governing management knew it.

Bertone not Bertoni

Maybe this need for a fresh perspective explained why PSA went to an independent Italian carrozzeria for the new car's design – perhaps a new start was best captured by Bertone's proposals rather than the internal studies at PSA?

Robert Opron and the then recently employed Jean Giret had begun to work on a new mid-range car in the mid-1960s – the GS resulted, but they also thought beyond that car early in the 1970s and drew up sketches and models of a more contemporary mid-sector Citroën. It is from these beginnings that the seeds of the BX idea grew.

Bertone must have charged Citroën for shaping the BX, but the truth is that the BX drew heavily on two previous Bertone concept cars created for other manufacturers. There was a clear visual link in terms of scale and stance to a project tagged FW11 for the British Reliant company. Even more obvious were the styling themes taken from Bertone's Volvo 'Tundra' styling exercise, particularly in terms of the cabin turret, lower panels and rear end styling. Was the BX a re-hash of a Volvoid idea from Bertone? Some might well argue it was, but it was none the worse for it at the hands of Bertone and Gandini.

Despite Bertone 'borrowing' aspects of the BX body style from a previous project, BX engineering design was full of the thoughts of Citroën's past and the inheritance of Lefebvre – yet paradoxically it was derided by some for its modernism. Was this a true Citroën, or a parts-bin amalgam of various in-house Peugeot-Citroën themes? It was indeed a Citroën, and although being a 1980s design under Peugeot's influence, there was plenty of the old spirit of the Bureau d'Études in the BX. Michel Harmand was lead interior and dashboard designer, and in his last year at Citroën, the veteran Henri Dargent also contributed details. In the BX, Harmand developed his instrument pod or 'lunule' idea and the fingertip control ergonomics first seen in the CX.

The BX was in production for thirteen years from 1982 to 1995. In total, 2,315,739 BXs were constructed during its production run, and the car received numerous facelifts and trim specification updates. It was also transfigured into a rally car, and a 4×4 turbocharged Gti machine of great potential.

Perhaps it was because, prior to the Xantia, the first car of the Peugeot-Citroën (PSA) merger was the LN (the 'hasty hybrid'), that some purists declined the BX's offering. Yet the

BX rode, handled, steered and went with true Citroën verve and passion, and it had real quality to its ride and handling set-up: the BX was a driver's car, and even the heavy diesel engines did not ruin its sweet balance.

The BX's engines were Peugeot-designed units and highly efficient. Citroën's old engines from the GSA had to go, their time was up, and in their place came water-cooled PSA-designed engines of XY, TU and XU(D) series. The 1.7 and 1.9-litre diesel incarnations turned out to be some of the best diesel engines ever made, while the 1.4-litre petrol unit was free-revving and smooth for a 4-cylinder unit, especially when this 1360cc engine was given fuel injection long before the fashion for injecting such small capacity engines took hold.

Plastic Surgery

For the BX, a super-computer CAD-aided design process brought great structural efficiency to its design. The floor pan was stiff, and the B-pillars saw early use of 'elephant's foot' design that widened the B-pillar at its base where it joined the sill. This increased the local stiffness and reduced intrusion in a side impact by providing internal resistance to the movement of the door as it was deformed into the cabin by crash impact forces. By using this new technique Citroën was ahead of the game in terms of side impact protection systems that were latterly so heavily marketed by some car makers.

Use of this reinforcement technique led Citroën to save weight in the construction of the doors, which led to a low quality feel when the door was slammed shut or leant upon, but underneath there *was* strength.

Safe in its Context

In order to save weight and increase fuel economy, the BX received a plastic-moulded bonnet, roof side panels at the C-pillar, and bumpers. This was the first mass-production car to deploy plastic/composite technology on such a large scale, and ranks as a forgotten 'first' for Citroën. The front and rear bumpers were large, one-piece, self-coloured mouldings that reached far back into the bodyshell – another advanced design that is today copied by all car makers. Over 20 per cent of the BX's non load-bearing structure was synthetic material.

ABOVE: **Inspired BX design detail. Glazed pillars, a very aerodynamic rear deck, door frame fillets and semi-spatted wheels. BX was a great piece of Citroën design.**

RIGHT: **This is a BX Mk2 TZI with front lip spoiler, rear deck spoiler and obvious Bertone lineage.**

The BX featured a large plastic rear hatch and bonnet and bumper panels to reduce weight.

So lightweight was the front bonnet that it was 75 per cent lighter than the steel equivalent and offered massive savings in terms of fuel economy. In order to retain some degree of stiffness, the hidden underside of the bonnet was reinforced with moulded-in aviation-style ribs – though even so, opening the BX's bonnet would see the entire panel twist alarmingly. This did not inspire confidence in the car's structure, but the facts were that underneath the lightweight exterior cladding, a strong, CAD, impact-resistant structure existed.

One of the problems of transverse-engined, front-wheel-drive cars under impact is rearward movement of the engine block, causing collapse of the floor/toe-board and scuttle. Citroën addressed this, and made sure that the deformation of a heavy impact was tailored to go down into the floor and not intrude at chest height in the cabin.

In a heavy crash, the BX's synthetic bonnet cracked and split like a wafer at a pre-determined point, yet underneath, a double bulkhead soaked up impact energy, and the steering column and facia bulkhead moved upwards to reduce intrusion and injury. In the offset frontal crash test, the BX's long A-pillars saw movement and vertical deformation, but channelled any intrusion down into the sills: therefore lightweight plastics had not compromised structural integrity, despite appearances.

Intriguingly, some of the early higher trim variant BX models featured a see-through plastic window set within the plastic C-pillar, but this was soon deleted. Citroën also threw advanced design at the car's interior. The instrument panel aped the GSA/CX design with satellite-type instruments and control pods beside the wheel. The rare BX 'Digit' featured a digital dashboard display – another early advance for the new car. Large front seats, moulded plastic cabin architecture, lots of padding and the versatility of a hatchback that was soon joined by an estate or 'BX Break' soon won the BX many loyal customers. Underneath it all was the fact that this was still a hydro-pneumatically suspended Citroën – and one with superb driving dynamics.

Revisions and a Change of Character

Four years into its production cycle, the BX was revised by Citroën, under Carl Olsen design leadership. The instrument panel was made more conventional, with dials replacing the revolving drum display. The Harmand-designed satellite keys to each side of the steering wheel were gone too, as a new dashboard moulding was introduced, and also conventional stalk-type controls. This aped changes first made to the GT models in 1985. Exterior mouldings were changed, with a new bumper and front spoiler moulding. New seats cured the backache that tall people had encountered in the original launch edition cars – but base model cars stuck with the spine-curving seats that were the osteopath's best friend.

By this time the BX estate with its massive plastic tailgate moulding and rather angular rear-end styling had become a firm favourite – especially with the 1.7 or 1.9 diesel engines in turbocharged form. These were hailed by press and owners alike as offering an unrivalled blend of torque, economy and speed, and with appropriate servicing, the correct oil blend, and relevant cam belt/tensioner changes, could easily achieve 200,000 miles (320,000km).

Aerodynamically Efficient

The BX proved that even square-cut cars could be wind cheating. With a small low front, smooth details such as the wind-

BX: THE CAR THAT SAVED CITROËN

screen seals, the moulded bumpers, and very careful attention to the base or wake drag off the rear windscreen and its airflow separation point, the BX was chamfered for smooth airflow, rather than lobed as in the GSA. On all BX hatchbacks, a discreet matt black infill panel at the base of the rear windscreen reaped massive rewards in drag reduction, and cost very little to make.

The BX estate featured a small rubber ridge spoiler at the top of the rear windscreen to tune the airflow separation off the roof and reduce drag and dirt-lifting turbulence.

The BX estate was a firm favourite, and in diesel version went on for hundreds of thousands of miles. This is the author's car.

The BX estate was a 'clean' design, yet sacrificed ultimate load-carrying ability with its angled rear end as opposed to a more conventional box-shaped compartment.

BX DRAG COEFFICIENTS

- Cd.0.34, as coefficient of drag on base model trim specification
- Cd.a 0.63 cross-sectional drag on all models
- Cd. rises to 0.36 for mid-range cars with wider tyres and body addenda, and Cd.0.37 for the 4×4 and bodykitted BX GTi variants. Due to careful rear-end design and wind tunnel work the estate did not suffer a fall-off in Cd. performance – at least not until it was fitted with roof bars

205

BX VARIANTS 1982–1995

BX 14 E /T
BX 14 RE
BX 14 TRE/TGE/TZE
BX 14i TE/TGE
BX15 RE/TRE –
  limited markets
BX 16 RE/RS/TRS/GTi
BX 16 TRI/TGI/TZI
BX 16 TXS/TXI –
  UK market
BX 16 Gti
BX SPORT
BX 17 D/TRD/TZ
BX17 TXD
BX 19 TRS/TGS/TRI/GTi
BX 19 D/TD/TRD/TGD/TZD
BX 19 DTR – UK market
BX 19 Gti 4×4/BX Gti 16V
BX4 TC

Timeline
October 1982
E/RE/R/, TRS

September 1983
19 D/RD

1985
BX SPORT
BX GT

BX DIGIT

Facelift August 1986
TRS/TRI/Gti
4×4 TC

July 1987
Gti 16V

February 1988
TRD Turbo

September 1989
TE, TGE
TGS, TZS
TZS
4×4
TGD
TZD

March 1990
TZi

September 1992
TXi

Key BX engine badges
BX, BX 14 (1360cc also
  with FI)
BX 16 (1580cc with variants
  in tune/bhp)
BX 19 – GT/Gti/16V(1905 cc)
BX Diesel – as
  TD/TRD/TGD/TZD/DTR
  1769/1905cc with Turbo, and
  D/RD/GD/without turbo

An early BX 16 TRS shows off the lobed form revealed from this angle.

MODEL BY MODEL

In what must have been one of the most complicated and confusing trim nomenclature ever forced upon a car (other than in the Ford ranges), the BX was presented in 1982 in a range of trim names. It started out as just BX 14, BX 16 and then BX 19 – all indicating engine sizes. These were then separated by trim indications such as E, TE and RE. Soon there was E, RE, RS, TRS, TRI and RD and RD. After the 1986 facelift came the BX TRD, TE, TGE, TGS, TZS, TZD and TZi, and in the end a TXi. By way of SPORT, 4×4 16 Soupapes (valves) and numerous special editions, BX ended up with over 200 possible trim, engine, body, drivetrain and limited edition variants.

A SPORTY BX?

Citroën soon realized that the BX could be tuned up, and with wider track and wheels, be made to handle – especially with added anti-roll stiffness added. The start of such thinking was the 1985 BX 'SPORT' range with 126bhp, a full 1980s-era body-kit and alloy wheels to match. BX SPORT was left-hand drive only, and 7,500 were sold between 1985 and 1987.

Next came a single carburettor version of the BX SPORT known as the GT. This car still had over 100bhp at 105bhp.

A further uprated version of the BX GT was the BX19 Gti. This stemmed from the success of the Peugeot 405 SRi range, and the BX 19 Gti was a 1.9-litre flyer of 122bhp. Again the

BX: THE CAR THAT SAVED CITROËN

ABOVE: **BX Sport** with all the kit and one of the fastest and best handling of the **BX** family.

RIGHT: **The BX Sport** boasted sports seats and this four-spoke steering wheel and conventional instruments beside the Mk1 side-panel fingertip controls.

BX: THE CAR THAT SAVED CITROËN

ABOVE: **The BX Digit was based on the MkI car with plastic glazed C-pillars, but offered a very early digital dashboard.**

LEFT AND BELOW: **Digital controls and displays were a 'first' for the BX.**

SPECIAL EDITIONS

Few cars have witnessed so many special editions being forced upon them. From minor upgrades in trim or with the addition of some stripes, through to the full embellishment of a luxury grade edition, the BX may hold a record, along with the Saab 900, for limited or special edition nomenclature. In some cases just a few hundred or a few thousand were made, in other variants, such as the *Leader* in two available versions, over 12,000 were produced in just one edition alone.

BX Special or Limited Editions

Athena	*Hurricane*	*Preview*
Calanque	*Image*	*Progress*
Cannes	*Leader*	*Routiere*
Chamonix	*Leader E*	*Select*
Chic	*Millesime*	*Sport*
Classic	*Olympique*	*St Tropez*
Deauville	*Pallas*	*Tecnic*
Digit	*Palm*	*Tonix*
Elegance	*Prestige*	

NOTE: Add-on bodykits in the form of plastic extensions to wheel arches and bumpers were available for fitment across the range, and several rear lip, wing and deck spoilers were marketed.

suspension was tweaked and a sub-GT version with the 1.6-litre 113bhp engine was launched.

These forays into tuning meant that Citroën came up with yet another tweak – the BX 16 valve of 1987. This was the first multi-valve head Citroën that took its technology from Peugeot 205 rally-car developments. Fully kitted out with spoilers, flares and increased suspension pressure, the BX 16V was another screamer of a Citroën with real performance. Sadly, like many tuned-up BXs, it was less than reliable if driven as intended. By 1988, the 16-valve head was fitted to the BX 19 Gti, which also took its cue from a Peugeot – the 405 Mi 16V.

BX Oddities

From the BX 'Digit' to stillborn coupés, and a range of ambulances and vans, the BX leant itself to numerous reinterpretations, not least those built by Heuliez.

In the 'Digit', a BX 19GT of 105bhp was kitted out with electronic equipment that supplied a digital display screen instrument cluster and also saw other functions slaved to this display. Equipment included digitized instruments and an 'open door' monitoring system. The standard BX19 GT centre console information display screen was linked to an instrument display with diagramatic and digital displays with the speed function in a small TV-type screen; there was also a 1980s Hi-Fi sound system with fashionable 'woofer' and headphones jack. Remote central locking was also a first.

The rare BX three-door vans were first produced by Heuliez in 1987, and ran for several years in limited numbers, notably on Dutch, Danish and Irish markets. Heuliez fitted a new, smooth, one-piece side panel over each rear side, disguising the rear side doors; this was no typical Citroën Enterprise van with welded up side doors and windows on show. In fact the BX van looked remarkably good, and came as a BX 19 TD Van and as a trimmed up 19TD Van Special with metallic paint. As such, it was an early precursor to the latter fashion for highly equipped vans – though now it is a very rare sight indeed.

- The Heuliez-built BX 4×4 estate was popular in Alpine regions and massively competent, the ability to raise the suspension adding to its appeal
- In 1982 the Citroën design team came forward with a proposal for a BX Coupé – some of the styling elements were incorporated into the design of the XM
- 'France Design', the brand of Henri Heuliez Automobiles, has had a long association with Citroën and was responsible for the BX 'Dyana', a cross between an estate and an MPV or even a van – as such it was an early precursor to later such cars
- The BX-based *Scarabée d'Or* was presented at the 1990 Geneva Motor Show. Based on a shortened BX 4×4 platform, the name recalled that of the Autochenille driven by Georges Marie Haadt and Louis Audouin Dubreuil, which led the first trans-Sahara crossing by car in 1922

RALLY SUCCESS

With Citroën having entered Group B rallying with the BX in 1986, a rally version was inevitable. This was the BX 4TC, and bore little resemblance to the standard BX. The car had a re-tooled nose to allow a bigger engine, and it featured a non-Citroën engine – a 2.2-litre unit from Peugeot's strange Simca-Chrysler (later Talbot-branded) sub-brand ownership. Various items from the SM rally experience years were dusted

BX: THE CAR THAT SAVED CITROËN

off the shelf, including gearbox components. For FIA Group B purposes, 200 BX 4TC were made for public sale, though many were taken back after group B was banned.

The 4TC was not successful in World Rally Championships, and the cancellation of Group B after the rising death toll of drivers forced Citroën's hand to cancel the car.

J. Andruet /A. Peuvergne finished sixth in the 1986 Swedish Rally, but in that year's Acropolis, Monte Carlo rallies, other Group B BXs failed to finish. Yet on some rally stages, BX 4TC was as fast as the competing Peugeot 205s and Audi cars. BX 4TC had promise, but too much complexity, and was handicapped by that old front-drive bugbear of a forward-biased engine and resultant handling compromises. Nevertheless, although BX Group B may not have been a success, it taught Citroën a lot.

An interesting performance BX 'one-off' was the 16V seen as a dealer/private entry in Scandinavia, tuned by an outfit called 'Custom Racing'. Driven by Magnus Gustafsson, the car campaigned up to 1992 and achieved several top placings in the Swedish national rally series, including one class win. This car was reputed to have been fitted with an early form of 'Hydractiv' suspension from the new XM range.

LEFT: **A BX trimmed for 'Classic Challenge' entry.**

BELOW: **The BX Group B rally car was not a competitive success but it did seed the ground for later wins by Citroën's rally team. Note the revised frontal design and rear wing to WRC Group B rules.**

210

CHAPTER THIRTEEN

XM AND C6

UNDERESTIMATED GRANDES ROUTIÈRES

XM AND C6 | UNDERESTIMATED GRANDES ROUTIÈRES

SOMEHOW IT IS fitting that the XM, perceived as perhaps the last grand Citroën before the subsequent re-birth of Citroën changed that fact, should be such an architectural car. After all, the stars of Citroën's design team had (and have) had a training, or interest in architecture.

How apt, then, that the respected British design critic and architectural expert Jonathan Meades owned a white XM *Exclusive*, and described the XM as being 'the last Gothic Citroën' as cited by the design guru Stephen Bayley. XM was a clever car and one much maligned for problems that were nowhere near as bad as a certain British perspective created for the car. In France and in Europe, XM remained a reasonable success, not problem free, but still a true inheritor of the ethos, and a fine Citroën. XM was also briefly present in America at a cost of $55,000 per car, via the Netherlands-based CXA (America) import company.

The record is that the XM did have build quality issues and required proper servicing. There *were* electrical component lapses, but the XM was not always the nightmare so often portrayed across its character. True, the electronic suspension sensing needed modification, and some trim items were low rent, but XM was far from being as unreliable as some people suggest, even if its electrics preferred warmer climates. It was galvanized and was initially rust resistant – far more so than the CX. Today, XMs are being restored and sold for strong prices (even in Britain).

The XM can now be seen as a great car. Like a proper large Citroën, its styling was a defining emotion, and for many it was indeed a spaceship of a car, just as the CX had been.

DEVELOPMENT OF THE XM

The XM was packed with details, and this came about from its parentage, because fittingly, given Citroën's history, XM was a Franco-Italian concept. It could have been a purely French concept but for the issues of a new corporate reality. This is because in the early 1980s with Jean Giret as the top design manager (Robert Opron had gone to Renault) within what was once the Bureau d'Études, the Citroën team had quietly hatched a scheme for a 'big brother to BX' as a *de facto* CX replacement. An elegant styling model was made, and some key themes for a new, large Citroën fastback saloon firmed up. However, under PSA fiscal control (and once discovered by Citroën's masters), this car – an offspring of the post-CX idea for a 'DX' or 'Projet E' thinking – was killed off.

So any successor to the CX was going to be a PSA-sourced car, and the resulting XM was a reaction to change within Citroën. Peugeot had built the very elegant Paul Bracq-styled 604 as its range topper, and would need a replacement. This would become the Peugeot 605 (and the long forgotten Talbot Tagora), but could this shared platform be used to create a new big Citroën? The PSA management were running the Peugeot design office and the Citroën styling centre. Art Blakeslee was the PSA design function leader and latterly ran the Citroën studio after Trevor Fiore and then Carl Olsen who was in 1983 Citroën's own *chef du style*.

Jacques Calvet would soon enter the scene as Citroën's new president as the XM idea developed. Orders were handed down to Citroën to create a new large car project under the code

XM has all the air of a grand Citroën, just like its CX predecessor with which this lovely blue XM is posing.

XM AND C6: UNDERESTIMATED GRANDES ROUTIÈRES

RIGHT: **The author's late 1980s sketch for a 'DX' design project for a new large Citroën aped CX and DS themes, but was nearer the subsequent XM motif towards the rear.**

BELOW: **The clever glazing and glasshouse is very apparent in this view of an architectural car.**

name of 'Y30'. Inside PSA's Peugeot/Citroën design department were also Dan Abramson and Geoff Matthews. Citroën design was on the cusp of change: should a big Citroën be a retro-vision of the DS, or a transformed CX? Or could something entirely new be created?

To aid that process, PSA took the decision to ask the BX stylists at the Bertone styling studio to tender ideas for the new car alongside Citroën's own designers' themes. Meanwhile, over at Peugeot, the elegantly proportioned but bland 605 was being shaped.

The Design Team

Citroën's team included the long-established Jean Giret, and less well known names such as the Californian Dan Abramson, and Monsieurs Perrier and Bouvier. Under Carl Olsen's lead, the team experimented with new forms and shapes, and particular emphasis on the role of the car's turret or glasshouse emerged. The use of 'graphical window' design techniques also came to the fore and led to the idea of a cleverly glazed cabin with some expensively curved glass on the front and rear side windows.

In parallel, and through a series of meetings, the Bertone offering explored similar themes as designers Marcello Gandini, and principally Marc Deschamps, whose ideas would emerge as the XM prototype. It is reputed that Deschamps created his XM genesis sketch in flight on a piece of lined notepaper. Perhaps thoughts of paper aeroplanes were an inspiration?

Of note, the rising waist-line at the C-pillar took form from Bertone's studio, although it must be said that a similar theme may have been reflected within Citroën's design function in some earlier Michel Harmand sketches for a big saloon, and then in sketches from the Velizy team, where men such as

213

LEFT: **French plates and slit headlamps – an XM moment.**

ABOVE: **XM ends.**

Abramson were also exploring the deep glasshouse with kinked front and rear styling elements. Olsen drew up a three-box suggestion and Abramson a more curved two-box idea (with hints of graphical window treatment), but in the end Bertone was chosen despite their car's long and narrow feel. The Citroën team at Velizy did, however, get to influence many of the exterior and interior styling details under Olsen, and brought harmony and integrity to the effects of such detailing. The SM-inspired rear-lamp décor panel was pure Citroën. After Olsen resigned, Art Blakeslee guided XM to production.

Drawing up the Prototype

The two design teams had presented styling bucks to PSA management in late 1984, and the sharper-edged Bertone shape won through over ideas that included Abramson's more curved post-CX design study of great elegance and proportion; what is obvious, however, is that both teams contributed to the car once the style was chosen, because elements of several proposals emerged into the resultant whole. The XM gained had a tapered and narrower rear section – a typical Citroën trait, and one less obvious in Bertone's original styling model proposal. The low belt-line, imaginative use of glass, and smooth panels were all classic Citroën CX-derived imagery.

XM was unusual in that it had a low front with thin lamps, a long bonnet rising into a black-pillared cabin technique, and an element of what felt like ecclesiastical architecture to the pillars and the supports to the roof. At the rear, shades of the SM were felt. A 'floating' design graphic for the roof was used, in that it was seen above blacked-out pillars with no obvious joining to the car's belt-line – something not repeated until recently in the DS3. Somehow the trick did not work quite so well in the XM estate styling.

Citroën's interior designers created a modern and upmarket feel for the interior, but the issues of PSA finances, and the fashions of the time, resulted in a toned-down salon featuring a fair amount of injection-moulded black plastic, however smartly shaped. The early cars had a more definitive dashboard design with a single spoke (and in the Mk1.5, a rare two spoke). Uniquely, XM was a *de facto* hatchback yet had a 'bustle' bootlid and an internal double windscreen that isolated the cabin from the exterior when the rear hatch was opened.

As a 'two-box' car in a world of 'three-box' shapes, Citroën's new saloon did indeed continue the idea of the saloon that looked like a coupé. Although it remained 'different', it was also not so avant garde as to completely put off non-French buyers. The fact that the car had a form of hatchback was not so obvious as the 'two-box' format might have created. There were two views of XM's styling: either it was a stylish non-retro

XM AND C6: UNDERESTIMATED GRANDES ROUTIÈRES

XM with revised grille and trims looking angular in an original brochure shot.

iteration of Citroën themeology, or it was still too much for a BMW or Mercedes buyer who wanted a 'three-box' saloon.

Like the SM, the front and rear styling of the XM did not seem to match, and yet as with the SM, it didn't matter because you only saw one end at a time! The XM was as different from the CX as that car had been from the SM, and yet all three share certain traits in scaling – with narrowing, truncated rear dimensions and long, low belt lines and front wing stances. Strangely the tensions and two-box scales of their vastly dif-

fering sculptures seem to match. Yet Citroën's success in making the XM 'not' a CX copy or derivative has to have been the correct decision.

With its chamfered side panels, sleek glazing and finely tuned curvatures to the intersection of glass and metal, the XM was a very clever design. In its Mk2 version, the black-coloured trim at the base of the front windscreen was instead painted body colour, and this change significantly altered the appearance and stance of the car. Black-painted door mirrors were used to

Some early XMs came with pale leather or fabric seat trims, which lifted the interior ambiance from dark to light.

215

blend in with the window graphics. Perhaps stained glass should have been offered as an option for those who could see the XM's cathedralesque architecture.

Excellent attention was given to bodywork detailing and rear airflow off the roof, and this gave the XM a Cd. of 0.28 in early form (which would rise above Cd.0.30 in production trims) and with a low cross-sectional Cd.a 0.60.

Drivetrain, Suspension and Structure

Incredibly, despite the PSA corporate issues, XM was to be hydro-pneumatically suspended but conventionally braked. It was also a coupé car in a three-box saloon segment – but then so were the Rover SD1, Lancia Gamma and the Audi 100 Avant. The money saving came, of course, under the skin, where lower-powered XMs had the PSA-series engines. A joint PSA floor-pan saved even more money across the XM range.

Carburettor and fuel-injected 2.0-litre power was the early XM standard, but a turbo and an underdeveloped V6 was also to be offered as a derivative from the PRV V6 unit, latterly with a 24-valve head – which was to suffer from an internal camshaft oil flow issue – and then with a new PSA/E series V6 engine. An early diesel version of 1990 saw the XUD 1.9 diesel engine enlarged to 2.1 litres (this engine block was angled or canted forwards and harder to work on). It was slow but simple and unlikely to go wrong. A later 2.5 D engine from Citroën's commercial engine range proved to be heavy but very economical. This had a Garret turbocharger, 3 valves per cylinder, twin-balancer shafts, hydro-elastic engine mounts and 217ft/lb of torque at just 2,000rpm – a proper van engine!

Just as the CX was an improvement on the DS's structural safety, so was the XM on the CX, by offering improved offset frontal crash performance. This was largely due to the XM having strong inner-wing housings and a specially designed kinked beam mounted at the rear of each front wheel-arch. This metal crush-member transferred offset-angled impact energy downwards and towards the centre of the car, and in doing so reduced cabin deformation and intrusion at the A-pillar. The sills were also increased in gauge thickness, as experience with the BX and CX had shown that they needed to be stronger; however, this did not stop many wet-climate XMs suffering terminal sill rot in later life. Blocked sunroof drains also caused big rust problems in the bodyshell. To save weight, XM followed BX practice and used a glassfibre bonnet and rear boot panel.

Electro-oleo-pneumatic Problems

Although hydro-pneumatic, the XM did not have double front wishbones, but a modified yet conventional front strut mechanism (which gave rise to typical strut mount corrosion); at the rear a more Citroënesque solution of rods and arms sufficed. Re-tuned, re-damped and with stronger anti-roll levels, XM's revised suspension system and its electro-signalling was a big advance.

Issues with electric systems were the XM's main problem, notably in 'H1' guise. Burn-out was a significant problem with

Under the bonnet with the 24-valve powerplant and green spheres.

the electronic valves and transistor, and revised parts were substituted. Also, early cars were often stuck in the firmer 'sport' suspension mode when the electro valve that controlled the extra sphere became jammed, but this could self-cure or be dealer fettled!

Across variants Mk1, the revised Mk1.5 and Mk2, faulty connections and sensing in systems mounted in the front wings and under the car proved the undoing of many an XM. Cars in the dryer south of France were less prone to ingress into the components. Citroën updated the ECUs on two occasions, and Bendix ABS sensors can be replaced with Teves brand.

The XM's version of 'Hydractive' suspension used sensors to monitor numerous suspension parameters, and those of brake, throttle and steering settings to create information for an on-board computer, which then either hardened or softened not just ride pressure in the hydro-pneumatic spheres, but also roll resistance as an inherent function. Sadly, climate, water and humidity affected the sensors and caused unreliability in the systems that were not modified. Use of a further 'anti-sink' Hydractive mechanism was seen on later XMs.

So it was a heavily revised version of the venerable hydro-pneumatics that was used in the XM's suspension, with much advanced tuning stemming from the BX and Xantia works. The green-painted spheres were still there, but pressures, sensing and wheel travel allied to tyre/wheel ratio were all expertly revised to give XM the best ride and handling compromise – one enhanced by the use of the self-sensing, electro-mechanically operated 'Hydractive' I/II system. You could even opt for 'comfort' suspension spheres on the XM to provide a more compliant ride.

British XMs were given the advanced 'active' suspension, but were not fitted with DIRAVI steering, as seen on top-spec European cars, except in the very last days of the Mk2 XM. XM was European Car of the Year in 1990.

The original XM interior with single-spoke wheel and black leather.

The later XM series 2 interior featured an airbag-equipped steering wheel and Xantia overtones.

For the 1995 model year a MK2 variant was launched in 1994; this had an air-bagged, four-spoke steering wheel – thus marking the end of the decades-old single-spoke motif – new dashboard mouldings and interior trims, and the more 'active' suspension to reduce roll. Also incorporated was the ZX/Xantia-derived 'rear steer' geometry. An unloved new nose cone was added, and for the European mainland, revised, more powerful headlamps.

Nearly 50,000 units were sold in the XM's first year of sales, and nearly 100,000 in the second year. But sales dropped by 45 per cent in year three, and by 1999 were below 10,000 a year; thus the car was hardly viable after just over 300,000 units had been made. In 1999 the XM, often wrongly called 'the last big Citroën', died a quiet death, though sales lingered into 2000. Along the way it had been beset with electronic connector failings, especially in northern climes, and had suffered a wider

---

MODEL DEVELOPMENT XM SALOON AND ESTATE

Key trim specifications:
i: Si: Sei: Si V6 Sei V6: Sei V6 24:V6 24V: D: SD; SeD
MK2: SX:VSX: *Exclusive*
French market special trim names: *Seduction, Harmonie, Ambiance, Exclusive*
Netherlands, Belgium trim names: *Seduction, Luxury, Pullman*
German market special trim names: *Classic, Tecnic, Pallas*

Special editions: 1992–94: Onyx, Premier, Prestige
Trim levels: VS, VSX and Exclusive. French launch 23 May 1989; British launch 29 September 1989

Model Dateline
Spring 1989: XM launched with 2.0-litre engine including injection, and V6 2.0-litre models including early carburettor cars in the UK prior to injection models.
1990: 24-valve V6 launched.
1991: Break (estate) launched – Heuliez-built.
1993: Turbocharged 2.0-litre launched.

Diesel variants: Early XM D featured the enlarged XUD engine at 2.1 litres with 110bhp. In 1996 the 2.5 D, with a claimed 130bhp for its commercial vehicle-derived engine, was focused on the British market and French farmers.

1995: XM was revised to 'Mk2' standard and given refreshed body mouldings, trim applications, and the use of the Xantia-derived 'Hydractive II' controlled suspension management system for hydro-pneumatics; however, the more advanced suspension from the Xantia Activa was not deployed other than on a handful of development cars.
1997: New PSA V6 across all PSA top range cars and used in the XM.

Late 1999: Production slows; some sales in early 2000.

NOTE: A series of rear-mounted aerodynamic devices were tried on the XM – perhaps with more marketing purpose than vital aerodynamic effect. On later cars an extended lip ridge was added to the trailing edge of the bootlid, and this offered significant airflow benefit. Some earlier cars had a pylon-supported rear wing device atop the lid

Engine Options
Citroën modified their petrol and diesel engine blocks on numerous occasions to produce the PSA 'D' series engine variants:

1989–94: XU series engines of 2.0-litre 8V, 2.0-litre 8V injection: 109bhp, 2.0-litre 8V injection 'C' spec 120bhp
1990–94: 2.0-litre 16V 130bhp
1989–94: 3.0-litre (2.9) PRV (PSA/Renault/Volvo) V6 12V 166bhp
1990–97: 3.0-litre V6 24V, 197bhp
1992–94: 2.0-litre Turbo (Garrett Airesearch) 16V with 143bhp
1994–2000: 3.0-litre (2.9) V6 12V 168bhp
1994–2000: 2.0-litre Turbo 16V with 143bhp
1994–97: 3.0litre V6 24V 197 bhp
1997–2000: 3.0-litre V6 E series 188 bhp

Diesel
1989–94: 2.1-litre XUD Diesel 80bp
1989–94: 2.1-litre XUD Turbo 109bhp
1994–99: 2.1-litre XUD B series 107bhp and Mitsubishi Turbo variant
1994–2000: 2.5-litre C Diesel series 127bhp and over 200lb/ft torque

malaise of poor quality trim items. However, when properly serviced and well looked after, the XM proved to have a loyal following – notably in the Netherlands and further south. The Heuliez-crafted estate or 'break' versions also continued the tradition of the large Citroën estate.

A galvanized car, XM resisted rot far better than the CX (not a difficult task…) yet now, two decades into XM, it has been found that the car rusts in the front suspension turrets and sills, and the rear subframes can be afflicted. The use of rubber bonding allowing moisture ingress caused the front strut top corrosion, but replacement materials can solve the issue.

XM Mk3?

As XM sales slowed in 1997 and the car's future was debated, Citroën funded a Mk3 facelift for the XM; however, this got no further than a styling studio model, crafted in 1998, in which a Xantia-style nose was grafted on, and bizarre tail-lamp strakes added at the rear. Most curiously, the black-painted glasshouse was replaced with body-coloured pillars and door frames. In fact the styling model was asymmetric, on one side featuring a mild restyle that retained the XM's creased skin pressings, and on the other a much more expensive, smoother Xantia-style body panel retooling proposal. But the whole XM effect and the original glasshouse graphical window treatment was destroyed, and the car looked instantly forgettable and could have easily worn a Renault badge: luckily the idea was discarded.

XM SPECIALS AND MODIFICATIONS

XMA Pallas/Vitesse

After the withdrawal of Citroën from America, the CXAuto company had imported CXs into America with relevant modifications – all via a Netherlands-based operating base. This company briefly flirted with imported XM cars into North America, and even took a stand at the 1991 New York Motor Show. A 2-litre injection-engined version tagged with the *Pallas* trim name was accompanied by the 3-litre V6 variant with *Vitesse* badging. It is reputed that a few XM *Exclusive* cars were imported in late 1992. Prices started at USD $55,000 and hard sales figures are difficult to ascertain. Ever-increasing emissions laws saw the XM cease to be available in America by late 1996.

XM Limousines

As early as 1992, Heuliez created a 'besuited and booted' limousine version of the XM. These were cars with extended bodies and conventional 'three-box' styling amid a sombre and conventional 'take' on the XM underpinnings.

The Tissier company also created a long body, booted XM tagged as 'Majesté' and weighing in at nearly 4,410lb (2,000kg).

Another XM body extension saw the car serve at the Élysée Palace in a fleet of presidential and ministerial XMs in true big Citroën style.

Extended wheelbase presidential limousine XM: note the double B-pillar insert.

XM Vans

As usual with nearly every Citroën, a van version for European tax-band consumption resulted in the inevitable XM 'Break Service', which on this occasion was created in the Netherlands to order by the Dutch Citroën concessionaire. It was constructed to order by a company called ASH as a basic cargo-floored van version that would make full use of the tax laws that encouraged such vehicles. The biggest structural alteration was a raised roof – one that expanded upon the original XM estate revised roof tooling. A lesser conversion with window blanks but retaining the furnished cabin was also offered.

In Slovenia, close to the output of the Citroën OltCit, the EME engineering company created long-wheelbase XM estate-based cargo carriers that were not unlike the special six-wheeled CX cargo vans that had been used by couriers and publishers for European night delivery runs. Long-wheel-based XM saloons were also created. The Heuliez-influenced XM estate (or Break) was a strong base for modification, and was used as the basis for private ambulances by independent coachbuilders such as Baboulin, GIFA and Petit.

Bodykit Cars

The 1980s fad for body-kitting cars even touched XM – thankfully via a reasonably restrained glassfibre/plastics range of stick-on addenda including rear wings, side skirts and new front valance and headlamps, created by the Belgian firm of Cituning.

OWNERS' IMPRESSIONS

A growing number of British and European XM enthusiasts have emerged; with a website forum and regular club meetings, the XM brigade has become a firm feature in the various Citroën car clubs. Russell Wallis, a Coventry trained automotive designer and well known Citroën illustrator says of the XM:

> Owners love these cars for their distinctive and individualistic Bertone styling. XM is quirky, yet it also manages to be somewhat discreet. It looks fast and purposeful. A traditional Citroën quirk of stubby rear and large front overhangs is retained. The design has real personality and character. Some might call it bland compared to the CX or DS, but the XM takes direct styling themes from the SM, so has every right to be considered a true Citroën. The design is unapologetically sharp, linear, crisp, low, sleek and importantly French! It has an arrogance to be something different from the usual executive cars of the time. However, the XM was a car that was meant to be more sober and approachable.
>
> It was meant to appeal to the successful executives of the era, and there is an element in the design which successfully combines both approaches. It is quirky but more conventional. Especially the interior.

Matthew Thomas is an architect, former Saab 900 owner, and true Citroën XM fanatic (he owns six XMs); he says:

> Although I never had other Citroëns, like many people I vaguely knew about the legendary DS and that most Citroëns were both quirky looking and technically innovative cars. Apart from another Saab, the only car that appealed was the XM.
>
> I just loved the shape, especially that sharp nose and other generally angled lines and the wrap-around glass, whilst the car seemed understated but also stood out in the crowd and was quite a rare sight even at that time. Our collection of XMs at one time reached seven cars, but currently we have six. I should add that the Citroën XM we own are very much daily drives. There is much pleasure (and support) available through the shared enthusiasm of fellow owners.

Darren Cross is another XM fanatic who is also touched by the XM's inter-galactic qualities:

> I remember passing an XM on the M1 motorway on my motorbike very slowly, taking in the styling and having a good stare. It was 1989 and the first time I had seen one, and just like the first time a CX Gti Turbo2 wafted past me several years earlier, the XM made an instant impression on me. It was the combination of the striking way it looked, and the way it seemingly floated along the motorway, I think the XM's striking lines polarize opinion – it's like a classic prog rock band: you either get it or you don't! From that first close encounter, I coveted an XM!
>
> Now when I look through the driver's side window of my XM at those sculpted black leather seats and interior cockpit, I am transported back in time for a split second, to 'Captain Scarlet', or 'Dan Dare'. There is something about the XM that evokes emotions of my 'sci-fi' boyhood in the late eighties.

OPPOSITE PAGE:
XM estate in Mandarin Red with revised grille and looking like a proper Citroën estate. Note the differing roof line and door/window frames.

XM AND C6: UNDERESTIMATED GRANDES ROUTIÈRES

SPECIFICATIONS — XM

Body
Five-door hatchback and five-door estate steel monocoque with composite panels. Production 1989–1999.

Engine
Front-wheel-drive transverse in-line 4-cylinder and v-angled V6s. In-line diesels 2.0/2.0 T/3.0 V6 12v/3.0 V6 24v/2.9 V6 24v/2.1 DT/2.5 DT

Transmission
Five-speed manual and four-speed automatic.

Suspension
Hydro-pneumatic with electro-mechanical signalling and ride control.

Dimensions

Length	185.4in (4,708mm) (hatchback); 195.4in (4,963mm) (estate)
Width	70.6in (1,793mm).
Height	54.8in (1,392mm); estate: 57.5in (1,466mm).
Wheelbase	112.2in (2,850mm).
Weight	2,888lb (1,310kg); 3,417lb (1,550kg). *(unladen)*

BERRY GOES XM

Jonathan Meades made me buy an XM. If you think you've heard the name before but are unsure where or how exactly, he's the unfashionably clever chap who occasionally appears on television. Static. Declamatory. Monochromatic. He's the reason I acquired an XM.

The first car I ever owned was a Citroën. It was an Ami 8 estate in 'washing machine' white. Crucially, it wasn't a Fiesta and used less fuel than Private Frazer's paraffin lamp in *Dad's Army*.

My father had bought it without consulting me. He told me I could pay him back 'as-and-when' but that didn't stop me from resenting its eccentric appearance, quirky controls and the utter absence of anything that might warrant the use of the word 'performance'. I was seventeen years old and (obviously) arrogance, ignorance and ingratitude were my default settings. Most definitely not a case of 'Mon Ami, Mate'. But I did want to make friends with a big, buxom, Bardo-esque Citroen DS.

This would be about the time that Paul Weller broke up The Jam, formed The Style Council, and released an album called *Café Bleu*. He seemed very taken with all things French, so long as they were from the France of the 1960s. I followed suit – a tight, black, three-button suit of the type still favoured by Monsieur Meades. I consumed Camus, Godard and Gainsbourg. I smoked Gauloise and drank Pastis, often at the same time. And I lusted after Françoise Hardy and the piano black DS with the blood red seats stolen by Alain Delon in *Le Samouraï*.

Meades could talk about anything, and often does, but his abiding obsessions are buildings and food. Poolside in Palm Springs, I bought an Onyx Blue XM. I bought it because Meades said cars are architecture just as much as any building of granite and glass – and because he also said that the Citroën XM was the last Gothic car.

The day I caught the train to Peterborough – where I was to collect this car I had neither seen nor driven, but had committed to buy – I stuffed a couple of old motoring magazines in my bag. I keep a man-sized pile of CAR from the eighties and nineties as I'd rather re-read Setright, Bulgin and May for the umpteenth time than tackle the guff that automotive-minded publications attempt to pass off these days. Pulling out the March 1997 edition of *CAR*, selected entirely at random, I learned that the Citroën XM was one of the 'Ten Worst cars of the Twentieth Century'. 'Inadequately-engined and difficult to drive' was the damning verdict. And if that was when they were new, what fresh horrors would a two-decade old example hold?

I like the XM's 'Job Centre Plus' aesthetic – acres of hard, shiny black plastic and doesn't-show-the-dirt upholstery. I've seen wood-and-leather interiors on more upmarket models and they look entirely unsuited for the inside of a car with such a super seventies space-age shape. I like the fact that it's the only car I've ever owned, driven, or seen on the street, or in a magazine or a movie about a dystopian future, with two rear windows. I like the way it skates around the city treating its crumbling infrastructure with impunity, nay, disdain. I call the car Gerard, by the way, because it's big, distinctive and very, very French.

I like the fact that if I had to I could live in it and would. I like the fact that it cost me next to nothing to buy and I can leave it parked in places you wouldn't walk your pit bull. I like the fact that men of a certain age will, on clocking me getting in, delay their progress so that a small child can experience the theatre of big Citroën dragging its arse of the floor and into the air.

STEVE BERRY, *Citroëniste, writer, biker, driver, broadcaster, XM owner*

XM RETROSPECTIVE

One thing is for sure, XM made many friends and is making more today as its qualities seem, quite paradoxically, to have imbued it with a contradictory classic, true 'old Citroën' status. Given its origins, this speaks volumes for its design and its driving.

A question remains, however: what was XM? A trick forced upon Citroën's purists by the heavy hand of PSA, or in fact a perfectly viable 'proper' Citroën that used a common, shared platform and mechanics for the basis of a stylish *grande routière*? Was XM a 'real' Citroën? These are the questions that Citroënistes ask and argue over, and probably always will.

Surely the answers to these questions lie in the 'grey' land that is between the black and white. True, XM used Peugeot mechanicals and engineering (even a Peugeot/Renault-Volvo engine) and therefore the purist can say it was not a 'real' Citroën – but by default if we use that definition, *no* car has been

XM AND C6: UNDERESTIMATED GRANDES ROUTIÈRES

since 1976 nor ever can be again, which is plainly too narrow a view. But XM *was* avant-garde, it was hydro-pneumatic, it was aerodynamic, it was bizarre in style and feel, and of course, it was fraught with occasional gremlins. So in all these respects, XM was indeed a 'real' Citroën. And who could argue with an XM *Exclusive* in white paint with black leather, or perhaps ultimately, an XM in mandarin crimson metallic hue, where the car looked like a true, grand Citroën.

XM had great style and shades of DS, CX, and even the four-door SM. For that, surely we can offer it a place in all but the most hardened of Citroën hearts.

C6: A RETURN TO GRAND FORM

In late 1998 XM was long in the tooth and about to be quietly culled, and Citroën did not have a big car. The Xantia V6 was also soon to be gone and the grand marque of France had no flagship. It was a bizarre situation made worse by the resurgence of competing Renault design ability, and the risk that Citroën was being perceived as moving down market. It seems that one fine corporate day, the powers that be at PSA decided to ask for the money to make another big Citroën, or rather a single example, a show car special designed to suggest what might be possible. And of a real car? There would be a caveat that this time it had to be fully developed with no nasty surprises lurking under the bodywork.

So was born the idea for what became Citroën C6 Lignage, that begat the C6, which itself evoked a 1920s name.

As the last year of the twentieth century approached, PSA's Jean-Marie Folz and Citroën's Claude Satinet took a decision that would lead to them tasking the Citroën design centre (by now a 'Centre de Creation') to present themes for a big new car – one that would put the press and public alike off the idea that Citroën would never build another grand land yacht car.

ABOVE: **Last of the line: XM 'Exclusive' shows off a rear design image that was very clever indeed.**

RIGHT: **C6 Lignage design concept defined a new design language for Citroën and influenced the C4 and the C6. The side pontoons and blades were very significant.**

Form and Function

The American designer Art Blakeslee would guide the creation of a big Citroën – and what an opportunity that was for a designer and team. It was a chance Blakeslee said he had waited for, for a long time. Yet the concept, and its creation and building into a 'show car one-off', would have to be done in weeks. Blakeslee and the team threw themselves into the challenge and created the Citroën C6 Lignage design in a few short weeks in early 1999.

Lead manager amongst the car's design team was Mark Lloyd, who joined Citroën in 1989 after graduating from the Royal College of Art Vehicle Design Unit; he then worked on the Activa 2 and Xanaé at Citroën advanced design at Velizy. But it was Marc Pinson who sketched and modelled the form of the C6 Lignage, and Vladimir Pirozhkov the lead interior designer who came up with the concept's radical cabin with its expansive sculpture and in-built bonsai tree! Pirozhkov's cabin was a blend of the exotic and the possible – perhaps reflecting his time as a design intern with Luigi Colani; Pirozhkov went on to lead interior design at Citroën, then at Toyota, and at the time of writing heads a leading Russian industrial design organization.

Blakeslee was clearly clever enough to avoid any hint of 'retro' – which would surely have destroyed Citroën's credibility. The Lignage concept car, and the consequent (delayed by five years) outcome as the C6, was a clever piece of innovative reverse engineering that captured the true spirit of Citroën in a stunning manner.

Marc Pinson developed a theme for Lignage and on through to C6 which evoked a hydrodynamic and aerodynamic feel – drawing heavily on Citroën's origins (as detailed herein). The idea of a land-yacht or even a catamaran was mooted by the designers. Pinson blended all the important styling elements together – A-pillars, side blades, and the traditional falling-away tail – yet C6 also had a spacious rear cabin with no loss of headroom or boot/trunk capacity. Overall it was a remarkable achievement, and one that also echoed the past in that it was translated from a few early sketches directly into model form, as Pinson and a modeller went straight from basic sketch to clay model.

The shape of the car was neither retro-pastiche nor derivative, it was a true reinvention of tradition, as is the best of Citroën design. With the chevron-themed large motifs and hints of vintage 'pontoon' styling in the arrow-edged front wings, which then led back into a fast-backed dome, there was much cleverness to the shape. The rear end was particularly clever in that it tapered but avoided being weak or thin in its graphics. Hints of Opron's SM dynamic lines sweeping downwards at the rear were obvious, and the ellipsoid rear windscreen was just very clever. Suddenly in one go, Citroën had an organic, cohesive, brilliant design icon: but would it remain a Geneva Motor Show exercise built on a modified XM platform, or would it become a new production car – and if it did, would too much be lost in translation?

With the new C4 range launching in 2004, Citroën was too busy trying to re-establish its mid-sector cars to finally create the offspring of Lignage until after the C4 was safely delivered.

Possessing its tapering form and exquisite scales and angles, the production C6 looked every inch (or centimetre) the grand Citroën: it can only be hailed as the finest return-to-form design exercise seen in years. Here were elements of CX, XM and SM, yet wrapped in an innovative package. With elegant headlamps, a new variation of the chevron, and fluted, Lalique-inspired rear lamps, C6 oozed French design couture.

At the rear, a concave, part-ellipsoid rear windscreen provided the usual advanced aerodynamic tuning and CX-style self-cleaning. On early high range cars a 'pop-up' rear spoiler on certain models aided downforce at higher speeds (lower spec non-spoilered cars had a different bootlid moulding, with a built-in Kamm-type ridge). A stunning set of cross-spoke alloy

C6 command post: subtle not overpowering.

XM AND C6: UNDERESTIMATED GRANDES ROUTIÈRES

LEFT: **The prototype show car's inspired interior, which was latterly translated into the C6 cabin under lead designer B. Rapatel.**

ABOVE: **The C6 retained much of the prototype's design. This dark blue paint seems to make the most of its elegance. The headlamps and chevron design motifs signal something very special indeed.**

RIGHT: **From the rear, with Lalique-inspired lights, a concave rear windscreen and emotive and dynamic body creases, C6 was a work of pure design brilliance to rival Citroën's best.**

225

Fluted lamps, curved glass and a 'pop-up' spoiler.

wheels set off the car, which had enough design in its statement to cause the same effect as a Rolls-Royce as it passed by. Here was an elegant, aerodynamic, stunning big Citroën: surely even the purists would not decry its PSA underpinnings?

Possibly the greatest sense of occasion came from the C6's interior: many owners opted for the light beige trimmed in full or part-leather, dependent on trim choice. With high-quality synthetic mouldings and a vast sense of room created by the pale colours, this interior created a relaxing ambiance of a true salon on wheels. The use of Mukonto wood shaped into half-circles on each door trim lent an Art Deco feel to the car, and the wood contrasted well with the polished alloy and chrome-effect trim fittings. The only other interior colour offered was a Germanic dark grey, which although it masked dirt and wear better, simply did not create the grand sensory event of the traditional light-toned interior. Some buyers wished Citroën would have offered a tan leather interior to mimic the effects of the SM and DS days, but it was not to be.

C6 was a car affected by colour. In black or dark blue it had the look of an imposing limousine, in grey paint it looked faster, yet in metallic crimson it looked very different indeed, and in particular the effect of the rear lamp motifs was lost because they blended into the paintwork colour. Some owners chose to order their C6s in white or gold, and these colours exposed the shut lines and detracted from the car's formal feel. At one stage Citroën offered a special edition C6 'Blanc et Noir', where the body was white topped with a gloss black painted roof:

Your carriage awaits: Citroën's interior design team for the C6 created a magical sense of occasion that the lighter-coloured interior exemplifies.

XM AND C6: UNDERESTIMATED GRANDES ROUTIÈRES

some thought this made the car look like a cheap hatchback, others liked it.

Given Citroen's architectural connections, perhaps it should not have been a surprise when the architectural company *Neutral* created a specially designed 'C6 garage'. Costing three times the price of the actual car to go in it, the structure was made from light-transmitting concrete, had a roof terrace and, according to its co-creator Christian Grou, allowed C6 owners to show off their cars, rather than hide them away as was traditionally done.

Powerplants

A PSA 3.0-litre V6 petrol engine option (deleted in 2009) offered real power and style to make the C6 an unsuspected getaway car, but in economic reality the 2.7 HDI diesel engine (latterly 3.0 litres) twin-turbo unit (jointly developed across a PSA/Jaguar/Ford investment) was the engine of choice.

From 2006 to 2008 a 2.2-litre diesel engine option with manual gearbox gave the C6 a slightly different character, but for many the ultimate car has to be the 3.0-litre HDI six-speed automatic. Yet it is perhaps the classic V6 petrol-powered C6 that retains its CX and XM affinity in a more real sense of grand Citroënism. Good as the 2.7-litre twin turbo diesel was, the driver had to compensate for its somewhat languid 'pick up'. Like the Jaguar S-Type with the same engine, the car was fast and economical and a fine cruiser, but its overtaking performance was handicapped by the sudden decline in diesel torque once a certain point had been hit in the torque graph.

Given that the XM had a 'Sport' mode to its suspension, a developed version was an obvious need for the C6, as were other tweaks to rates, sensing and signalling parameters in the hydro-pneumatic set-up: this was tagged 'Hydractive III+'.

Not all C6s were black or blue. Grey and crimson were a better choice than white or gold.

Building the C6 with structural elements visible.

Sales Figures

Fewer than 1,000 C6s were sold between 2006 and 2012 (an early sale in late 2005 is recorded) in Great Britain, with 973 claimed as sold, although the car achieved stronger figures in Europe where a total of 23,385 units was sold – and as usual with a big Citroën, it sold well in the Netherlands, not just in France. Sales in Cyprus, Greece and Italy were also evident.

The C6 was not immune from suspension and electronics issues, and was also subjected to a recall. Citroën absorbed many of the costs, but the car did retain a traditional requirement for visits to a dealer. To prove it was indeed a true Citroën, it was reputedly necessary to remove the rear seat and drop the fuel tank in order to change the rear ABS sensor!

C6 oddities in the British marketplace include two C6 2.2 diesels being ordered with manual gearboxes, and both with the special interior pack and its 'TGV'-style rear seat option. One British owner has converted his C6 petrol-V6 to LPG power.

C6 was also fitted with an electronic self-diagnosis system known as 'telemetric BSI', which allowed the car's parameters to be modified or re-set – everything from lighting combinations to the automatic function of options.

Manufacture of the C6 range was discontinued in April 2012, and in late 2013 Citroën dealers still had various new, demonstrator and used stock choices on hand.

C6 in different mood.

The Last Grand Citroen?

C6 has a dedicated following and is already a collectors item, but sadly in terms of sales, it did represent another chapter in the failure of the big French car concept to penetrate a world market. Whilst the DS (and CX) achieved this, the SM, XM and C6 did not. This should not detract from the design and driving brilliance of the C6, however, which to those in the know, remains an incredible Citroën. Was it the last true, grand, hydro-pneumatic Citroën land yacht? For the moment it was and remains so, but in coming years, and as the economic crisis eases, Citroën will surely give us another such car – one that may just stun the world in true 'DS' effect.

C6 MODEL DETAILS

Engines
3.0-litre V6 PSA E series, 200bhp.
2.2-litre diesel with manual and auto gearbox options.
2.7-litre V6 HDI twin turbo diesel, 201bhp.
3.0-litre HDI diesel 2992cc, 240bhp.

Notable features include a head-up display; tyre-pressure monitoring system; lane departure warning system; hydractive three suspension; automatic rear spoiler system; Xenon directional headlamps; 'pop up' bonnet design to reduce pedestrian injuries to a new EURONCAP standard. 'Lounge' pack offers reclining individual rear seats.

Model Life 2005–2012
2005: Late year launch for 2006 model year in France.
2006: Fully launched with Base, Lignage and Exclusive trim ranges.
2008: White paint offered in range. 2.2 HDI superseded.
2009: Lignage range trim dropped; V6 Petrol deleted for 2010 model year.
2010: 3.0-litre HDI variants with six-speed autoboxes as main range leaders.
2012: Production ends.

CHAPTER FOURTEEN

AX TO ZX

**VIA XANTIA
AND XSARA**

AX TO ZX | *VIA XANTIA AND XSARA*

AFTER THE PSA takeover of Citroën and the constraints placed on the old Citroën design unit function, change was to manifest, and with it came the years when Citroën was less able to perform its previous avant-garde design brief. This did not mean that the cars built in the new era were not good ones, but it did result in a period of more restrained design and engineering practice at Citroën: the resultant cars have been tagged 'dull' by some, but this is a generalization too far. A great deal of talented design work went into this period of Citroën's existence, but it has to be stated that it was a period devoid of Citroën's traditional output. We can lay the responsibility for that with accountants, managers and marketing men, and not with designers or engineers. And after all, Citroën, after its years of losses, needed to re-group and emerge to a new period of growth, which it has.

Because these cars are derived from pre-existing platforms and drivetrains, their stories are, by default, shorter, reflecting their differing engineering significance.

AX – THE 2CV REVERSE ENGINEERED?

The Citroën AX is often ignored, but it has a dedicated following amongst Citroën club members. So was it just another lightweight small hatchback of the type churned out by many manufacturers in the 1980s? The answer is that it was more than that because, just like the original 2CV, it was technologically advanced under its somewhat basic exterior.

The reality is that the AX was a surprisingly clever little car containing a lot of design. As such it was a long way ahead of the likes of the ancient Austin Metro/Rover 100, or cars like the Toyota Starlet or various small Euro-boxes. In effect it re-invented certain original 2CV characteristics; what cannot be denied is that the AX was a PSA car of ultra light weight built to meet the standards pertaining at the time. Today it has proved itself to be a long-lasting, durable little hold-all, and many are still providing strong service across Europe.

From 1986 to the 1999 model year, AX replaced the LNA and could be construed as a modern 'take' on the 2CV's principles; however, it was no real replacement for the bigger Visa range. Design studies had begun with the idea of creating a cross-branded Peugeot-Citroën replacement for the LNA, 104 and the Talbot Samba. Rationalization within PSA saw the AX appear as a stand-alone Citroën, while Peugeot went on to create the 106, which in itself became the Citroën Saxo.

Detailed Design

Following on from the BX, the AX used extensive portions of moulded plastics for its body panels including bumper aprons, rear hatch and other panels. The basic car weighed in at a stunning 1,410lb (640kg); adding a larger engine, sports wheels and trims and five doors would add up to 440lb (200kg) to that figure.

The body panel metal gauges were thinned down in non-critical areas and strengthened in others. The engine was mounted to the body to reduce the costs of having a heavy sub-frame, and even the dashboard was a thin, one-piece moulding of such fragility that it would split apart, and had to be upgraded to a new design. The styling met certain essential parameters for a low-drag small car, and the design team were discouraged from creating anything too *avant garde*. Despite these constraints, the AX was a finely tailored car with smart details and a neatness to its design. The body design was led by Geoffrey Matthews, and reputedly had input from some Fergus Pollock ideas, from his time in the unit.

Of particular interest was the car's aerodynamics, in that small cars are very difficult to make 'slippery', and achieving low drag in such a tiny car is a huge challenge to the designer. Citroen spent thousands of hours fine-tuning the AX's aerodynamics, and this included curved panels at the front, an integrated radiator flow path, and a defined critical separation ridge at the top of the rear roof allied to sculpting of the hatchback and under-car apron area. Panel gap tolerances were given special attention. Care was also given to window sealing and gutters and seams – and the combined result of all these measures was a stunning Cd.0.31.

By combining lightweight, efficient little engines and superior aerodynamics, AX became one of the most economical small cars on the market, and could be driven across a greater portion of Europe on one tankful of cheap petrol.

The car was available from its launch in late 1986 as a three-door hatchback with 1.0-, 1.1- and 1.4-litre PSA TU-series cambelt-equipped engines. Within two years a five-door model had arrived. Diesels were a PSA 1.4-litre, which soon became a 1.5-litre engine of supreme economy. The 1.4 (1360cc) TUD diesel engine broke the mythical 3ltr per 100km economy target by achieving 2.7ltr per 100km. In reality this meant that an AX could achieve over 85mpg (3.3ltr/100km) – and one car did just that in an economy trial from Britain to Spain by travelling 1,000 miles (1,609km) on 10gal (45.5ltr) of standard fuel at a near-constant cruising speed.

Although the suspension was entirely conventional, Citroën's engineers tuned in some excellent spring rates, damper rebound settings and typical long-wheel travel.

The AX – small, light, cheap and simple, but no 2CV nor real Visa replacement yet a good car in its own right.

No small car can offer the safety levels of a large car, with all its mass and larger deformation zones that will inevitably better absorb crash energy. AX was a small car, yet it offered acceptable crash performance in its day, and although potentially liable to the kind of footwell and steering wheel/dashboard intrusion to be expected in a small car impact, the tightly welded central hub with its thick B-pillar stood up well to impact and offered a better frontal offset crash performance than several of its major rivals. However, the fact remained that, as with any small car, big car levels of passive safety could not be achieved.

Developments

AX had distinct phases, first as a low-cost, basic economy car, then as fitted with bigger engines and sports-market trim affections, and finally as a facelifted, more comfortable baby hatchback in an increasingly busy marketplace.

Less than eighteen months after its birth AX became available as the AX Sport, with a 1.3-litre twin-carburettor, roller-skate packing of very nearly 100bhp (95bhp/71KW). The car came with Peugeot 205 Rallye-style white-painted wheels and a revised exhaust and inlet manifold. This was a true low weight to high power ratio, and was a car that soon found favour amongst the private rally fraternity in France. By late 1989 specification changes were made to the carburettor choice and trim items.

A lower-powered AX 14 GT with 85bhp/63KW was also created, and came with the first set of dedicated AX alloy wheels, yet had a single carburettor set-up. After late 1990 the use of fuel injection in these small engines reduced emissions but changed the behaviour of such small engines.

In late 1992 there were also changes to the hatchback moulding, revised bumpers and grilles, as well as seat designs and trims, and the revised dashboard moulding. These changes effectively created AX Mk2. In this period was also the birth of the fuel-injected, 100bhp, AX GTi which replaced the GT. The AX GTi was heavily marketed across Europe and was very popular in Great Britain. The AX was a big money earner for Citroën in the early 1990s.

Special Editions included *Chicago, Dimension, Echo, Elation, Forte, Las Vegas, Memphis, Spree, Spot* and *Tonic*.

Further European market/regional Special Editions included *Air France Madame, Audace, Chicago, En Vouge, Escapade, Flash, Hit FM, Image, Miami, Mutine, Olympique, Prestige, Piste Rouge* (AX 4×4), *Reflet, Thalassa* and *Vulcane*.

A limited AX range was offered from late 1995 in order to make way for the new Saxo, with production of the AX ending in 1998 after a twelve-year production run. A total of 2,425,138 units was manufactured.

This is the 'Reflet' special edition of the AX.

AX TRIMS AND DEVELOPMENT

1986 Launch: AX 10E:10 RE: 11 RE: 11 TRE: 14 TRS: 14 TZS. All three-door shell.
AX Diesel: 14 D, 14 RD and 14 TRD /DTR.
1988: Five-door bodyshell.
1989: GT five-door.
1990: AX rebadged: 10E, 10 RE, 11 TGE, 11 TRS, 14 TRS, Sport, GT, 14 D, 14 RD, 14 TRD/DTR.
1991: 14 TZX replaces 14 TRS.
1992: AX Sport replaced by the GTi with 100bhp and 119mph (190km/h) top speed.
1993: Limited production of 4×4 AX lhd only.
1993: Fuel injection across petrol range the petrol versions were all equipped with new monopoint fuel injection engines-except multipoint Gti.
1993: AX GT replaced by AX Furio.

Bizarre AX

The idea of an AX estate came as no surprise from Heuliez, who in 1988 created an AX 'Break' with raised roof line and large rear glass area. The car was the AX 'Evasion', but it evaded production status.

An AX Cabriolet?

The Citroën AX BB Cabrio was a small roadster derived from the AX (1988). In Portugal, Citroën dealership Benjamin Barral created an unofficial convertible version, called the BB Cabrio.

A second AX cabrio was privately built in the early 1990s by some Citroën dealers in the Benelux area. This featured a roll-over hoop via the retention of the B-pillar. The project was reputedly terminated by Citroën, which was probably the correct decision in both sales and structural terms!

Proton of Malaysia produced a locally built version of the Citroën AX, the 'Proton Tiara', from 1996 to 2000.

AX Rallying

From 1987 to 1993, AXs were entered in WRC class rallies across Europe. From Finland to Corsica to Portugal and Greece, Citroën-supported AX rally cars campaigned. AX was also popular in French privateer class rallying, and in other countries where its lightweight, cheap parts and nimble handling meant it was a superbly 'chuckable' little rally car, if somewhat fragile.

ZX: INTERIM PLOT

Like certain other post-Peugeot Citroën cars, the ZX is often undermined for being just that – an amalgam of PSA parts-bin components. But the fact is that ZX was not only a very good car, it was also arguably the first Citroën made to northern European build quality standards.

The ZX was neatly styled and its details were fully integrated. It was conventionally suspended using springs and dampers, yet it had great ride quality and excellent, pitch, rebound and roll control. The sportier versions with larger engines and wider wheels provided handling finesse to match their performance. ZX was available as a three-door and five-door hatchback as well as in estate or 'Break' form. It was trimmed from base model up to sport and luxury trim, and with its low maintenance costs, better build quality and combination of subtle style and economy, won many friends and sold very well across Europe and especially in Great Britain, where it revived Citroën's post-BX fortunes.

The VW Golf, Ford Escort or GM Astra may have been the default choices for many buyers, but word soon got out just how capable ZX was – especially in diesel configuration. ZX had a key advantage over its mass market rivals for it drove like a real Citroën with brilliant, pin-sharp steering, tuned handling and an amazing ride quality for a conventionally sprung car. ZX also had 'rear steer' suspension geometry, a very large boot area, and superb aerodynamics.

ZX was a smart and neat piece of styling, but **PSA** refused it the chance to be *avant garde*. Maybe at the time, that was what was needed.

The **ZX** interior was also neat yet tame, and provided many families with perfectly sound accommodation.

In the ZX three-door, a more dynamic side profile and window graphic was used, giving the car a more modern look.

Design

Created in the early 1980s, ZX was, according to Citroën's then design chief Carl Olsen, 'a very difficult design exercise'. It seems that the PSA marketing bosses wanted a car that would be blander and more acceptable, and that the BX's 1970s 'origami' school of styling should be abandoned for a more modern corporate face: BX had still been hydro-pneumatic, ZX would not be – complication was out. By this time Donato Coco had joined the styling team from his Royal College of Art course and award-winning Citroen design proposal, and began his input with working on the ZX.

Six styling proposals were presented to the Citroën management for ZX approval – three from the Citroën team at the Velizy design centre, two from the PSA advanced styling team, and one from Bertone. One of the three proposals by the Velizy team was chosen – but it was the least 'risky' one. The chosen ZX turned out to be smart and well crafted, but it was a contemporary car design that would age normally. One of the un-chosen Velizy proposals was for a fresh theme that would have been far more modern than the Golf, Escort Astra or their subsequent models. This advanced car from Olsen's team was tall, pert, and had a new design language that looked more late 1990s than late 1980s – indeed there are shades of Renault's later Clio and the 'top hat' vertically tailed, plump-rumped Megane Mk2 in this discarded prototype.

So PSA chose the competent but slightly safe, quieter design over something that was more advanced and yet which was *not* an avant-garde Citroën that might have put people off, but a clever new iteration for a new age, and which ten years later was aped by other car makers. It was offered with a range of petrol engines, and could be trimmed as a basic car or a sporty or luxury trim offering. The three-door cars are now very rare, and may become an appreciated modern classic. Many of the 1993-launched five-door ZX estate cars live on in daily use to date.

Trims and engines 1991–97: Reflex, Avantage, Aura, Volcane.
Furio: Revised trims and minor styling changes 1995.
Engines: 1.1, 1.4, 1.6, 1.8, 1.9D, 1.9DT, 2.0.
Special Editions: *Rallye Raid*, *Flash*, *Fugue*, *Prestige*, *Miami*, *Tonic*, *Audace*, *Harmonie*, *Temptation*.

Of all the ZXs, the diesel and turbocharged diesel-powered cars sold in greatest numbers. Although the heavier diesel engine robbed the car of some of its steering finesse and handling balance, many felt the sacrifice was worth it. The PSA XUD-type diesel engine was regarded as one of the best in the world, and provided it was properly serviced, would last longer than some of the ZX's other mechanical fittings. Huge mileages of up to 300,000 miles (483,000km) were possible on the engine, which also gave superb fuel economy if driven carefully.

A Peugeot 306 cabriolet-inspired ZX convertible was made by Heuliez and the American Sunroof Company in 1994 as a full open convertible known as the *West Wind*. It remained a stillborn concept.

Chinese ZXs

The ZX lived on in China via a curious batch of locally manufactured cars *circa* 2000–2004. Some were created with official Citroën involvement, others were locally procured, lightly modified 'copies', and this led to legal action by PSA and its Dongfeng Peugeot Citroën Automobile China corporation who had originally set up a joint venture to produce new Chinese-built ZXs from the original toolings.

In China, ZX has seen several 'variations' including this booted saloon version.

The authorized and updated ZX in China latterly saw the addition of the new corporate chevron frontal styling and revised rear lamp treatment, and the official Citroën Dongfeng ZX looked very good. Meanwhile, through a host of licensing and sub-licensing deals within the internal workings of a rapidly expanding domestic Chinese car industry, a series of re-engineered and re-engined ZX 'copies' appeared. These 'cloned' ZXs include the JM STAR M/JJ 7000 series, which is a booted ZX with a locally sourced engine. The car was available both as a hatchback and saloon, and the toolings were later purchased by Geely, when the car was renamed the *Maple Whirlwhind* SXE 7000 series. In yet another convoluted route for the old ZX tooling, by late 2005 it had become the Haiyu/Haixun/Haishang range, and something called a Marindo.

A further tooling rights iteration was a 2006 car named the Lifan – again based on the original ZX Fukang pressings. The new three-volume model followed in 2004, and was named *Maple Marindo* M303. The ZX 'clone', the Biaofeng, was reinvented several times. Along with the Visa, the ZX became a familiar sight in China, and we can only speculate as to whether 'copies' of the C6 will appear at bargain price.

Grafting current chevron graphics on to the Chinese ZX worked surprisingly well.

235

SAXO: BADGE ENGINEERING SUCCESS

Saxo was a so-called 'new' Citroën, yet in fact it was a very cost-effective reiteration of the Peugeot 106. By simply changing the shape of the rear three-quarter panel – a one piece pressing, yet leaving the interior panel unchanged but disguised by black paint and a printed window trim – the humble 106 was given a new rear style. This, allied to changes to headlamp, tail light and grille and trim items, saw a new car emerge from a pre-existing design. This was badge-engineering on a scale only previously aped by the LN/LNA and certain British cars.

Launched in 1996 and facelifted for the 2001 model year, Saxo was a three-door and then five-door small car to replace the AX range. At two extremes of the model line-up, Saxo won many conquest sales. Firstly as a small petrol- or diesel-engined variant it sold to young people, and as a 1.6-litre VTR 'hot hatch' fitted with alloy wheels, brave trim combinations and sporting pretension, the 129bhp Saxo VTR became a performance car modifier's dream, even if it was a touch tail-happy on throttle lift-off in mid-bend! The Saxo also created the 'Saxo Cup' one-make racing series, and was used in privateer rally classes; it even gave Sebastien Loeb a start as a Saxo rally car. Saxo was also made in electric versions as an early experiment in rechargeable technology, and was publicly trialled via a holiday hire car arrangement.

Saxo was also available in Europe as a van, electric vehicle, and in many special editions. It cannot be denied that it earned Citroën a great deal of money with its high sales figures, and it converted many new buyers to the brand – but neither can it be denied that if ever there was a PSA parts-bin Peugeot masquerading as a faux Citroën, Saxo was it. A good little car but no design star, Saxo was, for the true Citroëniste, a dull moment amid Citroën's survival.

Saxo models were the L, LX, VTS, VTR and Furio.

ABOVE: **The Saxo: with only one significant metal panel alteration, the Peugeot 106 begat the Saxo. This three-door is the electrically powered plug-in version.**

BELOW: **Saxo Mk2 seen in its rallying element.**

XANTIA: A REACTION

The Xantia was a curiosity in that it was a PSA-based car created in an era when the 'normalization' of Citroën using cost-effective parts-bin components was the ethos of the moment. Yet Xantia contained many core Citroën themes that were far from being the cheapest choice off the shelf. It was hydropneumatic, sleekly styled and aerodynamic, trimmed in true Citroën identity, and in terms of its size, shape and market position, actually unique. Designed from 1989 to 1992, Xantia reached the market in late 1992 and ceased production in 2001 – although a 2002 British-registered Xantia can be seen in the accompanying photographs. 1.2 million Xantias were built by Citroën. Like the Peugeot 405/406, Xantia had an after-life in Iran as the SKD-produced SAIPA-built version, which remained in production until 2009.

The Xantia's two-and-a-half-box 'liftback' shape with a sloped rear end terminating in a small boot box in a hatchback has

RIGHT: **Xantia was the beginning of a return to form. Stylish, roomy, and with a great engine and handling, it served Citroën well. This is the last-registered British market Xantia from early 2002.**

BELOW: **Neat, aerodynamic and individual in a bland market sector, Xantia was just different enough.**

always been credited to Bertone and Marc Deschamps. It is seen that the car is quintessentially Bertone in its proportions, but the influence of the Citroën styling centre's team and the ideas of Dan Abramson are evident in the Xantia's shaping and detailing. The smooth flanks, neat window graphics and elegant tail were a distinctive mark in a market over-populated with bland look-alike cars.

The ZX had been good but tame, according to the motoring press, so here, paradoxically, was a PSA-based Citroën, yet one with a more Citroën identity added.

Xantia's biggest commitment was in its use of a highly refined version of the old hydro-pneumatic suspension system. It was the last car to use the full suspension, braking and steering system of the old green fluid LHM version of the Citroën hydropneumatics. After decades of use and development, the addition of electro-mechanic sensors, valves and actuators to the system had been proven in the XM as 'Hydractive I/II'. For Xantia the system was further refined, and this was firstly an option to the higher specification Xantias, and then further developed for the later 'Activa' range. Two additional pressurized spheres were added to the suspension system, and these were programmed into a sophisticated computerized mechanism which eliminated body roll and pitch oscillations. Xantia also possessed rear self-steer.

The combined results were impressive, with the Xantia Activa taking on almost mythical status because in terms of its 'Hydractive +' handling and responses, it could steer, corner and manoeuvre faster than some supercars. The addition of 2.0-litre, low pressure turbocharged engines and also the lusty V6, soon created a subtle yet devastating road car of massive ability. Here was an act of true Citroën engineering on a decisive scale.

More humble Xantias used the PSA-XU engines as 1.6-, 1.8- and 2.0-litre variants. A 2.0-litre 16v powered the VSX model, and from 1997 to 2001 the 3.0-litre PSA V6 24V was crammed under the bonnet of left- and right-hand-drive Xantias. A personal right-hand-drive V6 Activa was built by British Xantia enthusiast Shaun Lilley. The venerable and still brilliant XUD diesel engines of 1.9D and 1.9 DT, and a rarer 2.1 TD, were ideal Xantia engines and made the Heuliez-built estate cars firm favourites across Europe until the debut of the HDI units. However, in 1997 Xantia was one of several cars to suffer very poor results in EURONCAP offset crash testing, and this reflected the car's older engineering origins.

The major styling facelift to the Xantia in 1998 also profiled the fitting of the new direct injection 1.6 and intercooled 2.0 HDI engines to the range. These, combined with structural reinforcement, new grille, revised lamps and trims, gave the Xantia a new lease of life. A top speed of 120mph (195km/h) shocked quite a few performance hatchbacks.

Xantia Special Editions (Europe market) were as follows: *Anniversaire, Prestige, Temptation, Audace, Harmonie, Athena, Plaisir, Seduction, Tendance.*

Xantia was also sold in Australia, where it enjoyed great success. A special edition celebrated Citroën's seventy-five years of Australian presence in 1998. The Australian seventy-fifth anniversary models featured the adaptive suspension and 2.0-litre turbocharged engine and numerous trim upgrades.

Smooth panels and special alloys mark this as the 'Activa' – active ride car.

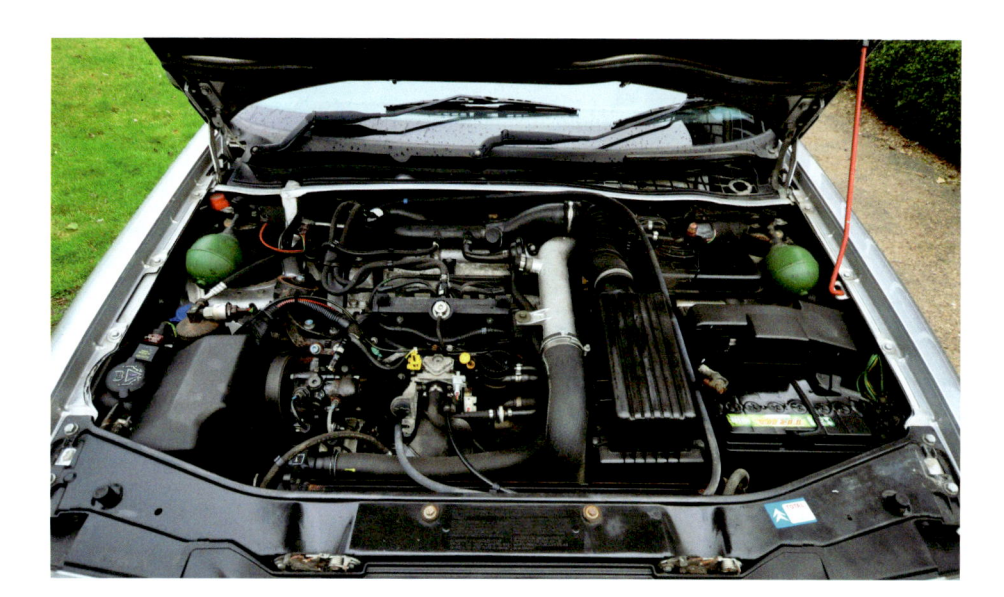

RIGHT: **Xantia Activa engine bay.**

BELOW: **Heuliez engineered the Xantia estate into a handsome machine.**

Heuliez Again

The Heuliez France Design function created the Xantia estate. Heuliez made major structural changes to the Xantia from the B-pillar rearwards, including longer door frames, reinforced floor and a strong rear hatch frame. The estate car offered an impressive 103,140cu in (1,690ltr) of boot space with the seats down, and only the angled rear windscreen design stopped the car carrying more. Heuliez built 147,260 Xantia estates, many of them in right-hand drive. Not available in right-hand drive were the rare, low-build numbers Heuliez Activa estate cars, which are now highly prized.

Keen to further the ground it made with its BX 4×4 estate, Heuliez built a special 4×4 Xantia estate with the curious name of *Buffalo*. This car had a special bodykit and a re-trimmed interior. The single prototype used a 2.1 TUD 12v engine. Citroën did not proceed with the project, and this one-off car remained dormant in the Heuliez collection until it was sold in 2012.

Xantia Rallycross 4×4

In 1993 Citroën developed a 4×4 Xantia from the idea of the BX 4×4, and created a competition car in the form of the

Xantia 4×4 Turbo for the French Rallycross Championship. This specially adapted car went through a number of engine and suspension set-up changes from 1993 to 1998: driven by Jean Luc Pallier, it won several European rallycross champions titles.

In 1999, Gilles Stievenert entered the European Rallycross Championship in his own Xantia 4×4, but finished off the podium; the race was won by Pallier in the factory-supported car.

THE XSARA

The Xsara was produced from 1997 to 2004. It was competent, comfortable and did well in EURONCAP testing. The styling was accomplished, yet the interior trim materials were somewhat dull. The steel-sprung ride was acceptable, as were most things about the car. Many chevron loyalists bought them, and so too did people who might have bought an Astra, Escort, Brava or Civic. Yet in its mainstream acceptability, Xsara did not excel in any particular area.

The car was built up from the Peugeot 306 platform, with that car's drivetrain and mechanicals. Xsara was available as a better-looking three-door coupé that was given a high trim specification and a range of alloy wheels, paints and seat trims to appeal to a wider market. A 2.0-litre 16V engine option in the post-2000 VTS model year soon became a niche car for those in the know. As a 1.9D hatchback, Xsara served many families well, as did the estate version, which was also available as a van.

In 2000, a Xsara Mk2 saw the car receive new front and rear styling motifs, reinforced bodywork and a new electrical system. The engine choice was expanded to include fuel injection on 1.6 base model engines and the venerable 1.8 was finally consigned to the scrap heap. An electrically powered Xsara based on the estate car bodyshell was also produced in limited numbers in 2000; was called the 'Dynactive' and it followed a hybrid prototype Xsara, the 'Dynalto'.

Further minor styling and specification changes were made in 2002, but by 2004, C4 was on its way and Xsara was gone.

The Xsara engines were 1.4, 1.6, 1.8, 2.0, 2.0 16V, 2.0 16V 165bhp/122KW, 1.9 D, 1.9DT, 1.6HDi, 2.0 HDi.

Perceived as competent but dull, Xsara did, however, leave two important legacies because it gave birth to the Xsara 'Picasso' MPV family vehicle which achieved massive sales and great popularity and spawned not just imitators, but a family of Citroen MPVs that were always at the top of their class (the C8 not included).

Xsara's second legacy was its success in rallying, the WRC profile and podium places and the legacy of the all-conquering Citroen rally team of *circa* 1999–2012.

Xsara was a hugely successful rally tool, and from 1999 to 2001 formed the basis of a rally car campaigned by Philipe Bugalski in the WRC F2 Group. A revised rally car design then led to Sebastien Loeb's 2004 WRC championship and the constructor's title for Citroen: Loeb won nearly thirty rallies in the Xsara, and three WRC titles. Other Xsara rally-car pilots included Jesus Puras, Carlos Sainz, Francois Duval and Petter Solberg.

Thanks to Citroen's Chinese joint ventures, Xsara was produced for the Chinese market by the Dongfeng Peugeot-Citroën company.

The Xsara: exotically named but trimmed to a market sector that defied adventurous design, Xsara was like ZX, utterly normal. This is the revised Mk2 styling.

CHAPTER FIFTEEN

C-SERIES CARS

C-SERIES CARS

FROM C1 TO C6 Citroën entered a new era via the C-series cars. Despite the fact that it launched these cars using non-sequential numbering, a range of cars defined by the letter C and a numerical model prefix became the mainstay of Citroën's recovery from losses and the more obviously PSA-derived cars such as the Xsara and Saxo. The Xsara Picasso range created a new niche of small MPVs, and has developed into variants of newer models. Key dates for the C series are as follows:

2001: C5	2006: C4 Picasso
2002: C8	2009: C3 Picasso
2002: C3	2009: C5 Mk3
2003: C2	2010: C4 Saloon South America
2004: C4	
2005: C6 and C1	2012–13: C4L and C-Élysée
2005: C5 Mk2	2013: C4 Picasso Mk2

Note: C-Crosser was a chevron-badged Mitsubishi Outlander

C3 THE FIRST OF A NEW ERA

Launched in 2002, C3 was a distinctive new shape that had a definite confidence about its design (reputed to Donato Coco, Jean Pierre Ploué and the design crew). Strong use of curves, hoops, graphical windows and chevron motifs signalled a new era for Citroën small car design. Underneath the expensive new pressings were some PSA 206 model items, but here was the new C3 platform and the engineering which would go on to form the basis of later cars – even the DS3.

Designed as a five-door (only) small hatchback bodyshell, C3 had big doors, a high roof, and just enough room to be used as a small family car for people with younger children. C3 also appealed to older people, not least as it was nimble, easy to see out of, higher off the road than many competitors, and easy to park. Despite the petrol engines being somewhat dull and ex-Saxo in their origins, the small 1.4 and 1.6 diesel HDI units that were offered went some way to brightening up the range, and all were given fuel injection. A Senso Drive transmission of electronically actuated semi-auto/manual operation also extended the car's options.

Engines included a base model 1.1i with 70bhp/53KW, a 1.4i 70bhp/53KW and 1.4 Di, a 1.6HDI 92bhp/69KW and a 1.6i 16v 92 bhp/69KW petrol were latterly offered not least in the C3 Pluriel derivative. A revised 1.4i offered 75bhp/56KW. C3 trims ranged from basic L, LX, SX, and from 2006 the VTR and XTR and a Stop and Start variant. The VTR and XTR came with 1.6i and 1.4i, 1.4HDI respectively.

C3 'Desire', 'Cool', 'Vibe' and 'Rhythm' trim variants were also offered in conjunction with various engine options; the SX version offered a 'proper' four-speed automatic gearbox. In 2006, C3 was given a late-life facelift with new lamp and trim designs. A new grille and bumper moulding was introduced. The dashboard and cabin mouldings and trims were heavily revised, and under the bonnet the new low emissions 1.6 HDI engine was made available for 2007.

The C3 Pluriel

In 2003 the boldly styled C3 Pluriel was brought out as a two-door bodyshell with a removable roof and side pillars. The car could be driven intact with the roll-back sunroof fully open, or have its side buttresses removed to create a fully open car. However, storing the roof pillars and buttress panes could

C3 signalled a new image and initiated a bolder design language for Citroën under the Donato Coco-led design crew.

Pluriel grew from C3's bold new start.

prove challenging. Pluriel was available in a range of single and two-tone colour schemes, and a new take on the old 2CV Charleston paint scheme.

Originally launched with petrol engines of 1.4 and 1.6 capacity, latterly a 1.4HDI option was offered. The Pluriel SensoDrive had a 1.6 petrol engine as standard. Citroën made numerous changes to the rubber sealing and the fittings of the roof supports, but the fact was that leaks occurred that let water into the cabin. Despite this, Pluriel was a huge success and won many new converts to the marque – paving the way for the DS3 to some extent before it was withdrawn in late 2009 (some remaining stock was available into 2010).

Like other PSA-era Citroën cars, Pluriel has its critics, but the reality is that at its time and in its marketplace, there was nothing else like it, therefore it was different – a true Citroën then.

C3 Series Two

The second series of the C3 was launched in late 2009 and boasted completely revised and much sharper styling – it looked very smart indeed for a small family car. Of note, lamp shapes, window treatments and a cut-way 'Visiospace' glazed roof panel added to the novelty. Top of the range cars had added 'bling' with trim strips and motifs. As early in its production life as 2013, C3 was revised with changes to lamps, grille and trim designs. Engines were the standard 1.1i, 1.4i, 1.4i 16v, 1.4 HDI, 1.6 HDI, and a 120bhp/89KW 1.6 16v petrol automatic range topper.

The main model range is badged as VT, Vti, Exclusive and Airdream+. A companion C3 variant is the Picasso which used the C3 platform but with a smart new mini-MPV bodyshell draped over it. This smaller, people-mover type car proved extremely popular with younger families, and with older

Brought to launch by Citroën's engineer-designer Estelle Rouvrais as product manager, the C3 in the second series is a small car jewel with distinct motifs.

people who liked its high entry and exit seating position and carrying capacity wrapped up in an easy-to-park package. A revised version was announced for 2014.

C2: OBSCURED HATCHBACK

Launched after the C3 as a derivative of the C3 platform, C2 used the C3's frontal structure allied to a truncated, three-door bodyshell. Designed in 2000–02, C2 was launched for the 2004 model year in late 2003.

C2 seemed to suffer from a lack of profile and promotion by its masters, yet it was a nimble replacement for the unloved Saxo, and particular emphasis had gone into the C3 and C2 to make it stronger and safer. Citroën added multiple reinforcement beams to the floor, doors and pillars, and achieved much better EURONCAP scores than they had with the Peugeot-derived Saxo.

Launched as L, LX and SX trims, C2 also continued the Saxo's Furio, VTR and VTS top-end trim offerings to go with larger engines offering 110bhp/82KW. The VTS model with an expensively trimmed interior, alloy wheels and 125bhp/93KW was a true 'hot hatch' with a 0–60mph time of an amazing 8.2sec.

British buyers were treated to a GT model available only in red, white or blue in 2004.

An interesting array of engine and transmission options included low-powered 1.1, 1.4, and 1.6 petrol engines, and diesel 1.4 and 1.6 HDI units offering great economy (also available in VTS sports trim as a rare sporty diesel small hatchback).

Citroën's 'SensoDrive' electronic gearbox was a manual transmission managed with electric clutch and shift engagement and actuation. The gearstick 'shift' is entirely false in that it actuates sensors, not a mechanical gear cog. This can be operated in semi-manual mode via steering column paddle-type devices, or left in fully automatic mode. In both the C3 and C2 the SensoDrive action was somewhat unrefined.

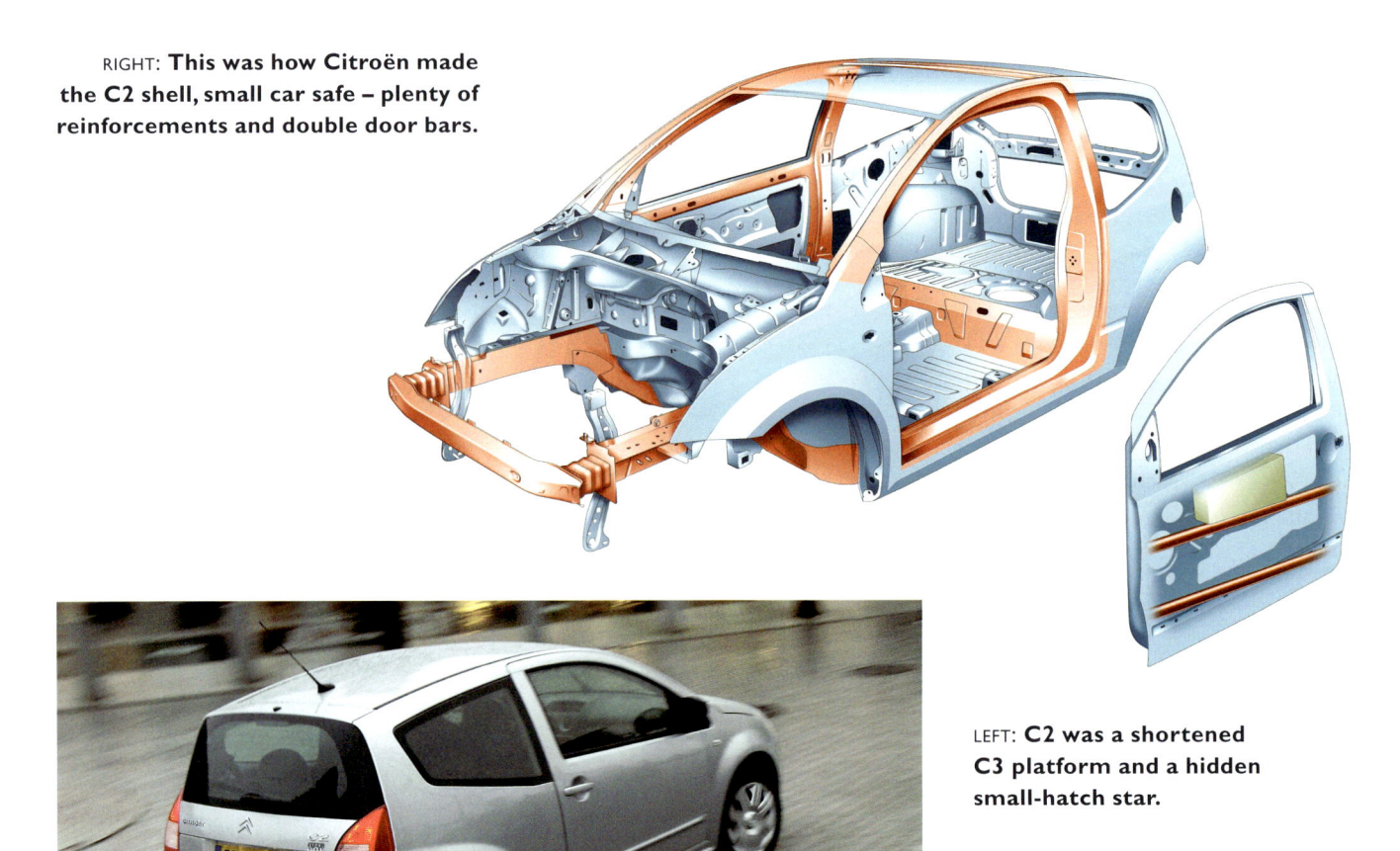

RIGHT: **This was how Citroën made the C2 shell, small car safe – plenty of reinforcements and double door bars.**

LEFT: **C2 was a shortened C3 platform and a hidden small-hatch star.**

From 2003–09, C2 was offered in the following variants: L, LX, SX, Furio, VTR, VTS, GT, Code, Stop and Start, Airplay, Design, Cool, Vibe, Rhythm, Cachet. Total C2 production was 676,004.

Rally Club C2

Perhaps the area where C2 gained more profile was on the rally scene. Building on the Saxo's record, the C2 became a Junior WRC entrant and WRC group class car. The C2 1.6 was a Citroën team car that won the Junior WRC in 2005 driven by Dani Sordo. Many privateers also ran C2s in national club level rally categories. In 2008, Sebastien Ogier again won the Junior WRC title, and Martin Prokop won in 2009

Chinese C2

The C2 was sold in China as part of the Dongfeng alliance. However, this was not the 'real' C2 on sale in the Chinese market, but a badge-engineered version of the old Peugeot 206 equipped with front and rear 'chevron' styling cues and Citroën trim items.

C5 – THE C CINQ

C5 was the largest Citroën to emerge from the initial effects of the PSA era, and was framed as a marketing concept across the days of Xavier Karcher's marketing-orientated leadership and Jacques Calvet's tenure. In design terms, C5 was an Art Blakeslee car that drew on the concept cars he had encouraged and overseen. As such there were styling elements of this period, and they derived from the curved and organic school of thought.

The impetus for the C5 came not as a stand-alone large car, but from the 'X' project to replace the Xantia. Early design studies for a Xantia replacement led to the larger car – the C5 itself. Strangely, this new big Citroën was neither a two-box coupé nor a full three-box concept. C5 had a boot or rear box, but one that not only truncated to look like a saloon, but actually disguised a hatchback.

Inside the car, the cabin was shaped and trimmed in a range of styles that took it from basic level up to leather and velour-clad opulence and 'haut de gamme' feel. High quality mouldings and trims masked some of the less attractive seat trim patterns and colours in the more basic specification cars. C5 has been accused by some of being typical of a duller period in Citroën design, but that is perhaps an unfair standpoint, because C5 did what it was designed to do, not at the behest of a team of engineers and designers, but at the command of a corporate system which realized that cheaper, more rational solutions were needed at that time. Underneath lay a shared Peugeot platform.

Suspension and Drivetrain

C5 in its top-of-the-range iteration was still hydro-pneumatically suspended, and used the advanced Hydractive III system developed from the XM/Xantia (Activa) – yet there were lower-end cars offered without the advanced electronic computer to alter ride height and roll response on the move, and the estates also lacked the 'Sport' suspension function.

The revised, Xantia-derived hydro-pneumatics were labelled 'BHI', or 'Built-in Hydractive Interface', and these used electro-valves controlling hydraulic actuation, electric height sensors, and a 'brain' that took parameters from the sensors to increase or decrease ride stiffness and to alter ride height. After the XM experience much work was put into improving the connectors.

At high speeds – above 65mph (110km/h) – the car is automatically lowered (by 15mm at the front and 11mm at the rear)

C5 in series one was distinctly curved in all its design points.

The current C5 is taughter in line, yet retains essential Citroën design cues.

into a nose-down/tail-up ride height setting to reduce drag, reduce lift and to lower the c.g. for safer handling. The system reverts once the car decelerates through the speed setting actuation. A series of control values and control laws provide reference datum points for the self-regulating hydro-pneumatic pump to work from. Citroën even changed the design of the suspension's pressurized spheres to create better responses and a longer life. A new fluid named 'LDS' replaced LHM/S in the hydraulic lines.

At the front the hydro-pneumatic set-up was mounted via a MacPherson type strut that was linked into a subframe and semi-wishbone location system for the front wheels and suspension components in an attempt to further reduce vibrational disturbances. At the rear a new multi-link, light alloy beam reduced weight and provided superior location and response for the wheel and suspension performance. The traditional suspension spheres were cradled in horizontal semi-trailing arms to reduce floor intrusion by removing the traditional strut top or housing in the load bay. As Hydractive was evolved, an extra sphere was added for each axle, which provided further sophistication to the control mechanisms because they and their effect could be almost instantaneously switched in and out of the system via microprocessor control units that sampled five ride, handling and movement parameters. This was advanced stuff, and it worked well unless age and gremlins took their toll.

The car was devoid of the traditional, hydro-pneumatically slaved brake and steering systems (it stopped very well on a cheaper-to-produce 'normal' system). Intriguingly, Citroën also offered a steel-spring, non-hydro-pneumatic on certain variants of C5 in Mk3 guises, which seemed a bizarre contradiction of principles.

A range of petrol and diesel engines were fitted with the C5, and variable valve timing camshaft actuation made an appearance. Common-rail direct injection 'HDI' diesel technology really highlighted the C5 diesels out in the marketplace.

Opting for a V6 petrol-equipped C5 seemed an odd decision, given how good the HDI engines were, but Citroën has always offered such a choice. In the V6 2946cc ES-series engine, major work went on to reduce weight and emissions, and the addition of a fly-by-wire electronic throttle further improved economy. The options of HDI engines ranging from the 1.6 litre through to 2.0 and 2.2 litre catered for all tastes, and yet petrol power was available through the 1.8-litre, 2.0-litre and 3.0-litre V6. A diesel particulate filter and Eloys DPF/EGR reservoir were also installed amid an EGR regeneration/cleaning function, which as in so many other manufacturers' applications, could lead to problems of clogging.

Structure

After the Xantia had suffered from unfortunate results in the first phases of the EURONCAP offset crash tests in the mid-1990s, Citroën worked hard to ensure that the C5's structure was better able to withstand the by then impending offset frontal impact testing. It designed a very stiff monocoque central section, which not only had a lateral transverse reinforcing ring around the roof, B-pillars and floor (with a roll-hoop function), but the energy-absorbing bearer arms were engineered to run from the bulkhead and A-pillars down into the floor pan to greatly stiffen the cabin.

Citroën fitted four such special beams (as opposed to the more usual two), and these improved not just cabin safety-cell strength but also energy dissipation. Very high strength steel was also placed strategically around the cabin apertures to improve resistance to intrusion. The bonnet was aluminium and reduced weight by nearly 18lb (8kg) compared to a steel unit. Each front wheel arch has specially shaped 'crush-can' sections and Z-shaped beams to channel offset impact forces. All four doors were equipped with anti-intrusion bars and lateral compression paths in their metal pressings.

Equipped in this manner, C5 was the strongest, safest Citroën bodyshell ever manufactured to that date; it easily exceeded the new crash test legislation, and was on a par with the better recognized safety focused brand names.

With a Heuliez-engineered estate of massive proportions, a fine range of diesel engines, and capacious seating for five in a hatchback body that looked like a saloon, C5 won many friends and became a popular family car. It did not, however, really break in the corporate or company car market for Citroën. Despite a tidy restyling and refreshing in late 2004, C5 remained a bit of an oddball. All that changed with the launch of the very different C5 Mk3 was a range of booted saloons and very elegant estates. The car was in fact also slightly lengthened at the rear, and the front and rear restyling aped the new C4 corporate motifs and enlarged chevron treatment.

C5 Series Three, 2008

The new C5 of 2008 was in fact the Mk3 version of the C5 model range. This was a very different car. It was a blatant attempt by Citroën to tap into the corporate car market by producing a car styled to resemble a typical northern European executive saloon. Citroën invested large amounts of money in improving the build quality and interior design.

Despite the claims of being a Germanic car, the new C5 contained a host of Citroën design details – not least an ellipsoid self-cleaning, low drag rear windscreen taken from C6 and CX practices; C5 was beautifully crafted with careful attention to scaling and sculpture in its metal work. The estate or 'Tourer' was very stylish and provided an interesting alternative to Swedish and German offerings. Some issues have become apparent, including a 'rocking' sensation in certain suspensions that seems to stem from suspension sphere pressure and sensing, but this has been addressed by Citroën under warranty with upgraded components. In the main, the new C5 has been a car of reliable and economical success, and in 2013 received minor trim and specification improvements.

Lower-trimmed versions of the car were also available, with conventional steel springing for the suspension, and yet the C5 is, of course, hydro-pneumatically suspended car across its main model variants. Following American practice, the new C5 was equipped with an electronic emergency notification system set off by impact and an on-line breakdown assistance capacity.

The new Hydractive III+ system features electrovalves for the fluid intake and for the fluid exhaust. Electromagnetic force actuates immediately and the spheres have new diaphragms that are non-nitrogen permeable. This offers a constant calibration to the system.

C5 MODEL DEVELOPMENT

C5 Mk1/Mk2 facelift produced 2001–08: Revised styling with longer front and rear ends late 2004.
Engines: 1.8- and 1.6-litre in-line 4-cylinder petrol; 3.0-litre V6 petrol; 1.6, 2.0, 2.2-litre HDI diesels. Five-door three-box hatchback – 187in (4,745mm) length – and extended wheelbase five-door estate – 191in (4,839mm) length.
Model trim range: VS, VX, VXS, VTR: Exclusive.

The C5 Mk 3

Launched in late 2008 as a 2009 model year car; a new bodyshell offering three-box saloon and five-door estate variant was launched. Launched with a steel springing suspension option as well as hydro-pneumatic specification available.

Engines: Petrol engine as base 2.0-litre 16V, which was replaced by a 1.6-litre THP engine in 2010. Diesel option of a 2.7-litre joint Ford/PSA AJD DT17 engine, which was superseded by 3.0 HDi-litre diesel in 2009. 2.0- and 2.2-litre diesel engines were replaced by a single 2.0-litre HDi with six-speed autobox or manual transmission. In 2012, new 2.0 and 2.2 Hdi (200hp) and a 1.6 Vti petrol engines were all introduced.

Manual, automatic and six-speed sequential adaptive automatic transmissions were offered.

In 2012 there were minor specification changes and styling changes to grille, badges and motifs. The Chinese market version received a revised grille, badging and interior trim materials.

C1: A CITROËN CONUNDRUM

C1 is an odd sort of Citroën. Somehow it has shades of the 2CV, somehow it doesn't. Or is it an AX reborn? Not quite. A perfectly adequate runabout with some fun to be had, the points about the C1 are like the car itself – short and to the point, and unlikely to be of historical note.

A typical 'joint venture' car, C1 was a PSA/Toyota car designed with youth and city appeal. They called it the 'B-Zero Project' (B being below C as in C series). Peugeot, Citroën and Toyota all market their own versions of the car with small changes to light motifs, bumpers and trims. With a body design created under Donato Coco's crew, three and five-door versions are available, and all share a thrummy little 3-cylinder engine and responsive handling at the low velocities attainable from the 1.0-litre engine. A 1.4 HDI version felt a bit front heavy but put out very impressive mpg figures.

The rear hatchback is all glass, the bumpers one-piece mouldings, and Citroën's variant had unique rear lamp/C-pillar panels.

This Citroën is built with its badge-engineered mates in the Czech Republic, and has been around since 2005. Citroën recently subjected their C1 to a second extensive make-over, and after over eight years in the market, it still provides basic cheap motoring and adequate cabin and safety standards. But things have moved on: C1 wore the chevrons, but not really, and it is due to die soon.

Needless to say, beyond the VT, Vibe, Rhythm and Code trim ranges, Citroën made the C1 a Special Edition billboard for *Splash Cool*, *Airplay* editions. An electrically powered C1 has been developed in the UK, and Swiss designer Sbarro created a C1 GT concept. A van version of the C1 with the diesel engine has proved a superb workhorse for small businesses in Europe.

Thus the C1 was cheap, nippy and safe, it had youth appeal and a degree of 'design' – but no one will ever write a book about it, surely. Was this the LNA of its day? You might think so.

THE C4: A NEW BEGINNING

If a VW Golf was the default choice, it should not have been, for Citroën should surely have reincarnated the GS years ago. But PSA did not let it happen. Gladly PSA sanctioned the C4 and in 2005 it became a turning point: here at last was a return to true Citroënism. Based on the Peugeot platform it may have been, but C4 was packed with new design, new ideas and a general sense of reinvigoration. Designed at the same time as the C6, C4 had shades of GS in its architecture and packaging.

C4 was the concept of the design crew led by Donato Coco and Jean Pierre Ploué. In five-door form it closely matched elements of the GS, and had a distinctive rear body style. In three-door form, the little C4 hatchback had overtones of coupé style and an Ami-inspired reverse rake rear windscreen. The interior design was common to both body variants, and featured a newsworthy non-rotating hub to the steering wheel in which driver functions were located. The sensation of the steering-wheel rim rotating round a static central hub took some getting used to, but it was very effective in ergonomic terms and allowed a new design of airbag that was tailored to offer better interaction with the driver in an impact. The instrument displays were a centrally mounted digital/analogue affair. C4 also offered a range of electronic aids including a lane departure warning and an electronic stability programme.

C4 was highly aerodynamic, especially in the three-door long-canopied roof variant; Cd. 0.28 was claimed. It was unusual in offering laminated side window glass in the non-executive car sector, and this feature greatly reduced wind and road noise.

Engines were 1.4i, 1.6i, 1.6 THP, 2.0i, 1.6 HDI and 2.0 HDI. Transmissions included five and six-speed manual, a four-speed automatic and a six-speed electro-mechanical semi-auto.

For the model year 2009 (late 2008) the C4 was refreshed with new grille and headlamps that reflected the new DS3 design motifs. The C4 three-door was dropped in favour of the DS3 offering. The new diesel 'Airdream' emissions package was fitted to revised engines and petrol engines with variable valve timing, and 'THP' turbocharging technology was developed.

The original C4's styling team included J. Blondel, A. Malaval and B. Rapatel. C4 Mk2 was shaped by M. Hossann, N. Gonzales and S. Johnson. The C4 Picasso was worked on by V. Gritt, R. Linari and N. Gonzales. The C4 bodyshell was superseded for 2011 by a new, larger design that also spawned the DS derivative, which used similar front bodywork but a revised canopy and rear end style.

Of particular sales success have been the Europe model C4 VTR/VTS and 'Loeb' editions, featuring upgraded trims and engines. The C4 Picasso derivative in long- and short-wheel-base variants has been a huge success as a superbly packaged MV, and the 2013 model brings new standards of design, use and handling to the sector.

C4 continued to provide Citroën with WRC Rally Championship drivers and constructor' world titles, and created a huge following on the rally circuit for the Citroën team.

C Series beyond Europe

As a further tangent, Citroën is designing in China at its new Shanghai styling satellite and manufacturing local market specification cars in Argentina, China and Russia.

C4 Saloon

Using the European market C4 Mk1 platform and part-bodyshell, a special South American specification C4 saloon was created in 2009. This used the C4 bodyshell with the addition of a very large, elongated rear boot/trunk, unique rear lamp motifs, and higher ride height with revised spring and damper rates to cope with rural roads. The car was manufactured alongside the Argentinian-built Picasso range. The Argentinian variant is also sold across South America and in Hungary and Turkey, where it is badged as the 'C4 Pallas' – an illustrious Citroën name used to describe a slightly more humble product.

C-SERIES CARS

LEFT: **C4 in three-door performance trim guise. Here was the new, more dominant chevron branding and fresh face.**

RIGHT: **The 'Picasso' range of MPVs has proved to be a huge hit for Citroën. This one is Argentinian built.**

BELOW: **The latest model C4 Picasso raised the MPV class stakes even higher with its blend of fine design, strong engines, brilliant handling and superb accommodation.**

249

SPECIFICATIONS — C4 SERIES

Body
Five-door hatchback and three-door semi-hatchback coupé. Picasso MV five-door; C4 Mk2 variant as five-door and Picasso only. Production C4 series 1/2 from 2005 to date

Engine
Front-wheel-drive transverse in-line: 1.4, 1.6, 2.0, 1.6 HDi/2.0 HDi diesel

Transmission
Five-speed manual, six-speed manual, four-speed automatic, six-speed semi-auto

Suspension
Conventional springs and strut

Dimensions

Length	168in (4,260mm) (hatchback); 168.3in (4,274mm) (coupé)
Width	69.6in (1,769mm)
Height	59.4in (1,510mm) (hatchback); 57.4in (1,458mm) (coupé)
Weight	2,315lb (1,050kg).

Citroën C4L

The new 2010 European model C4 bodyshell was used to create a new car for the Chinese market. The bodyshell was given new frontal styling, a newly tooled, high-built rear boot/trunk, revised C-pillars and rear side doors, and a longer wheelbase. Aimed at the lucrative upper sector, the C4L is the first production Citroën to come from the Shanghai styling centre satellite. It has an innovative rear 'lounge' seating concept with backrests angled at 29 degrees.

C4L uses the new THP 150 and 170 petrol engines (jointly developed with a BMW project) and a VTi 135 performance option: six-speed and sequential automatic transmissions are offered. The C4L has the air of a DS-line car in that it resembles a DS4 but with a saloon body. It began manufacture in China at the Wuhan plant in 2012, and will be built by Citroën Russia at the Kaluga plant in 2013.

C-Élysée

C-Élysée uses an amalgamation of body pressings and model-specific tooling to create a booted three-box saloon for a world-wide market. A long wheelbase (104in (2.65m)) gives class-leading cabin space, and together with the long-travel suspension (conventional springing), a comfortable car is created suitable for use on local and rural roads as well as on motorways. Extra protection has been built into the floor pan and engine bay to ensure reliability in harsh road conditions. Petrol and diesel engine options are available. The car is built in Spain and marketed in southern Europe and north Africa.

C4L was a booted C4 manufactured in Argentina.

CHAPTER SIXTEEN

CITROËN CONCEPT CARS AND DS-LINE

A NEW HALLMARK

CITROËN CONCEPT CARS AND DS-LINE

A NEW HALLMARK

CITROËN HAS ALWAYS built concept cars – those design specials or experiments designed to showcase a company's talents. With Citroën, the concept car story began decades ago with the Coccinelle, André Lefebvre's brilliant true genius of future vision. The 2CV had been a triumph of minimalism or marginal motoring in that it offered advanced results in a basic package. But since the launch of the 2CV the world had changed, not least as high speed roads, autoroutes, autobahns or motorways had begun to criss-cross Europe. The 2CV with its 'barn-door' aerodynamics and ancient mechanics was hardly suited to a new 1950s age of smooth, streamlined style.

PROJECT CS

Project CS – or Coccinelle – was Lefebvre's inspired answer to the quandary of creating an advanced car with 'super car' design details in a more basic package. As such it was a work of genius because it pre-dated so many of today's design themes and ecologically driven design parameters. First drawn up in 1953, this new idea for a frugal but fast, small family car seems to be the ultimate incarnation of Citroën thinking. Conceived just as the DS was becoming real, the CS or Coccinelle project was so named because of its resemblance to a ladybird (*coccinelle* in French): the car's shape extended the Art Deco *gouette d'eau* motif into a late twentieth-century shape.

Lefebvre used post-war advances in mathematical calculation to create a body design by calculus and wind-tunnel flow tests, rather than by Bertoni 'in the clay' sculpting. This resulted in a shape and structure of form and function that was in unison and highly efficient. The original design for intended production was to have a Becchia-developed Citroën engine, but as the design progressed and its fate became less certain, a normal 425cc flat twin power plant was installed in the fore to mid position under the driver's seat and directly above the drive line.

The car's internal structure was built in duralumin alloy supported by aircraft fuselage-type reinforcing members in steel and alloy. To minimize difficult alloy welding, a new aerospace glue known as Redux (also used in the de Havilland Comet jetliner and the Sud Aviation Caravelle) was employed, creating a truly 'bonded' structure. Draped over this was the sleek shape of the metal and plastic-clad body. Perspex windows (also taken from aviation technology) and gull wing-type doors were key elements of the design. Such design techniques meant that the car had an empty weight of just 842lb (382kg), a cruising speed of over 60mph (100km/h), and much improved fuel economy figures over the standard 2CV engine installation.

The car lacked windscreen wipers to preserve smooth frontal airflow, and a 'drooping' windscreen mechanism was intended to allow the driver a view through the open slot

Coccinelle was true 1950s future vision by Lefebvre as an 'eco' city car of advanced technology. As such it was a design pathfinder.

created by the lowered windscreen – yet once kept free of ingress, the smooth laminar type flow up the windscreen was essentially correct.

With four or five seats, plenty of room for family baggage and a layout that tapered towards the single rear wheel, the Coccinelle had elements of many strands of low cost, yet high design thinking. There were the inevitable handling issues with the front-biased wheel and suspension layout – despite the use of a three-sphere hydropneumatic system allied to front double wishbones, which was more evidence of truly advanced design research thinking.

In the cabin, plastics and light support structures were utilized, as well as a centrally mounted instrument pod.

Sadly an early prototype crashed during a handling test, but it is believed that ten prototypes were made. Incredibly for a company on the cusp of launching the DS, Citroën's management shied away from commissioning the Coccinelle into production, and Citroën, France and the world were denied a car that might have usurped the impact and fame of the 1955 DS.

In the Coccinelle we see much that is normal today and much that is the future of mass transportation. It seems incredible that André Lefebvre should have done all this in 1953.

The engineers behind 'Project CS' were Lefebvre, Bucan, Estaque, Laroy, Lauran, Leonzi and Roche.

The Jacques Né designed Mini-Zup of 1972 was another example of Citroën's amazing design skills.

After Coccinelle, it would be 1972 before the small city car idea resurfaced as a concept car at Citroën in the form of the Jacques Né/Henri Dargent designed Mini-Zup. Later in 1972, Mario Bellini designed the Kar-A-Sutra concept car for Citroën, but after this busy year, Citroën concept cars were in temporary abeyance.

CARS AND THEIR CREATORS IN THE RECENT ERA

From 1974 to 1976 the Citroën styling centre at Velizy existed under the PSA corporate umbrella and had to create cars based on Peugeot underpinnings – but it would be wrong to suggest any lack of creativity in the Velizy centre, or in the Advanced Design Studio facility during the 1980s, and indeed throughout and beyond the 1990s. PSA later funded an Advanced Design Network studio at Velizy in 2004.

From the likes of Art Blakeslee, Trevor Fiore, Carl Olsen, Geoff Matthews, Donato Coco, Dan Ambramson, Mark Lloyd, and onwards to Jean Pierre Ploué, Alex Malaval, Thierry Metroz and others, the dedicated Citroënistes of the styling team (divided into exterior, interior, advanced and commercial vehicle design teams) produced a range of production vehicles and concepts that were second to none in terms of the intelligence that went into their designs. It is correct to observe that cars such as the AX, ZX, Xsara, Picasso, C3, C5, *were* derived from their respective PSA-base platform engineering origins, but it is not correct to suggest that they were in any sense 'lesser' in terms of styling, aerodynamics or design characteristics.

Because such cars lacked hydro-pneumatics (except the C5) and the more overt avant-garde styling of their illustrious predecessors, it has become fashionable to call them 'dull'. However, that comparison comes from the very high arts of earlier Citroënism, one that was unsustainable in raw commercial terms, particularly after the consumer market changes of the 1980s and the need to provide higher build quality and earn profits within the PSA corporate pyramid.

Was the C3 Pluriel a 'real' Citroën? Of course it was, for it had innovation in its design. Was the Peugeot 106 based Citroën Saxo a dull, humble, badge-engineered car created from a low budget brief to change its badges, trims and a one exterior rear side panel pressing to create a so-called 'new' model? Yes of course it was, but it didn't stop it selling even if it really wasn't a 'true' Citroën: perhaps cars like the Saxo *did* detract from the Citroën legend, but few car makers have made every one of their models a space-ship of innovation – except Citroën in a previous life, of course, and therein lay the unfairness of expectation being heaped upon subsequent offerings.

During the late 1980s through to the early years of the new twenty-first century, Citroën was rebuilt and its masters allowed it to stretch its wings again. This was leveraged by a range of stunning concept cars that the Velizy design unit produced in the 1980s and beyond into the era framed by the 'Centre du Style' and the 'Centre Création'. Therein lay the proof that within the PSA behemoth, Citroën's spirit, that old savvy of the Bureau d'Études, was not lost.

The defining marque hallmark of the chevrons also changed their form several times across the decades. Recently they have been redesigned and given a wing-like emblematic form, and

CITROËN CONCEPT CARS AND DS-LINE: A NEW HALLMARK

starting with the C4, a new frontal setting of the chevrons as an integrated styling hallmark has been created under the pen of Citroën's graphic designer Charles Aouad, who correctly observed that the chevrons are a 'complex' entity.

Concepts of the Best

Citroën has turned out an unusual number of concept car designs over the years – more than any other car maker – ranging from Activa to Xenia and Xanea.

There are many names associated with Citroën design, and space constrains the telling of each of their respective stories, yet we should briefly alight upon the names of men and women, young and old, who have worked for Citroën and who touched and have been touched by its history after the end of the Bureau d'Études years and the closing of its chapter. At this time, many of Citroën's older designers were on the cusp of retirement or of moving on: Dargent, Giret and Harmand were names that would soon leave the unit.

The cachet of having worked for Citroën's design function is large: for example, since 2012 **Giles Taylor** has been design director at Rolls-Royce cars, yet his career began at Citroën via Coventry University's transportation design course and the Royal College of Art Vehicle Design Unit, from which he graduated in 1992. From the RCA he joined PSA and worked as an exterior designer at Citroën, where his input involved concept and production cars until 1997, when he moved to Jaguar. So even Rolls-Royce's top designer started out at Citroën.

1980: Beginning the Fightback for Citroën Design

Trevor Fiore was the Englishman of Italian maternal descent whose name was an Anglo-Italian reflection of his roots; with British car design work and Loewy Bureau experience behind him as the 1970s turned into the 1980s, Fiore headed the advanced Citroën design at a most difficult time in Citroën's corporate evolution under PSA. As *chef du style* from 1980 to 1982 he created many exquisite themes, notably Karin and Xenia, both concept cars of incredible design quality and originality.

ABOVE: **Trevor Fiore's Karin created a much needed profile for Citroën design in the early days of the PSA dominance.**

LEFT: **Karin's interior with Michel Harmand input was startling, and 'wowed' the design world.**

The long-established designer **Geoffrey Matthews** rose to become exterior design chief at Citroën and influenced a number of key themes in the 1980s, notably leading on the AX and contributing to the XM. He had framed the Espace idea for Renault, and at PSA produced the future vision of the 1986 Citroën Eole economy car concept. With input from Citroën designers, Matthews shaped the AX as Citroën's new lightweight small car for the 1980s, and influenced a resurgence in design for the chevron. Geoff Matthews also laid down the original sketches for the Eole concept car – one that would emerge as a prototype with a Cd.0.19, a fantastic achievement at the time.

The American **Carl Olsen** became Citroën's design chief while Citroën's design hand was still very much within PSA control. Much of the work was tweaking and 'face lifting' existing cars, and the chance to really make big, bold, expensive car design statements was not easily come by at Citroën *circa* 1982 when Olsen arrived as Fiore left. Olsen was appointed to Citroën and brought an appreciation of detail, sculpting and integrated forms to the work at Velizy. He also had a touch of mid-Atlantic style, being an American with British affiliations. At the time of his appointment, Citroën had few new production cars to champion.

Olsen's first works at Velizy were to refresh the BX into its Mk2 iteration and to create a BX-based coupé. In an interview with *Car Styling* he said that the design was undertaken to 'restore confidence in the Velizy design team'. Olsen cites Dave O'Connell as the lead designer on the BX coupé idea. A Cd.0.25 was claimed – a huge advance over the standard BX. The BX coupé was created in weeks. Olsen also managed the Eole project for an advanced eco-friendly car. This prototype body may have been the first to be milled using the new computerized milling or carving process now so familiar.

Olsen also oversaw the AX, which had had major input from Geoff Matthews as its exterior stylist, also Fergus Pollock (who went on to Jaguar fame), Jean Giret, Michel Harmand, Victor Nacif (now head of design for Nissan in Los Angeles), and a Monsieur Moreau. An AX-based youthful open-top project car – a sort of beach 'ute' – was named Xantia 84, and was also styled under Olsen's lead before he resigned.

Dan Abramson, an American, was a product of the Los Angeles Art Center College Body Design Unit; he worked for Chrysler and then in Subaru's US design studio before accepting an offer from PSA. Working in the advanced design area, Abramson created further profile for Citroën on the international stage, not least through his Activa and Activa 2 concepts. Other Abramson concepts included Berlingo Bulle and the clever ellipsoid Xanae, which was a pointer to the Donato Coco team led, Xsara 'Picasso' design. And while many credit Bertone for the neat Xantia shape, it was Abramson's pen that created much of Xantia's style.

Abramson was also a lead contributor to the Xanae concept car which ranks as one of the cleverest and most influential of such concept ideas because it so heavily imprinted the subsequent Xsara Picasso and later MPV types from Citroën (other manufacturers followed its lead). Citroën's research department under its manager M. Violini was a vital part of this future-proof study. Luc Epron was a key figure in engineering a working prototype of Xanae.

Abramson would go on to lead Citroën's large car design unit and influence smaller car design. Under Art Blakeslee, Abramson would add his input to Marc Pinson's C6 design and contribute to the Berlingo. But Abramson's earlier and brilliant Activa shapes were a lost opportunity for Citroën, in that they had all that was needed to create a new DS, a *grande routière* of a Citroën. But to make these cars would have compromised the XM and cost more money than PSA would have allowed at the time.

Art Blakeslee was another American in Paris. Before that, by 1965 he headed Chrysler's international design studio, and after a decade of design and concept experience, was appointed Director of Design. Then came a European sojourn via Chrysler's Talbot function, and with that marque's purchase by Peugeot, the door was open to a French experience. Having headed the PSA design function, Art Blakeslee went to head the Citroën design centre, and faced the difficult job of addressing the legacy of issues and the thinking that still ran through Citroën's design function: Bertoni's model-making prowess over the use of sketch techniques was still in evidence, it seems.

Blakeslee's skills in scaling, sculpture and graphics saw the emergence of new design lineage for Citroën, such as the C5 which he led on, and emphasis on the use of a more dominant chevron logo as a styling hallmark. After the departure of Xavier Karcher as Citroën's corporate chief, it appears that PSA gave a longer leash to Citroën design, and a rash of concept cars resulted under Art Blakeslee's direction.

One of Blakeslee's other legacies for Citroën was to create a sponsored design study in various university or college courses across a wider Europe. This resulted in a Citroën-led emergence of young design talent which saw several recruits to the Velizy Centre de Création. Having overseen the production of the XM and a new resurgence of models culminating in the C4, Blakeslee was also the lead influence in making the C6 Lignage and resultant C6 production car.

Mark Lloyd was a graduate of Cambridge University and the Royal College of Art Vehicle Design Unit. He began his career at Jaguar, joined Citroën in 1989 as an exterior designer working on concepts and production cars, and was named lead designer of Concept Cars in 1999, overseeing the many concepts from C6 Lignage, Osmoose and a host of others. He is now a senior figure within Citroën design as head of design, and recently range manager for advanced projects since 2009, with input into concept cars and the work of the Shanghai design unit project.

Marc Pinson is a graduate of École Supérieure de Design Industriel Paris, and joined Citroën in 1992 working on interiors including the revised Xantia and the Picasso cars. Five years later he became an exterior designer and achieved impact with the C6 Lignage and consequent C6. Such successes led him to head a design team, and then to join the Advanced Design unit in 2002; he is now a senior design manager.

Frédéric Soubirou, **Pascal Grappey** and **Gilles Vidal** are recently prominent names in shaping DS-Line cars under **Jean Pierre Ploué**. Ploué is PSA Group Design Director, a position he reached via a tenure of design leadership at Citroën's studio with focus on advanced design. Ploué earlier guided the Citroën styling renaissance for nearly a decade – influencing the C5, C4 and C4 Picasso. His earlier claim to fame was leading on the design of the Renault Twingo. He recently moved to head the advanced design function across PSA as the lead director of styling for both Peugeot and Citroën.

Alexandre Malaval is a senior design figure within not just Citroën but also Peugeot, where he directs PSA design. Malaval was encouraged and assisted into his design career by his family's friendship with Michel Harmand, the great Citroën interior design genius who worked for Citroën from 1964 to 1987. Harmand was an artist and sculptor who also designed many exterior car body proposals and contributed to the SM, as well as creating a GS coupé and influencing other projects. Malaval is also an architecture enthusiast, and after working on the C5 Mk3 and then directing the DS5 project from 2007 to 2010, he moved to a senior PSA/Peugeot studio role.

Gilles Vidal joined PSA after graduating from the Art Centre College of Design (Switzerland) in 1996, and in the subsequent years worked on the C3, Pluriel, C2, and Piccasso ranges before working on the Osmose design study and other concepts prior to leading the advanced design unit and output such as C-Cactus and C-Metisse. He was appointed a lead design manager in 2010, and along with people such as Pascal Grappey and Domagoj Dukec, represents a seasoned sense of Citroën design couture. Vidal now contributes to Peugeot.

Thierry Metroz was a senior Renault design unit figure before joining Citroën. Another graduate of École Nationale Supérieure des Arts Appliqués et des Métiers d'Art, he has worked in design units across the world. Metroz is guiding DS-Line and a possible DS reinvention.

ABOVE: **Metropolis, the Citroën Shanghai design unit super saloon concept left behind old themes and evoked a new language.**

LEFT: **Metropolis made a massive statement of intent as a three-box shape that eschewed the normal Citroën coupé format.**

KEY NAMES OF THE CENTRE DU STYLE DESIGNERS 1979–2005–2014

The following figures (in alphabetical order) worked variously on the BX, AX, Xantia, XM, Xsara, Picasso, Berlingo, C2, C3, C5, C6, and the concept cars respectively. H. Dargent retired in 1984, and in 1985 J. Giret retired and M. Harmand moved to Peugeot.

Dan Ambramson	Henri Dargent	Matthais Hosnnan	Carl Olsen	Andreas Stamp
Luciano d'Ambrosio	Trevor Fiore	Mark Lloyd	Alex Padwa	Urs Stemmler
N. Bauchet	Jean Giret	Geoffrey Matthews	Eugene Pagliano	Lars Taubert
Mario Bellini	Ivo Groen	M. Moreau	Cyril Pietton	Giles Taylor
Art Blakeslee	Murat Gunak	Gunvant Mistry	Marc Pinson	Scott Yu
Oliver Boulay	Michel Harmand	Victor Nacif	Vladimir Pirozhkov	
Donato Coco	Shaun Hensridge	David O'Connell	Fergus Pollock	

Recent Designers

As Citroën entered its next phase and had more freedom to express itself after 2004, a new cast of design staff complemented previous experts. These more recent Citroën designers include:

Patrick Arnaud	Laurent Duquenne	Sean Johnston	Pierre Monferrini	Anne Ruthmann
Charles Aouad	Domagoj Dukec	C. Layarol	Kevin Nougarede	Frédéric Soubirou
J. Blondel	Leighanne Earley	Thomas Leret	Marc Pinson	Oleg Son
Carlo Bonzanigo	Julien Famchon	Mark Lloyd	Vladimir Pirozhkov	Lars Taubert
Sebastian Buffet	Pascale Grappey	Vincent Lobry	Steve Platt	Celine Venet
Christophe Cayroll	Vincent Grit	Cathal Loughnane	Jean Pierre Ploué	Gilles Vidal
Fabien Coradin	Nicholas Gonzales	Guillaume Lemaitre	Christophe Poinlane	Oliver Vincent
Andrew Cowell,	Christian Guidima	R. Linari	Muriel Prodault	Mathieu Wandon
Bertrand Dantec	Magalie Hayley	Alexandre Malaval	B. Rapatel	Takumi Yamamoto
Frederic Duvernier	Thomas Haussey	Thierry Metroz	E. Ruis	

CITROËN CONCEPT CARS AND DS-LINE: A NEW HALLMARK

RIGHT: **The DS4 concept created by Ugo Spagnolo with Aurelien Petit, Benoit Louzaouen and Guillaume Vasseu reeked of advanced Citroënism.**

LEFT: **Survolt, electric racer and a riot of design themes for a possible future.**

BELOW: **Ora Ito Design – Ito Morabito created a stunning alchemy of Citroën themes in his speculative, unofficial concept.**

258

A New Citroën Van Icon

In 2012 the Citroën Global Van Design Project set Royal College of Art design students the task of creating a new Citroën van icon. One of the students was a member of the Peugeot family, and the eventual winner from all the students was Alexander Ibett. Citroën's Alexandre Malval and Andrew Cowell oversaw the project with Professor Dale Harrow, head of vehicle design at the RCA. All agreed that the ideas the students presented were of the highest quality, and framed fresh possibilities for a new era in design.

Another exciting Citroën student design project was that for a 'DS24' concept created by Ugo Spagnolo, with Aurelien Petit, Benoit Louzaouen and Guillaume Vasseu. Their stunning DS24 concept was anything but retro, and was packed with innovative yet original themes. These four students were from the Institut Supérieur de Design and their ideas made a huge mark on Citroënism.

In 2013 Citroën itself showed Wild Rubis as a potential 4×4 'soft roader' design with body styling led by Kevin Nougarede as a concept for Citroën's entry into this new market sector.

Concept Car Design Survolt

For the 2010 Salon d'Genève Motor Show, Citroën did something new by blending sporting design and aerodynamics with an all-electric car concept. This was the 'Survolt', a low-slung car with overt 'hyper car'-type styling amidst its riot of curves, scales and shapes. Survolt was shaped on the outside by Frédéric Soubirou, designed on the inside by Julien Famchon, had colour and trim items by Vincent Lobry, and graphics by Mathieu Wandon. The project's chief designer was Bertrand Dantec, and the Survolt artwork and publicity photography was by Laurent Nivalle.

Survolt impressed the industry, and gave notice that there was more to the 'new' Citroën than DS-Line alone.

Ora Ito's Futurology

Ito Morabito is a French designer with a reputation for creating new iterations of luxury-brand design motifs, and for producing new hallmarks that are instantly recognizable as belonging to the brand they frame.

Working under the design atelier name of Ora Ito, in 2010–11 Morabito created two stunning, speculative Citroën design proposals of his own in order to frame a vision of Citroën. The 'UFO' concept mixes classic DS imagery with a futuristic body as a 'genetic transformation'. The styling elements are a wonderful blend of themes that make you think of DS and SM: the rear canopy and shapes could only say Citroën. The reaction on-line and to a Parisien street show in 2011 was massive.

Morabito's second Citroën idea is EVO-MOBIL, and like UFO, is an investigation into themes for design not seen before. It takes its inspiration from the Traction Avant's monocoque bodyshell and the twin frontal body structure support arms that stick out from the bulkhead – the 'jambons' as they have become known.

DS-LINE AND BEYOND

Like others such as Saab Porsche, BMW and Mercedes Benz, Citroën's design team did not invoke or respond to the ideas of marketing or 'customer clinics'. Design was informed by, and prescribed from *designers* – not short-term fashion or the court of public opinion or perceptions of the moment; by ignoring such dangerous design arbiters, Citroën design did not fall into the trap of being the creator of fashion-sensitive, quickly dating trends.

Style not Fashion

Citroën's design leaders today are Thierry Metroz, Alexandre Malval, Andrew Cowell and Mark Lloyd, with Carlo Bonzanigo, Bertrand Dantec, Pascal Grappey, Marc Pinson, Pierre Monferrini, Frédéric Soubirou, Gilles Vidal and their teams – and all know what it is that makes a Citroën, of that specific philosophy.

There is still the question of tradition in modern car design: can the Citroën ethos constrain or advance its design future? Surely the answer is that the lithe and efficient design and engineering hallmarks of past Citroëns are far more worthy than the bloated modernism of the design themes of others. By respecting its past design traditions, Citroën's new cars remain lithe and efficient, whereas other designs have taken on the 'bling' motifs that will briefly be in fashion for a market whose new urban peoples have little concept of car design or its traditions. Why else would other, once sacrosanct design icons festoon their previously pure designs with over-large badges, gawping grilles, bejewelled motifs and all manner of tattoos and ungainly adornments of passing fetishism?

That way lies no-man's land. But Citroën knows that the future can learn from the past, and that the retro-pastiche, just like the faux school of design, has no part in true automotive excellence. As Alexandre Malval, the Citroën/PSA design leader, recently said:

We have to find a different aesthetic for the future: the Chinese market is far more fashion led, but that fashion can change really fast, and we have to be a little bit careful because of that speed of change. China is open to new silhouettes, new technology – so many things. But we must also remember our heartland in Europe, where proportions and volumes of scale are so important. We must tread that path carefully.[15]

Current Citroën thinking is to avoid retro-pastiche and build a new iteration or idiom of the grand Citroën philosophy. But this does not mean building boring cars to keep corporate accountants happy – it means designing and making cars that are so special, people want to buy them, they *prefer* them. The old world of a radical Citroën whatever-the-costs is gone, but that is no reason to be dull. This is why the C3 has given birth to the hugely successful DS3, the C4 became the sculptural DS4, and why DS5 and the new 'Picasso' ranges contain style draped over proven, reliable mechanicals. The latest 2013 C4 Picasso has raised the stakes in the people carrier or MPV category, and with strong press reviews, has not only gone to the top of its class, it has actually moved the standard on.

The DS-Line has a global reach for a new Citroën in new markets with new buyers. It is proof that PSA has finally let Citroën fly again, and in 2013 DS-Line was even given its own new chief: Yves Bonnefont. Bonnefont will oversee the return of sales and marketing in a specific niche from the PSA function to a distinct Citroën unit with its eyes set on China and emerging markets as well as securing its traditional place in the premium European sector. DS-Line is in essence a very clever separate brand yet one that complements and preserves the Citroën heritage without in any way being a marketing 'con'.

DS3: ANTI-RETRO RE-INVENTION

If the new BMW Mini was cheeky, it was also hamstrung by its retro imagery and ride and accommodation compromises. In the new DS3, Citroën created a genuine rival to the chuckable Mini, yet one which offered a better cabin and improved ride – and there was nothing retro about the way DS3 looked. DS3 was based on the Citroën C3 platform, which was developed and expanded under Gilles Le Borgne as lead engineer and then head of advanced concepts engineering. After DS3's 2010 launch, Le Borgne would go on to create the new PSA EMP2 platform, and then in 2012 head the advanced vehicle engineering and design projects department; by 2013 he was Executive Vice President of Research and Development.

Above all, however, it was the style of the DS3 that was fun but fresh: it contained new graphics and motifs which overnight moved Citroën design on. Under Mark Lloyd's exterior design lead, with input from others including Frédéric Soubirou, DS3 was genuinely new. Surely, Opel's 'Adam' followed DS3's path? The inspired interior design was by Christophe Poinlane and offered a range of cloth, leather and combination surfaces allied to chromed fittings and expensively textured plastics.

In addition, Citroën created a paint and graphics package that allowed the customer to make the most of the car's styling, allied to personal preferences. A torsionally rigid three-door shell with good EURONCAP ratings (achieving a high 89 per cent occupant protection score) and effective side impact and roll-over protection meant that the fast little car was as safe as it could be.

DS3 – an amazing new face for Citroën – not retro yet certainly a Citroën, it has proved massively popular and won many new brand converts.

The first clues to DS3 came from the DS Inside concept car, and by late 2009, DS3 was ready. The car had 'floating' roof graphics, blacked-out roof pillars and an intriguing B-pillar that was truncated into a fin-type motif. At the front and rear the car was given expensive lights and badges. Inside, a high-quality interior with body colour or colour-coded finishes allowed the customer to personalize their car in the same way they could apply their taste to the exterior: with twelve colours, nine roof graphic designs and a range of alloy wheels, buyers could create their own unique vehicle. The three trim packages were DSign, DStyle and DSport, with each adding equipment and trim items up to the DSport as top trim variant.

Under the bonnet were to be found a range of punchy petrol engines, turbocharged units, and the excellent 1.6 HDi diesel unit. From 1.4 litre to 1.6 litre, turbocharged and then to the performance versions, DS3 offered an engine for everybody, not least via the DS3 Racing capable of 146mph (235km/h).

Launched globally in 2010, the DS3 caused a sensation and huge profile for a 'new' Citroën – opening up a fresh chapter in the marque's history and winning new, more youthful converts to the brand. Some DS3 customers had no idea what a DS or a CX was – all they knew was that here was a car to take on the Mini, and a range of sporting supermini class cars. DS3 also reinvigorated the Citroën rally team and provided fresh impetus to its World Rally Championship campaign.

DS3 might not quite have had the 'point and shoot' character of a performance-badged Mini, but it was not far off, and even the ever-critical men of the BBC's *Top Gear* soon voted the DS3 their 'Car of the Year' in 2010, and the 'Small Car of the Year' award as well. Here was a Citroën that had youth appeal, handled well, was safe, sporty and fun, and which truly opened up a new chapter in the Citroën story. Surely DS3 deserves recognition by even the hardest-hearted classic car purist.

Also in 2010 the Citroën rally team adopted the DS3 WRC, with Loeb and Ogier taking five wins each in the championship, Loeb retaining the world championship, and Ogier finishing third. Citroën took the manufacturer's crown in 2012 with the DS3-based rally car team with, Ogier replaced by Mikko Hirvonen.

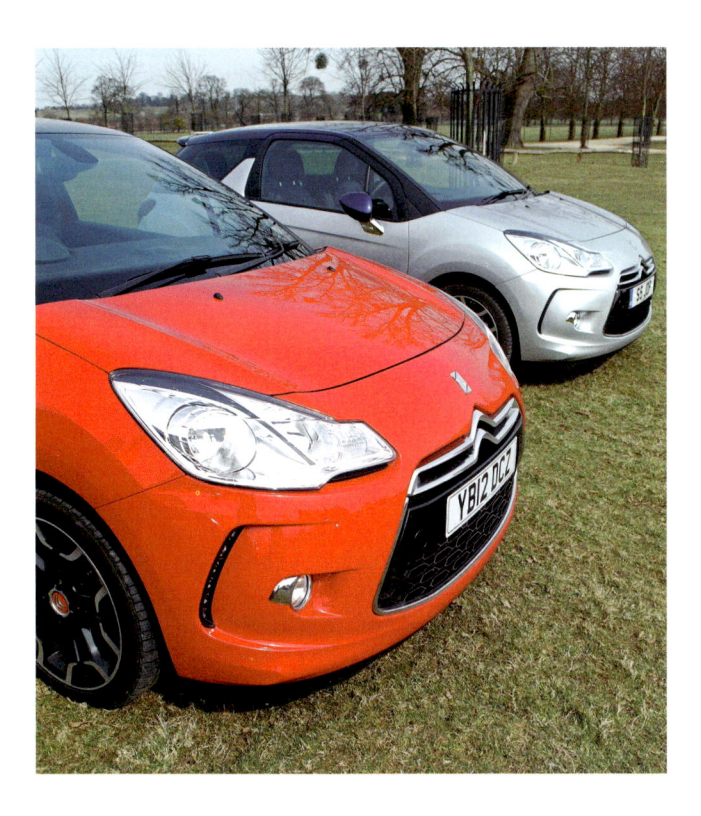

ABOVE: **DS – different shades. Colour changes the new 'face' of Citroën.**

RIGHT: **Bejewelled baby? DS3 with floating B-pillar and roof graphics.**

DS3 allowed the customer to tailor the car to their tastes. This is the 'loud' Racing trim version.

DS3 MODEL DEVELOPMENT AND DETAILS

2009 for 2010 model year: VTI 95: 1397cc, 94bhp/70KW.
VTI 120: 1598cc, 118bhp/88kw/VTI120 automatic.
THP 150/155: 155bhp/115KW 205.
THP 207: 204bhp/152 KW turbocharged.
2011 Model year sees 1.2 engine offering as 1.2 Vti.
HDI 90: 1,560cc. 89bhp/66KW.
HDI 110: 1.560cc. 108 bhp/81KW.

Diesel 'Airdream' models featured bhp/KW increases, lower emissions and increased torque.

DS3 Racing with 207bhp/154KW was introduced in 2010 as a road-going version of the DS3 rally spec car. Orange/black and white/grey were initially offered with a graphics package and a cabin trim/seat upgrades and unique alloy wheel design. DS3 Racing reflects DS3 rally car specifications.

DS3 RRC rally car programme introduced in 2012 with reference to DS3 WRC package. Road-going-spec to brakes, aerodynamic addenda and reduced engine output of 205bhp as opposed to 315bhp of WRC rally-spec DS3 for competition use.

Transmissions: Five-speed manual, six-speed manual, five-speed automatic.

Model range
1.2 VTI 82 DSign
1.6 VTI 120 DStyle
1.6 THP 155 DSport
1.6 e-HDI90 Airdream DStyle/95g/km Co2
1.6 e-HDI Airdream DSport
DS3 Racing and 'Grey' 'Red' 'Black' special editions as issued
Cabriolet range across engine and trim specifications

The DS3 went from strength to even better, with new engines, new models, the performance version DS3 Racing, and in 2012, the new cabriolet model with roll-back roof. DS3 has an active owners' club and has brought Citroën ownership and enthusiasm to a whole new demographic, who have embraced what some call 'DS – Different Spirit'. In 2013 DS3Sport owner and artist Peter Valliant created his unique DS3 covered in his own artwork.

Dyed-in-wool Citroën purists may want to look the other way, but the DS3 and the DS-Line cars are creating and securing Citroën as a modern marque, and not as a classic car memory – however wonderful that memory may be.

CITROËN CONCEPT CARS AND DS-LINE: A NEW HALLMARK

SPECIFICATIONS — DS3/DS3 RACING: PIERRE BUDAR

Body
Steel monocoque three-door hatchback and two-door convertible with fabric/synthetic roll-back roof section. Production 2009 to date.

Engine
1.4i 16V; 1.6i 16V; 1.6THP 16V; 1.6HDi diesel.

Transmission
Five-speed/six-speed manual; five-speed automatic.

Suspension
Conventional spring and strut.

Dimensions
Length   155.5in (3,950mm).
Width   67/3in (1,710mm).
Height   57.5in (1,460mm).
Wheelbase 97in (2,464mm)

Under the guidance of DS3 development engineer Pierre Budar, the limited edition DS3 Racing used a tweaked version of the 1.6bhp engine. Two production batches totalling 1,000 cars were created. The output numbers are impressive with 202bhp in the first production batch and 205bhp in a further second limited-edition run. Re-mapping of the engine leads to 203lb ft torque – matching the bhp figure.

Other changes include 18in wheels, 30mm wider track and a freer exhaust flow. Upgraded brakes include bigger front discs of 323mm. A 15mm lower ride height with firmer spring and damper rates complements the set up.

Citroën modellers shaping the DS4 coupé roof canopy section.

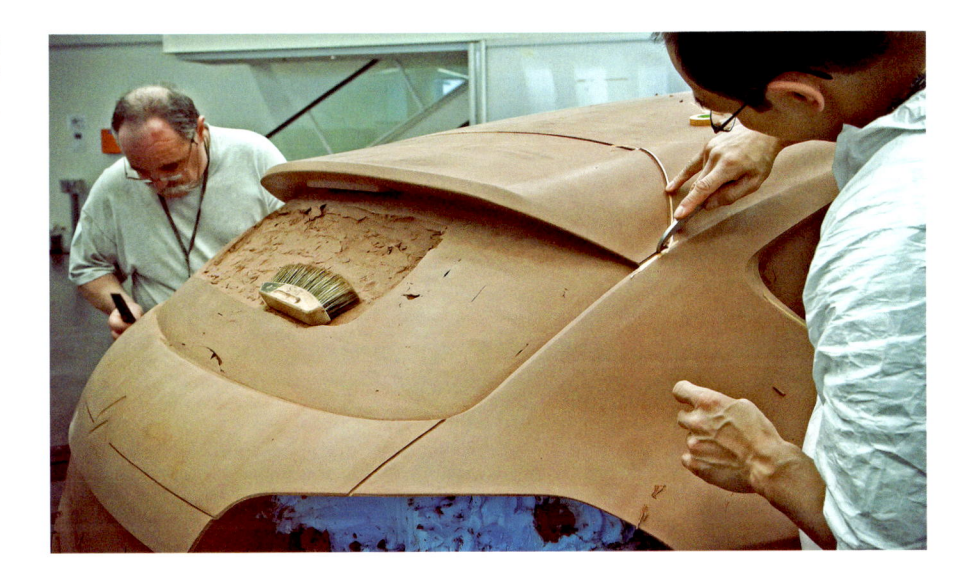

DS4: SCULPTURAL STYLE

DS4 mixes an urban theme with the grace of a saloon coupé. Is this the first non-conformist mid-range Citroën since the GS or CX? Maybe it is.

Thomas Leret DS4's colours and materials stylist says: 'The aim was to make a luxury object. We took inspiration from leather-work, from haute couture, jewellery and clock making. This car is a really unique object – you haven't seen anything like it before. I think every designer deserves the chance to work on a project like DS4.'[16]

Magalie Hayley says of her DS54 colours and material stylist work: 'The design is very precise, almost chiselled and plays with the light. The light slides over it.'[17]

263

DS4 is a clever stand-alone based on existing underpinnings. Every aspect of this design is honed and tailored to a new level.

The DS4 has evolved into a classy upmarket car and a plastic-clad, higher-riding soft roader. It comes with the current range of Citroën petrol and diesel engines, and has sold strongly in Europe; however, it has not caught on so well in Great Britain.

DS5: DYNAMIC STYLE

Of all the DS sub-brand cars so far, it is perhaps the DS5 that seems the cleverest. Like the original DS, it has made an impact because it is new and cannot be easily categorized. Built on the joint PSA Platform 2, DS5 offers petrol, diesels and hybrid powerplants. THP 155bhp and 200bhp petrol engines, as well as HDI 110bhp and HDI 160bhp diesels, form the core range which is now supplemented by a 'Hybrid 4' variant with a 165bhp HDI engine and a rear-mounted 37bhp electric motor.

Stemming from the Sport Lounge concept car, DS5 seems to have shades of the great Citroën design motifs, yet also creates new ones. The glasshouse and cabin turret elements make clear references to aviation design, cockpit windows and sweeping fuselage forms. The interior is also modelled on cockpit themes and has a riot of textures and details, and notably, a reversion to tan-coloured, pleated leather in true 'big Citroën'

The DS5 defied design conventions and spawned the DS5LS, a new model DS5 saloon derivative launched in China in 2014.

DS4 and DS5 both feature this upmarket 'Habana'-pleated, tan leather interior trim option that has many echoes of Citroën's past interior treatments.

style (first tried out in 'Habana' pleated leather on the front sets of high-end DS4s).

In the main body we see shades of DS and Opron-esque dynamic swage lines: the 'chromed' or steel-effect blade running from the bonnet/hood up into the windscreen area is both an innovative idea yet seems entirely fitting. The aerodynamic styling of the rear canopy and tail are superb examples of integrating form with essential aerodynamics.

The design team behind the DS5 were Andy Cowell (Design Manager) Pierre Monferrini (Project Manager) and Frédéric Soubirou (Exterior Manager). The DS5 is neither a people-carrier nor an estate car: somehow it was a saloon if it wanted to be, or a sports estate or wagon for other moods and purposes. A bit like the Range Rover, the DS5 is equally at home in a chic city setting or out in the country. It was launched with petrol and diesel power, and in 2012 also became available as a hybrid vehicle. DS5 Hybrid 4 has combined diesel-electric technology with a 15 per cent reduction in CO_2 emissions through direct-injection HDi technology. With 99g per kilometre, DS5 Hybrid 4 beats the 100g barrier.

The only obvious flaw in DS5's jewel is that it is steel-sprung and has succumbed to the fashion for large alloy wheels of low profile aspect ratio. So DS5 does not ride like a DS! But surely Citroën will be producing a hydro-pneumatic version – maybe even a Pallas, to top the range? After all, if they can make the new C5 with or without hydro-pneumatics, can they not do the same for DS5? Despite the shock of steel suspension, DS5 remains a major achievement, and signals huge intent.

RALLY CITROËN

Citroën's competition history goes right back to the 1920s and the days of a special-bodied Rosalie competing at Monthléry. The 'Raids' across the world and one early foray at Le Mans did not signal a desire to form a Citroën racing team. However, decades of rally, trials and speed and endurance entries, and even SMs at Le Mans, gave Citroën's non-official activities a veneer of *de facto* factory support. From Jack Weaver racing modified Traction Avants in New Zealand, to the Citroën DS winning the Monte Carlo as a Citroën-branded entry, and René Cotton's management of the Citroën team, the marque has a long history in competition.

The DS was extensively rallied – across Europe in national rallies and club events, as well as in the 1968 London to Sydney Rally. French driver Jean-Pierre Bugnot campaigned the DS to many club and group level podium places. A DS23 won the 1974 London to Munich Rally. As recounted earlier in the book, GS and CX were rallied, notably in Australia. Citroën also appointed Marlene Cotton (latterly Marlene Wolgensinger) to manage its 'works' rally projects.

Perhaps it was the successes of the DS, GS and Visa rally cars that finally encouraged Citroën into re-creating its own rally/racing team for a wider series of international events.

Having built a special 'Raid' rally concept car over ZX mechanicals in 1991, the ZX RAID, as it has become tagged, took top honours in the Dakar Rally by winning in 1991, 1994, 1995 and 1996. Other victories were in the 1992 Rally of Tunisia and

Rally Citroën – WRC multiple World Champions. In 2014 Citroën is entering the World Touring Car Championship.

the Paris-Moscow-Beijing Rally of 1992. Citroën won the separate WRC 'Raid' championship with drivers Ari Vatanen and Pierre Lartigue. By 1998 Citroën had withdrawn from this series and created a 'Citroën Sport' project which would be based around the new Xsara, which it would enter in the French Rally Championship and the World Rally Championship series. Philippe Bugalski won the French title in 1998 and 1999, and by 2001 a certain Sebastien Loeb would join the Citroën team. He won the French driver title in 2001.

Citroën's small cars, the Saxo and C2, and even the AX, had all enjoyed Club level success across the European scene. The Saxo VTS 1.6 litre was turned into a 'Citroën Cup' car for a one-make series at national club event level. A Saxo 'F2' was a heavily modified shell and in later variant a sequential shift gearbox and 2.0 litre power. The Saxo was variously campaigned from 1997 to 2001 and Sebastien Loeb gained valuable early rally experience in the Saxo as early as 2001 in the Monte Carlo Rally where he came 15th. For the 2002 season a Saxo VTS rally car was also campaigned by Citroën.

Citroën entered the Xsara in WRC stages and Patrick Magaud, Phillipe Bugalski, Jesu Purass and Fabien Doenlen all competed in the Corsican, Catalunya and San Remo rallies. A developed Xsara T4 was launched in 2001 to enter the WRC series. Puras won the Corsica Rally, and Loeb finished in second place on his and the car's first WRC outing.

The Xsara T4 won the Monte Carlo rally but was penalized for an infringement and demoted. In 2002 Citroën entered only half of the WRC series, but 2003 was the first full year when the Citroën rally team entered the full WRC series and campaigned in all events. New drivers were Colin Macrae and Carlos Sainz. Citroën took all three podium places in the Monte Carlo Rally, and won the German rally, San Remo rally and Turkish Rally. Although Loeb did not win the WRC Driver's Championship, Citroën did take the manufacturer's crown.

In 2004 the two-car Xsara team, now driven by Loeb and Sainz, won seven WRC rallies, including the arduous Cyprus, Argentina and Australia rallies. Loeb won the first of his WRC championships in this year, and again Citroën took the manufacturer's title. In the junior league JWRC the C2 was entered by the Citroën team; it also enjoyed national rally success in privateer hands – just as had the Visa and the Saxo.

In the 2005 season the team's lead drivers were Sebastien Loeb and François Duval. The team won ten rallies, and Citroën secured another manufacturer's crown. Carlos Sainz also joined the driver line-up. After this incredible year, Citroën had a quiet 2006, during which it developed a new car, while the new adjunct team of Kronos Citroën competed via official Citroën support. A third driver, Dani Sordo, joined the driver line-up.

In 2007 Citroën abandoned the Xsara and started its new WRC campaign with the three-door C4 WRC series car. This led to a battle with Ford and Marcus Gronholm, with Loeb and Citroën triumphing and securing a fourth consecutive WRC title. By 2008 the C4 WRC had won the Monte Carlo rally and enough rounds of the championship to yet again win both the driver's and manufacturer's main WRC titles.

In 2009 the dominance of the C4 WRC continued, despite occasional failures; and in 2010 both Loeb and Sordo continued to campaign, with the addition of Sebastien Ogier from the

Citroën junior rally team. For 2011 with the new DS3 WRC on the team, the two Sebastiens – Loeb and Ogier – constituted the main thrust: Loeb took another WRC title, and Ogier came third, both men achieving five wins each. For 2012 Ogier decamped to VW Rally and Ford's Mikko Hirovenen took his DS3 place. Loeb won the Monte Carlo (again) but Citroën lost Hirvonen's Portugal Rally win for a technical infringement. By 2013, Citroën's own rally team had won sixty-five rallies, eight constructor's titles and eight driver's titles (with Loeb's ninth on hand).

2013 sponsorship includes the Total/Abu Dhabi/Red Bull/Michelin/Eurodata branding, and the co-drivers of Daniel Elena, Jarno Lehtinen and Carlos de Barrio. Team principal was Yves Matton, and technical director Xavier Mestelan-Pinon (previous rally team directors Olivier Quesnel and Guy Frequelin having left).

Only the thought of a 4×4 DS5 WRC car could be more tempting…

CORPORATE CITROËNISM

Held back post-1976 within PSA for entirely rational fiscal considerations, within the last decade Citroën has been set free again by its PSA masters. In 2011, PSA handed semi-autonomous control of sales and marketing back to a dedicated Citroën management team and structure, as well as supporting the DS-Line brand to expand.

The result of the new freedoms has meant new resources for design, even if the engineering structure for new cars remains a joint Peugeot-Citroën PSA platform basis. Other expansions have seen Citroën take part in the joint PSA-Toyota deal in 2004, which resulted in the C1, and Citroën also signed an electric car development project with Mitsubishi Motor Corporation, resulting in the Citroën-badged version of the Mitsubishi i-MiEV city car in 2001. The Citroën C-Crosser was a badge-engineered Mitsubishi Outlander built in the Netherlands.

Deals to build a production plant in Russia were also a product of this era. In 2010 Citroën signed a deal with China Changan Auto Group, which added to the existing Dongfeng set-up. In 2011 Citroën agreed to enter an engine and hybrid powerplant development deal with BMW. In 2012 PSA agreed an intention to co-operate with General Motors (GM) in the European market, a move that echoed André Citroën's early discussions in the 1920s with GM. Could this agreement be the gateway to a re-launch of Citroën in the USA?

Citroën has produced cars in Chile, Argentina, Australia, Ireland, Romania, South Africa, Spain, Thailand, Yugoslavia and Zimbabwe. It has set up a Shanghai design and production base, and a wonderful 'DS World' Shanghai showroom. Citroën's China Tech Center has 1,000 engineers and designers constituting the first PSA design centre outside Europe. An early outcome was the suave Citroën Metropolis concept. Citroën has forged links with the Automotive Institute of Tongji at the University of Shanghai to train the next generation of engineers and designers. PSA has three production sites in China. Citroën also continues to build cars in Russia and Argentina, with special models for local markets, which did at one stage include the bizarre variant of the Peugeot 206-based but chevron-badged Citroën.

In Europe, Citroën still has links with FIAT via the Sevel Société Européenne de Véhicules Leger SA (SPA), and this is jointly owned by FIAT, Peugeot and Citroën. From this group comes the range of badge-engineered vans such as the Ducato, Boxer, Dispatch, Qubo, Nemo and Bipper ranges. Citroën is also a part of the joint production agreement with Toyota for the badge-sharing C1/107 and Aygo cars built by Toyota Peugeot Citroën Automovile (TPCA) in the Czech Republic.

The closure of Citroën's British manufacturing base signalled a change in the brand's British position. For many more recent years Citroën in Britain positioned itself as a supplier of cheaper cars that were heavily discounted from new. Yet the BX was sold to business users as well as private British buyers. The risks of heavy new-car price discounting, poor residual values, and brand perceptions leading to such were latterly realized and a repositioning attempted, not least through the DS-Line cars.

But despite the world recession and decline in European sales, Citroën heads towards 2020 with an inventory of great cars, an inspired design portfolio, and more to come. The glossy brand of clever cars, the philosophy of design and a particular charm of the Citroën car lives again, and André Citroën would surely approve.

CITROËN'S MAIN LEADERSHIP 1919 TO THE PRESENT DAY

André Citroën	Jean Baratte
Pierre Michelin	Jacques Calvet
Pierre Jules Boulanger	Xavier Karcher
Robert Puiseux	Jean-Martin Folz
Pierre Bercot	Claude Satinet
Claude Alain Sarre	Christian Streiff
Francois Rollier	Philippe Varin
Raymond Ravenel	Frederic Banzet
Georges Taylor	Yves Bonnefont
Jacques Lombard	

TAILPIECE

Our journey through the Citroën story closes here in the present, yet with the company well placed to survive the economic crisis of the world, and already designing its way out of trouble into a glittering future that reflects its wonderful past. Is the DS5 one of the most individual statements of bravery in recent car design – emphatically so; can the DS Numero 9 be the next DS? We can only implore Citroën management to make it so.

For owners and enthusiasts everywhere, Citroën remains an affair of the heart or an enigma of the mind. Few car manufacturers have such an illustrious history of innovation and of effect upon people and their transport. Be it a Traction Avant, 2CV, DS, SM, CX, or a Visa, a BX, or a DS5, or a van, or any Citroën (except one or two of the offerings from the doldrum years), the fact is that we can simply stand and stare at a Citroën and see something far more than a piece of planned obsolescence. Others like Renault may now also show great design skills, but surely Citroën was, and is, a French icon and a specific philosophy, something far beyond just making cars.

The children of famous parents often have a tough time, and Citroën is no different. Some thought its best years were behind it, but they were wrong. Fiscal reality may prevent another totally revolutionary 'moment' in history, but as the offspring of the genius André Citroën and all his men, Citroën is a child that has stood tall on its own, and will continue to do so. And perhaps another great design event may not be far off. For Citroën is not in the shadow of its illustrious forebears, but instead in the protection of their philosophy and its aero-auto-scientific thinking of the new.

For the essence of these cars is that grand, tactile sense of occasion, and of innovative design that was, and remains, encapsulated by one word and all that it means – **CITROËN**.

DS9 – new beginning of an old legend?

REFERENCES

1. Citroen DS5 on-line media design conversation 2012.
2. *Classic and Sports Car* July 2012. Haymarket Media, London.
3. Auto Club de l'Ouest archive.
4. Loubet, Jean-Loius. *Citroën dans les années trente ou comment restructurer une enterprise*. Histoire, économie et société. 1996, 15e année, n2. pp 281–297
5. Berk, Gijsbert-Paul: *André Lefebvre and the cars he created for Voisin and Citroën*. Veloce Publishing Ltd, 2009.
6. Winstone, D. R. A. *Gerin*. Faustroll Publishing 2012.
7. Archives P. A. F. Cayla at Service Historique de la Défense/Archives Centrales de la Marine. Sheldon-Duplaix P. A. Charge d'Études avec Geneste P., Conservateur des Archives Centrales de la Marine.
8. Shelton, T. *Automobile Utopias as Traditional Urban Infrastructure Visions of the Coming Conflict 1925–1940*. TDSR Vol xxII:No.II: 2011.
9. Winstone, D. R. A. *My 1000 Cars* Gabriel Voisin. English Reference Edition. Faustroll Publishing 2012.
10. Bertoni, Leonardo. *Flaminio Bertoni – la vitta il genio e le opere*. Macchioni, Milan. 2002.
11. Norbye, Jan P. *The Wankel Engine*. Chilton Book Co., Radnor Penn, USA, 1971.
12. SM Club of Europe/SM Club Netherlands archives and member communications.
13. Scarlett, M. Mère Peugeot's Citroën's gap-filling international Visa. *Autocar* 30.09.1978.
14. *The Citroënian Magazine*. Vol LXXII, November 2012.
15. Malaval, A. Citroën Media statement 2011.
16. Leret. T. Citroën Media statement 2011.
17. Hayley, M. Citroën Media statement 2011.

BIBLIOGRAPHY

Aalderink, S. Personal communications Project M-35.
Abramson, D. Personal communications.
Adams, K. T-Bar treasure. *Octane* Vol. 110 August 2012.
Andrade, J. 'Wind tunnel tests and body design' *Journal Society Automotive Engineers*. Vol 29 1931.
Bader, D. Sir (the late) Personal communications.
Bel Geddes, N. Archive at Humanities Research Centre, University of Texas, Austin.
Berk, Gijsbert-Paul *André Lefebvre and the cars he created for Voisin and Citroën*. (Veloce Publishing Ltd, 2009).
Bertoni, Leonardo *Flaminio Bertoni – la vitta il genio e le opere* Macchioni, Milan, 2002
Besson, Vice Admiral Article *Visionaire du Vice Amiral Besson sur 'L'aviation dans la Marine' Le Petit Journal*, 26 Mai 1912.
Brioult, Roger (the late) Personal communications and *l'Histoire et les Secrets de son Bureau d'Études 5/6*. EDI 1987.
Broustail, Joël, and Greggio, Rodolphe *Citroën: Essai sur 80 ans d'antistratégie*. Libraire Viubert, Paris 2010.
Brownhill, D. Personal communications.
Bush, D. J. *The Streamlined Decade*, New York, Braziller, 1975.
Car Styling (Quarterly) San'ei Publishing Co. Ltd, Tokyo. Numerous volumes 1981–1989.
Cass, B. SM Club GB Personal communications.
Citroën Archives, Paris/Conservatoire Citroën/Roger Huille.
Citroën publications, papers, technical documents 1925–2013.
Citroën: Meetings of the Board of Société Anonyme André Citroën, 11 June 1934, 13 December 1934, January 1935 and 4 June 1936.
Citroënet on-line archive, Julian Marsh.
Classic and Sports Car July 2012, Haymarket Media, London.
Cats, Jeroen (the late), 2CV research.
Cayla, P. A. F. Patent application 1923.
Cayla, P. A. F. *La Technique Moderne annoté par Cayla* (1911), extrait de la Revue de la Technique Aéronautique, 15 Janvier 1911.
Coco, Donato. Interview with L. Cole for *Autocar* and Royal College of Art Auto Design Unit research 1984.
Cole, L. F. New 2CV design proposal for Citroën. Eric Dymock report *Classic Cars* September 1994.
Cole, L. F. *Secrets of the Spitfire*, Pen and Sword 2012.
Cole, L. F. Selected articles *The Independent* 2005–2006.
Cole, L. F. Personal Citroën archive and design research 1984–2012.
Conway, C. David. Personal communications/private archive.
Conway, C. David. Citroën *The First 90 Years* (Zeteo Publishing 2011).
Curtis, W. J. E. *Le Corbusier Ideas in Form* (Phaidon 1986).
Eiffel, G. *Mémoires de la Société des Ingénieurs Civils de France* Paris 1911.

Esnault-Pelterie, *Mémoires de la Société des Ingénieurs Civils de France* Paris 1912.
Georgano, N. *Beaulieu Encyclopaedia of the Automobile* Stationery Office London.
Giedion, S. *Mechanisation Takes Command: A Contribution to Anonymous History* Oxford Publ 1948.
Green, E. *A Bootful of Right Arm* Cassell, Australia 1975.
Harmand, M. 'Epochs and Styles', *Auto and Design* February 1996.
Heuliez. Archive material.
Jammes, P. Personal communications and DSinAsia.com
Knight, P. Coltman, D. Levieux, E. *Le Corbusier, The Radiant City* Trans. Dover Publ. New York 1967.
Les Amis de Gabriel Voisin.
Loheac Museum, France.
Long, B. and Claverol, P. *SM Citroën's Maserati-engined supercar* Veloce Publishing 2006.
Loubet, Jean-Loius. *Citroën dans les années trente ou comment restructurer une enterprise*. Histoire, économie et société, 1996, 15e annee, n2 pp 281–297
() Margolius, I. *Automobiles designed by Architects* London, Wiley, 2000
Miekle, J.L. *20th Century Limited* Temple University Press 1971.
Morabito, Ito. Ora Ito Design Personal Communications 2013.
Mullin, P. Museum Voisin Exhibition 2012.
Noblet, J. de, Dir Centre de Recherche sur le Culture Technique. Editor *Industrial Design Reflections of a Century*. Flammarion APIE Paris. 1993.
Norbye, Jan P. *The Wankel Engine*. Chilton Book Co, Radnor Penn, USA. 1971. Also Norbye on Citroën SM.
Office National d' Etudes et des Recherches Aerospatiales (O.N.E.R.A.) Archives.
Pijlman, Peter, I. *Robert Opron, Automotive and Art*. Sagitta Productions, Rotterdam, 2007
Posthumus, C. *Prophet without honour, the 1923 Voisin Laboratoire*. The Motor 1923.
Pressnell, J. *Citroën DS, The Complete Story* The Crowood Press 1999.
Revue Aeronautique Trimestrielle des Vieilles Tiges Voisin, Gabriel, 1966, 'Henry Farman (1874–1960)' No.7, January 1966 pp 8–16.
Romani, I. *Les Essais aerodynamiques des voitures automobiles, maquettes et vehicles reels, union Technique de l'Automobile et du Cycle* Vol 11, 1950.
Reiner, S. *La Tragédie d'André Citroën* AMOIT, 1954.
Rocher, C. *L'Affaire d'André Citroën souvenir d'collaboration* Edits Lajeussor Paris.
Rouxel, Jean-Christophe *L'Espace Tradition de l'École Navale* (Cayla).
Royal College of Art Vehicle Design Unit M.A. Course works and tutors' personal communications.
The Automobile November 2011.
Rugg. P. and F. Personal communications/archives.

Sabates, F./Bertoni. L. *Flaminio Bertoni 30 ans de style Citroën*.
Scarlett, M. Mère Peugeot's Citroën gap-filling international Visa *Autocar* 30.09.1978.
Scarlett, M. (the late) Personal communications.
Scibor-Rylski, A. J. *Road Vehicle Aerodynamics* Pentech, 1975.
Schwietzer, S./Sabates, F. *André Citroën les chevrons de la glorie* 1980.
'Service Historique de la Défense Archives Centrales de la Marine', Sheldon-Duplaix P.A. Charge d'Études avec Geneste P., Conservateur des Archives Centrales de la Marine.
Shelton, T. *Automobile Utopias as Traditional Urban Infrastructure Visions of the Coming Conflict* 1925–1940, TDSR Vol xxll, No.11, 2011
Sobey, J. Personal communications and archive.
'Soufflerie Aérodynamique de Chalais Meudon' Archives.
Texas University, Austin. Exhibition: 'Norman Bel Geddes Designs America' September 2012–2013.
'The Citroën Bijou' *The Motor* 4 Jan 1960.
The Citroënian Magazine Archives, Citroën Car Club Ltd.
Totivy, E. Personal communications at Malestroit, Bretagne.
Voisin, E. G. *Mes 1,000 Cerfs-Volants* Gabriel Voisin 1963.
Voisin, E. G. 1966, Henry Farman (1874–1960) *Revue Aéronautique Trimestrielle des Vieilles Tiges* No.7, January 1966 pp 8–16.
Winstone, D. R. A. *Gerin* Faustroll Publishing 2012.
Winstone, D. R. A. *My 1000 Cars* Gabriel Voisin, English Reference Edition. Faustroll Publishing 2012.
Winstone, D. R. A. Personal communications.
Wolgensinger, J. *Citroën 1919–39* Delpine 1967.
Wolgensinger, J. *André Citroën* Flammarion Paris 1991.

INDEX

Aaltono, R 146
Abramson, D 213–215, 238, 253, 255
Academie Grande Chaumiere 102
ACB 61
Adler 53, 55, 95
Advanced Design Network 253
AEAT 61
Aerodinamica Pininfarina 150, 169
Aerodynamics 11, 49–50
Aerodyne 39
Africar 72, 78
Albertus, Mnsr 134, 155
Alfa Romeo 57, 128, 131, 150, 170
AlfaSud 150
Alfieri, G 132, 140
Aligé, M 96
Allera, H 96, 132
American Sunroof Company 234
Andreau, J 21, 30, 52, 55
Andruet, J 210
Antem, J 31, 61
Aouad, C 257
Art Deco 10
Art Nouveau 10
Artaud, E 20, 21
Ateliers de Batignoles 120
Audinet, M 157, 163
Aulnay-sous-Bois 168
Austin 150
Automobiles Crajova 196
Bader, D 14
Baert, P 96
Banzet, F 267
Baratte, J 267
Barker, R 12
Barottio Carrozzeria 54
Barral, B 232
Barron, Mnsr 103

Barry, J 9, 14, 137
Barthelemy, A 170
Bauchet, N 257
Bayley, S 12
Becchia, W 64, 68, 97, 252
Bechereau, Mnsr 39
Beckwith, M 147
Behr, G 33
Bel Geddes, N 40
Bellini, M 253, 257
Bercot 94, 99, 116, 128, 132
Berliet Co. 91, 168
Bernard, M 43
Berry, S 14, 222
Bertone Design 202, 212, 238
Bertone, N 164, 202
Bertoni, F 31, 10, 32, 53, 54–55, 64–68, 84, 88, 95, 97, 98, 114, 125, 128–129, 152
Bertoni, L 55
Beutler Bruder 61
Bianchi, L 112
Bigrat, J 146
Bingen, G 18
Bionier, L 125
Birotor 157, 163, 164
Bishop, G 12
Blakeslee, A 212, 214, 224, 245, 255
Blanc, R 14, 148
Bleriot, L 31
Blondel, J 248
BMW 95
Boas, A 18
Bond, J (007) 14
Bonnefont, Y 260, 267
Bonzanigo, C 257
Bosseart 105, 143
Bouffard, A 179
Bouffard, G 179
Boulanger, P J B 32, 34, 64, 67–68, 85, 95
Boulay, O 257

Boullay, Mnsr. 103
Bouquet, J C 68
Bouquet, Mnsr 68
Bourgeois-Luchard 30
Bouvier, Msr 213
Bouzinac, Mnsr 96
Bracq, P 135
Bradford, R 181
Brasier, H 18
Braux, C 179
Brezhnev, L 14
Briggs Streamliner 40
Bristol Co. 42
British Leyland 155
Brittany Ferries 148
Brodie, A 12, 141, 147
Broglie, M 23, 33, 65
Brouse (Mehari) 78
Brownhill, D 94
Brull, C 33
Bucan, Mnsr. 252
Budar, P 263
Budd Co. 24
Bugalski, P 240
Bugatti, E 128
Bugno, J-P 147, 265
Bureau d'Etudes 9, 16, 85, 101–102, 128, 184, 186, 196, 200, 202, 253
Burnell, J J 14, 181
Byrd, R 29
Cabaillot, Mnsr 20, 21
Cadiou, J 33, 85
Calvet, J 212, 245
Camargue (Bertone) 164
Campbell Motors 17
Caneau, Mnsr 68
Cardinal, J-P 96
Cass, B 137
Cassiat, Mnsr 130
Caudo, J 147
Cayla, P 31, 43–45

Centre Creation 253
Centre du Style 253
Challenger Motors 179
Chapron, H 105–107, 142
Charbonneaux, P 72
Charles, M, 112
Charles, Y 194
Charreton, J 129, 134, 155
Chataigner, Mnsr 68
Chausson 128, 133, 142
China 232–234
China Changan Auto Group 267
China Tech Centre 267
Chinon, Mnsr 65, 103
Chirac, President 14
Citracit 29
Citroën Great in Britain 78
Citroën in America 179
Citroën in Argentina 70
Citroën in Japan 27–28
Citroën, André 7, 9, 18–34, 19, 52, 267, 268
Citroën, L B 18
Citroën production models pre-1934
  A Types 20–23
  B Type s 22–23
  C Types 10–12, 23.24
  Kegresse Types 28–29
  Rosalie 24–25, 32– 34
Citroën production models post-1934:
  2CV 64–82
  Ami 116–126
  AX 230–
  Bijou 81–82
  BX 202–210
  C1 27–248
  C2 244–245
  C3 242–244
  C4 248–250
  C5 245–247
  C6 223–228

C8 242
C-Crosser 242
CX 168–18
Deux Chevaux 64–82
DS 94–112
DS3 260–263
DS4 263
DS5 264–265
Dyane 124–126
GS 150–166
GS Birotor 163–164
LNA/LNA 185–186
M35 120–125
Mehari 75–78
OltCit/Axel 187, 196–200
Picasso 240
Plureil 242–243
Saxo 236
SM 128–148
Traction Avant 52–62
Visa 184–200
Xantia 237– 240
XM 212 –227
Xsara 240
ZX 232–235
Citroën commercials 1918-2013:
  Autocars 84
  Berlingo 92
  Brouette 85
  C25 92
  H van 84–92
  Jumpy 92
  Livarasion 84
  Normandie 84
  Terrassier 85
  Tractor 85
  TUB 85
  TUC 85–86
  Type 23 84
  Types 29, 32, 45, 46, 48, 60 84–86
  Visa 92
Citroën concepts 252–259

INDEX

Citroën projects:
C 152
CS/C10 252
F 152
L 172
TA 200
TPV 54
VD 186
VGD 97
Y 186
Citroën specials 71–73
Citroënet 179
Citroëneta (Chile) 72
Cituning 220
Clabot, R 30
Claveau, E 39
Clement, A 19
Clemont-Ferrand 67–68
Clerc, Mnsr 68
Coanda, H 31, 39
Coco, D 234, 242, 248, 253
Colin, A 96
Coltellini, P 112
Comotor 120–122, 163, 184
Composite (plastics) 202–204
Cook, P 14
Cordier, P 33, 170
Corot, J 40
Costa, A 146
Costin, F 82
Cotton, M 144
Cotton, R 111, 265
Coty, President 14
Cowan, A 180
Cowell, A 259
Cowey Co. 44
Crespelle, F 27
Croissere Jaune 25
Croissere Noire 25
Cross, D 220
Cubism 10
Cugnot, N-J 52
Cuinet, R 33, 53
Currs, Carrosserie 90
Curtiss Wright 120
CXA Company 178
d'Aubaurde, P 33, 53
D'Ambrosi, L 257
Dacia 196
Dagonet, J 74
Danh, P 194
Daninos, J 33, 53
Dantec, B 259
Dargent, H 96–98, 102, 114, 125, 155, 186, 189, 202
Daunat, F 140
de Bladis, A 121, 155
De Gaulle, President 14
Delage 30, 128
Delahaye 30
Delaisse, C 30, 105
Delassus Mnsr 134

Delcourt, P 31
Delgarde, L 96
Delpeuch Co. 44
Depailler, P 163
Deperdussin, J A 39, 56
Derreumaux, B 134
Deschamps, M 213
Deschaseaux 133, 238
Descotte, Mnsr 103
Designers: Citroën Listing 257
Deudeche 10, 64
DIRAVI 133, 172
Docksteader Motors 179
Dommiec, A 33
Don, M. 12
Dongfeng-PSA 234
Dore, Mnsr 96
Dorigo, D 194
Dreptin, P 31
Driguet 30
DS Numero 9 268
DS-Line 259
Dubernard, Y 142
Dubreil, A 25
Ducassou-Pehau, R 125
Duchemin, 61
Duclos, J 68
Dufresne, L 19, 33
Dukec, D 257
Dunlop 19
Dupin, Mnsr 155
Duquenne, L 257
Duralinox 65
Durand 61
Duriez 61
Duval, F 240, 266
Duvernier, F 257
Dynactive 240
Dynauto 240
École des Arts le Metier 10, 41
École des Beaux Arts 10, 41
École Grande Polytechnique 10, 41
École National Superieure des Aeronautique et de Construction Mecanique 10, 36, 41
École National Superieure des Arts Appliques et des Metiers d'Art 10
École Superieure des Arts Graphiques et Architecture Interieur et Design 10
Eiffel, G 41
Elizabeth II, Queen 14
EMP2 Platform 260
Esclassan, H 31
Esnault-Peltrie 39
Estaque, A 114, 170, 184, 187, 189, 252

Exposition Internationale des Arts Decoratifs et Industriels Modernes 40
Facel 53
Falaschi, J 30
Famchon, J 259
Farina, Battista 30
Farman, H 39
Fauborg St-Denis 19
Faulks, S 14
Fenaille, P 52
Fenwick Co. 86
Ferguson, J Co. 178
Ferté Vidame, La 66, 68–69
Fiat 184–186
Figoni et Falaschi 61
Figoni, J 30
Fiore, T 212, 254
Folz, J-M 223, 267
Forceau, A 33, 65
Ford 18–2, 53
Forest, Belgium 87
Fortin, R 33
Foucher 155
France Design 202
Franchiset, P 53, 64, 85, 87, 102
Frequelin, G 267
Frere, P 112
Fressyinet, H 40
Frua, P 143
Fukang 235
Gandini, M 202, 213
Garbe, L 81, 179
Garnier, A 179
Gaston Mtrs 27
Gautier Mnsr 155
Geel, Mnsr 68
Geely 235
General Motors 27, 267
Gerin, P F 11, 44–48, 103
Girard, L 97
Girardeau, Mnsr 68
Giret, J 155, 184, 186, 187
Gonzales, B 187
Gonzales, N 248
Graber 61
Grappey, P 256, 257
Gregoire, J-A 52
Gresley, N 40
Gritt, V 248
Gromik, R 129, 169, 170
Gropius, W 7
Grosseau, A 128, 170
Grou, C 227
Grummer, G 31
GS M7 4×4 164
Guigario, G 150, 171
Guillot, L 23, 33, 41
Guinness, A 14
Gustafsson, M 210
Haardt, G 20, 25
Hadid, Z 7

Hailwood, M 14
Hamilton Gould, C 22
Hanroiud, J-P 146
Harker, M 200
Harmand, M 102, 129, 170, 187, 197, 202–204, 254
Harrow, D 259
Hathaway, J & S 144
Hatherley, W 140
Havel, B 140
Hayley, M 263
Helig, H 179
Hermet, A 96
Heuliez 90, 141–142, 164, 177, 209, 234, 239, 247
Hickman, R 82
Hinstin, 18, 28
Hollnade, President 14
Hondet 155
Hopkirk, P 180
Hossann, M 248
Houdin, C 33, 155
Hruska, R 150
Hume, D 140
Hutton, R 133, 147
Hydractive 238, 247
Ibett, A 259
Ingeneau, P 68, 85, 87
Ingenieurs Arts le Metiers 9
Institut Superieure de Design 10
Irat, G 61
Issy-les-Moulineaux 10, 21, 38, 39
Jamblime, R de 146
Jammes, P 13, 108–110
Janes, J-C 133
Jaray 37
Jaray, P 31
Javel, Quai de 19
Jiane 126
Johnson, M 4
Johnston, S 248, 257
Joly, Mnsr 133
Joanny et Breal 61
Jouan, A 125
JouetsCitroën 31
Jouffret, H 23, 4
Jowett Javelin 98
Juchet, G 187
Julien, M 33, 53
Junkers, H 39
Kamm, W 115, 155
Kandinsky 7
Karcher, X 245
Karin 254
Kazimierczak, Mnsr 33
Kegresse Types 28–29
Kegresse, A 28
Kegresse-Hinstin 29
Kirwan-Taylor, P 81–82
Kleinmann, A 18
Klinjntun, J-P 144

Koundadze, M 179
Labourdette & Son 30
Lachaize, Mnsr 9, 96
Laisne, L 61
Lalique 25, 225
Lanchester, F 31
Lancia Aprillia 57
Lancia Gamma 155
Langenthal 58
Lartigue, P 266
Lattay, Mnsr 114
Laubard, P 23
Lauve de Segur, H 129, 134
Le Bastard, Carrosserie 90
Le Borgne, G 260
Le Breton, Mnsr 133
Le Corbusier 7, 48, 64
Le Mans 32
Le Tourneur, JM 30
Le Tourneur, M 30
Le Zebre 19
Lecot, F 61
Lefebvre, A 9, 12, 37–38, 53, 56, 64, 96, 252
Lefebvre, M 97
Leffondrie, Carrosserie 90
Lemaire, P 31, 53
Leno, J 14
Leonzi, J 68, 252
Leret, T 263
Leroy, G 87, 252
Levallois 19
Levassor, E 31
Levavsseur, L 31
Ligier 146
Lignage Prototype 224–225
Lihou, JP 160
Lilienthal, O 31
Lillet, S 238
Linari, R 248
Lincoln Zephyr 98
Lindbergh, C 20
Llewellin, P 12
Lloyd, M 224, 255
Lobry, V 259
Loeb, S 236, 266
Loewy, R 40
Lombard, J 267
Lopez, F 194
Loucheur, L 19
Louis, A 33
Louis, A 33
Louys, P 25
Lowdell, B 140
Lowdell, R 140
Loysen, A 31
Lutz, R 25
Lycee Concordat 18
Lycee Louis le Grand 18
Macrae, C 266
MacLeod, P 140
Magault, M 146
Mages, P 64, 155

INDEX

Mages, P 9, 65, 103–14, 155
Maignan, Mnsr, 103
Maillou, Mnsr 155
Malaval, A 248, 253, 256
Malleret, G 132
Mannessius 30
Martin, A 96
Martin, M 146
Martin, Mnsr 75
Martin, P 185
Maserati 132–144
Maserati Quattroporte 143
Mathis 55
Matthews, G 213, 230, 255
Matton, Y 267
Maxim Motors 165
Meades, J 14, 222
MEP 165
Mercier, P 33, 65
Meslet, P 194
Mestelan-Pinon, X 267
Metroz, T 253, 256
Meunier Mnsr 96
Michel, E 25
Michel, M 101
Michelin 33, 67, 105, 134, 184
Michelin, A 32, 34
Michelin, P 34
Mistry, G 257
Mitchell, R J 39
Mitre, L 61
Mitsubishi Motor Corp 267
Monceau et Truchot 61
Monferrini, P 265
Monte Carlo Rally 146, 266
Monteil, M 33
Monthléry 32, 122, 265
Morabito, I 258, 259
Morane Co. 23, 41
Morel, J 25
Morris 150
Mors 18
Moss, R 155
Moteur Flottant 31
Moyet, E 20, 33, 65
Mullin, P 42
Muratet, J 33, 65
Nacif, V 257
NASA 134
Ne, J 120, 144, 253
Netret, R 146
Nicolas, J 130–132
Niort, France 85
Nivalle, L 259
Noel, A 179
Nordinger, T 33
Norroy, M 23
North, O 39
Nougarede, K 259
Nougarou, J 120
Nozati, Mnsr 155

NSU 121, 121, 184
NSU Prinz 122
NSU Ro80 121
O'Connell 257
O'Sullivan, J 166
Ogier, S 266
Oleo-pneumatic suspension 104–105
Olsen, C 202, 204, 212, 234, 255
ONERA 97
Opel 27, 34
Opron, R 128, 131, 170, 184, 224
Orsi 132
Paget, A 96
Pajot, J-C 133
Palais (Presidential) 14
Pallier, J-L 240
Panhard 19, 30, 124, 125
Panhard-Levassor 31
Paradis, M 179
Pardevi 184
Paris Motor Show 94
Parthenon Motors 179
Paul, Mnsr 137
Paulin Ratier co 31
Paulin, G. 30
Peacock Co. 52
Penaud, A 31
Perkins, E 165
Perrier, Mnsr, 213
Persson, K 194
Persu, A 31
Peuch, C 96
Peugeot 50, 52
Peugeot 104 184–188
Peugeot SA(PSA) 184–187, 202, 212, 227, 230, 242–248
Peuvergne, A 210
Pezous, Maurice 165
Pinson, M 224, 255
Piquet, A 137
Pirozhkov, V 224
Plassard, J 144
Ploue, J-P 24, 253, 256
Poillot, Mnsr 96
Poinlane, C 260
Pollock, F 230
Pompidou, President 14
Portout, G 30
Poype, de la, R 76
Prandtl, L 39
Preston Motors Pty 25
Prince, Le 146
Project C 152
Project F 152
Project L 172
Proton Tiara 232
Provost, P 33
Prud'homme, R 33, 53, 65, 130

Puech, C 96, 101
Puiseux, R 9
Purass, J 266
Quesnel, O 267
Quingard, T 147
Quinn 155
Raba, R H 101–102
Rafael, G 137
Rally Citroën 265–266
Rapatel, B 225, 248
Ratier 31
Ravenel, R 103, 267
Red Bull 266
Reddiex, J 165
Regembeau, G 140
Regembeau, P 140
Reliant FW11 202
Renard, M 61
Renault 16 152
Renault SA 184
Renault, Leon 65
Renault, Louis 49
Renner, J 14
Rennes la Janais 116, 121
Rheims Cahthdral 40
Ricard, J 61
Ricardo 33
Richmond, J 27
Ricou, A 105
Riffard, M 31
Riveria Motors 179
Robin, L 33
Roche, A 155, 252
Rochet-Schneider 19
Rollier, F 267
Rolls-Royce 42
Rosengart, L 23, 28
Rougier, H 38
Rouvrais, E 243
Rover SD1 155
Royal College of Art, Vehicle Design Unit 10, 224, 234, 254
Rugg, P 181
Ruis, E 257
Rumpler 37
Saab 95
Sager, F 146
Sagis, Carrozzeria 90
Sainturat, M 33, 53, 64
Sainz, C 240, 266
SAIPA Co 37
Sallot, G 33
Salomon, J 33
Saoutchick, Iakov (Jacob) 30
Sarkozy, President 14
Sarre, C-A 179, 267
Sason, S 95
Satinet, C 23
Sauvagnargues, J 144
Sayer, M 144

Sayette de la, Henri 32
Sayle, A 14
Scarlett, M 133
Schneider et Cie 29
Schrieck, van der, R 146
Self, W 14
Sellier, A 33
Sensaud de Lavaud, D 10, 32, 120
Sensodrive 244
Serre, Mnsr 134, 179
Setright, L J K 12
Seznec, H 96
Shanghai Design Centre 267
Shenstone, B S 40
Sical (Carrosserie) 33, 53
Sizaure-Naudin 18
Skoda 34
Sloan, E 163
Slough 11, 90, 108, 179
Smith, K 79, 81
Sneddon Motors Pty 27
Sobey, J 88, 90
Societe Anonyme des Engrenages Citroën 19
Solberg, P 240
Somerset-Leake, N 81–82
Son, O 257
Sordo, D 266
Soubirou, F 7, 255, 259, 260, 265
Soufflerie Aerodynamique de Chalais Meudon 56
Soufflerie Aerodynamique Gustave Eiffel 130
Spagnolo, U 259
St Gobain 110
St Ouen-Gare 24
Staudt Co. 70
Steck, M 68
Steel, I 165
Stokoe 140
Streiff, C 267
Systeme Chevaux 23
Systeme Panhard 43
Talbot 128
Talbot Tagora 212
Talbot-Lago 30
Tatin, V 31
Taubert, L 92
Taylor, G 254, 257, 267
Teague, W D 40
Terramorsi, J 146
Terrason, P 33, 65
Theux, L 25
Thierry, P 142
Thimonier, P 146
Thomas, M 220
Tissier Co. 219
Tjaarda van Starenorgh, J 40
Toivonen, P 112

Tonneline, E 61
Touret, Mnsr 137
Toyota (TPCA) 267
Trautman, R 146
Trend Imports Co 178
Truillet, Mnsr 13
TTT 61
Tunman, K 165
UMAP Co 74–75
Valiant, P 262
van der Hoek Ostende, P 144
Varesina, Carrozzeria 54
Varilla, E B 31
Vatenen, A 266
Vavon, J-P 33
Velizy 222–226, 253
Venet, C 257
Verrier, G 146
VGD 96, 97
Vidal, G 256
Vinatier, J 146
Vincent, O 257
Visiospace 243
Voisin C25 42
Voisin C28 42
Voisin C-series/Laboratoire 37, 38, 42, 48
Voisin Myra 57
Voisin, E G 9, 19, 30, 31, 41–43, 53, 96
Volvo 34
Volvo Tundra 202
Vutotal 30
Waldegaard, B 144
Wallis, R 220
Walter, D 140, 144
Wandon, M 259
Wankel, F 152, 157
Weaver, J 27, 265
Welles, O 14
Wellinski, A 165
Westwood, N 27
Wilson, C 110
Wilson, G H 165
Winstone, D R A 41
Wolf, C 32
Wolgensinger, J 96, 137
Wolgensinger, M 265
Worfblaufen 61
WRC 266–267
Wright, O & W 7
Wuhan 250
Wuling Co. 19
XUD/Y series engines 202
Yacco Oil Co. 32
Yamamoto, T 257
Yamanouchi 28
Yareb Co. 178
Yu, S 257
Zhukovskii, N 3